All-in-One DevNet Associate Exam

DEVASC Exam 200-901 V1.0 Cert Guide

1st Edition

ISBN: 9798704466710

Our Cisco DevNet Certifications Catalog

Our Cisco Next-Level Certifications Catalog

Contents at a Glance

Table of Contents

About the Author

Muhammad Afaq Khan started his professional career at Cisco TAC San Jose and passed his first CCIE in 2002 (#9070). He held multiple technical and management positions at Cisco San Jose HQ over his 11 years of tenure at the company before moving into cloud software and data center infrastructure IT industries.

He has worked at startups as well as Fortune 100 companies in senior leadership positions over his career. He is also a published author (Cisco Press, 2009) and holds multiple patents in the areas of networking, security, and virtualization. Currently, he is a founder at Full Stack Networker and a vocal advocate for network automation technologies and NetDevOps. He is a Cisco Certified DevNet Associate[1] and was among the first 500 people #DevNet500 worldwide to pass the exam.

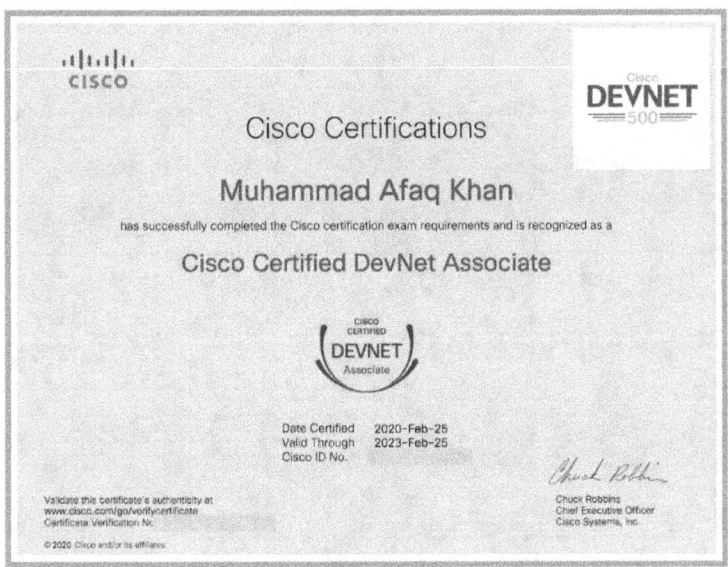

---

[1] https://bit.ly/2Pt7R9J

Preface

Congratulations! You have taken your first step towards preparing and passing the Cisco DevNet Associate (DEVASC) 200-901 V1.0 Exam.

Did you just purchase a copy? **Interested in getting access to a complimentary DEVASC Exam Quiz and a Learning Plan?** Register here[2] and then send us an email at support@fullstacknetworker.com to get started.

This study guide is dedicated to all *those souls who will never settle for less than they can be, do, share, and give!*

---

[2] https://fullstacknetworker.com/user-account

Introduction to Cisco DevNet Certification Track

Just to recap, Cisco announced the DevNet program back in June this year at Cisco Live in San Diego, after tinkering around with DevNet initiative for about 5 years. Like the Network side of things with CCNA and CCNP tracks, DevNet program also contains Associate and Professional tracks with several exams depending on the certification level.

Well, Cisco knows, like every other networking vendor, that networking hardware and even software have now become commoditized, thanks to Cloud that made owning infrastructure a stupid thing of the past and likewise SDN that helped us move away from black boxes with proprietary operating systems to mostly branded white boxes with highly programmable operating systems such as Arista EOS or Cumulus Linux. Now, keep in mind that Cisco didn't arrive at this conclusion overnight, obviously, their profit margins were tied up into infrastructure and they still are, but they seem to now have embraced the subscription-based pricing model.

Anyhow, with DevNet, Cisco is hoping to turn their products into platforms where they can focus on providing the APIs and let the infrastructure and application software developers do the integration work. Cisco now claims that they have well over 500K members enrolled in their DevNet initiative, obviously, a lot of them come from channel partners. What I also noticed is that Cisco is walking a fine line here, they are not going all out and saying network engineers should all become developers or that developers should consider becoming CCIEs.

The most critical question is what it all means for you as a Network Engineer. Regardless of what Cisco's party line is, the DevNet certification program represents a tremendous opportunity for you to graduate out of being a networker to an Automation Engineer or a Network DevOps.

If you are clueless about programming, DevOps, encoding formats such as JSON, and APIs, then you want to start with the Associate track. But, if you find yourself writing python code during downtime, or perhaps you came from a coding background like I did, then you can venture straight into the Professional track. Another way to figure this out is to simply read through the Associate exam topics, if you find a lot of unfamiliar jargon in it, then congratulations you have hit the jackpot. I personally think, most network engineers would want to start at the Associate level.

Now, you can become Cisco Certified DevNet Associate or CCDA by just passing DEVASC 200-901 exam. This exam is about APIs, Infrastructure, deployment, software development principles and obviously knowing your network fundamentals, i.e., knowing your protocols and some of the bits and bytes.

Cisco Certified DevNet Professional track, or path to CCDP, requires passing not just one but two exams. You need to pass one Core exam, i.e., DEVCOR 350-901 and one concentration exam. The only key difference between the two exam topics, i.e., Associate exam versus DevNet Core exam is the level of difficulty as knowledge domains remain the same with the exception of Network fundamentals. For Professional track, you are expected to know your networking protocols and devices.

As for the concentration exam, Cisco has offered 8 exam choices and all you need to do is to pick one from either list. If you are familiar with the DevOps tooling ecosystem, then you can pick DevOps. Likewise, if you find yourself deeply interested in pursuing network automation, go for the Enterprise (ENAUTO) exam.

Below, I have broken down the actual domains of knowledge that you need to master to get DevNet certified. The foundation of all is still networking, but then the meat of it is around programming, which is mostly Python and corresponding libraries, DevOps toolchain, becoming familiar with the infra APIs and application deployment. If you prefer the DIY approach, you can create your syllabus and google every topic until you are ready. On the other hand, if you like a more structured approach, then feel free to check out our DevNet Associate Course.

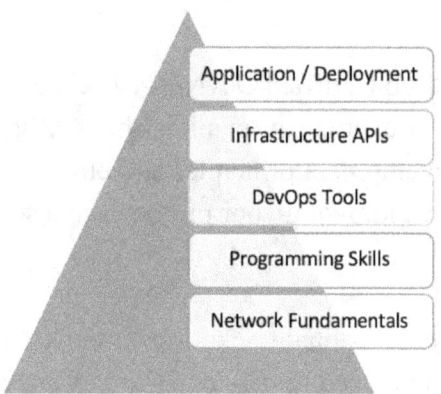

Let me summarize.

- DevNet certification program offers two tracks, Associate track, the entry level, and the next step up, the Professional track.
- While Cisco doesn't explicitly say so, Network Engineers, please pay attention to DevNet track and network automation, if you don't want to witness your job getting automated.
- Associate requires passing one exam, whereas Pro track requires passing two.

What this Study Guide contains

This guide will help you comprehensively prepare for the DEVASC exam. As you may already have noticed on the "Contents at a Glance" page that this guide has been formatted around the Cisco's official DevNet Associate 200-901 official exam topics or curriculum[3]. The benefit? Well, as you read through the various topics, you will know exactly where you're within your learning journey.

All contents are carefully covered with core concepts, code snippets, and topic summaries to help you master the skills so you can confidently face the pressures of the Cisco exam as well as its real-world application. DevNet jargon is going to be uncharted territory for most network engineers, perhaps to the point, that it may be taken for typos at first glance. For this reason, I'd strongly suggest looking up all the terms that appear foreign to you.

How to use this Study Guide

This guide is for anyone who's studying for Cisco DevNet Associate 200-901 exam. I strongly suggest taking a methodical approach for exam preparation, i.e., start with a target date or when you would like to sit for the actual exam and then work backwards to see what kind of study plan would work for you. To augment this study guide, I have put together a 200 hours learning plan[4] consisting entirely of public resources, something that you can download today and follow along.

DevNet Associate DEVASC 200-901 V1.0 Exam Topics Bodies of Knowledge	Exam Weight
Software Development and Design	15%
Understanding and Using APIs	20%
Cisco Platforms and Development	15%
Application Deployment and Security	15%
Infrastructure and Automation	20%
Network Fundamentals	15%

---

[3] https://bit.ly/36Q8O1X

[4] https://bit.ly/3clJq4H

What's available on the Full Stack Networker website

FullStackNetworker.com carries the supplemental resources (sold separately) that go hand in hand with this study guide to further ensure your exam success.

- All-in-One Course[5] that covers all concepts and hands-on labs for the DEVASC Exam
- 6x Practice Quizzes (one for each section as per the official curriculum)
- 1x Exam Simulation (to help you prepare to face the pressure of a real Cisco exam)
- Hands-on Labs with cloud-hosted IDE for immediate Python code execution
- Code snippets hosted as the GitHub Gists that you can clone/fork for modification

---

[5] https://bit.ly/2vMTkPz

CHAPTER 1 SOFTWARE DEVELOPMENT AND DESIGN

This chapter covers the following exam topics from Cisco's official 200-901 V1.0[6] DevNet Associate exam blueprint.

- Compare data formats (XML, JSON, and YAML)
- Describe parsing of common data format (XML, JSON, and YAML) to Python data structures
- Describe the concepts of test-driven development
- Compare software development methods (agile, lean, and waterfall)
- Explain the benefits of organizing code into methods / functions, classes, and modules
- Identify the advantages of common design patterns (MVC and Observer)
- Explain the advantages of version control
- Utilize common version control operations with Git
    - Clone
    - Add/remove
    - Commit
    - Push / pull
    - Branch
    - Merge and handling conflicts
    - diff

---

[6] https://bit.ly/2uh1Zcv

Compare data formats (XML, JSON, and YAML)

When using Application Programming Interfaces (or APIs) through software, it is super critical to receive and transmit data in forms that are standards-based and machine and human readable.

Let's go over a few reasons why it is so.

- It allows use of off-the-shelf software tools to convert and accept them into native data structures (e.g., JSON value/pairs to Python dictionaries)
- It makes it easier to write code that communicates with messages in format that another remote endpoint can easily consume
- It is easier to read and manipulate received messages
- It makes it easier to detect malformed messages

Extensible Markup Language (XML) and JavaScript Object Notation (or JSON, pronounced as Jay-sun) and YAML Ain't Markup Language (YAML) are the main data encoding formats used in remote APIs today. JSON is both a human-friendly and machine-readable format and sends data in name-value pairs.

JSON and YAML can be converted to each other without much effort. JSON is best known for the curly brace syntax. It is popular because it is easier to read and natively maps to Python dictionary data structure. However, XML is bit of an outlier, it is less simple to parse and convert to JSON or YAML. It is an older format so there are plenty of mature APIs that still use it.

Parsing JSON, YAML and XML is a common requirement of interacting with REST APIs.

XML Example

XML is the parent of HTML. It is generic method to wrapping textual data in symmetrical tags to indicate semantics. XML files typically carry an extension of .xml.

```xml
<?xml version="1.0" encoding="utf-8"?>
<root>
 <persons>
  <element>
   <gender>male</gender>
   <name>Jeff Bezos</name>
  </element>
  <element>
   <gender>male</gender>
   <name>Elon Musk</name>
  </element>
  <element>
   <gender>female</gender>
   <name>Jessica Alba</name>
  </element>
 </persons>
</root>
```

XML Prologue

The first line in XML file is known as the XML prologue. It has a special format and bracketed by <? and ?>. It contains the tag name xml and attributes stating the version and a character encoding. Normally, you'd find the version to be "1.0" and the character encoding to be "UTF-8" or 8-bit Unicode Transformation Format.

XML Comments

XML files can include comments, much like their HTML counterpart, they are enclosed in <! -- and --> tags.

XML Body

Everything after the prologue is considered to be the XML body. The individual elements are surrounded by symmetrical pairs of tags, the opening tag < and the closing tag > symbols. The closing tag includes a "/" preceding the closing tag.

The main body of the document as a whole is always surrounded by an outermost tag pair, e.g., <root> and </root> in the example.

The structure of an XML document is like a tree with branches (known as elements) containing further branches (known as sub-elements), e.g., <element></element> are elements whereas <gender></gender> are sub-elements.

```
<persons>
        <element>
                <gender>male</gender>
                <name>Jeff Bezos</name>
        </element>
        <element>
                <gender>male</gender>
                <name>Elon Musk</name>
        </element>
        <element>
                <gender>female</gender>
                <name>Jessica Alba</name>
        </element>
</persons>
```

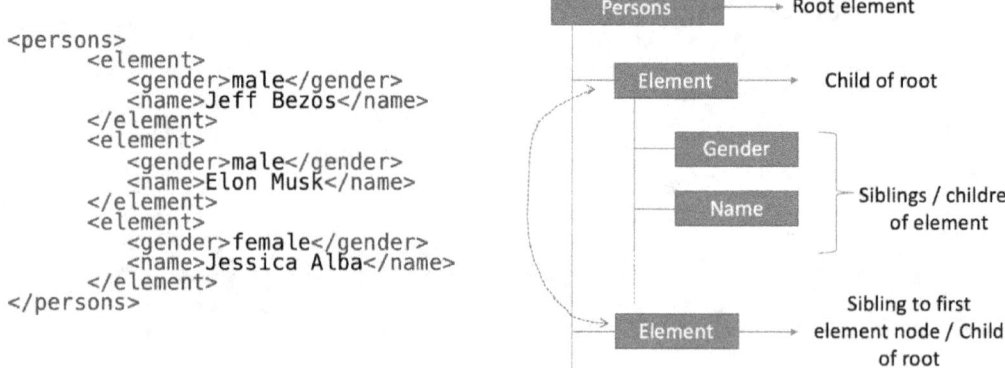

XML Attributes

XML allows you to embed attributes inside the tags to convey additional information. Version and the encoding types in the XML prologue are examples of attributes. Attribute values are carried inside double quotes and an element can have multiple attributes each with a unique name.

XML Namespaces

Some XML messages or documents incorporate a reference to a specific namespace to convey how they should be consumed. Namespaces are defined by standard bodies such as the IETF, e.g., xml:ns:netconf for NETCONF.

JSON Example

Now, let's convert above XML into JSON.

```
{
  "persons": [
    {
      "name": "Jeff Bezos",
      "gender": "male"
    },
    {
      "name": "Elon Musk",
      "gender": "male"
    },
    {
      "name": "Jessica Alba",
      "gender": "female"
```

```
      }

    ]

  }
```

JSON Data Types

JSON data types include numbers, strings, and boolean (True or False). JSON filenames typically end in ".json".

JSON Objects

Much like JavaScript, individual objects comprise of key/value pairs surrounded by braces e.g., {"key":"value"}.

JSON Maps and Lists

Objects can also contain multiple key/value pairs, separated by commas, similar to Python dictionaries. JSON values can also contain lists of data objects.

Unlike XML or YAML, JSON doesn't support adding any kind of comments. JSON format also doesn't give any significance to whitespaces, so you can ident your JSON data using tabs or spaces or nothing at all.

YAML Example

YAML format is like a superset of JSON but even easier to read. One of the most commonly known use of YAML is configuration files and particularly for writing declarative automation templates such as Ansible playbooks. YAML parsers can also parse JSON but not vice versa.

YAML File Structure

YAML files open with "---" and end with "...". You can also have multiple YAML documents within one file where each document is separated by "---". YAML filenames typically end in ".yaml".

YAML Data Types

YAML data types include numbers, strings, and Booleans. Strings don't need to be quoted, quotes are only needed when strings contain characters that have meaning in YAML.

YAML Indentation and File Structure

YAML uses indentation to describe hierarchies. Items indented below a label are considered members of that labeled element. There are no specific requirements for indentation amount, you can use a space or a tab. However, the best practice is to use two spaces per indent level.

YAML Maps and Lists

YAML maps can contain multiple key/value pairs and ordered lists. Maps are expresses over multiple lines, beginning with a label key and a colon, followed by members.

```
1   this-is-a-map:
2     key: 5
3     anotherkey: Full Stack Networker
```

Lists are represented in a similar way, but members are preceded with a hyphen (dash) and a space.

```
1  this-is-a-list:
2   - 1
3   - 2
4   - 3
5   - 5
```

Maps and lists can also be written in flow syntax (much like Python).

```
1  this-is-a-map: { key: 5, anotherkey: Full Stack Networker}
2  this-is-a-list: [1, 2, 3, 5]
```

YAML Comments

Comments in YAML can be inserted anywhere inside the document with the exception of in a long string. All comments are preceded by the hash sign.

```
1  # YAML is fun
2  this-is-a-map: { key: 5, anotherkey: Full Stack Networker}
3  this-is-a-list: [1, 2, 3, 5]
```

Now, let's convert our JSON document into YAML.

```
persons:
    -
        name: 'Jeff Bezos'
        gender: male
    -
        name: 'Elon Musk'
        gender: male
    -
        name: 'Jessica Alba'
        gender: female
```

Describe parsing of common data formats (XML, JSON, and YAML) to Python data structures

As we discussed earlier, XML is a markup language much like HTML and consists of a set of rules for encoding documents that are human and machine-readable. XML was formally defined in W3C specifications. Using XML, you can define your tags or elements, their order, and how they are supposed to be processed or displayed on screen. XML encoded file can live on a server or take on a transient when being transmitted between two machines.

One of the most distinguishing characteristics of XML is that it allows you to define your tags or elements, as opposed to HTML where tags are standardized. It is similar to HTML, but at the same time more flexible, i.e., it is both a language as well as a meta-language where you can define other languages using as it the basis, for example, RSS or XSLT.

XML Parsing in Python

Parsing means analyzing a message and breaking it into its components. When messages are transmitted over the wire, they are communicated as a stream of characters. Upon arrival, they need to be parsed into a semantically appropriate data structure where each component is recognized as an integer, float, string, and so on.

Compiling source code is also a type of parsing. Serialization, on the other hand, is about converting a data structure into a format that can be transmitted. When you use a REST API which reads data from Python dictionaries and output them as equivalent JSON/YAML/XML in string form to the remote resource – when you are serializing, you are actually encoding. Deserialization is a particular type of parsing (or decoding); it takes serialized data and recreates the original data structure from it.

Python allows you to parse, modify and build XML documents. Your XML document can be stored in a file or the form of a string. There are two well-known methods to parse XML with Python, i.e., you can use the ElementTree (ET) APIs or the Minidom module to load and parse XML.

The XML data format is hierarchical and the most fitting way to represent that data is with a tree. ET has two classes to help break that hierarchy down into two levels, i.e., ElementTree which represents the whole XML document as a tree and Element which represents a single node in that tree.

Interaction with the entire document, such as reading and writing files, is commonly done using the ElementTree, whereas interactions with a single XML element (or child) or sub-elements (or sub-child) are carried out using the Element level.

Using the ElementTree APIs to parse XML

XML Document

```
<persons>
 <element>
  <gender>male</gender>
  <name>Jeff Bezos</name>
 </element>
 <element>
  <gender>male</gender>
  <name>Elon Musk</name>
 </element>
 <element>
  <gender>female</gender>
  <name>Jessica Alba</name>
 </element>
</persons>
```

Python Code

```
1   import xml.etree.ElementTree as ET
2   tree = ET.parse('persons.xml')
3   root = tree.getroot()
4
5   print(ET.tostring(root, encoding = 'utf8').decode('utf8'))
6
7   print('\nNumber of Elements:')
8   print(len(root))
9   print('\nNumber of Sub-Elements:')
10  print(len(root[0]))
11
12  print('\nElem/Sub-Elem Data:')
13  for elem in root:
14      for subelem in elem:
15          print(subelem.tag + ":" + subelem.text)
```

Code Output

```
<?xml version='1.0' encoding='utf8'?>
<persons>
    <element>
        <gender>male</gender>
        <name>Jeff Bezos</name>
    </element>
    <element>
        <gender>male</gender>
        <name>Elon Musk</name>
    </element>
    <element>
        <gender>female</gender>
        <name>Jessica Alba</name>
    </element>
</persons>

Number of Elements:
3

Number of Sub-Elements:
2

Elem/Sub-Elem Data:
gender:male
name:Jeff Bezos
gender:male
name:Elon Musk
gender:female
name:Jessica Alba
>
```

Using Minidom Module to parse XML

You can also use Minimal Document Object Model (or Mini DOM) module to parse XML documents, however, for security reasons, it is preferred to use the ElementTree module instead.

Using Minidom, you can achieve parsing in three simple steps.

- Import xml.dom.minidom module
- Utilize the function parse (i.e., minidom.parse) to parse the document (minidom.parse ("persons.xml")
- Get the XML Elements using doc.getElementsByTagName("element")

Python Code

```
1  from xml.dom import minidom
2
3  doc = minidom.parse("persons.xml")
4
5  elements = doc.getElementsByTagName("element")
6  for element in elements:
7    name = element.getElementsByTagName("name")[0]
8    gender = element.getElementsByTagName("gender")[0]
9    print("name:%s, gender:%s" %
10   (name.firstChild.data, gender.firstChild.data))
```

Code Output

```
Python 3.7.4 (default, Jul  9 2019, 00:06:43)
[GCC 6.3.0 20170516] on linux


name:Jeff Bezos, gender:male
name:Elon Musk, gender:male
name:Jessica Alba, gender:female
>
```

JSON Parsing in Python

JavaScript Object Notation (or JSON) is language-agnostic is documented as its data encoding standard. It supports primitive types such as strings and numbers along with nested lists and objects.

Python includes a native JSON package that you can use to both encode and decode data. You can use "import json" to import the entire package and parse JSON data into a python dictionary or list. You can parse the JSON file using the json.load() into python dictionary data structure which is organized in key-value pairs. You can also read and write JSON strings using json.loads() and json.dumps methods respectively.

JSON Document

```json
[
  {
    "gender": "male",
    "name": "Jeff Bezos"
  },
  {
    "gender": "male",
    "name": "Elon Musk"
  },
  {
    "gender": "female",
    "name": "Jessica Alba"
  }
]
```

Python Code

```
1  import json
2  with open('persons.json', 'r') as f:
3    my_dict = json.load(f)
4
5  for distro in my_dict:
6    print(distro['gender'])
7    print(distro['name'])
```

Code Output

```
Python 3.7.4 (default, Jul  9 2019, 00:06:43)
[GCC 6.3.0 20170516] on linux
male
Jeff Bezos
male
Elon Musk
female
Jessica Alba
>
```

YAML Parsing in Python

YAML Ain't Markup Language (or YAML) is the most human-friendly data encoding or serialization standard out there. Much like JSON, it is also a language-agnostic data encoding method. You can use the PyYAML library to read and write YAML data.

You can import pyYAML library using "import yaml" and then load YAML file into python dictionary object or data structure using yaml.safe_load() method. You can use yaml.dump() method to write YAML.

YAML Document

```
1   ---
2 - - gender: male
3     name: Jeff Bezos
4 - - gender: male
5     name: Elon Musk
6 - - gender: female
7     name: Jessica Alba
8   ...
```

Python Code

```python
1   import yaml
2 - with open('persons.yaml', 'r') as f:
3     my_dict = yaml.safe_load(f)
4
5 - for distro in my_dict:
6     print(distro['gender'])
7     print(distro['name'])
```

Code Output

```
Python 3.7.4 (default, Jul  9 2019, 00:06:43)
[GCC 6.3.0 20170516] on linux
male
Jeff Bezos
male
Elon Musk
female
Jessica Alba
>
```

Further Reading

Python syntax, I/O, conditionals, and functions[7]
Python data structures and loops[8]
Parsing JSON using Python[9]
XML Basics[10]

Describe the concepts of test-driven development

The primary goal behind testing is to make sure that the software works the way it's supposed to work. Software testing can be divided into two categories.

- Functional testing
- Non-functional testing

Functional testing is about determining whether software works correctly, i.e., it behaves as intended in the logical sense. It encompasses the lowest level of detail examined with unit testing to the higher levels of complexity commonly explored in integration testing.

Non-functional testing examines aspects of usability, security, fault tolerance, compliance and many more issues. It is critical to understand that non-functional testing doesn't have to wait until most of the software is ready or finalized.

There are two most common types of software development methodologies, i.e., Behavior-Driven and Test-Driven Developments, commonly known as BDD and TDD respectively.

---

[7] https://bit.ly/339zydy

[8] https://bit.ly/2TGYN3H

[9] https://bit.ly/3cTRMUU

[10] https://bit.ly/2wTrJwg

BDD is a set of software practices that target to reduce resource waste in activities such as rework due to requirements not being clear, hesitance to refactor code or slower feedback cycles primarily due to organization silos and multiple hand-offs. BDD is about testing the behavior or outcome as opposed to the implementation.

Now, you may have heard about various testing techniques such as unit or integration or acceptance testing. As the name suggests, unit testing is about testing a "unit" of code, where the unit refers to a function in an object or a module. By narrowing down the scope of testing such as a single function, unit testing is simple to write and perform. There may be multiple unit tests, but they are isolated from each other.

Unit testing can be performed using home-grown scripts or industry-standard tools depending on the coding language being used. For example, you can use Mocha or Jasmine or Karma for JavaScript, and Microsoft Unit Testing Framework or NUnit for the .NET framework which can work several languages such as C#, C++, F#, and VB.NET.

The integration test is about testing multiple pieces of code together. Acceptance (or functional) test is about testing the entire system, the purpose of such testing is to assess the overall system's compliance with the known business requirements and evaluate if the entire system (such as an app) is acceptable to delivery. It is crucial to note that unit tests are typically written by the software programmer who's implementing the software, whereas integration and acceptance tests are written by software QA teams.

Now, these testing techniques are not to be confused with BDD or TDD as they are orthogonal to testing techniques. TDD is about "when" you are testing, whereas unit testing, for example, is about "what" you are testing. Just to make this point clear, you can write a unit test before, during or even after you write code.

Test-Driven Development (or TDD) is a software development methodology that uses repetition of quick development cycles that starts off writing a test case first. It is about letting your tests drive your software design and development. You will typically accomplish this using unit, integration and functional testing techniques combined. Last but not least, the spirit of TDD is not just about "writing" the testing code before application coding starts, it is actually about testing *drive* your coding or software development.

TDD approach can be broken down into three core steps which repeat endlessly until the development goals are achieved.

1. Initial Test (or Unit test)
2. Coding
3. Refactor Code

Now, we can break each of those stages into smaller action steps.

- Initial Test (or Unit test)
  - Writing a test that fails (if it passes, rewrite it until it fails)
- Coding
  - Run the test and witness it fail
  - Write enough production code to ensure that it can pass the test (or tests)
- Refactor Code
  - Refactor (improving code efficiency or internal structure of the code while preserving the external behavior). Idea is to improve code by taking many smaller steps)
  - Run the test(s) and ensure that it passes
  - Check in code

TDD cycle repeats indefinitely among those three stages so when the final code is checked in, the cycle starts again from writing a test that fails.

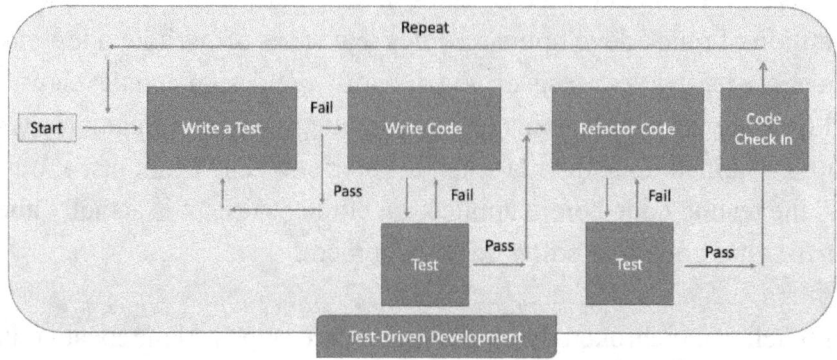

Let's now go through TDD application in practice with the help of a unit test.

In Python, you can carry out TDD by using built-in methods and libraries. For unit testing, you may use any of the methods that start with assert<blah>, assert() allows you write your assertions (there are more methods, but they are outside the scope of this example). For libraries, you can use nosetest, unittest and pytest.

The testing workflow includes three main steps.

1. Define a class TddPython derived from unittest.TestCase
2. Add methods that start with test_ (required by nosetest library)
3. Execute tests by adding unittest.main() at the end of our python test script (test_calc.py)

Define a class TddPython derived from unittest.TestCase

To perform the unit testing, we will create one project and two packages inside it. Let's call them testapp and test. To create importable python packages, you need to add an empty file known as __init__.py (two underscores before and after) inside each testpp and test directories.

Let's now create a python file called test_calc.py which would include our test code.

Python Code (test_calc.py)

```
1   import unittest# importing standard unittest module from python
        library
2
3 ▾ class TddPython(unittest.TestCase): #our class that would contain
        multiple test cases
4
5 ▾     def test_calc_subtract_method(self): #test method
6           calc = Calculator()# initiliate the Calculator
7           result = calc.subtract(4, 1)
8           self.assertEqual(3, result)
9
10 ▾ if __name__ == '__main__':
11     unittest.main()# execute test
```

Our unit test didn't complete successfully since we didn't import the Calculator.

Code Output

```
Python 3.7.4 (default, Jul  9 2019, 00:06:43)
[GCC 6.3.0 20170516] on linux
E

======================================================================

ERROR: test_calc_subtract_method (__main__.TddPython)
----------------------------------------------------------------------

Traceback (most recent call last):
  File "main.py", line 6, in test_calc_subtract_method
    calc = Calculator() # initiliate the Calculator
NameError: name 'Calculator' is not defined

----------------------------------------------------------------------

Ran 1 test in 0.001s

FAILED (errors=1)
repl process died unexpectedly: exit status 1> █
```

Let's now define calculator in calculator.py file and add the file to testapp directory.

Python Code (calculator.py)

```
1  class Calculator(object):
2    def subtract(self, x, y):
3    pass
```

Python Code (test_calc.py)

```
1   import unittest# importing standard unittest module from python
        library
2   from testapp.calculator import Calculator #import
3
4   class TddPython(unittest.TestCase): #our class that would contain
        multiple test cases
5
6       def test_calc_subtract_method(self): #test method
7           calc = Calculator()# initiliate the Calculator
8           result = calc.subtract(4, 1)
9           self.assertEqual(3, result)
10
11  if __name__ == '__main__':
12      unittest.main()# execute test
```

Now, when the test is run again, it is telling us that subtract method is returning pretty much nothing at the moment.

Code Output

```
Python 3.7.4 (default, Jul  9 2019, 00:06:43)
[GCC 6.3.0 20170516] on linux
F
===================================================================
FAIL: test_calc_subtract_method (__main__.TddPython)
-------------------------------------------------------------------
-----
Traceback (most recent call last):
  File "main.py", line 11, in test_calc_subtract_method
    self.assertEqual(3, result)
AssertionError: 3 != None

-------------------------------------------------------------------
-----
Ran 1 test in 0.001s

FAILED (failures=1)
repl process died unexpectedly: exit status 1>
```

Now, we modify our calculator.py file to include the following.

Python Code (calculator.py)

```
1 ▾ class Calculator(object):
2 ▾   def subtract(self, x, y):
3       return x - y
```

Now, let's rerun the test and see what we get.

Code Output

```
Python 3.7.4 (default, Jul  9 2019, 00:06:43)
[GCC 6.3.0 20170516] on linux
.
-------------------------------------------------------------------
-----
Ran 1 test in 0.000s

OK
```

Great! As we modified our code, our test passed successfully. As you can notice, TDD along with the unit testing, can be both fun and at the same time immensely beneficial to the quality of your code.

Co-evolving test and application code provides several benefits.

- It compels developers to consistently think about customer requirements.
- It helps constrain what application code needs to do.
- It forces creation of highly testable code.

Compare software development methods (Waterfall, Agile, and Lean)

Software development i.e., Software Development Life cycle (or SDLC), is the process of building software, i.e., going from an idea to a high-quality fit and finished product. It is much more than just writing code, it starts with the actual customer requirements behind the idea, to creating a proof of concept, performing the tests, and eventually squashing bugs.

There is no standard as such for SDLC or the exact phases, but the most common consensus comprises of the following six.

- Requirements and Analysis
- Design
- Implementation
- Testing
- Deployment
- Maintenance

Today, SDLC is nothing more than a common-sense abstraction that is put into practice in the form of rules, steps and principles. For example, the individual steps can be repeated or even performed in reversed order. Let's now look at each of those phases and what they mean.

Requirements/Analysis phase is where the product team gathers requirements for the software. These requirements should be based on the needs of the target customer along with the feedback from the in-house experts and any other sources that can provide the specific information and industry best practices. Sadly, often times the requirements come from the coder or the personal insights of the product team members, i.e., "if you build it, they will come". Anyhow, the goal of the requirements and analysis is to define the problem by answering the following questions.

- Who are the stakeholders?
- What are their top challenges?
- How are they meeting those challenges today, have they tried a solution, are they using a solution, what would it take to displace it?
- What are their constraints, i.e., cultural, or technical, and their appetite for change?
- What's the organization's current infrastructure and application choices?
- What's their current IT process, roadmap and roles?
- What features would they like to be included, and how many users?
- Are there any preferences around user experience for web, desktop and mobile applications?
- What are their integration requirements with regard to other applications that they already use today?
- What are their expectations with regard to scale?

You will need to iterate over the requirements by digging deeper into both software's front-end (the parts that users interact with) and backend (software that's hidden away performing heavy lifting around data processing, storage, etc.).

Once the requirements are gathered, then you need to analyze the results to ascertain the following:

- Is it possible to build the software based on requirements and the budget?

- What are the major risks to development schedule?
- What are the test requirements? How will the software be test?
- What are the estimated delivery dates? How will the software be delivered?

Generally, at the conclusion of the requirements and analysis phase, you will need to document the requirements, and it can happen in one of two ways, i.e., legacy or modern ways. In the legacy approach, you will jot down your requirements in the form of a software requirement document or software requirements specifications. In case of more modern approaches such as Agile, your target will be put together a minimum viable product (or MVP).

The design phase is about taking the requirement document and turning it into a software design document, something that may include building a proof-of-concept product. Now, with the legacy SDLC approaches, the design phase is used to put together the High-Level Design (or HLD) and Low-Level Design (or LLD). LLD is just the detailed version of the HLD where software's individual components, protocols and other aspects of the required design are documented. In case of modern SDLC approaches such as Agile, this phase is going to be about designing and delivering the high priority features for MVP.

The implementation phase is about the actual coding or development of software based on the deign put together in the previous phase. Test engineers also write their test plans during this phase. At the end of the phase, all functional code is ready to be tested.

Testing phase is about taking the software code produced in the implementation phase as input and test engineers install the code in their test beds and perform testing according to their test plans. There are four types of testing that takes place during this phase.

- Functional testing
- Integration testing
- Security testing

At the conclusion of the phase, it is expected that high quality and defect-free code is ready for production. This obviously sounds over the top, as code is never bug free and bug fixing requires plenty of back and forth between the developers and testers.

The deployment phase is about taking the supposedly bug-free software from the testing phase and push it into the production i.e., release to the customers and end users.

Last but not least is the Maintenance phase, which is about providing support to customers, fix customer-found defects, work on software improvements and eventually gather newer requirements for the next iteration. In case of modern SDLC approaches, the teams close the loop immediately and continue to deliver fewer features with each sprint.

Software development methodologies can play a crucial role in providing the structure, processes, and discipline to developing software. Many methodologies are in use today and the best methodology for one organization can be different from another, as cliché as it sounds, one size doesn't fit all. Every methodology has its advantages and disadvantages.
Now, picking the right methodology for your organization depends largely on the following criteria and the desired software development lifecycle (or SDLC).

- Team size and location (small or large, all in one campus or dispersed across the globe)
- Scale and scope of development (size of the project)
- End users (customer expectations and desired feature velocity)
- Time frame (short-term or long-term)

There are over a dozen frameworks out there including agile, lean, waterfall, rapid, spiral, scrum, rational, extreme, prototype, dynamic, feature-driven, etc. For this discussion, we will only focus on agile, lean and waterfall models.

Waterfall Method

Waterfall was created back in the 1970s and is the most traditional or old school choice for the software development. It consists of several stages that are mostly followed in sequence (hence the name waterfall) which requires a lot of discipline and planning in advance. It consists of about half a dozen stages and they are to be followed in a pretty rigid manner allowing little wiggle room to accommodate last-minute changes.

- Requirements analysis
- Design
- Implementation (or Coding)
- Verification (or Testing)
- Deployment and Maintenance

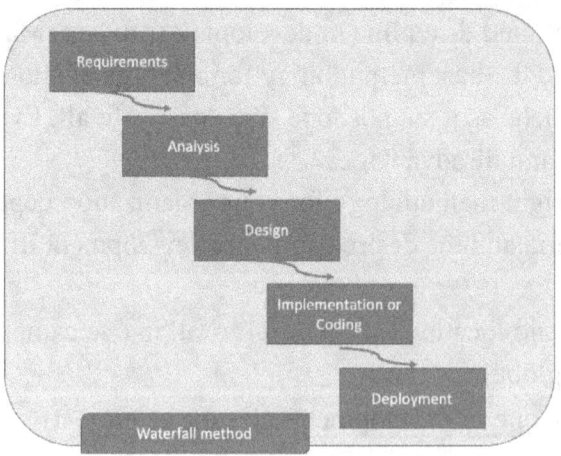

Waterfall is simply just one iteration of SDLC. In some literature, it is also broken down into seven steps or phases.

- System requirements
- Software requirements
- Analysis
- Program design

- Coding
- Testing
- Operations

Now, let us go over the pros of cons of the waterfall method.

Pros

- Scope of the project is understood in advance
- Serialized execution which can help with organization and work assignments in larger teams
- Simple to understand due to rigidity with deliverables and review process

Cons

- Any changes past the implementation stage, require a full restart
- There is no delivery until the very end of the cycle
- Not suitable for larger and ongoing projects. Often customers don't know what they want in the early stages of product development, or perhaps never for a breakthrough product that is 10x better than the previous generation.

Agile Method

Agile methodology was born out of dissatisfaction with the classic waterfall method; thus, it is perfectly suitable to accommodate changes and the need to produce and deliver code faster. Using the agile approach, software teams develop software in what's known as "sprints" or "iterations" which can last from a week to a month in most cases.

Agile requires a lot of collaboration among the teams and stakeholders involved to deliver both working and tested features faster. Agile method didn't become official until 2001 when 17, shall we say frustrated software engineers, banded together to figure out a solution to legacy SDLC approaches. They published their recommendations in the form of Agile Manifesto. As per the manifesto, Agile is about four key values.

- Individuals and interactions (over processes and tools)
- Working software (over comprehensive documentation)
- Customer collaboration (over contract negotiation)
- Responding to change (over following a plan)

Now, in order to accomplish their ambitious manifesto, they included 12 principles.

- Customer focus (early and continuous delivery of valuable software)
- Embrace change and adapt (changing requirements are welcome)
- Frequent delivery of working software (delivery working software as fast as possible)
- Collaboration (Product managers and software engineers must work together)
- Motivated teams (motivated individuals are what you need to get the job done)
- Face to face conversations
- Working software (it is the only way to measure progress)
- Work at a sustainable pace (aim to maintain a constant pace indefinitely)
- Agile environment (attention to technical excellence)
- Simplicity
- Self-organizing teams
- Continuous improvements (tune and adjust continuously)

Fast forward to today, there are four popular Agile methods.

- Agile Scrum
- Lean
- Extreme Programming (XP)
- Feature-Driven Development (FDD)

The scrum methodology focuses on small, self-organizing teams that meet daily and work in iterative sprints. The Agile Scrum is the most popular Agile methodology.

The lean methodology, unsurprisingly, is based on Lean manufacturing. It emphasizes elimination of wasted effort throughout the life cycle execution. The extreme programming (or XP) is rather prescriptive as far as the coding best practices and quality of life issues are concerned such as overwork, toil, dependency management, etc. Last but not least, FDD is a process of modeling used to estimate and plan the feature delivery.

Agile methodology uses a unique set of terms to describe the overall process.

- Sprints
- Backlog
- User stories
- Scrum teams

In the agile model, the SDLC still applies but they are more like many quick iterations of the SDLC. Each of those iteration is known as a sprint. The purpose of using sprints is to fulfill the agile principle of frequent delivery of working software. Typically, a sprint lasts anywhere from two to four weeks. During each sprint, the team takes on as many tasks or user stories as they can accomplish within the agreed-upon duration of the sprint. Each sprint is expected to produce a working and deliverable software; however, it doesn't mean that it will always be delivered.

The backlog is a prioritized list of all of the features based on the Requirements and Analysis phase. It is worth noting that features within a backlog are not necessarily included in the immediate release. It is the job of the product owner to create backlog.

When a feature reaches the top of the priority list, it needs to be broken down into smaller tasks known as user stories. Each user story should be small enough that a single team can execute it within a single sprint. The user stories consist of simple statements of what a user needs and why using the following template.

As a <user|role>, I would like to <action>, so that <value|benefit>.

Let's write a couple of statements using this template.

- As an admin of the software, I would like to see the list of windows machines that are part of the active directory, so that I can maintain effective user or group policies.
- As a user of the software, I would like to be able to install and uninstall the app, so that I can troubleshoot any app related issues.

Last but not least, scrum teams are made up of people with different roles so entire SDLC can be executed. These teams are cross-functional, collaborative, self-empowered and they are accountable for the completion of the user story part of a sprint. It is recommended that scrum teams are not larger than 10 individuals.

Scrum teams are supposed to have a daily standup, which is a meeting that should not last more than 15 minutes. The goal behind the daily standup is to keep all team members abreast of what each individual has accomplished since the last standup and what they are going to work on until the next standup.

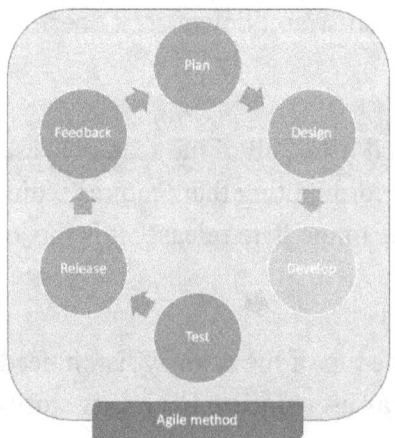

Pros

- It can gracefully adapt to changing customer requirements
- It relies on user stories (step by step use cases) leaving little to no room for any guesswork
- Faster, high quality delivery

Cons

- Unlike the waterfall, it is not a plan-driven approach per se. It is optimized for producing features faster with or without elaborate documentation
- It requires more time and commitment from everyone
- Final product can be way different than what was initially intended

Now, before we move onto lean methodology, let's review the similarities and differences between waterfall and agile.

	Waterfall Methodology	Agile Methodology
Sequential	Yes	No
Flexible	No	Yes
Change friendly	No	Yes
Requirements are defined	Yes	No
Delivery quality software	Yes	Yes
Continuous evolution	No	Yes
Rigid execution	Yes	No

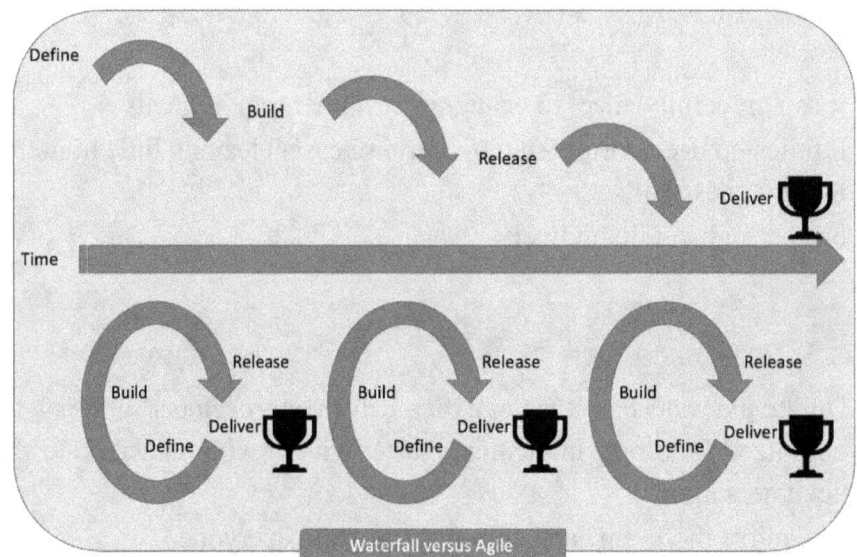

Waterfall versus Agile

In summary, agile is a better approach as long as it is feasible to implement.

Lean Method

The lean method was pioneered by Toyota for car manufacturing and focuses on minimizing waste and maximizing value to the customer. It was applied to software development by Mary and Tom Poppendieck, in their book Lean Software Development: An Agile Toolkit, published in 2003. They outlined seven principles for lean.

- Eliminate waste
- Amplify learning
- Decide as late as possible
- Deliver as fast as possible
- Empower the team
- Build integrity in
- Optimize the whole

Eliminate Waste

Waste is anything that doesn't add customer value. As per Poppendiecks, "eliminating waste is the most fundamental lean principle". They outlined seven wastes of software development.

- Partially done work
- Extra processes (just like a bunch of paperwork)
- Extra features (if customer didn't ask for it, then it doesn't provide any value for them)
- Task switching (For humans, time spent switching contexts is a waste)
- Waiting (any type of delay is a waste)
- Motion (people physically moving and artifacts such as code moving from one person to another)
- Defects (or bugs are waste because of the impact of the defect both internally and when faced by the customer)

Amplifying learning with short sprints

Writing software is a learning process and it takes several tries to get it right. So, in order to accelerate learning and tune software, there should be frequent and short iterations of working software. With short iterations, the developers can learn faster, customers can give their feedback sooner than later, and finally features can be adjusted to maximize value for the customers.

Decide as late as possible

It is better to base decisions on facts rather than opinions or speculation. This lean principle dictates that when there is uncertainty with not enough data available to make a decision, it is better to decide later than sooner. The delayed decision-making can also help with changing requirements.

Deliver as fast as possible

It enables customers to provide feedback, developers to amplify learning, and rest of the lean principles that we have discussed.

Empower the team

Expertise lies within the team, so it is best to let them make their own decisions as opposed to centralized decision making. Avoid micromanagement as it lowers the overall efficiency.

Build integrity in

The concept of integrity in software development is about the alignment between the software features and what the customer needs.

Optimize the whole

This principle is about the focus on the big picture. Each expert must take time to see the big picture so that software can be built cohesively.

When applied to software development, Lean focuses on the creation of easily changeable code. As we discussed, one of the core principles of lean SDLC is to develop software in one-third of the time, with a limited budget and an assumption that you don't need to know everything about the development cycle so you can learn as you go.

Lean method essentially helps agile work at scale across a big organization. It operates from a top-down approach as opposed to bottoms-up. Like waterfall and agile, lean also has its pros and cons.

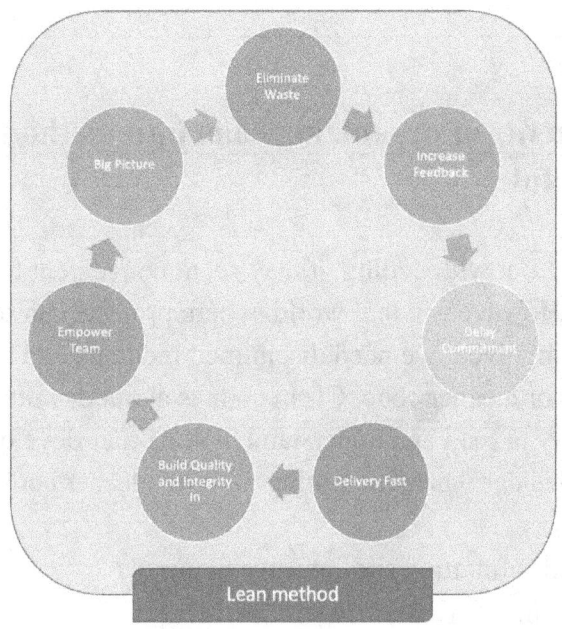

Pros

- Elimination of waste
- More features in less time, developers have lots of autonomy
- Fits well with agile and DevOps

Cons

- Very much team dependent, requires an excellent team which can tie any loose ends
- Requires that business requirements are both documented (by a business analyst) and understood by the development team

	Lean Methodology	**Agile Methodology**
Primary focus	Waste	End users
Scope	Process	Uncertainty
Outcome	Value	Functional product
Negative connotation	Cost reduction	Chaos
Known vulnerable point	Doing Lean for Lean's	Taking Agile as a

	sake	religion

Explain the benefits of organizing code into methods, functions, classes, and modules

When we're starting out with coding, it may seem convenient to throw code in a file and execute it. However, in real world, where projects can be large and multiple teams are involved, we need disciplined methods and best practices that help us write better or cleaner code. Clean code is about developers trying to make their code easy to read and understand by the other developers. There are few key areas to consider when attempting to write cleaner code.

- Standardized formatting and intuitive naming
- Overall organization
- Modularity
- Self-documentation (comments etc.)

Methods, functions, classes, and modules are ways of achieving source code level modularity so that it is easier to read and modify. In the words of Harold Abelson,

"Programs must be written for people to read, and only incidentally for machines to execute."

Now, let's understand those constructs one by one with Python examples. Both Methods and functions are blocks of code that perform task when executed. Code that performs a specific task, regardless of its frequency, could be a candidate for encapsulation inside a function. On the other hand, code that is used more than once should be encapsulated inside a function or a method. The powerful utility about functions and methods that they can be written once and executed as many times as needed.

Another feature related to functions and methods is their ability to execute the encapsulated code based on the values of the variables passed in on execution. These variables are known as arguments. The arguments are what you define as a developer when creating a function or a method as its acceptable parameters. Thus, arguments passed must match the data type(s) excepted by the method or function.

As you can see below, we're defined our function with several parameters, and then calling it with three arguments, i.e., an integer, a string and then a key/value pair.

```
1   #Function defintion
2 - def func_name(parameter1, ..., parameterN):
3     #your code goes here
4
5     #Function call
6   func_name(50, "argument2", {"argument": "5"})
```

Methods and functions can also return a value using the "return" keyword followed by a variable.

```
1 - def func_name(parameter1, ..., parameterN):
2       #block of code
3       var = paramter1 + parameter2
4       return var
5
6   myvar = func_name(5, 6, {"argument": "5"})
```

Methods

Methods almost always belong to a class or another object. They always include an object or variable when called, even if they don't include an explicit object, the "self" object is included by default. The primary purpose of calling a method is to manipulate the object.

```
1 ▾ class fsn:
2 ▾    def foo_method(self):
3        pass|
```

Functions

Functions are simply a block of code that only runs or executed when it is called. Functions may or may not have parameters, however, if any data parameter or object is passed, it is passed explicitly. Moreover, a function doesn't have to be a part of a class.

```
1 ▾ def subtract(self, x, y):
2        return x - y
```

Both methods and functions can be either user-defined or built-in included within standard or native python libraries.

There are two key differences to note between the methods and functions.

- Functions can be called by name only, as they are defined independently, however, methods are defined within a class hence referencing them require a class reference as well.
- Functions and methods may look similar, both defined by "def" keyword, but the key difference is the concept of the class and object as shown in the coding examples.

Classes

Since python is an object-oriented language, everything is an object with properties and methods. We used the "self" parameter in the earlier examples, it is nothing but a reference to the current instance of the class and is primarily used to access variables that are part of the class.

In python, all classes a built-in _init_ function which is always executed when the class is being initiated. You can use the _init_() function to assign values to object properties. Let's go over an example so you understand the concept.

```
1  class Persons:
2      def __init__(self, name, gender):
3          self.name = name
4          self.gender = gender
5
6  person = Persons("Elon Musk", "male")
7
8  print(person.name)
9  print(person.gender)
```

Modules

Module is a file that contains python definitions and statements. You can pick any name you want but it must end with a .py extension. Now, every time you create a main module (your actual python script), you can import that module into your main module using the "import" statement.

Please note that by default python will only search the current directory for module files, i.e., the directory where your main python script is located. However, you can use the sys module and sys.path.insert function to import a module from another directory should that be needed. Alternatively, you can also include as a package using "from <file-path> import <function-name>" as well however that mandates that you have an _init_.py file.

Last but not least, you can also use a module without importing it into your main python script by referencing it at the end of your .py file as shown below.

```
1  if __name__ == "__main__":
2      import sys
3      fib(100)
```

Let's now create a module named fibonacci.py and import it into our main python script using the "import" statement.

Python Code (fibonacci.py)

```
1 ▾ def fib1(n): #print Fibonacci series up to n
2       x, y = 0, 1
3 ▾     while x < n:
4           print(x, end = ' ')
5           x, y = y, x + y
6       print()
```

Python Code (fibo.py)

```
1   import fibonacci# import our module and all its functions(hint:
        there is only one)
2
3   fibonacci.fib1(10)
```

Now, let's execute our python script and see what we get.

Code Output

```
Python 3.7.4 (default, Jul  9 2019, 00:06:43)
[GCC 6.3.0 20170516] on linux
0 1 1 2 3 5 8
▸ ▯
```

Let's add another function and import only fib2() function into our main script.

Python Code (Fibonacci.py)

```
1  def fib1(n): #print Fibonacci series up to n
2      x, y = 0, 1
3      while x < n:
4          print(x, end = ' ')
5          x, y = y, x + y
6      print()
```

```
1  def fib2(n): #return Fibonacci series up to None
2      result = []
3      x, y = 0, 1
4      while x < n:
5          result.append(x)
6          x, y = y, x + y
7  return result
```

Python Code (fibo.py)

```
1  from fibonacci import fib2# only import fib2 function
2
3  print(fib2(10))
```

Now, let's execute our python script and see what we get.

Code Output

```
Python 3.7.4 (default, Jul  9 2019, 00:06:43)
[GCC 6.3.0 20170516] on linux
[0, 1, 1, 2, 3, 5, 8]
```

Now, let's summarize all of the concepts that we have learned so far with the help of an illustration as shown below. Framework is made of libraries, libraries are made up of packages, and packages are made up of modules.

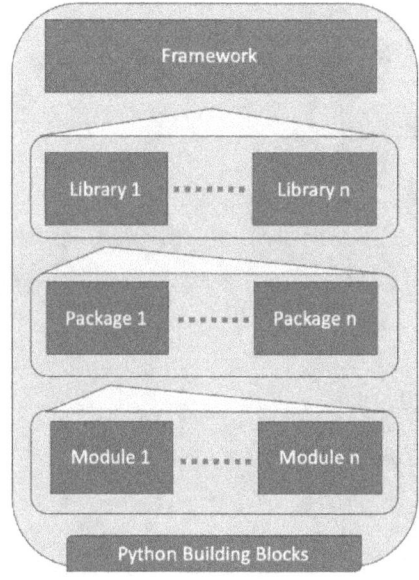

Identify the advantages of common design patterns (MVC and Observer, MVP, MVVM)

Design patterns are language-independent and thus can be implemented with any general-purpose software language. There are three main categories of patterns.

- Creational (patterns used to guide and abstract software object creation at scale)
- Structural (patterns that allow use of objects and classes for various projects)
- Behavioral (patterns that detail how objects can communicate and work together)

Model View Controller (MVC), Model View Presenter (MVP), Model View View-model (MVVM) and Observer are design patterns that relate to the presentation layer thanks to the popularity and importance of UI-centric design and its application to mobile software. Let's tackle them one by one.

Model View Controller (MVC)

As the name goes, the MVC model breaks up the overall design pattern into three components i.e., Model, View, and Controller. It is also known as architectural design pattern. The goal is to simplify application development that use graphical user interface (or GUI). Each of the three components communicates with the other two in one direction. The benefit of the MVC design pattern is that each component can be built in parallel since they are abstracted, i.e., built around the input/output from the two other modules.

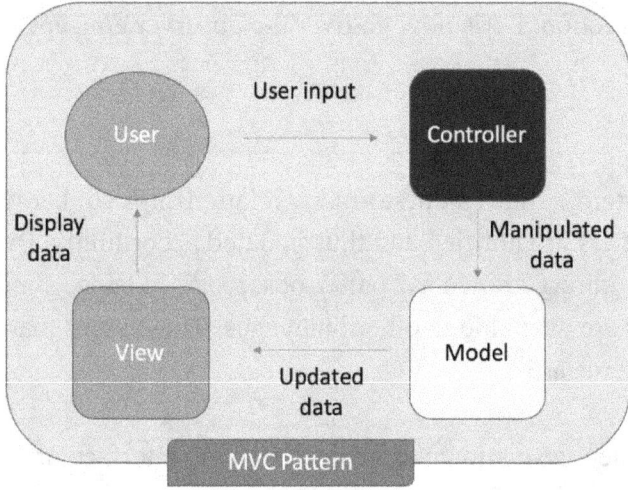

The execution of the MVC model goes like this.

1. The user provides input
2. The controller accepts the input and manipulates the data
3. The controller sends the data to the model
4. The model accepts the manipulated data, processes it, and then sends over to the view.
5. The view accepts the data and makes it available to the user.
6. The user sees the updated data as a result of his/her input.

Model simply means the data that is required to display in the view. Model consists of a bunch of classes that describe the business logic as well as business rules for data with things such as how the data can be manipulated. It is the application's data structure.

The view represents the UI components such as XML, HTML, etc. It presents the data that is received from the controller. In MVC, view monitors the model for state changes and displays update when there is one. Now, model and view interact with each other using what's known as the observer pattern. The Model makes use of the Observer pattern so that it can keep the observers updated while maintaining abstraction. Let's now go over the observer concept.

The Observer Pattern

The observer pattern defines a one-to-many relationships so that when one object changes state, others are notified and thus updated accordingly. Python comes with an observer library known as "patter-observer", likewise similar implementations are available in other languages. The classes that make up of the observer patterns are

- Observable – also known as subject, it is the interface or class that defines operations for attaching and un-attaching observers to the client.
- ConcreteObservable – It is another class that maintains the state of the object and if and when a change occurs it notifies the attached observers.
- Observer – It is the interface or abstract class that defines the operations that are to be used to notify the object.

It is easier to understand this model using the following diagram.

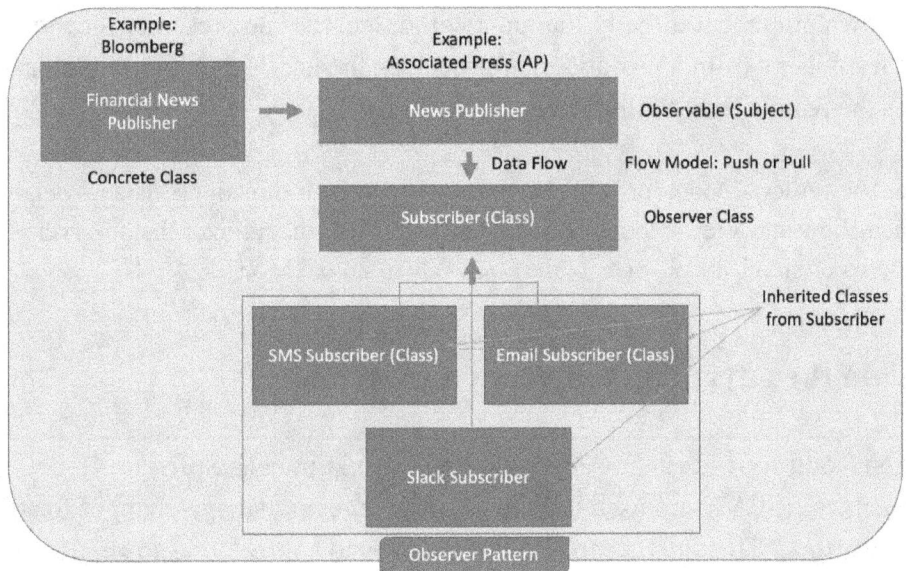

The benefit of the observer pattern is that observers can get real time data from the subject when a change happens. Subscription or push method provides better performance than the pull (or polling) method. We witness observer patterns every day in the form of social media such as Facebook, where you (the user) is the observer who follows another user (the subject). When the subject posts something on their news feed, the system notifies all of the observers (or users) that there is a new post.

Now, the last component within the MVC is the controller. The controller is responsible to process the incoming requests, so it processes the user's data via Model and passes back the results to View, thus acting as a middleman between View and the Model.

Model View Presenter (or MVP) is derived from MVC however with one exception and that is the controller is replaced by the presenter, so instead of Model-View-Controller it instead has Model-View-Presenter aspects.

The model represents a set of classes that communicates the business logic and the data. Again, much like MVC, it also governs the rules for data updates and data manipulation.

The View component directly interacts with the user. The presenter receives input from users from View and then processes the user's data via Model and passes the results back to the View.

Model View View-Model (or MVVM) pattern supports bi-directional data association between View and View-Model. View-Model is the one that utilizes the observer pattern to communicate changes in the View-Model to the Model.

Explain the advantages of version control

Version Control Systems (VCS), sometimes also known as Software Code Management (SCM), are used to help a software team manage changes to source code over time. They help keep track of changes to source code so should there be a mistake made by one of the members of the team, code can be rolled back before those changes were committed thus minimizing disruption.

In a medium to large software project, at any time, several code changes are simultaneously happening.

- New source code for newer features
- Changes to source code to fix bugs
- Re-factoring old code for better readability and organization
- New source code that requires testing before it can be allowed into the main code (branch)

As you've witnessed in all of the python examples so far, source code lives in files and version control systems (VCS) help track changes to those files. There are many version control systems in use today, however, the most popular ones are Git and Apache Subversion (SVN). Mercurial, Perforce and CVS are other examples. In this discussion, we will focus only on Git.

Git is a free and open source and supports dozens of operations that can be performed to enforce source code version control in a distributed manner. Some of the benefits of Git and other VCSs are as follows.

- Long-term change history of every source file made by anyone on the team. It includes history relating to the creation, deletion, and edits. The metadata generally includes author name, date, and purpose.
- Branching and merging are common operations that are performed by developers all the time. Branching is usually done for either writing new features or new release (more common). Once all the necessary code is added and tested, it is then merged back into the main branch.
- Traceability is yet another benefit of CVS where each change is traceable and at the same time linked to a bug tracking system such as Jira. If each change is annotated with a note that describes what it is doing, then it goes a long way to find the root cause when things don't work out as planned.

Utilize common version control operations with Git

You can put Git to paces in two different ways, i.e., self-host a Git server or let a provider host it for you i.e., Git-as-a-service. Self-hosted servers require you to use your server (or a VM) and require a little more knowledge than provider-hosted counterparts, but they are mostly light-weight software and free. There are also some hybrid Git servers like GitLab, which can be self-hosted (for free) or web-hosted (for a cost, generally billed as $ per user).

For self-hosted variants, I'd strongly suggest you consider using GitLab, Gitea (one that I am using, and you will see it throughout this guide) or Gogs. In case you're curious, they are all freeware. For web-hosted, you've GitHub, and then plenty of GitHub-like alternatives such as GitLab, BitBucket, SourceForge, Launchpad, etc.

Some of the benefits of the version control systems are:

- Collaboration (multiple people can work on a project at the same time)
- Accountability and visibility (changes can be tracked)

- Work in isolation (new features can be built without affecting existing software)
- Safety (changes can be undone if there is a mistake)
- Work anywhere (all you need to work is a working copy)

There are three main types of version control systems.

- Local
- Centralized
- Distributed

A local version control system tracks files within a local file system, it is like a making copy of a file before you modify. This approach allows you to revert back to the previous version. It obviously doesn't provide most of the benefits that we have discussed above. Centralized version control system uses a client/server model. The repo is stored in a centralized system. Every time an individual wants to make a change to a file, they need to get a working copy of the files from the central repo to their local machine. In a centralized system, only one person at a time is allowed to modify a particular file. When you need to make changes, you checkout the file which results in a lock on the file and then you check it in when you are done.

The distributed version control, unlike centralized variant, is based on a peer-to-peer model. In this model, when an individual wants to make a change to a file, they must first make a copy or clone the full repo to their local machine. Multiple people can clone remote repos to their local machines. Each individual can work on any file without needing any locking, when they are done making changes, they can just push the repo to the remote or main or hosted service.

Before we proceed, it is important to understand what a Git repository or repo is. If you recall, the purpose of Git is to help you manage a software project with the help of version controls by way of manipulating the graph of commits. With Git, a project is nothing but a set of files that change over the lifetime of the project and Git stores this information in a data structure called repository or repo.

A Git client must be installed on the client machine before someone can make a clone a repo. Git clients are widely available for windows, macOS and Linux/Unix. It is worth noting that some clients offer a GUI, but main focus remains on command line interface (or CLI).

Git repo is stored in the same root directory as the project itself, but inside a folder or sub-directory if you will, known as .git. Anyhow, a Git repo contains, among other things, the following components.

- Set of commit objects, for example
  - Set of files that reflect the current state of the project
  - References to parent commit objects
  - 40-character name that uniquely identifies the commit object in the form of a SHA-1 hash. If two commits are identical as far as commit objects are concerned, they will produce identical hashes.
- References to commit objects that are known as heads, for example
  - Head is just a reference to a commit object, by default each folder contains a head known as "master". "HEAD" in uppercase is used to denote the current or active head for the given repo.

You can use git status, git ls-files and git worktree list –porcelain commands to display Git worktree details.

```
netdevops@netdevops-VirtualBox:~/project$ git status
On branch dev_branch
Your branch is up to date with 'origin/dev_branch'.

nothing to commit, working tree clean
netdevops@netdevops-VirtualBox:~/project$ git ls-files
.drone.yml
ansible.cfg
group_vars/all.yaml
host_vars/Dev_Switch.yaml
host_vars/Prod_Switch_1.yaml
host_vars/Prod_Switch_2.yaml
host_vars/Prod_Switch_3.yaml
host_vars/Test_Switch_1.yaml
host_vars/Test_Switch_2.yaml
inventory_dev
inventory_prod
inventory_test
playbooks/roles/common/tasks/main.yaml
playbooks/site.retry
playbooks/site.yml
netdevops@netdevops-VirtualBox:~/project$
netdevops@netdevops-VirtualBox:~/project$ git status
On branch dev_branch
Your branch is up to date with 'origin/dev_branch'.

nothing to commit, working tree clean
netdevops@netdevops-VirtualBox:~/project$ git worktree list --porcelain
worktree /home/netdevops/project
HEAD 06f9d8ebefd1e3eca754a9c43826a00387e4e160
branch refs/heads/dev_branch

netdevops@netdevops-VirtualBox:~/project$
```

Now, let's review some common source code operations that you can perform with Git. You can consider all of the Git operations as options that you will add to your "git" commands.

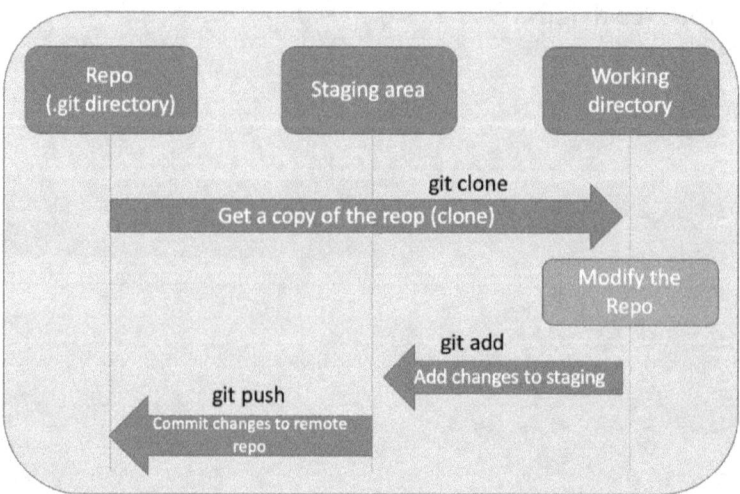

The git repo resides in a hidden .git directory, it holds metadata such as the files, commits and logs that contains commit history. The working directory is the folder that contains the working copy of the files on the local machine. The staging area stores the information that an individual wants to either add, update, or delete in the repo. It is not a folder or a directory, staging area is just an index file located in the .git directory.

Each of the three stages mentioned are associated with three states within Git.

- Committed (the version of the file that has been saved in the repo)
- Modified (the file that has changed before it is added to the staging area)
- Staged (the modified file that is ready to be committed to the remote repo)

Clone Operation

As the name implies, the "clone" option allows you to clone or duplicate a repo to your local machine. Please note that repo in question could be located on your local file system or a remote server. You can access the remote repo via HTTP/HTTPS or SSH protocols.

You can find the complete link of your GitHub repo as shown below.

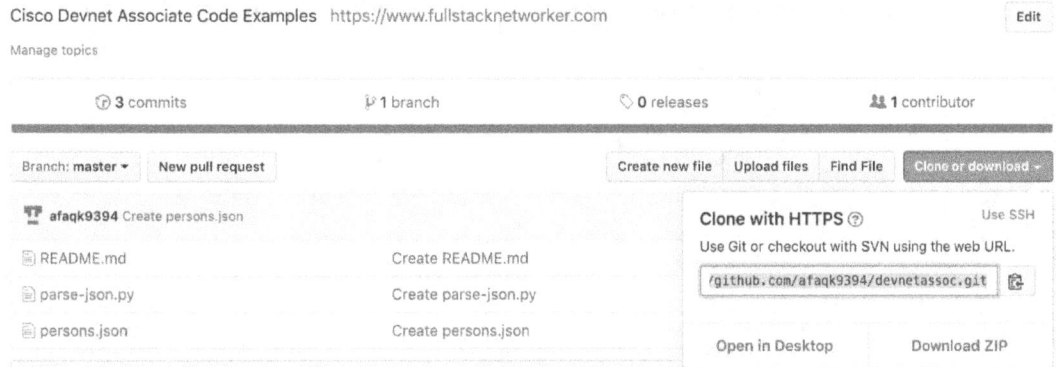

$ git clone https://github.com/afaqk9394/devnetassoc.git

```
netdevops@netdevops-VirtualBox:~/GitExamples$ git clone https://github.com/afaqk9394/devnetassoc.git
Cloning into 'devnetassoc'...
remote: Enumerating objects: 9, done.
remote: Counting objects: 100% (9/9), done.
remote: Compressing objects: 100% (7/7), done.
remote: Total 9 (delta 1), reused 0 (delta 0), pack-reused 0
Unpacking objects: 100% (9/9), done.
```

```
netdevops@netdevops-VirtualBox:~/GitExamples$ cd devnetassoc/
netdevops@netdevops-VirtualBox:~/GitExamples/devnetassoc$ ls -lah
total 24K
drwxr-xr-x 3 netdevops netdevops 4.0K Sep 24 19:45 .
drwxr-xr-x 3 netdevops netdevops 4.0K Sep 24 19:45 ..
drwxr-xr-x 8 netdevops netdevops 4.0K Sep 24 19:45 .git
-rw-r--r-- 1 netdevops netdevops  154 Sep 24 19:45 parse-json.py
-rw-r--r-- 1 netdevops netdevops  192 Sep 24 19:45 persons.json
-rw-r--r-- 1 netdevops netdevops   14 Sep 24 19:45 README.md
netdevops@netdevops-VirtualBox:~/GitExamples/devnetassoc$
```

Add/remove Operations

Git add allows you to add a file to the staging area, and Git remove works on the working directory as well as the staging index.

In the example below, "git add -u" command only adds currently tracked files (the modified ones) to the staging area and checks if any of the files have been deleted. It doesn't add any of the new files to the staging area. Once "git add" is completed, you can view results using the "git show" command as shown below.

```
netdevops@netdevops-VirtualBox:~/project$ git add -u
netdevops@netdevops-VirtualBox:~/project$ git show
commit af9f244130560a401697dc2de989439de72d8376 (HEAD -> dev_branch, origin/dev_branch)
Author: git <netdevops@server.local>
Date:   Mon Oct 22 19:43:43 2018 -0700

    ETV1.1-DEMO1

diff --git a/group_vars/all.yaml b/group_vars/all.yaml
index 875d65f..c40b281 100644
--- a/group_vars/all.yaml
+++ b/group_vars/all.yaml
@@ -10,6 +10,6 @@ ansible_become_method: enable
 ansible_become_pass: netdevops
 contact: NetDevOps Team
 mgmt_interface: FastEthernet0/0
-read_community: NewSecureRead
-write_community: NewSecureWrite
+read_community: ETV1.1SecureRead
+write_community: ETV1.1SecureWrite
 servers: 10.0.10.1
netdevops@netdevops-VirtualBox:~/project$
```

Git remove is the exact opposite of Git add, with add you track a file for changes whereas with remove to untrack it.

Commit Operation

Git commit command records all of the file changes in the local repo along with a hash that serves as the tag for identifying the commit. These commits can later be pushed to a repo or merged from a repo etc.

Please note the difference between "git add" and "git commit", former simply add your modified files to the queue that can be committed later whereas the later commits the files into the index to the local repo.

Git commit command can be used with a flag, such as -a or -m. "-a" is used to add all the files to the staging area whereas "-m" allows you to add (or commit) all the changed files to your version history along with a commit message. Last but not least, if you can combine staging and commit by using both flags together i.e., "git commit -am".

In the following example, a git commit is taking place for the changes (two lines containing Read and Write SNMP strings) that were previously only added ("git add -u").

```
netdevops@netdevops-VirtualBox:~/project$ git commit -m "Updated SNMP Community Strings"
[dev_branch 06f9d8e] Updated SNMP Community Strings
 1 file changed, 2 insertions(+), 2 deletions(-)
netdevops@netdevops-VirtualBox:~/project$ git show
commit 06f9d8ebefd1e3eca754a9c43826a00387e4e160 (HEAD -> dev_branch)
Author: git <netdevops@server.local>
Date:   Tue Sep 24 12:47:45 2019 -0700

    Updated SNMP Community Strings

diff --git a/group_vars/all.yaml b/group_vars/all.yaml
index c40b281..1252054 100644
--- a/group_vars/all.yaml
+++ b/group_vars/all.yaml
@@ -10,6 +10,6 @@ ansible_become_method: enable
 ansible_become_pass: netdevops
 contact: NetDevOps Team
 mgmt_interface: FastEthernet0/0
-read_community: ETV1.1SecureRead
-write_community: ETV1.1SecureWrite
+read_community: devnet-assoc-read
+write_community: devnet-assoc-write
 servers: 10.0.10.1
netdevops@netdevops-VirtualBox:~/project$
```

You can view commit hashtag using the "git log" command as shown below. Note the line that starts with "commit" and includes "☐06f9d8ebefd1e3eca754a9c43826a00387e4e160".

```
netdevops@netdevops-VirtualBox:~/project/group_vars$ git log -1
commit 06f9d8ebefd1e3eca754a9c43826a00387e4e160 (HEAD -> dev_branch, origin/dev_branch)
Author: git <netdevops@server.local>
Date:   Tue Sep 24 12:47:45 2019 -0700

    Updated SNMP Community Strings
netdevops@netdevops-VirtualBox:~/project/group_vars$
```

Push / Pull Operations

Git push command executes the already committed changes to your branch, in this case, we're pushing them to "dev_branch". While it is outside the scope of git push or pull, committing changes essentially kicks off our Continuous

Integration and Continuous Delivery (CICD) pipeline as shown in the Gitea and
Drone (self-service CD platform) GUI screenshots.

```
netdevops@netdevops-VirtualBox:~/project$ git push origin dev_branch
Username for 'http://10.0.2.15:3000': netdevops
Password for 'http://netdevops@10.0.2.15:3000':
Counting objects: 4, done.
Delta compression using up to 2 threads.
Compressing objects: 100% (3/3), done.
Writing objects: 100% (4/4), 392 bytes | 392.00 KiB/s, done.
Total 4 (delta 2), reused 0 (delta 0)
To http://10.0.2.15:3000/netdevops/switch_configuration.git
   af9f244..06f9d8e  dev_branch -> dev_branch
netdevops@netdevops-VirtualBox:~/project$ git show
commit 06f9d8ebefd1e3eca754a9c43826a00387e4e160 (HEAD -> dev_branch, origin/dev_branch)
Author: git <netdevops@server.local>
Date:   Tue Sep 24 12:47:45 2019 -0700

    Updated SNMP Community Strings

diff --git a/group_vars/all.yaml b/group_vars/all.yaml
index c40b281..1252054 100644
--- a/group_vars/all.yaml
+++ b/group_vars/all.yaml
@@ -10,6 +10,6 @@ ansible_become_method: enable
 ansible_become_pass: netdevops
 contact: NetDevOps Team
 mgmt_interface: FastEthernet0/0
-read_community: ETV1.1SecureRead
-write_community: ETV1.1SecureWrite
+read_community: devnet-assoc-read
+write_community: devnet-assoc-write
 servers: 10.0.10.1
netdevops@netdevops-VirtualBox:~/project$
```

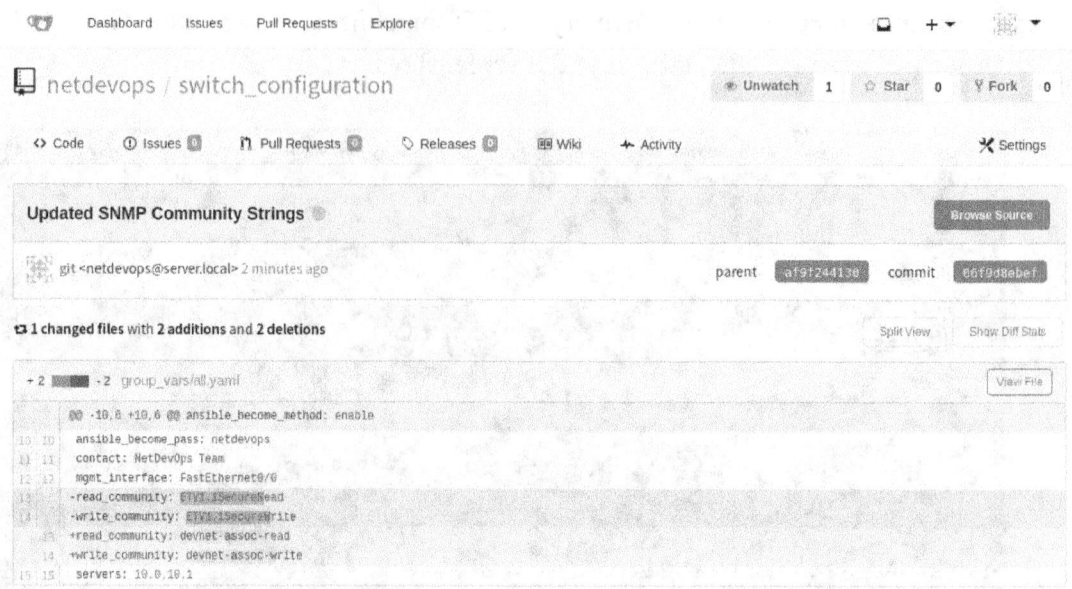

Dashboard   Issues   Pull Requests   Explore

netdevops / switch_configuration   Unwatch 1   Star 0   Fork 0

<> Code   ① Issues 0   ⋔ Pull Requests 0   ♢ Releases 0   ▦ Wiki   ✦ Activity   ✕ Settings

Updated SNMP Community Strings   Browse Source

git <netdevops@server.local> 2 minutes ago   parent af9f244130   commit 66f9d8ebef

⇄ **1 changed files** with **2 additions** and **2 deletions**   Split View   Show Diff Stats

+ 2 ▬▬▬ - 2 group_vars/all.yaml   View File

```
       @@ -10,6 +10,6 @@ ansible_become_method: enable
10  10   ansible_become_pass: netdevops
11  11   contact: NetDevOps Team
12  12   mgmt_interface: FastEthernet0/0
13       -read_community: ETV1.1SecureRead
13       -write_community: ETV1.1SecureWrite
    14   +read_community: devnet-assoc-read
    14   +write_community: devnet-assoc-write
15  15   servers: 10.0.10.1
```

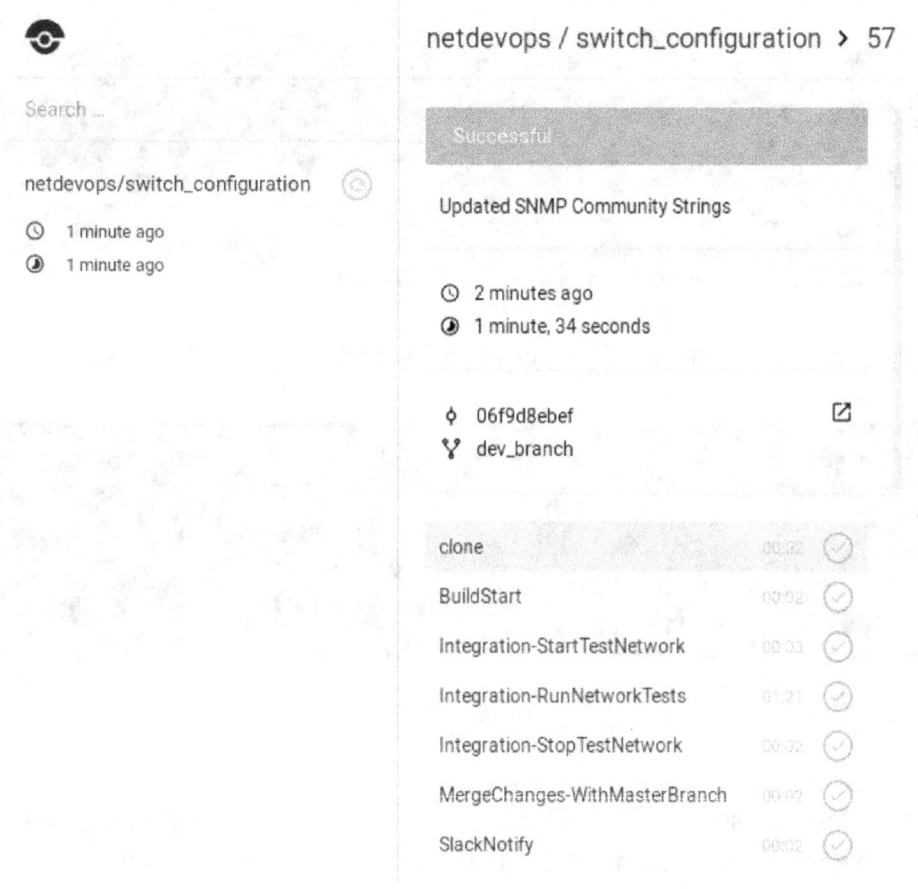

Git pull command fetches remote changes to your local repo. Note the new file persons.xml was pulled from the GitHub repo branch master.

```
netdevops@netdevops-VirtualBox:~/GitExamples/devnetassoc$ git pull https://github.com/afaqk9394/devnetassoc.git
remote: Enumerating objects: 4, done.
remote: Counting objects: 100% (4/4), done.
remote: Compressing objects: 100% (3/3), done.
remote: Total 3 (delta 1), reused 0 (delta 0), pack-reused 0
Unpacking objects: 100% (3/3), done.
From https://github.com/afaqk9394/devnetassoc
 * branch            HEAD       -> FETCH_HEAD
Updating 3bb47de..7f481e5
Fast-forward
 persons.xml | 14 ++++++++++++++
 1 file changed, 14 insertions(+)
 create mode 100644 persons.xml
netdevops@netdevops-VirtualBox:~/GitExamples/devnetassoc$
```

Like we did before, you can verify the changes by peeking inside the git logs.

```
netdevops@netdevops-VirtualBox:~/GitExamples/devnetassoc$ git log -1
commit 7f481e52a60d07e27bc7952fe417035816bf275f (HEAD -> master)
Author: afaqk9394 <46501831+afaqk9394@users.noreply.github.com>
Date:   Tue Sep 24 22:02:11 2019 -0700

    Create persons.xml
netdevops@netdevops-VirtualBox:~/GitExamples/devnetassoc$
```

Branch

Git stores its data as a series of snapshots, so when you make a commit, it stores the commit object which contains within it a pointer to the snapshot of the content (or changes) you staged.

A branch in Git jargon is nothing but a movable pointer to one of the commits, the default branch name is in Gitea is "master" (same on GitHub by the way). The name "master" traces its roots into "git init". Branches enable git users to work on code independently without affecting the main code in the repo.

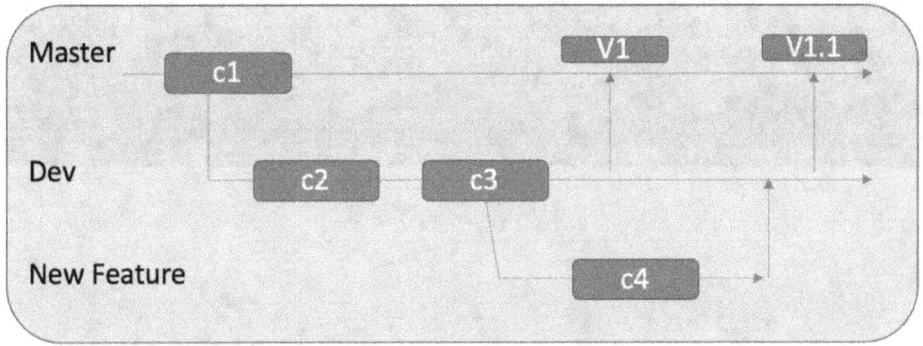

Let's visualize the relationship among commit objects, commits, snapshots, and master branch. Git knows your current or active branch by way of HEAD which is pointing to the master branch.

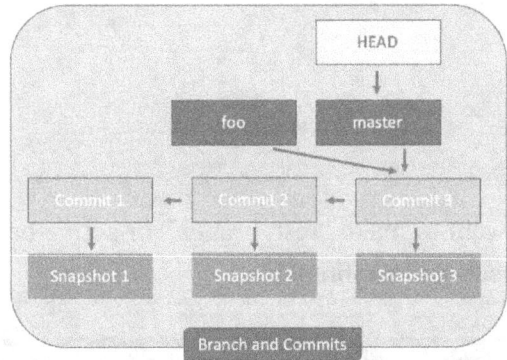

In this example shown below, our changes were committed to dev_branch and were merged into master after they were successfully tested using our Drone-based CICD pipeline.

```
netdevops@netdevops-VirtualBox:~/project/group_vars$ git show-branch
* [dev_branch] Updated SNMP Community Strings
 ! [master] drone testing phase
--
*   [dev_branch] Updated SNMP Community Strings
```

Let's now add a new branch name "test_branch" by using "git branch test_branch" command.

```
netdevops@netdevops-VirtualBox:~/GitExamples/devnetassoc$ git branch test_branch
netdevops@netdevops-VirtualBox:~/GitExamples/devnetassoc$ git show-branch
* [master] Create persons.xml
 ! [test_branch] Create persons.xml
--
*+ [master] Create persons.xml
netdevops@netdevops-VirtualBox:~/GitExamples/devnetassoc$
```

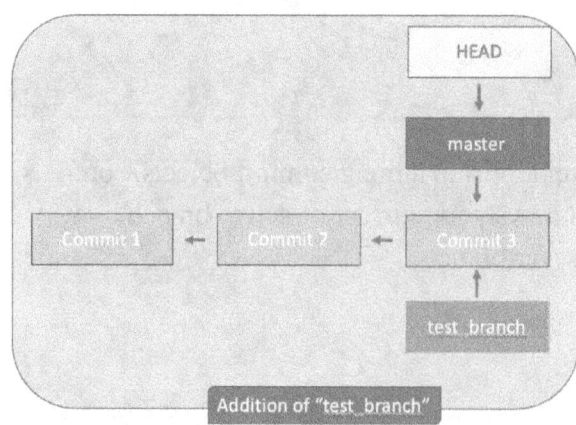

Now, let's say if we want to make "test_branch" or active branch, which can be
done by using 'git checkout test_branch".

```
netdevops@netdevops-VirtualBox:~/GitExamples/devnetassoc$ git show-branch
* [master] Create persons.xml
 ! [test_branch] Create persons.xml
--
*+ [master] Create persons.xml
netdevops@netdevops-VirtualBox:~/GitExamples/devnetassoc$ git checkout test_branch
Switched to branch 'test_branch'
netdevops@netdevops-VirtualBox:~/GitExamples/devnetassoc$ git show-branch
 ! [master] Create persons.xml
* [test_branch] Create persons.xml
--
+* [master] Create persons.xml
netdevops@netdevops-VirtualBox:~/GitExamples/devnetassoc$
```

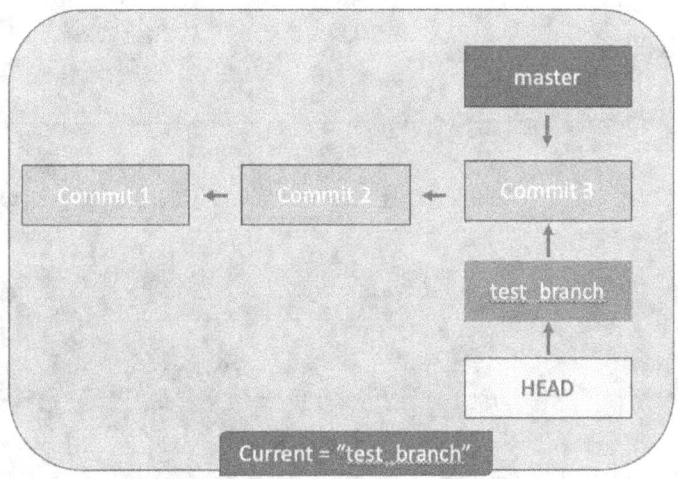

Now, if you make a change and commit to our test_branch, then our test_branch will point to a new commit 4 (added "Richard Branson" to persons.xml file), while the master will continue to point to commit 3.

Commit 4 was assigned a hashtag ⬚of
425a91fc654801e18be3ea8c7b51f18b0775cb52.

```
netdevops@netdevops-VirtualBox:~/GitExamples/devnetassoc$ cat persons.xml
<persons>
    <element>
        <gender>male</gender>
        <name>Jeff Bezos</name>
    </element>
    <element>
        <gender>male</gender>
        <name>Elon Musk</name>
    </element>
    <element>
        <gender>female</gender>
        <name>Jessica Alba</name>
    </element>
    <element>
        <gender>male</gender>
        <name>Richard Branson</name>
    </element>
</persons>
netdevops@netdevops-VirtualBox:~/GitExamples/devnetassoc$ git commit -a -m "added Richard Branson"
[test_branch 425a91f] added Richard Branson
 1 file changed, 5 insertions(+)
netdevops@netdevops-VirtualBox:~/GitExamples/devnetassoc$ git show-branch
 [master] Create persons.xml
 * [test_branch] added Richard Branson
--
 * [test_branch] added Richard Branson
+* [master] Create persons.xml
netdevops@netdevops-VirtualBox:~/GitExamples/devnetassoc$ git log -1
commit 425a91fc654801e18be3ea8c7b51f18b0775cb52 (HEAD -> test_branch)
Author: git <netdevops@server.local>
Date:   Tue Sep 24 22:40:13 2019 -0700

    added Richard Branson
netdevops@netdevops-VirtualBox:~/GitExamples/devnetassoc$
```

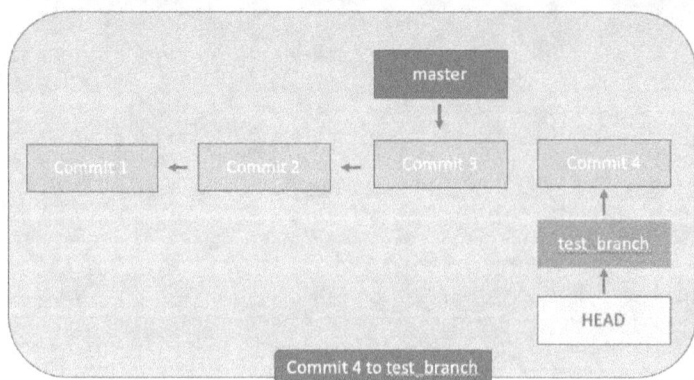

Merge and handling conflicts

Git uses merge as a way to put forked history back together again, fork simply
refers to cloning or copying a branch. However subtle, there is a difference

between fork and branching, former is an independent copy of the repo where later is simply a way to adding some code, say a feature that will eventually be merged back into the main branch.

In the real world, there are two primary reasons why you'd fork a repo, i.e.

- You want to propose or contribute changes to someone's project or code
- You want to use someone else's project as a starting point for your own (e.g., Ubuntu Linux is a fork of Debian distro, likewise CentOS is a fork of Red Hat Enterprise Linux)

Now, in order to demonstrate a merge, we're going to run through the following set of actions.

- Add a new branch (anothertest_branch)
- Checkout anothertest_branch (so it becomes current, using "git checkout anothertest_branch" command)
- Add yet another name to persons.xml (Oprah Winfrey) and save it as persons1.xml
- Track our new file (persons1.xml) using "git add"
- Commit our change (addition of Oprah Winfrey within the new file persons1.xml, using "git commit -a -m "added Oprah Winfrey")
- Finally, merge anothertest_branch into master using "git merge anothertest_branch"

```
netdevops@netdevops-VirtualBox:~/GitExamples/devnetassoc$ git add persons1.xml
netdevops@netdevops-VirtualBox:~/GitExamples/devnetassoc$ git commit -a -m "added Oprah Winfrey"
[anothertest_branch cb0cf78] added Oprah Winfrey
 1 file changed, 19 insertions(+)
 create mode 100644 persons1.xml
netdevops@netdevops-VirtualBox:~/GitExamples/devnetassoc$ git show
commit cb0cf788e19c1ec8406c71f2910b7d09a7fae725 (HEAD -> anothertest_branch)
Author: git <netdevops@server.local>
Date:   Tue Sep 24 23:00:50 2019 -0700

    added Oprah Winfrey

diff --git a/persons1.xml b/persons1.xml
new file mode 100644
index 0000000..5d5fad9
--- /dev/null
+++ b/persons1.xml
@@ -0,0 +1,19 @@
+<persons>
+    <element>
+        <gender>male</gender>
+        <name>Jeff Bezos</name>
+    </element>
+    <element>
+        <gender>male</gender>
+        <name>Elon Musk</name>
+    </element>
+    <element>
+        <gender>female</gender>
+        <name>Jessica Alba</name>
+    </element>
+     <element>
+        <gender>female</gender>
+        <name>Oprah Winfrey</name>
+    </element>
+</persons>
+
Applications netdevops-VirtualBox:~/GitExamples/devnetassoc$
```

```
netdevops@netdevops-VirtualBox:~/GitExamples/devnetassoc$ git branch
* anothertest_branch
  master
  test_branch
netdevops@netdevops-VirtualBox:~/GitExamples/devnetassoc$ git branch master
fatal: A branch named 'master' already exists.
netdevops@netdevops-VirtualBox:~/GitExamples/devnetassoc$ git checkout master
Switched to branch 'master'
Your branch is ahead of 'origin/master' by 1 commit.
  (use "git push" to publish your local commits)
netdevops@netdevops-VirtualBox:~/GitExamples/devnetassoc$ git branch
  anothertest_branch
* master
  test_branch
netdevops@netdevops-VirtualBox:~/GitExamples/devnetassoc$
netdevops@netdevops-VirtualBox:~/GitExamples/devnetassoc$ git merge anothertest_branch
Updating 7f481e5..cb0cf78
Fast-forward
 persons1.xml | 19 ++++++++++++++++++++
 1 file changed, 19 insertions(+)
 create mode 100644 persons1.xml
netdevops@netdevops-VirtualBox:~/GitExamples/devnetassoc$
```

Diff Operation

Git diff command shows the file differences or changes that are not yet staged (or tracked or added), changes between files in the staging area and the current version, and the differences even between branches.

In the example below, we made changes to parse-json.py script as highlighted with red (-) and green (+) and corresponding line items or contents.

```
netdevops@netdevops-VirtualBox:~/GitExamples/devnetassoc$ git add parse-json.py
netdevops@netdevops-VirtualBox:~/GitExamples/devnetassoc$ git diff test_branch
diff --git a/parse-json.py b/parse-json.py
index baae765..dece3ae 100644
--- a/parse-json.py
+++ b/parse-json.py
@@ -1,7 +1,7 @@
 import json
 with open('persons.json', 'r') as f:
-    my_dict = json.load(f)
+    my_dictionary = json.load(f)

-for distro in my_dict:
+for distro in my_dictionary:
     print(distro['gender'])
     print(distro['name'])
```

In the example below, we requested the diff between two of our branches, test_branch, and anothertest_branch.

```
netdevops@netdevops-VirtualBox:~/GitExamples/devnetassoc$ git diff test_branch anothertest_branch
diff --git a/persons.xml b/persons.xml
index e4037e0..b2d6fdf 100644
--- a/persons.xml
+++ b/persons.xml
@@ -11,9 +11,4 @@
         <gender>female</gender>
         <name>Jessica Alba</name>
     </element>
    <element>
        <gender>male</gender>
        <name>Richard Branson</name>
    </element>
 </persons>

diff --git a/persons1.xml b/persons1.xml
new file mode 100644
index 0000000..5d5fad9
--- /dev/null
+++ b/persons1.xml
@@ -0,0 +1,19 @@
+<persons>
+    <element>
+        <gender>male</gender>
+        <name>Jeff Bezos</name>
+    </element>
+    <element>
+        <gender>male</gender>
+        <name>Elon Musk</name>
+    </element>
+    <element>
+        <gender>female</gender>
+        <name>Jessica Alba</name>
+    </element>
+    <element>
+        <gender>female</gender>
+        <name>Oprah Winfrey</name>
+    </element>
+</persons>
+
netdevops@netdevops-VirtualBox:~/GitExamples/devnetassoc$
```

Merge conflict results from competing changes, say developer A deletes a file in branch A and developer B edits the same file in branch B where both branches A and B are part of one repo. This scenario forces a decision of whether to delete or keep the removed file in a new commit. You can display merge conflict using the "git status" command.

You'd need to resolve the conflict before a commit will be allowed. You have two choices, either you keep (git add <file>) the file from branch B or remove it (git rm <file>). Now, before we move on, it is important to summarize the various Git operations we have covered in this section.

Git Operation or Concept	Git Command (without options, operable to currently checkout branch)	Description

Project	n/a	Everything, a folder where your .git/ folder lives
Repo	git init	Directories and files that are version controlled within .git/ folder. It can contain multiple branches. This allows a team to work together, i.e., divide and conquer feature development.
Branch		Multiple versions of repo, say feature-1, feature-2 etc.
Fork		Duplicate a repo so you can experiment with or modify code without affecting the original repo.
Clone	git clone	Duplicate a repo (say copy from remote to local drive). Git clone command includes a bunch of other tasks, think of it as a wrapper around init, add, fetch, and checkout git operations.
Add	git add (or git stage) git add -A git add . git add -u	Tracks or Stages all file(s) for changes Stages all Stages new and modified, without deleted Stages modified and deleted, without new
Remove	git remove	Untrack file(s) for changes
Commit	git commit	Saving tracked changes to local repo
Push	git push	Upload locally saved changes to remote repo
Pull	git pull	Download saved changes from remote repo
Merge	git merge	Merging saved changes from one or

		more branches into one
Diff	git diff	It runs a diff on data sources such as commits, branches, files etc.

GitOps

Now, before we move on, there is one more topic that's worthy of mention in this section, and that is GitOps. It is a way of implementing continuous deployment for cloud native applications. The central idea of GitOps is having a Git repository that acts as single source of truth with declarative descriptions of the infrastructure currently desired in the production environment and an automated process to make the production environment match the state stored inside the repo.

The main benefits of GitOps approach are:

- Versioned deployments and change history
- Rollbacks by using Git
- Out of the box access control
- Policies for deployment

There are two ways to implement GitOps, i.e., push and pull-based deployments. Both methods are similar except the how the deployment pipeline works. If you use a traditional build tool such as Jenkins or TravisCI are triggered by an external event such as when new code is pushed to the software repo. With pull-based deployment, there is a new role of an operator which takes over the role of the pipeline by continuously comparing the desired state in the environment repo with the actual state in the deployed infrastructure.

Further Reading

Introduction to Git[11]

Git Reference[12]

[11] https://bit.ly/3aR1Agi

[12] https://git-scm.com/doc

Chapter Summary

- eXtensible Markup Language (or XML) is a markup language much like HTML and consists of a set of rules for encoding documents that are human and machine-readable.
- There are two well-known methods to parse XML with Python, i.e., you can use the ElementTree (ET) APIs or the Minidom module to load and parse XML.
- JavaScript Object Notation (or JSON) is language-agnostic is documented as its data encoding standard.
- YAML Ain't Markup Language (or YAML) is the most human-friendly data encoding or serialization standard out there
- There are two most common types of software development methodologies out there, i.e., Behavior-Driven and Test-Driven Developments, commonly known as BDD and TDD.
- TDD approach can be broken down into three core steps which repeat endlessly until the development goals are achieved.
    o Initial Test (or Unit test)
    o Coding
    o Refactor Code
- Agile requires a lot of collaboration among the teams and stakeholders involved in order to deliver both working and tested features faster.
- Lean method essentially helps agile work at scale across a big organization. It operates from a top-down approach as opposed to bottoms-up.
- Methods, functions, classes, and modules are ways of achieving source code level modularity which in turn makes it easier to read and modify.
- MVC model breaks up the overall design pattern into three components i.e., Model, View, and Controller.
- Git is a free and open source and supports dozens of operations that can be performed to enforce source code version control in a distributed manner.
- Git add allows you to add a file to the staging area, and Git remove works on the working directory as well as the staging index.

CHAPTER 2 UNDERSTANDING AND USING APIs

This chapter covers the following exam topics from Cisco's official 200-901 V1.0 DevNet Associate exam blueprint.

- Construct a REST API request to accomplish a task given API documentation
- Describe common usage patterns related to webhooks
- Identify the constraints when consuming APIs
- Explain common HTTP response codes associated with REST APIs
- Troubleshoot a problem given the HTTP response code, request and API documentation
- Identify the parts of an HTTP response (response code, headers, body)
- Utilize common API authentication mechanisms: basic, custom token, and API keys
- Compare common API styles (REST, RPC, synchronous, and asynchronous)
- Construct a Python script that calls a REST API using the requests library

Construct a REST API request to accomplish a task given API documentation

Application Programming Interface (or an API) is an interface mechanism and a protocol to carry out communication between a server and a client with the primary purpose of simplifying the software development of client-side software.

API determines what type of data, services, and functionality the application exposes to 3rd parties. Here are a few common use cases for the APIs.

- Task automation
- Data integration (between two applications)
- Functionality (one application can integrate functionality from another application)

APIs have been around for decades, but their usage has grown exponentially over the past decade. Modern APIs are coded into the product from day one and very reliable to use. Another factor for the popularity is the ease of use, e.g., you can use APIs with simpler coding languages such as Python or even without writing a single line of code with tools such as Zapier.

APIs are broadly split into internal and external based on how they are used and shared in a system. Internal and external APIs are also known as private and public. Private APIs are exclusively meant to be used for building applications that are to be used within a company.

Public APIs, on the other hand, are for open use by all third parties who may be interested in building applications that use the company's services. Outside organizations are expected to use these APIs to build or extend beyond the original intent.

All major operations systems such as macOS, Windows, iOS, and Android have both private and public APIs. The use of private APIs by anyone outside the organization is frowned upon, and for mobile development, it simply means that your app will be rejected by iOS or Android approval teams. However, there was one famous example, where late Steve Jobs personally intervened and approved an app then known as "Knocking Live Video".

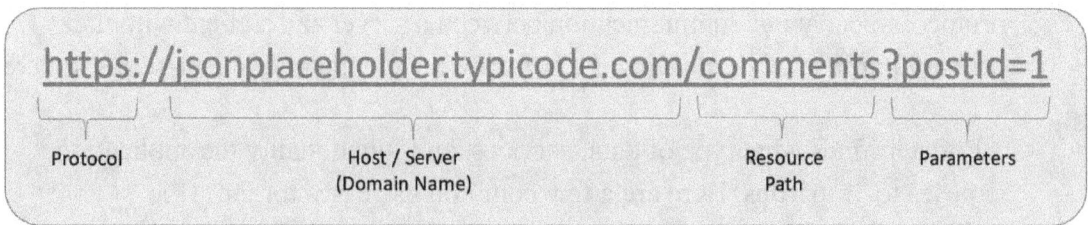

Let's now use cURL to issue a REST API request, cURL is a "client for URLs", or a command-line utility to transfer data using various protocols. Here we will use cURL to perform a GET operation (using the -I option tells it to only pull the HTTP headers or HEAD method). The response you see below is what is sent by the web server in response.

```
MAK1-MBP:~ afaqkhan$ curl -I https://jsonplaceholder.typicode.com/comments?postId=1
HTTP/2 200
date: Fri, 27 Sep 2019 04:24:48 GMT
content-type: application/json; charset=utf-8
set-cookie: __cfduid=d538016e77932f4322c8dc1440542615f1569558288; expires=Sat, 26-Sep-20 04:24:48 GMT; path
=/; domain=.typicode.com; HttpOnly
x-powered-by: Express
vary: Origin, Accept-Encoding
access-control-allow-credentials: true
cache-control: public, max-age=14400
pragma: no-cache
expires: Fri, 27 Sep 2019 08:24:48 GMT
x-content-type-options: nosniff
etag: W/"5e6-4bSPS5tq8F8ZDeFJULWh6upjp7U"
via: 1.1 vegur
cf-cache-status: HIT
age: 19
expect-ct: max-age=604800, report-uri="https://report-uri.cloudflare.com/cdn-cgi/beacon/expect-ct"
server: cloudflare
cf-ray: 51cab5c91917e4d4-LAX
```

Describe common usage patterns related to webhooks

A webhook is simply an HTTP callback to a specified URL that notifies your application when a specific activity or even takes place. Webhooks enable applications to receive real-time data as the trigger takes place. It is the opposite of the polling or pull mechanism.

You can think of webhooks as reverse APIs, because server calls the client application when the target activity or event occurs. The URL called by the server is actually an API on the application side that the server calls. For example, Cisco DNA Center platform and WebEx Teams provide webhooks that third-party applications can use to receive data when a network related event occurs, or a new message is posted in a particular room respectively.

Webhook events are triggered by some action taken by a user or a machine on one system which communicates some kind of unstructured or structured data (such as JSON) to another system. The underlying transport protocol is HTTP or HTTPS and the method used is POST.

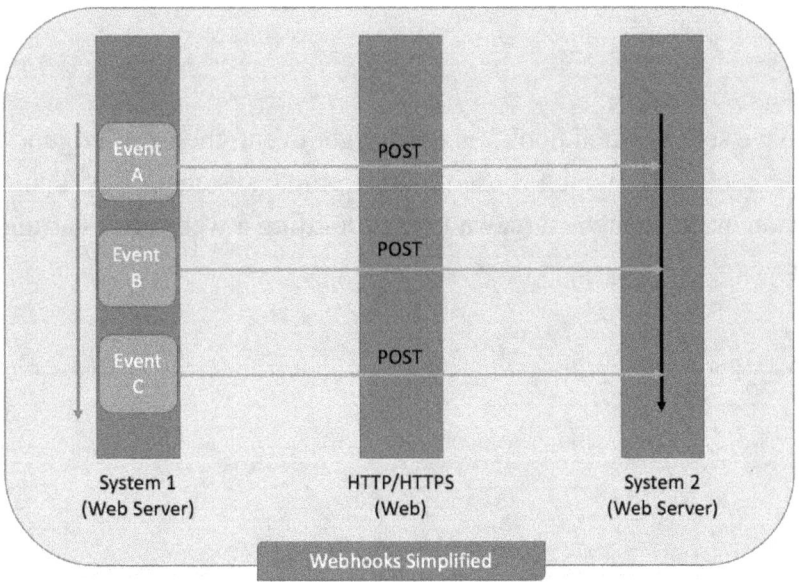

An example of webhook creation on Zapier platform.

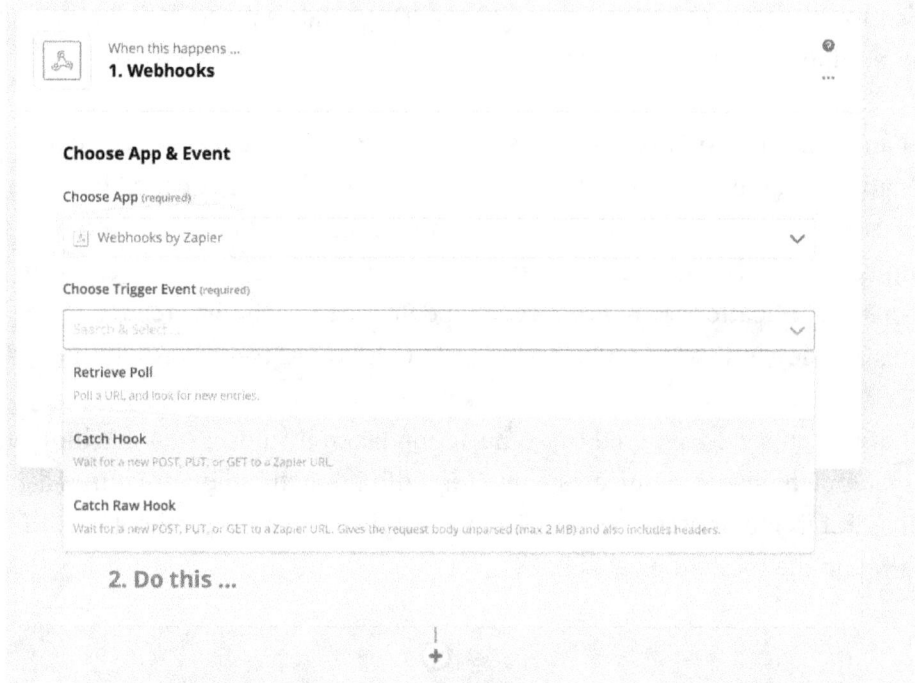

Now, once we select "catch hook" as our trigger event, then Zapier generates a random webhook URL, which is used by the remote system to POST into Zapier every time an event of interest (say a user submitting a web form) is triggered on that system.

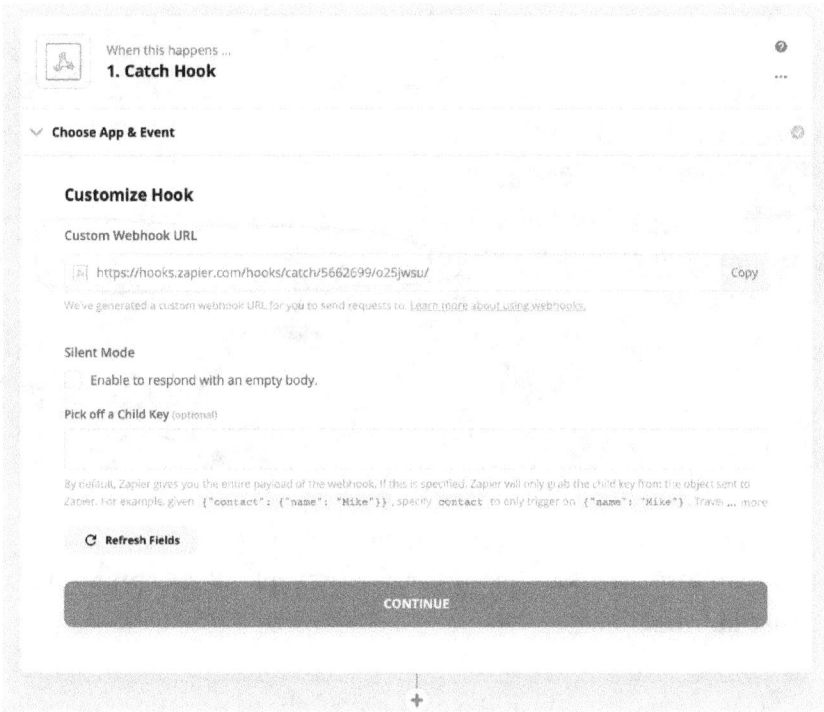

Even as a web user, you trigger multiple webhooks each day while browsing through the web. How? Let me give you a few examples.

When you go to Cisco certification page where Cisco has a call to action "Stay Informed", and when you fill up that form and hit submit, a "new subscriber" webhook is called into Cisco's email marketing platform (say MailChimp) and your submitted data such as your names, email address and certification status are populated within new subscriber fields.

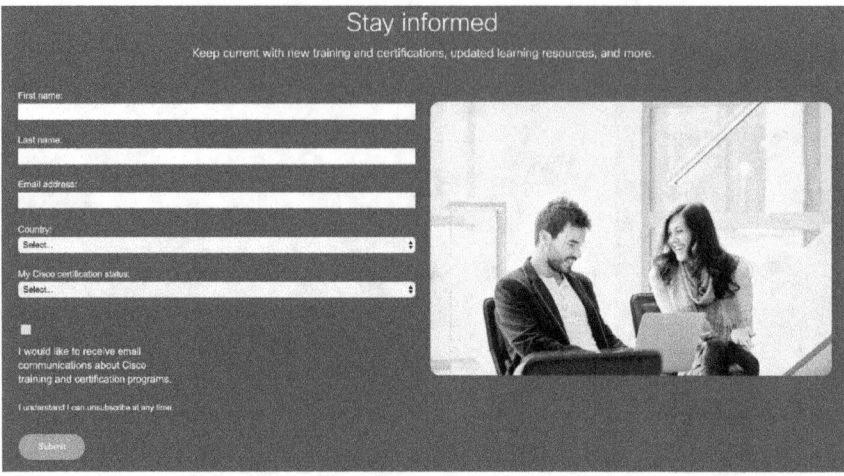

Another example is each time you submit an order on Amazon or Shopify. Your order submission form invokes perhaps multiple webhooks, captures and processes that information.

Last but not least, you may revisit the concept of observer pattern from the last section and think "hey, they look similar" and yes, they do, but an observer pattern could be implemented for just about any event-driven systems but webhooks are as the name says, for the "web".

In case of the web, the browser (subject) notifies the user (the observer) when an event takes place. Do you ever recall going to a website and receiving the following notification?

Instead of polling the web server, in this case, the web server is offering an option to push notifications to your browser or even desktop when there is an event.

Just to recap, the consumption of a webhook requires meeting some of the following requirements.

- The application must be up 24x7 to receive the HTTP POST
- The application must register a URL on the webhook provider so the provider where to send a notification when the target event occurs.
- The application must be able to handle the incoming payload.

Identify the constraints when consuming APIs

API constraints refer to the architectural constraints or design guidelines that should be followed when using the APIs. In this section, we will be using REST or RESTful APIs to discuss constraints.

Representational State Transfer (or REST) was described by Roy Fielding in 2000 as part of his PhD dissertation. He described six constraints or principles for REST (not to be confused with REST APIs!). These constraints can be applied to any protocol and when that happens, it is known as RESTful.

- Client/server
- Stateless
- Cache
- Uniform interface
- Layered system
- Code-on-demand

Let's understand each of those constraints one by one.

The client and the server should be independent of each other, e.g., where one client can be built for multiple server platforms. Client/server refers to the assumption that clients and server applications MUST be able to evolve and develop independently, a client only needs to know the resource URIs.

The requests from the client to server must be standalone, i.e., there is no concept of a session. The server cannot contain session states. Make all client/server interaction stateless, but why? Because if you make a client app stateful, then it needs to communicate the entire lifecycle of user states to the remote server which isn't good for the server as a client should simply store the user states while no context is stored or preserved between REST requests.

The server dictates if the response is cacheable or not, if it is cacheable then client can use the data from the response for another request later on. Caching can be implemented on the client or server-side, and it is hugely useful for performance reasons including minimizing some client/server communication. The uniform interface, i.e., the interface between the client and the server, is based on four principles of its own.

- Identification of resources
- Manipulation of resources through representations
- Self-descriptive messages
- Hypermedia as the engine of application state

The system is made up of different layers and where each layer under provides services only to the layer above it (much like what happens in case of OSI stack). REST allows the use of layered system architecture, i.e., a web server where APIs are actually hosted may store its database on another server and authentication information on yet another one without exposing any of this to the client.

Lastly, the code-on-demand is an optional constraint and simply describes the fact that information returned by a REST service can include executable code, or link to code, etc. Code-on-demand is used by payment gateways such as Stripe, where they send in a JavaScript file that is downloaded and executed by the client. There is no doubt that if used without security measures, code-on-demand can become a security risk.

REST web service API or REST API is a programming interface that adheres to the principles of REST and communicates over HTTP. REST APIs use the following components of the HTTP.

- HTTP requests/responses
- HTTP verbs or methods
- HTTP status codes
- HTTP headers/body

There are four major components of a REST API call.

- Uniform Resource Identifier (URI)
- HTTP method
- Header
- Body

The URI or URL identifies which resource the client wants to manipulate. The URI syntax consists of the following components:

- Scheme
- Authority
- Path
- Query

With all of the four pieces together, it looks like the following.

scheme:[//authority][/path][?query]

or

https://fullstacknetworker.com:443/v1/products/?q=DevNetAssociate

The scheme refers to the transport protocol, for REST APIs, there are only two choices, HTTP or HTTPS (HTTP with TLS). The authority or destination consist of two parts, the host and port. The path, also known as resource path, simply represents the location of the resource, or data or an object. The query and the parameter are optional. If a query is present, it is preceded by a question mark (?) as shown in the example above.

Further Reading

Getting Started with APIs[13]

Explain common HTTP response codes associated with REST APIs

HTTP Method	Action (CRUD)
POST	Create (C)
GET	Retrieve (R)
PUT	Update (U), existing resource
PATCH	Update (U), partial update on a resource
DELETE	Delete (D)

In summary, the HTTP response or status code means the following.

- 1XX: Informational (e.g., 101 means Switching Protocols)
- 2XX: Success (e.g., 200 means OK)
- 3XX: Redirection (e.g., 301 means Moved Permanently)
- 4XX: Client Error (e.g., 401 Unauthorized, 403 Forbidden, 404 Not Found etc.)

---

[13] https://bit.ly/2TVkn3o

- 5XX: Server Error (e.g., 500 Internal Server Error, 502 Bad Gateway, 503 Service Unavailable etc.)

Now, let's look at some of the specific response codes and their description.

HTTP Response Code	Status Message	Description
200	OK	Good
201	Created	New resource created
400	Bad Request	Invalid request
401	Unauthorized	Missing/Incorrect authentication
403	Forbidden	Not allowed
404	Not Found	Resource not found
500	Internal Server Error	Something wrong with the server
503	Service Unavailable	Server is unable to complete request
504	Gateway Timeout	Server timeout

Troubleshoot a problem given the HTTP response code, request and API documentation

In the previous section, we learned about the HTTP response codes that we expect to receive from the API server such as 2xx, 4xx and 5xx codes. What if, the API server or service can't be reached at all? Well, in that scenario, you will not receive an HTTP status code because the API server is not available to send back a response.

Anyhow, troubleshooting APIs is about investigating two sides of the communication, i.e., the client and the server sides. In case of the client-side errors, here is a list of things that can go wrong.

- User error (is the URI correct? Has this request worked before?)

- Connectivity issues (are there any proxy, or firewall or VPN devices in the middle? Is there an SSL certificate error?)

Once you've verified the client-side, you can look for some of the possible server-side errors.

- API service status (is the server up? Is the network down?)
- Connectivity issues (is server IP and domain accessible from client side?)

If you are able to receive a response code from the API server, then you take the following steps to troubleshoot issues.

- Check the return code (from the API service)
- Check the response body
- Check the HTTP status code

Let's now construct a simple HTTP GET with a valid URL to GitHub and see what we get in response. As mentioned earlier, HTTP 200 means file or resource was found and all OK.

Python Code

```
1  import requests as req
2
3  response = req.get('https://github.com/apps/devnet-app')
4  print(response.status_code)
5  if response.status_code == 200:
6    print('Success!')
7  elif response.status_code == 404:
8    print('Not Found.')
```

Code Output

```
https://REST-API-authentication-basic-userpwd.fsnetwc  [⧉]

Python 3.7.4 (default, Jul  9 2019, 00:06:43)          [→] [×]
[GCC 6.3.0 20170516] on linux
200
Success!
> []
```

Now, let's modify the app web URL by adding a "blah" at the end and see how our HTTP response code changes. HTTP status code 404 simply means file or resource was not found.

Python Code

```python
1   import requests as req
2
3   response = req.get('https://github.com/apps/devnet-app/blah')
4   print(response.status_code)
5
6 ▾ if response.status_code == 200:
7     print('Success!')
8 ▾ elif response.status_code == 404:
9     print('Not Found.')
```

Code Output

```
Python 3.7.4 (default, Jul  9 2019, 00:06:43)          [→] [×]
[GCC 6.3.0 20170516] on linux
404
Not Found.
```

Identify the parts of an HTTP response (response code, headers, body)

REST API responses are HTTP response, and they communicate the results of a client's HTTP request. REST API responses are similar to the requests and are made up of three components.

- HTTP status
- Header
- Body

RSET APIs use the standard HTTP status codes in the response to inform the client whether the request was successful or not. HTTP status codes are always three digits as we discussed in the earlier section.

Just like the request, the response's header also uses a standard HTTP header format. There are two types of headers.
- Response headers
- Entity headers

Response headers contain additional information that doesn't relate to the content of the message. Let's go over two examples of response headers.

Key	Example Response header
Set-cookie	Sessionid=902387459037;Path=/
Cache-control	Cache-control: max-age=1440,pubilc

Entity headers are additional information to describe the details of the body such as the response's content-type.

Key	Example Response header
Content-type	Application/xml

The body of the REST API is the actual data that the client requested in the API request. The data type used by the body is described in the entity header.

If the APIs need to send back a large amount of data, such as in response to a search request, the APIs may paginate the response to reduce the bandwidth requirement. The use of pagination helps breakdown the data in smaller chunks, say 75 or 100 records at a time. But what if the server needs to send a large amount of data that can't be paginated? Well, then it can use compression to reduce the bandwidth requirement. The data compression can be requested by the client in the accept-encoding field as part of the request header. Following are the valid values for it.

- gzip
- Compress
- Deflate
- Br
- Identity
- *

If the server supports compression, then it will send compressed data along with the content-encoding field, in the response header, set to the type of compression used. You can also view HTTP headers (requests and responses) using the Inspect function within the Chrome browser.

Before we wrap up this section, let's compare all of the HTTP methods side by side in terms of Request and Response headers. Idempotent is a fancy word but what it means is that an HTTP method is idempotent by definition if an identical request can be made either once or many times over with the same effect while the server state is not changed. Except for the POST method, all other HTTP methods are not idempotent.

HTP Method	Request Has Body	Successful Response Has Body	Idempotent	Cacheable
GET	No	Yes	Yes	Yes
POST	Yes	Yes	No	Only if asked
PATCH	Yes	Yes	No	No

PUT	Yes	No	Yes	No
DELETE	May be	May be	Yes	No

Utilize common API authentication mechanisms: basic, custom token, and API keys

Before we discuss API authentication, it is crucial to understand what authentication is and how it is different from authorization.

Authentication is the process of verifying a user's identity, i.e., you are proving that they are who they say they are. For example, when you go to sit a Cisco exam, the Pearson VUE testing center asks for two forms of identifications so they can ascertain that you are the person who booked the exam online.

Authorization is the user proving that they have the permissions to perform the action. For example, when you go to a concert, all you need to show is your concern ticket to prove that you are allowed in. You don't have to prove your identity.

The REST APIs can be authenticated in many different ways, but the most common ones are using one of the following.

- Basic Auth (where the access token is sent as the username, identifies a user)
- Bearer Authentication or Access token (identifies a user that is using the app)
- API keys (identifies the app or site that's making the API call)

Basic authentication or Basic Auth, uses standard HTTP authentication scheme. It sends credentials as username/password pairs separated with a colon with Base64 encoding.

In REST API request, the Basic Auth information is provided in the header.

Authorization: Basic <username>:<password>

It is the simplest form of authentication but carries credentials without any encryption and thus is almost always used with HTTPS.

Bearer authentication or token authentication uses standard Bearer authentication scheme. It uses a bearer token which is a string generated by an auth server such as an identity service. It is more secure than basic auth and typically used with oAuth and SSO.

In REST API request, the bearer authentication information is provided in the header. It is recommended to use HTTPS with bearer just like basic auth.

Authorization: Bearer <bearer token>

The API key or API token authentication is yet another authentication mechanism. API key is a unique alphanumeric string generated by the server and assigned to a user. To receive the API key, a user needs to log into the service and request their token. All REST API requests for this user must provide the same key as the form of authentication. It is also recommended to secure this key with HTTPS.

There are two types of API keys, public and private. The public key can be shared with others and it enables others to get public information about you. Your private key is much like your password and must not be shared with anyone. If someone gets access to your private key, then they can access the system as you indefinitely.

Open Authorization or what's known as oAuth, combines authentication and authorization. oAuth is the recommended form of authorization for REST APIs. There are two versions of oAuth, i.e., oAuth 1.0 and oAuth 2.0. oAuth 2.0 is the most prevalent version used by the REST APIs.

oAuth allows pre-registered applications to get authorization to perform REST API requests on user's behalf, i.e., without needing the user to share his/her credentials with the application itself. The user provides credentials to the authorization server (such as IdP and IdS), obtains an access token and uses that from inside the application to access the service.

Most API services also implement some form of API rate limiting as a best practice for the following reasons.

- Avoid a server overload (let's say a server receives an API-driven DDoS against the service)
- Improve response and better uptime for everyone

Python Code using token sent as username

```
 1  import requests
 2  import json
 3
 4  token = 'N3h5OJYadMUFBYqhxkX6XOozRBI4RJSZlsB3'
 5  url = 'https://gorest.co.in/public-api/users'
 6  data = {
 7     "email": "email7@example.com",
 8     "first_name": "devnet",
 9     "last_name": "associate",
10     "gender": "male"
11  }
12  result = requests.post(url,
13     headers = {
14        'Content-Type': 'application/json',
15        'Authorization': 'Bearer {}'.format(token)
16     }, data = json.dumps(data))
17  print('Code: ', result.status_code)
18  print('Content: ', result.content.decode()[: 500] + '...')
```

Code Output

As you can notice, new user email7@example.com was successfully added.

```
Code:  200
Content:  {"_meta":{"success":true,"code":200,"message":"OK. Everything
 worked as expected.","rateLimit":{"limit":30,"remaining":28,"reset":4}
},"result":{"id":"2044","first_name":"devnet","last_name":"associate","
gender":"male","dob":null,"email":"email7@example.com","phone":null,"we
bsite":null,"address":null,"status":null,"_links":{"self":{"href":"http
s://gorest.co.in/public-api/users/2044"},"edit":{"href":"https://gorest
.co.in/public-api/users/2044"},"avatar":{"href":null}}}}...
>
```

If we modify the access token, the user doesn't get added and we receive an error message instead.

Python Code

```python
1   import requests
2   import json
3
4   token = 'B3h5OJYadMUFBYqhxkX6XOozRBI4RJSZlsB3'#
5   wrong token supplied
6   url = 'https://gorest.co.in/public-api/users'
7 ▾ data = {
8     "email": "email8@example.com",
9     "first_name": "devnet",
10    "last_name": "associate",
11    "gender": "male"
12  }
13  result = requests.post(url,
14 ▾   headers = {
15      'Content-Type': 'application/json',
16      'Authorization': 'Bearer {}'.format(token)
17    }, data = json.dumps(data))
18  print('Code: ', result.status_code)
19  print('Content: ', result.content.decode()[: 500] + '...')
```

Code Output

```
Code:  200
Content:  {"_meta":{"success":false,"code":401,"message":"Authenticatio
n failed."},"result":{"name":"Unauthorized","message":"Your request was
 made with invalid credentials.","code":0,"status":401}}...
> 
```

Let's also explore all of the token authentication mechanism together with one
GitHub app example. We will break down the overall approach into six steps.

1. Register a GitHub app ("devnet-app" app) using
   github.com/settings/apps
2. Create a private API key for our app
3. Install the "devnet-app" app and authorize it for R/W permissions for
   repo and labels etc.
4. Load the private key file (devnet-app.2019-09-28.private-key.pem) using
   the Python Crypto module (cryptography.hazmat.backends)
5. Get the app installation id and app access token and use them to
   construct our authorization headers so we can perform an HTTP GET on
   our target repo (devnetassoc)
6. At this point, we've R/W access to our GitHub repo remotely via REST
   APIs via the devnet-app. We can modify the devnetassoc repo, add
   labels, etc. using HTTP POST.

Screenshots shown below highlight the GitHub side of tasks that are required to
accomplish the above steps. Once you've done that, you can move to build
Python script.

Settings   Developer settings   GitHub Apps   **devnet-app**

General
Permissions & events
Install App
Advanced
Public page ⬚

About

Owned by: @afaoki9394

App ID: 42354

Client ID: Iv1.8a277bd82900fddd

Client secret: a4aacbd08c048d12ee9bc8c1b3e69c2238b02f71

[Revoke all user tokens]   [Reset client secret]

GitHub Apps can use OAuth credentials to identify users. Learn more about identifying users by reading our integration
developer documentation.

Basic information

GitHub App name

devnet-app

The name of your GitHub App.

Write Preview	📝 Markdown supported

devnet-app for testing response codes

Homepage URL

https://www.fullstacknetworker.com

The full URL to your GitHub App's website.

User authorization callback URL

https://www.fullstacknetworker.com/blah1

https://www.fullstacknetworker.com/blah2

Events will POST to this URL. Read our webhook documentation for more information.

Webhook secret (optional)

Read our webhook secret documentation for more information.

SSL verification

🔒 By default, we verify SSL certificates when delivering payloads.

🔘 **Enable SSL verification**   ⚪ Disable (not recommended)

[Save changes]   Cancel

Display information

Upload a logo...

You can also drag and drop a picture from your computer.

Drag & drop

Private keys

[Generate a private key]

You need a private key to sign access token requests. Learn more about private keys.

🔑
Private

Private key 39:a1:0d:7d:d6:7e:df:e7:e1:43:59:51:07:67:8e:17:d5:66:96:e5
Added 6 hours ago by afaqk9394

[Delete]

Settings   Developer settings   GitHub Apps   **devnet-app**

General

Permissions & events

Install App

Advanced

Public page

Permissions

Changes to permissions will be applied to all future installations. Current users will be prompted to accept any changes and enable the new permissions on their installation.

Repository permissions

Administration ⓘ
Repository creation, deletion, settings, teams, and collaborators.

Access: **Read & write** ▾

Checks ⓘ
Checks on code.

Access: **No access** ▾

Content references ⓘ
Get notified of content references, and create content attachments.

Access: **No access** ▾

Contents ⓘ
Repository contents, commits, branches, downloads, releases, and merges.

Access: **No access** ▾

Deployments ⓘ
Deployments and deployment statuses.

Access: **No access** ▾

Issues ⓘ
Issues and related comments, assignees, labels, and milestones.

Access: **Read & write** ▾

Metadata ⓘ
Search repositories, list collaborators, and access repository metadata.

mandatory   Access: **Read-only** ▾

Pages ⓘ
Retrieve Pages statuses, configuration, and builds, as well as create new builds.

Access: **No access** ▾

Pull requests ⓘ
Pull requests and related comments, assignees, labels, milestones, and merges.

Access: **Read & write** ▾

Webhooks ⓘ
Manage the post-receive hooks for a repository.

Access: **No access** ▾

Settings   Developer settings   GitHub Apps   **devnet-app**

General

Permissions & events

Install App

Advanced

Public page

Install devnet-app

Choose an account to install devnet-app on:

afaqk9394   installed   ⚙

Settings   Developer settings   GitHub Apps   **devnet-app**

General

Permissions & events

Install App

Advanced

Public page

Recent Deliveries

⚠️ ✉️ 6e7ed5f0-e283-11e9-9dde-4c09a64e8026   2019-09-28 23:36:13 ⋯

| Request | Response `404` | | | Redeliver | 🕐 Completed in 1.0 second. |

Headers

```
Request method: POST
content-type: application/json
Expect:
User-Agent: GitHub-Hookshot/3afdf3c
X-GitHub-Delivery: 6e7ed5f0-e283-11e9-9dde-4c09a64e8026
X-GitHub-Event: installation
```

Payload

```
{
  "action": "new permissions_accepted",
  "installation": {
    "id": 2278268.
    "account": {
      "login": "afaqk9394",
      "id": 46501831,
      "node_id": "MDQ6VXNlcjQ2NTAxODMx",
      "avatar_url": "https://avatars3.githubusercontent.com/u/46501831?v=4",
      "gravatar_id": "",
      "url": "https://api.github.com/users/afaqk9394",
      "html_url": "https://github.com/afaqk9394",
      "followers_url": "https://api.github.com/users/afaqk9394/followers",
      "following_url": "https://api.github.com/users/afaqk9394/following{/other_user}",
      "gists_url": "https://api.github.com/users/afaqk9394/gists{/gist_id}",
      "starred_url": "https://api.github.com/users/afaqk9394/starred{/owner}{/repo}",
      "subscriptions_url": "https://api.github.com/users/afaqk9394/subscriptions",
      "organizations_url": "https://api.github.com/users/afaqk9394/orgs",
      "repos_url": "https://api.github.com/users/afaqk9394/repos",
      "events_url": "https://api.github.com/users/afaqk9394/events{/privacy}",
      "received_events_url": "https://api.github.com/users/afaqk9394/received_events",
      "type": "User",
      "site_admin": false
    },
    "repository selection": "all",
```

afaqk9394 / devnetassoc   👁 Unwatch ▾ 1   ★ Star 0   ⑂ Fork 0

‹›Code   ⓘ Issues 2   ⑄ Pull requests 0   ▣ Projects 0   ▤ Wiki   Security   ⓘ Insights   ⚙ Settings

Options

Collaborators

Branches

Webhooks

Notifications

Integrations & services

Deploy keys

Moderation

Interaction limits

Installed GitHub Apps

GitHub Apps augment and extend your workflows on GitHub with commercial, open source, and homegrown tools.

🔲 devnet-app   Configure

Services

Services are pre-built integrations that perform certain actions when events occur on GitHub.

Note: GitHub Services have been deprecated. Please contact your integrator for more information on how to migrate or replace a service with webhooks or GitHub Apps.

The Email service has been replaced by repository notifications. Settings have been migrated on your behalf and can be configured there.

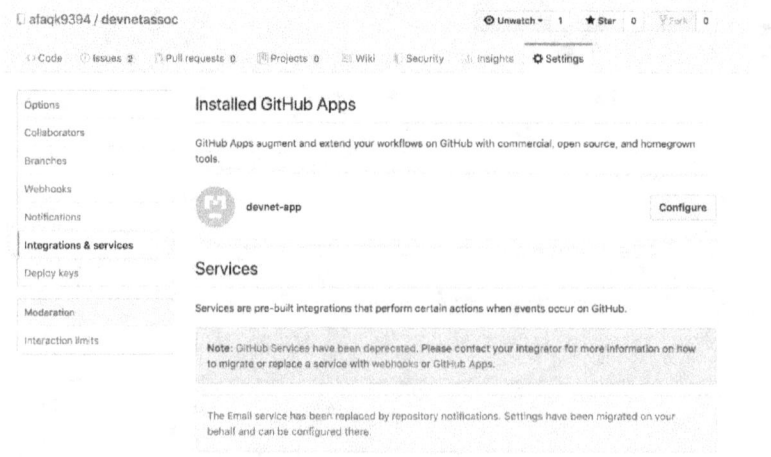

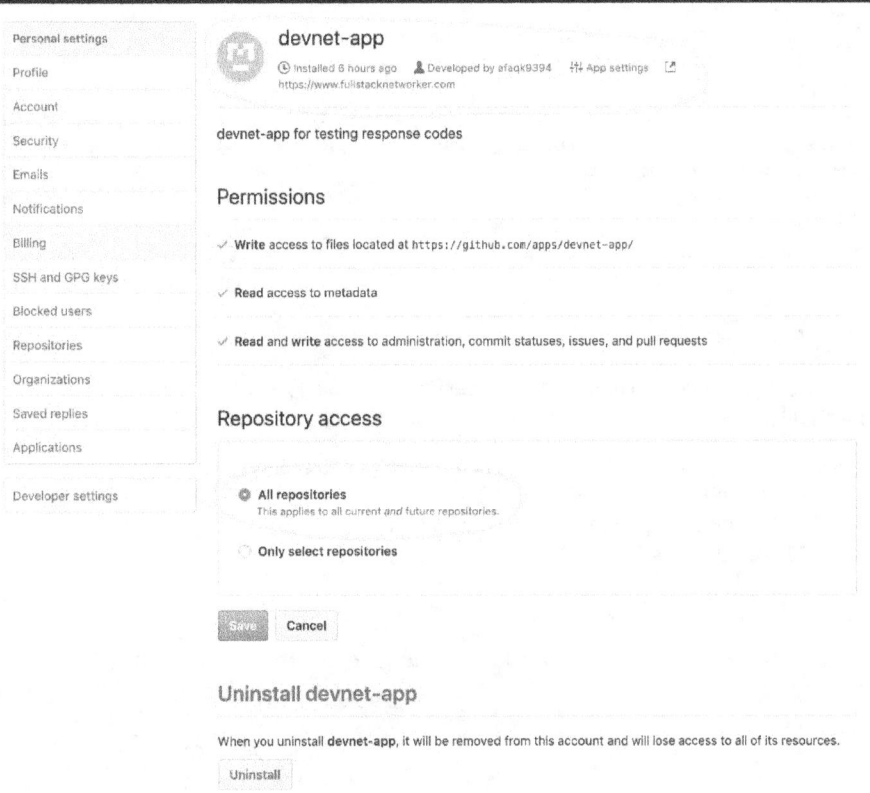

Python Code

```python
1   import requests
2   from cryptography.hazmat.backends import default_backend
3   import jwt
4   import time
5
6   fname = 'devnet-app.2019-09-28.private-key.pem'
7   pem_str = open(fname, 'r').read()
8   pem_bytes = pem_str.encode()
9
10  private_key = default_backend().load_pem_private_key(pem_bytes,
        None)# Encode * anything * using the requires RS256 algorithm
11
12  def app_headers():
13
14      time_since_epoch_in_seconds = int(time.time())
15  payload = {
16      #
17      issued at time 'iat': time_since_epoch_in_seconds,
18      #JWT expiration time(10 minute maximum)
19      'exp': time_since_epoch_in_seconds + (10 * 60),
20      #GitHub App 's identifier
21      'iss': '42354'
22  }
23
24  actual_jwt = jwt.encode(payload, private_key, algorithm = 'RS256')
25
26  headers = {
27      "Authorization": "Bearer {}".format(actual_jwt.decode()),
28      "Accept": "application/vnd.github.machine-man-preview+json"
29  }
30  return headers
31
32  resp = requests.get('https://github.com/apps/devnet-app', headers =
        app_headers())
33
34  installation_id = 2278268
35  resp = requests.post('https://api.github.com/installations/{}
        /access_tokens'.format(installation_id),
36      headers = app_headers())
37
38  headers = {
39      "Authorization": "token {}".format("v1
            .91d1033fc5a6089aea61bb3364231feba0d69012"),
40      "Accept": "application/vnd.github.machine-man-preview+json"
41  }
42  print(headers)
43  resp = requests.get('https://api.github.com/installation
        /repositories', headers = headers)
44  resp = requests.post('https://api.github.com/repos/afaqk9394
        /devnetassoc/issues/2/labels',
45      json = ["bug"], headers = headers)
46  print('Code: ', resp.status_code)
47  print
```

Let's now analyze the above code piece by piece.

Import Modules

```
import requests
from cryptography.hazmat.backends import
default_backend
import jwt
import time
```

Import private key file (.pem)

```
fname = 'devnet-app.2019-09-28.private-
key.pem'
pem_str = open(fname, 'r').read()
pem_bytes = pem_str.encode()
```

Get ready to encode everything using our private keys (TLS)

```
private_key =
default_backend().load_pem_private_key(pem
_bytes, None)
# Encode *anything* using the requires
RS256 algorithm
```

Function definition

RS256 (RSA Signature with SHA-256) is an asymmetric **algorithm**, and it uses a public/private key pair: the identity provider uses a private (secret) key to generate the signature, and the consumer of the JWT uses a public key to validate the signature. Epoch is unix time in seconds.

```
def app_headers():

    time_since_epoch_in_seconds = int(time.time())
    payload = {
    # issued at time
    'iat': time_since_epoch_in_seconds,
    # JWT expiration time (10 minute maximum)
    'exp': time_since_epoch_in_seconds + (10 * 60),
    # GitHub App's identifier
    'iss': '42354'
    }

    actual_jwt = jwt.encode(payload, private_key,
    algorithm='RS256')

    headers = {"Authorization": "Bearer
    {}".format(actual_jwt.decode()),
    "Accept": "application/vnd.github.machine-man-
    preview+json"}
    return headers
```

Issuing a REST GET to our app (devnet-app) and then posting the response along with the app installation ID

```
resp =
requests.get('https://github.com/apps/devnet-
app', headers=app_headers())

installation_id = 2278268
resp =
requests.post('https://api.github.com/installat
ions/{}/access_tokens'.format(installation_id),
headers=app_headers())
```

At this point, if everything goes OK (200), we're above to successfully HTTP GET the repo details.

```
headers = {"Authorization": "token
{}".format("v1.1b4ecb5123751885cb8e4c8b6e5
bccdce95c9c21
"),
"Accept": "application/vnd.github.machine-
man-preview+json"}
print(headers)
resp =
requests.get('https://api.github.com/insta
llation/repositories', headers=headers)
```

Shows two repos ("total_count":2), "demo" and "devnetassoc".

```
Python 3.7.4 (default, Jul  9 2019, 00:06:43)
[GCC 6.3.0 20170516] on linux
{'Authorization': 'token v1.1b4ecb5123751885cb8e4c8b6e5bccdce95c9c21',
'Accept': 'application/vnd.github.machine-man-preview+json'}
Code: 200
Content: {"total_count":2,"repository_selection":"all","repositories":
[{"id":211567090,"node_id":"MDEwOlJlcG9zaXRvcnkyMTE1NjcwOTA=","name":"d
emo","full_name":"afaqk9394/demo","private":false,"owner":{"login":"afa
qk9394","id":46501831,"node_id":"MDQ6VXNlcjQ2NTAxODMx","avatar_url":"ht
tps://avatars3.githubusercontent.com/u/46501831?v=4","gravatar_id":"","
url":"https://api.github.com/users/afaqk9394","html_url":"https://githu
b.com/afaqk9394","followers_url":"https://api.github.com/users/afaqk939
4/followers",...
>
```

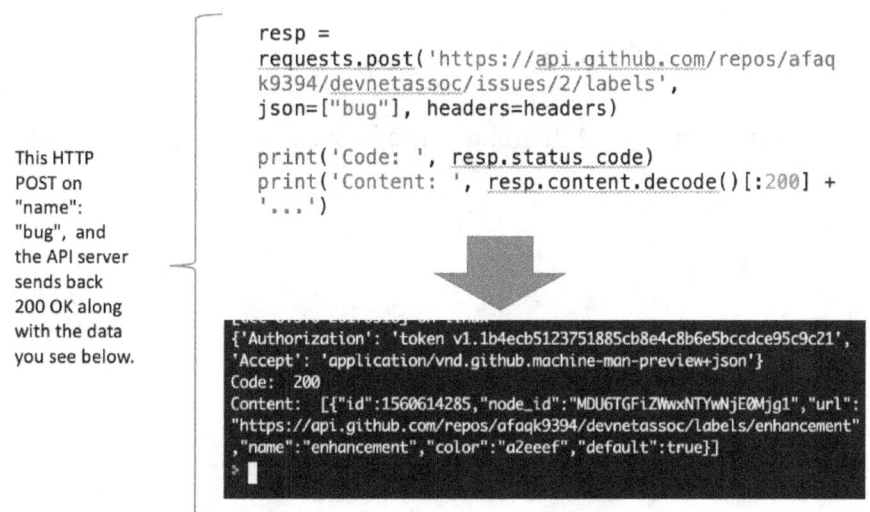

This HTTP POST on "name": "bug", and the API server sends back 200 OK along with the data you see below.

Finally, if you browse directly to the GitHub API URL using a browser, you also get the following JSON encoded output similar to above.

https://api.github.com/repos/afaqk9394/devnetassoc/issues/2/labels

JSON for "devnetassoc" repo via API URL

```
[
{ "id": 1560614276,
"node_id": "MDU6TGFiZWwxNTYwNjE0Mjc2",
"url": "https://api.github.com/repos/afaqk9394/devnetassoc/labels/bug",
"name": "bug",
"color": "d73a4a",
"default": true }
]
```

Compare common API styles (REST, RPC, synchronous, and asynchronous)

The APIs may use HTTP, SMTP or another communication protocol to exchange the data between a desktop or a mobile and a remote service.

- Simple Object Access Protocol (SOAP)

- Remote Procedure Call (RPC)
- Representational State Transfer (REST)

REST APIs are the most popular API architecture in use today.

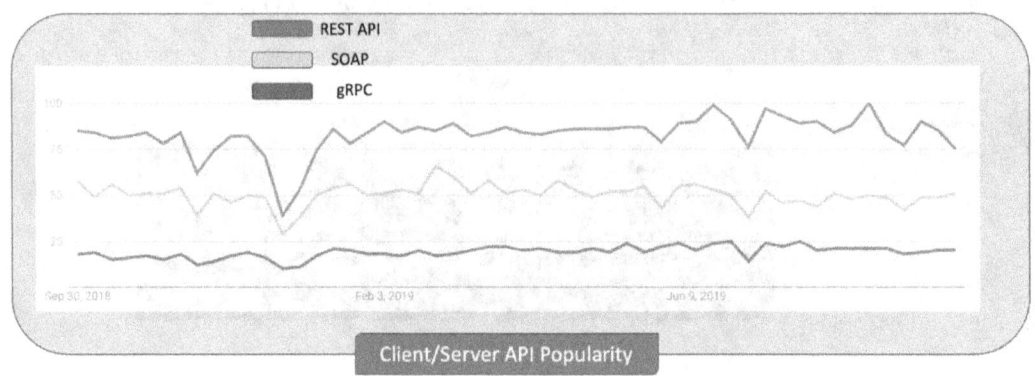

Client/Server API Popularity

There API types differ in many ways but one of the most fundamental aspects is about what data transfer formats are used or supported for request-response messaging.

API Type	Supported Data Encoding Formats
SOAP	XML
REST	JSON, XML etc.
JSON-RPC	JSON
gRPC	ProtoBuf, JSON etc.
GraphQL	JSON
Thrift	JSON or binary data

A common example used to describe the differences between SOAP and REST is that the former is like using an envelope to send information whereas the latter is like using a postcard.

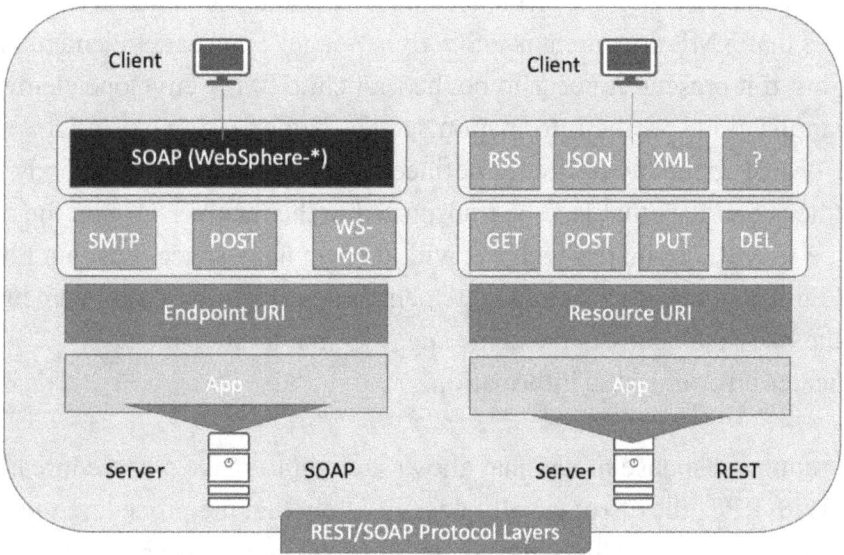

SOAP is a messaging protocol and is based on XML. It was developed by Microsoft and is commonly used with HTTP transport. It has three well-known characteristics.

- Independent
- Extensible
- Neutral

SOAP was designed so all kinds of diverse applications can communicate with each other. It is based on XML, so it can be extended where you can add features such as reliability or security on top of it. It can be used with just about any protocol, e.g., HTTP, SMTP, and TCP/UDP.

SOAP messages are nothing but XML documents and can contain four elements.

- Envelope
- Header
- Body
- Fault

The envelope must be the root element of the XML and it includes a namespace that defines that XML document is a SOAP message. The header element is optional, but if it present, it needs to be the first child of the envelope element. It contains application specific information such as authorization, specific attributes or just about any attributes defined by the applications. The body contains the actual data that is to be transported to the receiver. Again, the data needs to be in XML format as well but with its own namespace. Last but not least, the fault is yet another optional element and needs to be a sub-element or a child of the body element. As the name suggests, the fault element communicates error or status information.

RPC is a request-response model that allows a client to make a procedure call to a server. With RPC, the client usually doesn't know that the procedure request is being executed remotely. Under the covers, for the client, it is simply a method with arguments however the method is executed remotely, and the results are returned. In most cases, with RPC, the client makes a synchronous API call to the server and is blocked while the processes the request. RPC is an API style and can be applied to a number of different transport protocols such as XML-RPC, JSON-RPC, NFS and SOAP.

Web APIs are further divided into client and server-side APIs. Client-side APIs are used to extend the functionality of the browser whereas server-side performance a similar function for server-side APIs.

There are tons of client tools that can be used to test REST APIs, let me summarize a few notable ones.

Postman is a cross-platform REST client that used to be a Chrome extension, you can use it to send a POST request to your web server and it will provide you back with the response. You can configure or set up your HTTP request with all the headers and cookies that your API expects.

SoapUI is a headless REST client that lets you create complex testing scenarios. It is available both as an open source as well as paid (Pro) flavor.

Tricentis Tosca is a continuous testing platform for both Agile and DevOps. It supports HTTPS, JMS, AMQP, Rabbit MQ, SOAP and REST protocols. Katalon and Apache's JMeter are also other notable testing tools.

API calls can be synchronous or asynchronous. Synchronous API calls mean that the application code execution will block or wait for the API call to return before continuing execution. Now, it may sound counter-intuitive, since based on that description, from a user point of view your application will appear as unresponsive while it is waiting for the API to return data so why even go down that path? Well, synchronous APIs are used primarily when further code execution depends on the data returned by the API. The synchronous APIs respond to a request directly and usually providing data or another appropriate response.

On the other hand, asynchronous API calls do not block or wait for the API call to return from the server. Thus, code execution continues and when the API call returns data from the server, a "callback" function is executed. With asynchronous APIs, the client can will receive and act on the data once the server has processed the request. APIs are designed to be asynchronous when the request is an action that takes some time for the server to process or perhaps the data isn't readily available e.g., when the server has to make a request to a remote service to fetch the data. There can be a variety of client-side designs that can be used with asynchronous APIs, i.e., a client may need to queue to store the requests to maintain the order of processing or perhaps employ a polling mechanism to find out the status or progress of a given request.

Further Reading

Using Postman[14]

Construct a Python script that calls a REST API using the requests library

---

[14] https://developer.cisco.com/learning/lab/hands-on-postman/step/1

REST API POST Operation

The HTTP POST method sends data to a web server. The type of the body of the POST request is indicated by the Content-type header. Here we're creating a new user (em@example.com) and the web server will create the user including assigning it an ID which you can see in the response header. Please note the status code 200 (OK) in the response header.

Python Code

```python
1   import requests
2   import json
3
4   token = 'z8-sXMth942nOiQqXuikCNjbamrAlI2IjS7g'
5   url = 'https://gorest.co.in/public-api/users'
6   data = {
7      "email": "em@tesla.com",
8      "first_name": "elon",
9      "last_name": "musk",
10     "gender": "male"
11  }
12  result = requests.post(url,
13    headers = {
14       'Content-Type': 'application/json',
15       'Authorization': 'Bearer {}'.format(token)
16    }, data = json.dumps(data))
17  print('Code: ', result.status_code)
18  print('Content: ', result.content.decode()[: 500] + '...')
```

Code Output

```
Code:  200
Content:  {"_meta":{"success":true,"code":200,"message":"OK. Everything wo
rked as expected.","rateLimit":{"limit":30,"remaining":28,"reset":4}},"res
ult":{"id":"1571","first_name":"elon","last_name":"musk","gender":"male","
dob":null,"email":"em@tesla.com","phone":null,"website":null,"address":nul
l,"status":null,"_links":{"self":{"href":"https://gorest.co.in/public-api/
users/1571"},"edit":{"href":"https://gorest.co.in/public-api/users/1571"},
"avatar":{"href":null}}}}...
>
```

REST API GET Operation

The GET method requests a representation of the given resource thus it is only used to retrieve data. In the example below, we retrieve metadata for user #1571 (Elon Musk).

Python Code

```
1   import requests
2   import json
3
4   token = 'z8-sXMth942nOiQqXuikCNjbamrAlI2IjS7g'
5   url = 'https://gorest.co.in/public-api/users/1571'
6   result = requests.get(url,
7     headers = {
8       'Content-Type': 'application/json',
9       'Authorization': 'Bearer {}'.format(token)
10    })
11  print('Code: ', result.status_code)
12  print('Content: ', result.content.decode()[: 500] + '...')
```

Code Output

```
Code: 200
Content: {"_meta":{"success":true,"code":200,"message":"OK. Everything wo
rked as expected.","rateLimit":{"limit":30,"remaining":29,"reset":2}},"res
ult":{"id":"1571","first_name":"elon","last_name":"musk","gender":"male","
dob":null,"email":"em@tesla.com","phone":null,"website":null,"address":nul
l,"status":null,"_links":{"self":{"href":"https://gorest.co.in/public-api/
users/1571"},"edit":{"href":"https://gorest.co.in/public-api/users/1571"},
"avatar":{"href":null}}}}...
>
```

REST API PATCH Operation

The HTTP PATCH method is for applying partial information to a web resource. The type of the body of the PATCH request is indicated by the Accept-Patch header. In this example, we patch and add a phone number for our user #1571 (Elon Musk).

Python Code

```python
1   import requests
2   import json
3
4   token = 'z8-sXMth942nOiQqXuikCNjbamrAlI2IjS7g'
5   url = 'https://gorest.co.in/public-api/users/1571'
6   data = {
7       "phone": "510-123-4567"
8   }
9   result = requests.patch(url,
10      headers = {
11          'Content-Type': 'application/json',
12          'Authorization': 'Bearer {}'.format(token)
13      }, data = json.dumps(data))
14  print('Code: ', result.status_code)
15  print('Content: ', result.content.decode()[: 500] + '...')
```

Code Output

```
Code:  200
Content:  {"_meta":{"success":true,"code":200,"message":"OK. Everything wo
rked as expected.","rateLimit":{"limit":30,"remaining":29,"reset":2}},"res
ult":{"id":"1571","first_name":"elon","last_name":"musk","gender":"male","
dob":null,"email":"em@tesla.com","phone":"510-123-4567","website":null,"ad
dress":null,"status":null,"_links":{"self":{"href":"https://gorest.co.in/p
ublic-api/users/1571"},"edit":{"href":"https://gorest.co.in/public-api/use
rs/1571"},"avatar":{"href":null}}}}...
>
```

REST API PUT Operation

The HTTP PUT method is for creating a new resource (if one doesn't exist) or replacing information for a given web resource that already exists. In this example, we replace our older user (#1571) with a new one (Jessica Alba). You can notice that the fields, such as phone #, that were not explicitly provided by our code, didn't change because of the PUT request.

Python Code

```
 1   import requests
 2   import json
 3
 4   token = 'z8-sXMth942nOiQqXuikCNjbamrAlI2IjS7g'
 5   url = 'https://gorest.co.in/public-api/users/1571'
 6 ▾ data = {
 7     "email": "ja@honest.com",
 8     "first_name": "Jessica",
 9     "last_name": "Alba",
10     "gender": "female"
11   }
12   result = requests.put(url,
13 ▾   headers = {
14       'Content-Type': 'application/json',
15       'Authorization': 'Bearer {}'.format(token)
16     }, data = json.dumps(data))
17   print('Code: ', result.status_code)
18   print('Content: ', result.content.decode()[: 500] + '...')
```

Code Output

```
Code:  200
Content:  {"_meta":{"success":true,"code":200,"message":"OK. Everything wo
rked as expected.","rateLimit":{"limit":30,"remaining":29,"reset":2}},"res
ult":{"id":"1571","first_name":"Jessica","last_name":"Alba","gender":"fema
le","dob":null,"email":"ja@honest.com","phone":"510-123-4567","website":nu
ll,"address":null,"status":null,"_links":{"self":{"href":"https://gorest.c
o.in/public-api/users/1571"},"edit":{"href":"https://gorest.co.in/public-a
pi/users/1571"},"avatar":{"href":null}}}}...
>
```

REST API DELETE Operation

The HTTP DELETE method is for deleting an existing resource. In this example, we simply delete our user Jessica Alba (or #1571).

Python Code

```
1   import requests
2   import json
3
4   token = 'z8-sXMth942nOiQqXuikCNjbamrAlI2IjS7g'
5   url = 'https://gorest.co.in/public-api/users/1571'
6   result = requests.delete(url,
7     headers = {
8       'Content-Type': 'application/json',
9       'Authorization': 'Bearer {}'.format(token)
10    })
11
12  print('Code: ', result.status_code)
13  print('Content: ', result.content.decode()[: 500] + '...')
```

Code Output

```
Code:  200
Content:  {"_meta":{"success":true,"code":204,"message":"The request was h
andled successfully and the response contains no body content.","rateLimit
":{"limit":30,"remaining":29,"reset":2}},"result":null}...
>
```

We can also verify that the resource (user) was indeed deleted by issuing an HTTP GET which results in status code 404 (Not Found).

Python Code

```
1   import requests
2   import json
3
4   token = 'z8-sXMth942nOiQqXuikCNjbamrAlI2IjS7g'
5   url = 'https://gorest.co.in/public-api/users/1571'
6   result = requests.get(url,
7     headers = {
8       'Content-Type': 'application/json',
9       'Authorization': 'Bearer {}'.format(token)
10    })
11
12  print('Code: ', result.status_code)
13  print('Content: ', result.content.decode()[: 500] + '...')
```

Code Output

```
Code:  200
Content:  {"_meta":{"success":false,"code":404,"message":"The requested re
source does not exist.","rateLimit":{"limit":30,"remaining":29,"reset":2}}
,"result":{"name":"Not Found","message":"Object not found: 1571","code":0,
"status":404}}...
>
```

Further Reading

Python and REST APIs[15]

---

[15] https://bit.ly/2W7Mejl

Chapter Summary

- Application Programming Interface (or an API) is an interface mechanism and a protocol to carry out communication between a server and a client with the primary purpose of simplifying the software development of client-side software.
- Webhooks are ways for apps to communicate with each other in an automated fashion
- API constraints refer to the architectural constraints or design guidelines that should be followed when using the APIs.
- CRUD stands for Create, Retrieve, Update and Delete.
- HTTP 200 means file or resource was found and all OK.
- Idempotent means is that an HTTP method is idempotent by definition if an identical request can be made either once or many times over with the same effect while the server state is not changed
- Client-side APIs are used to extend the functionality of the browser whereas server-side performance a similar function for server-side APIs.
- Postman is a cross-platform REST client
- The HTTP POST method sends data to a web server. The type of the body of the POST request is indicated by the Content-type header.

CHAPTER 3 CISCO PLATFORMS AND DEVELOPMENT

This chapter covers the following exam topics from Cisco's official 200-901 V1.0 DevNet Associate exam blueprint.

- Construct a Python script that uses a Cisco SDK given SDK documentation
- Describe the capabilities of Cisco network management platforms and APIs (Meraki, Cisco DNA Center, ACI, Cisco SD-WAN, and NSO)
- Describe the capabilities of Cisco compute management platforms and APIs (UCS Manager, UCS Director, and Intersight)
- Describe the capabilities of Cisco collaboration platforms and APIs (WebEx Teams, WebEx devices, Cisco Unified Communication Manager including AXL and UDS interfaces, and Finesse)
- Describe the capabilities of Cisco security platforms and APIs (Firepower, Umbrella, AMP, ISE, and Threat Grid)
- Describe the device level APIs and dynamic interfaces for IOS XE and NX-OS
- Identify the appropriate DevNet resource for a given scenario (Sandbox, Code Exchange, support, forums, Learning Labs, and API documentation)
- Apply concepts of model driven programmability (YANG, RESTCONF, and NETCONF) in a Cisco environment
- Construct code to perform a specific operation based on a set of requirements and given API reference documentation such as these:
    - Obtain a list of network devices by using Meraki, Cisco DNA Center, ACI, Cisco SD-WAN, or NSO
    - Manage spaces, participants, and messages in WebEx Teams
    - Obtain a list of clients / hosts seen on a network using Meraki or Cisco DNA Center

Construct a Python script that uses a Cisco SDK given SDK documentation

Cisco DevNet has divided the overall Cisco portfolio into eight Dev Centers, one representing each technology group.

- Cloud
- Collaboration
- Data Center (UCS, NX-OS, IOS XE, etc.)
- IoT and edge computing
- Networking (IOS XR, IOS XE, NX-OS)
- Security
- Wireless and mobile
- Application developers

SDK stands for Software Development Kit, it is a package integrated with libraries, documents and code examples. It is different from APIs, which are a documented set of URIs where developers only need a reference guide and a resource address to get started.

SDKs	APIs
Set of tools that can be used to develop or create applications	It is an interface that allows software applications to interact with each other
Contains all APIs	Purpose built for specific use or a feature
More robust, with tons of utilities	Lightweight and fast
Primarily used to create new applications	Primarily used for adding specific functions to an existing application

Cisco provides a wide range of SDKs on different Cisco platforms, here is a non exhaustive list.

- WebEx Teams SDK
- Jabber web, Guest SDKs
- DNA Center SDK
- UCS Python SDK
- APIC Python SDK
- IMC Python SDK
- Instant Connect SDK

Currently, Cisco has provided us with three programmability solutions that we can use to interact with Cisco devices and platforms.

- Device by device approaches
  - On-box (such as executing CLI via Python)
  - Off-box (such as leveraging one of the many standard interfaces using NETCONF or RESTCONF APIs)
- Controller or Network-based approach (such as using Cisco DNA Center or OpenDaylight using REST API)

However, technically speaking and in terms of SDKs and toolkits, we have access to the following frameworks.

- Cobra SDK
- NX Toolkit
- ACI Toolkit
- YANG Development Kit (or YDK)

Cisco APIC Python SDK (Cobra SDK)

The key component within Cisco Application Centric Infrastructure (or ACI) is the Application Policy Infrastructure Controller (or APIC). APIC supports the deployment, management, and monitoring of applications with a unified operations model for physical and virtual infrastructure components. The ACI policy model is based on promise theory which is about scalable control of objects rather than using the top-down paradigm.

APIC is aware of both the configuration commands and the state changes for the underlying objects. With promise theory, underlying objects handle configuration state changes, as initiated by the APIC in the form of desired state changes. With this approach, objects are also responsible for sending in exception and faults back to the control system (call it bottoms-up approach if you will) in addition to enabling greater scale by enabling the methods of objects to request state changes from one another.

Cobra SDK comes in two installable .egg files with the following installable packages.

- acicobra (main Cobra SDK with three of the following namespaces)
  - cobra
  - cobra.mit
  - cobra.internal
- acimodel (Python package that includes ACI Management Information Tree or MIT)

Going by the GitHub repo (datacenter/cobra), it seems a bit stagnant where last commit took place over two years ago.

NX Toolkit

NX Toolkit is a bunch of python libraries that allow configuration of Cisco Nexus 9K and 3K series switches. It is based on NX-API REST which is used in ACI and the Cisco NX-OS and provides a framework for network programmability and automation.

You can clone the nxtoolkit.git repo from GitHub or just download it as a zip file. Alternatively, you can also do a docker pull on docketcisco/nxtoolkit. Going by the GitHub repo, it seems nothing has been added to it by Cisco over the past four years.

ACI Toolkit

ACI toolkit is a collection of python libraries that allow the configuration of the APIC controller. It is based on the REST API. The overall toolkit model is divided into three components.

- Application Topology Object Model
- Interface Object Model
- Physical Topology Object Model

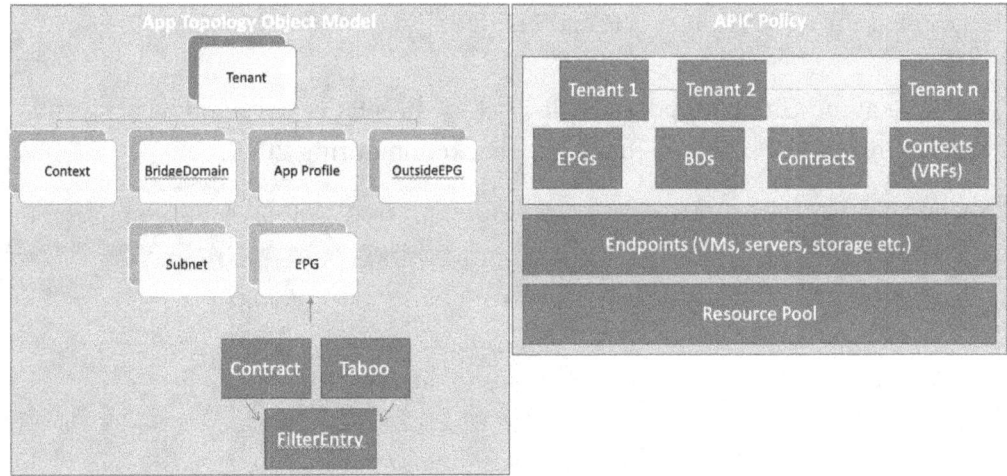

Looking at the diagram on the left, the tenant is the root class within the toolkit, this is where all of the configurations take place as far as application topology is concerned. AppProfile is what contains the actual configuration. Endpoint Group (EPG) is the object where you define configuration for what happens when an endpoint is connected to the ACI fabric. Context is pretty much like VRFs in Cisco jargon. EPGs provide or consume the network services as defined in the Contracts (Taboos, as the name implies, are network services that can never be provided or consumed by the EPGs). FilterEntry defines the traffic profile that either a contract or taboo applies. Much like the application topology object model, there is also the top-down APIC policy taxonomy on the right side to lay out the scope of various ACI objects.

There is also an ACI toolkit interface model (physical and virtual) and a physical topology model (pod, node, link) as part of the ACI toolkit object model.

YANG Development Kit (or YDK)

YANG Development Kit (or YDK) is an SDK that provides APIs that are modeled in YANG to reduce the complexity with the help of APIs, by abstracting out the protocol or encoding details. SDK consists of a core package that defines services and providers. In addition to the core package, there are a bunch of other modules that provide the YANG modeling. YDK is currently supported for IOS XE, IOS XR and NX OS.

Looking at the GitHub repo, it seems that the project is alive and kicking and there were several commits that were checked in during 2019.

CiscoDevNet / ydk-py		Used by ▾ 12	Watch ▾ 49	★ Star 124	Fork 40
‹› Code	ⓘ Issues 2	Pull requests 0	Projects 0	Wiki	Security	Insights

Branch: master ▾ ydk-py / core ydk /		Create new file	Upload files	Find file	History
abhikeshav 0.8.3 (#44) ⋯			Latest commit 57bb46f on May 31		

..			
_core	0.8.3 (#44)		4 months ago
entity_utils	Creating 0.8.2 branch		7 months ago
errors	0.7.1 (#34)		2 years ago
ext	0.6.0 (#28)		2 years ago
filters	0.6.0 (#28)		2 years ago
logging	0.6.0 (#28)		2 years ago
models	0.7.1 (#34)		2 years ago
path	0.8.3 (#44)		4 months ago
providers	Adding branch 0.8.1		8 months ago
services	Adding branch 0.8.1		8 months ago
types	0.8.3 (#44)		4 months ago
__init__.py	0.6.0 (#28)		2 years ago
exthook.py	0.6.0 (#28)		2 years ago

Python SDK generated from YANG data models.   http://ydk.io

yang   python   ydk   ios-xe   ios-xr   catalyst   nx-os

⑦ 131 commits	ⅈ 4 branches	♡ 22 releases	ⅈⅈ 6 contributors	⚖ View license

Branch: master ▾	New pull request		Create new file	Upload files	Find File	Clone or download ▾

👤 abhikeshav 0.8.3 (#44) ⋯				Latest commit 57bb46f on May 31
📁 cisco-ios-xe	0.8.3 (#44)			4 months ago
📁 cisco-ios-xr	0.8.3 (#44)			4 months ago
📁 cisco-nx-os	0.8.3 (#44)			4 months ago
📁 core	0.8.3 (#44)			4 months ago
📁 gnmi	0.8.3 (#44)			4 months ago
📁 ietf	0.8.3 (#44)			4 months ago
📁 openconfig	0.8.3 (#44)			4 months ago

For SDK-based programmability, we will simply use the easiest method
available to us by Cisco to do so and that is to use on-box Guest Shell on Cisco
IOS XE 16.7.x (or otherwise known as Fuji). Please note that you can use Python
library on-box or off-box which happens via SSH/NETCONF interface.

Guest Shell is a virtualized Linux-based (LXC) container environment that runs
side by side the IOS XE, that separation allows secure execution of various
scripts (such as Python) and other software packages. CSR1000v running IOS
XE 16.7.x uses a CentOS 7.x minimal rootfs.

Enabling the Guest Shell depends on what platform and IOS XE version you're
using. If you're using a version before Fuji, you'd need to use first use "iox",
followed by "guestshell enable" along with virtualportgroup IP addresses. Once
that's set up, you can pre-installed Python 2.7.x or install Python 3.x package
using "guestshell run python3" command.

Now, for CSR1000v and IOS XE Fuji and later, you can enable and configure
Guest Shell using the following steps.

- Run "iox" and enable guest shell using "guestshell enable" command
  along with the app-hosting appid guestshell"

- Configure Virtual Port Group by assigning it an IP address
- Optionally, you can configure NAT so that your Guest Shell container stack can access the internet and download other installable packages

CSR1000v Configuration

CSR1Kv(config)# iox

interface VirtualPortGroup0
ip address 172.16.30.1 255.255.255.0

ip nat inside
ip nat inside source list GS_NAT interface GigabitEthernet1 overload
ip access-list standard GS_NAT permit 172.16.0.0 0.0.255.255
guestshell enable

app-hosting appid guestshell
vnic gateway1 virtualportgroup 10 guest-interface 0 guest-ipaddress 172.16.30.2 netmask
255.255.255.0 gateway 172.16.30.1 name-server 8.8.8.8 default
resource profile custom cpu 1500 memory 768

Python 2.7 (pre-installed version) can be launched using the "guestshell run python <script.py>" command.

Now, let's put together a few lines and execute Python script to retrieve some IOS XE specific information. In the example below, we're using the CLI module to issue configure a new loopback interface (lo100) and then retrieving system clock information.

>>> import cli
>>> cli.clip('configure terminal; interface loopback 100; ip address 172.17.1.1 255.255.255.255')

```
*Oct 13 18:39:48.518: %LINEPROTO-5-UPDOWN: Line protocol on Interface
Loopback100, changed state to up

>>> cli.clip('show clock')
'\n*18:11:53.989 UTC Sun Oct 13 2019\n'
>>> output=cli.cli('show clock')
>>> print(output)
*18:12:04.705 UTC Sun Oct13 2019
```

Instead of using cli.cli function, you can also use cli.clip function to directly display information on the Guest Shell console.

Describe the capabilities of Cisco network management platforms and APIs (Meraki, Cisco DNA Center, ACI, Cisco SD-WAN, and NSO)

Historically, network devices have been configured in a device-by-device manner manually. While this worked well in smaller networks and before anything cloud-native was available, it doesn't work anymore. The growing network complexity, the ever-expanding DevOps/IaC software tooling ecosystem, simpler to use programming languages and APIs, most applications moving to the cloud and software-defined virtualized infrastructure, make a perfect case for making the leap towards network automation at scale. With automation, not only we can achieve better uptime but also drastically reduce network OPEX.

Following are among the few key use cases for applying network automation.

- Device provisioning (configuration management)
- Device software management (firmware management)
- Compliance (auditing networks)
- Reporting
- Troubleshooting (reactive and proactive)

- Data collection and streaming telemetry

Cisco Meraki

Meraki's cloud-based management platform offers centralized visibility and control over the entire wireless networking infrastructure without having to deal with on-site Wireless LAN Controllers (or WLCs). You can launch the dashboard inside a browser.

Every Meraki device, i.e., APs, ethernet switches and security appliances connect over the internet to the Cisco Meraki cloud-based management platform.

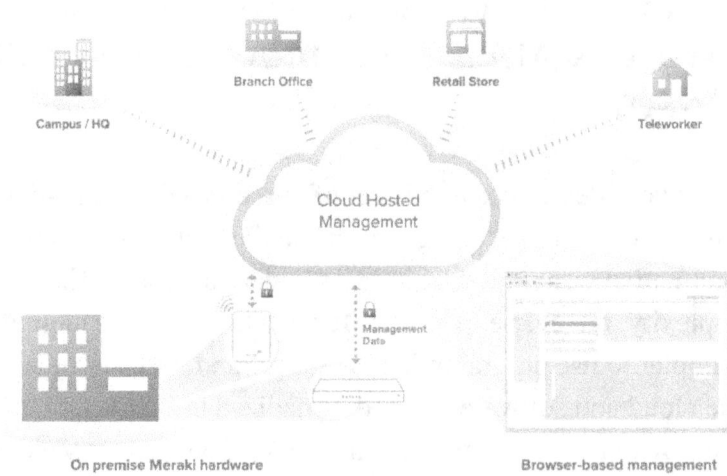

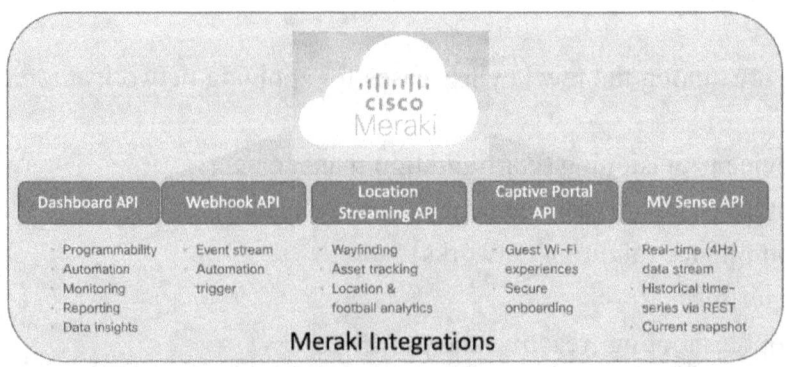

The Meraki enterprise cloud-managed networking service has five different API for integration.

- Dashboard API (device provisioning, management and monitoring)
- Webhook API (real-time notification system for network alerts and events)
- Location streaming API (Wi-Fi and BT client location information)
- External captive portal API (build custom engagement models at Wi-Fi access points)
- MV Sense API (REST API and real-time MQTT stream supporting oversight of physical space)

Let's now go over a live example of Meraki deployments as witnessed through various Dashboard options.

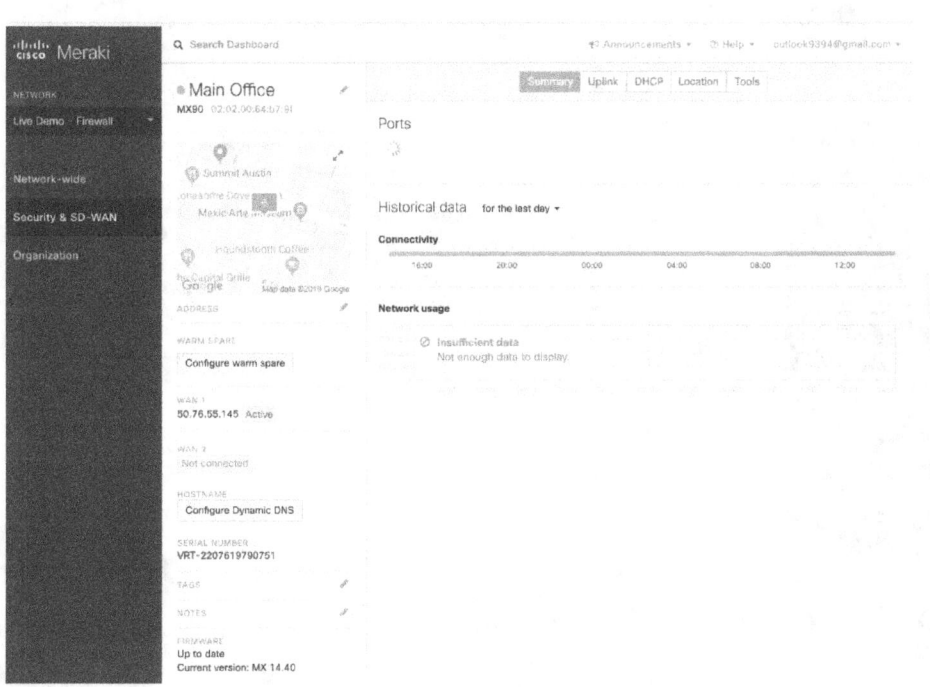

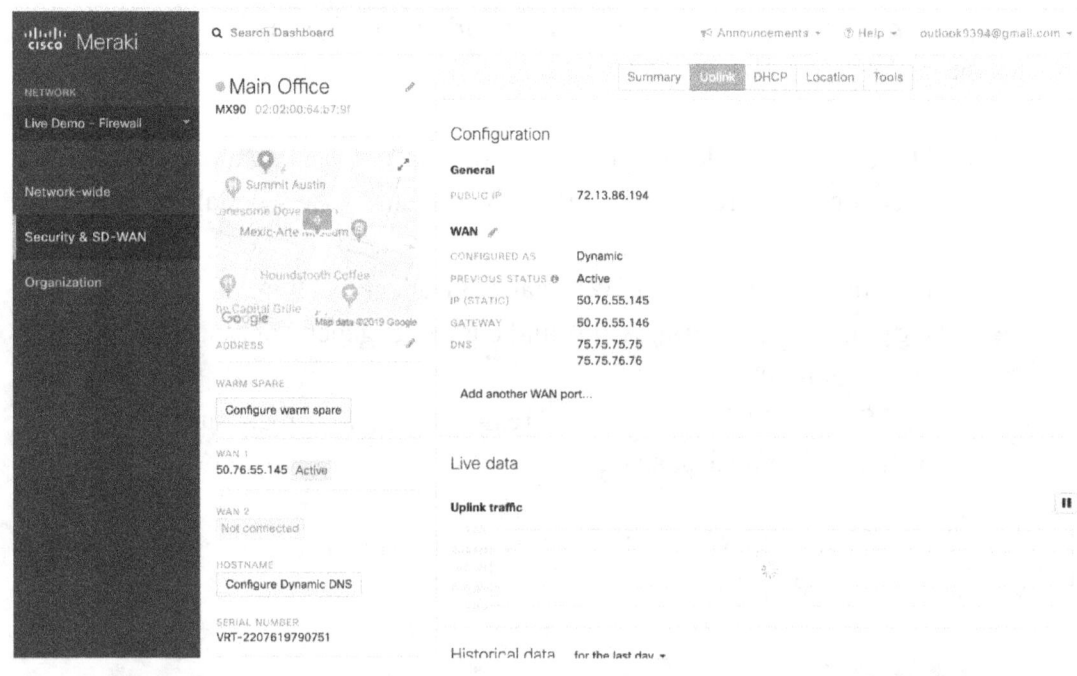

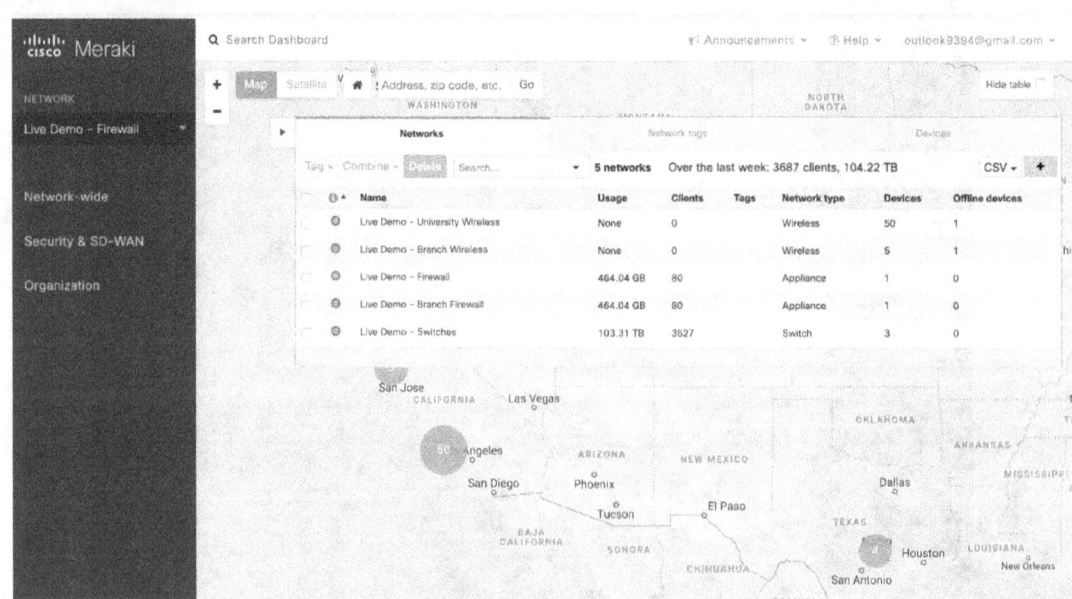

Let's now go over each of the five API resources starting with the dashboard
API.

Meraki Dashboard API

You can use Organization > Configure > Settings to enable REST API access to Meraki cloud platform.

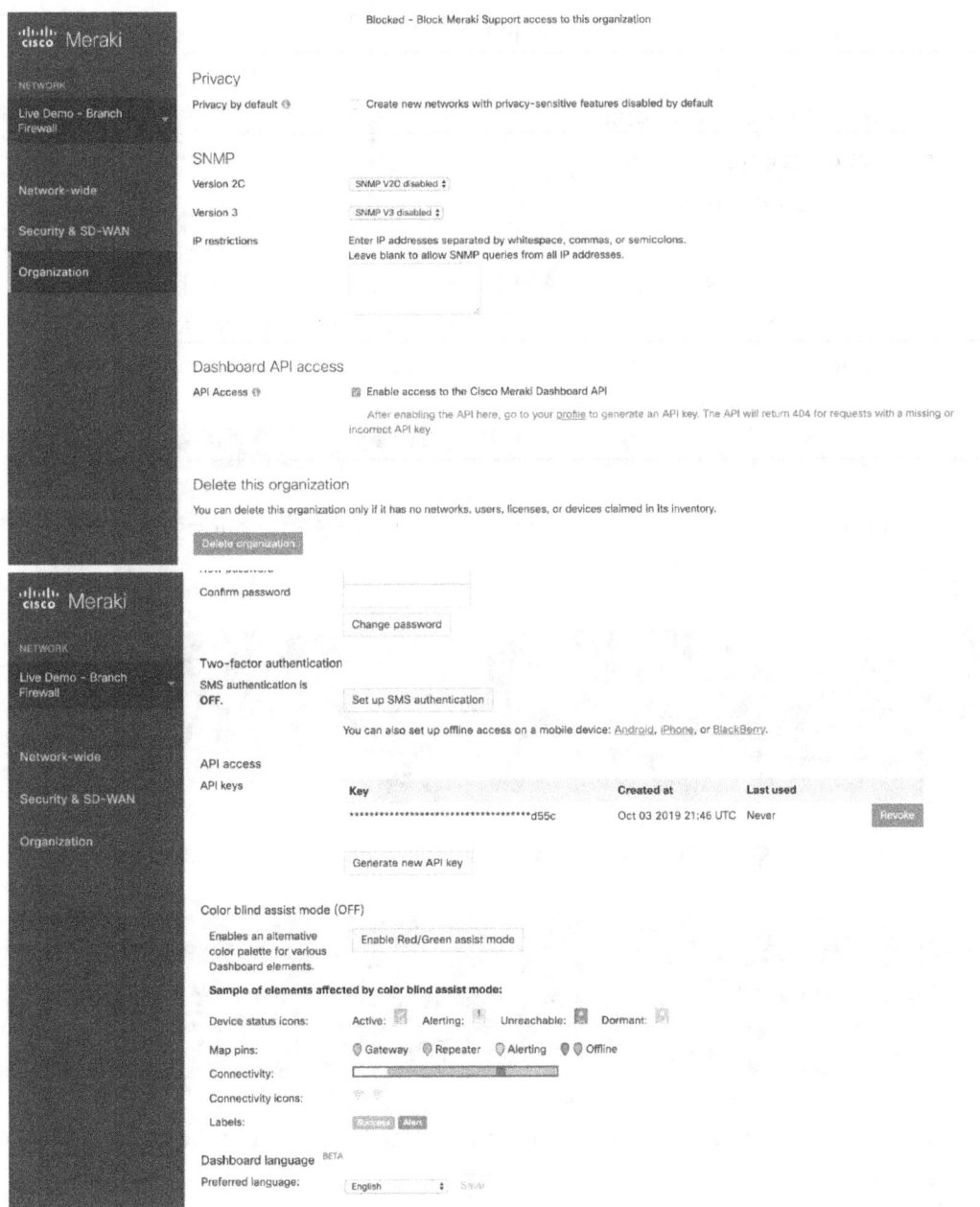

Once you've generated Meraki cloud platform access REST API key, you can use either a Python script (with request module) or use Postman to access various Meraki information such as

- Get Organization ID
- Get the list of networks inside an Org
- Get the Org inventory
- Get network information
- Get device information
- Get SSID information

Every API request must specify an API key via the HTTP request header. If API key is missing, you will receive an HTTP 404 status code as opposed to a 403. This behavior helps hide the existence of a resource to an authorized user.

```
X-Cisco-Meraki-API-Key: <secret key>
```

You can use curl, postman, or a Python script to make API requests. Let's try a curl to retrieve the organization list.

```
curl --request GET -L \
  --url https://api.meraki.com/api/v0/organizations \
  --header 'X-Cisco-Meraki-API-Key:
8f90ecec4fca692f606092279f203c6020cad55c'
```

If you have the organization ID, you can request organization's metadata.

```
curl --request GET -L \
  --url https://api.meraki.com/api/v0/organizations/641762946900403561 \
  --header 'X-Cisco-Meraki-API-Key:
8f90ecec4fca692f606092279f203c6020cad55c'
```

Likewise, you can make API calls to list networks as well using the organization id as part of the URI.

Meraki Webhook Alerts API

With Meraki webhooks, you can set up systems that subscribe to Meraki cloud alerts. You can configure timing threshold value for the alerts, e.g., you may want to wait for a few minutes before firing off a downtime alert.

Meraki Location Scanning API

The Meraki cloud uses the physical location of access points to estimate the location of a client. It is a best effort estimate since the geo-location data accuracy can vary based on a number of factors that are hard to control.

Meraki captive portal API allows you to create a splash page, the first page you see when you access a Wi-Fi hotspot. By configuring a captive portal, you can redirect all inbound traffic to a particular URL. Following are the typical examples of what you can put on the URL.

- Customer survey (for cafes or restaurants)
- Choose and purchase a billing plan (e.g., for paid roaming hotspots)
- Serve an Ad
- Accept a set of terms of service (perhaps the most common element that we witness on every captive portal page)

Meraki MV Sense API

Meraki smart camera can perform object detection, classification and even tracking. The MV Sense API can server historical, current and even real-time data generated in the camera for enhanced security. The API endpoints in MV Sense provide access to machine learning and computer vision data for use in applications. The API endpoints support REST and MQTT protocols.

RESTful APIs offer an on-demand service, so you can access historical or near real-time object detection from the camera. MQTT-based endpoints use a publisher/subscriber model. With MQTT-based API endpoints, you can access real-time feed of people detection and their locations in addition to light-level readings. Here a few examples of how you can use MV Sense camera APIs.

- Detect one or more people an object and set off an alarm if people get closer to it.
- Detect several people standing in one location and correlate that with customer wait times.
- Deliver better lighting by integrating MV light readings into general smart lighting systems.

Meraki has published python modules for accessing various resources within the Meraki ecosystem, e.g.

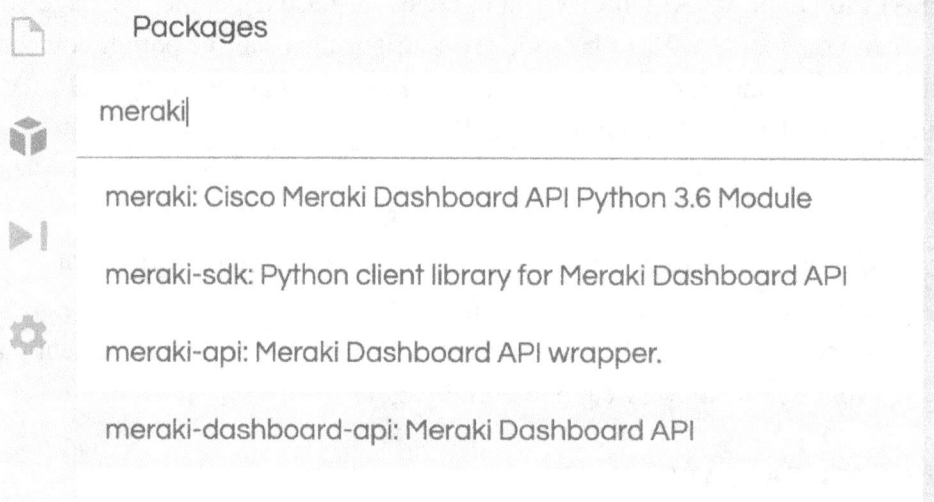

Let's now carry out a few small tasks using the REST API and Meraki python module.

Python Code

```
main.py          saved    ▼
1    from meraki import meraki
2
3    apikey = "2b925f015ec2645e9e1ab70e5db6de40273fc5ef"
4    myOrg = meraki.myorgaccess(apikey)
5    print (myOrg)
```

Code Output

```
Python 3.7.4 (default, Jul  9 2019, 00:06:43)
[GCC 6.3.0 20170516] on linux
Organization Operation Successful - See returned data for results

[{'id': '641762946900403561', 'name': 'outlook9394@gmail.com - Li
ve Demo'}]
‣ 
```

Python Code

```
1    from meraki import meraki
2
3    apikey = "2b925f015ec2645e9e1ab70e5db6de40273fc5ef"
4    orgid = 641762946900403561
5    Networks = meraki.getnetworklist(apikey, orgid)
6
7    print (Networks)
```

Code Output

```
Python 3.7.4 (default, Jul  9 2019, 00:06:43)
[GCC 6.3.0 20170516] on linux
Network Operation Successful - See returned data for results

[{'id': 'N_641762946900876737', 'organizationId': '64176294690040
3561', 'name': 'Live Demo - University Wireless', 'timeZone': 'Am
erica/Los_Angeles', 'tags': None, 'productTypes': ['wireless'], '
type': 'wireless', 'disableMyMerakiCom': False, 'disableRemoteSta
tusPage': True}, {'id': 'N_641762946900876738', 'organizationId':
 '641762946900403561', 'name': 'Live Demo - Branch Wireless', 'ti
meZone': 'America/Los_Angeles', 'tags': None, 'productTypes': ['w
ireless'], 'type': 'wireless', 'disableMyMerakiCom': False, 'disa
bleRemoteStatusPage': True}, {'id': 'N_641762946900876739', 'orga
nizationId': '641762946900403561', 'name': 'Live Demo - Firewall'
, 'timeZone': 'America/Los_Angeles', 'tags': None, 'productTypes'
: ['appliance'], 'type': 'appliance', 'disableMyMerakiCom': False
, 'disableRemoteStatusPage': True}, {'id': 'N_641762946900876740'
, 'organizationId': '641762946900403561', 'name': 'Live Demo - Br
anch Firewall', 'timeZone': 'America/Los_Angeles', 'tags': None,
'productTypes': ['appliance'], 'type': 'appliance', 'disableMyMer
akiCom': False, 'disableRemoteStatusPage': True}, {'id': 'N_64176
2946900876741', 'organizationId': '641762946900403561', 'name': '
Live Demo - Switches', 'timeZone': 'America/Los_Angeles', 'tags':
 None, 'productTypes': ['switch'], 'type': 'switch', 'disableMyMe
rakiCom': False, 'disableRemoteStatusPage': True}]
```

Python Code

```python
1    from meraki import meraki
2
3    apikey = "2b925f015ec2645e9e1ab70e5db6de40273fc5ef"
4    netid = "N_641762946900876737"
5    dList = meraki.getnetworkdevices(apikey, netid)
6    print (dList)
```

Code Output

```
Python 3.7.4 (default, Jul  9 2019, 00:06:43)
[GCC 6.3.0 20170516] on linux
Network Operation Successful - See returned data for results

[{'lat': 34.4495289477602, 'lng': -119.659931659698, 'address': '
955 La Paz Rd., Santa Barbara, CA', 'serial': 'VRT-2207619790745'
, 'mac': '02:02:00:64:b7:99', 'lanIp': None, 'networkId': 'N_6417
62946900876737', 'name': 'Student Center, floor 1, NE', 'model':
'MR16', 'firmware': 'Not running configured version', 'floorPlanI
d': None}, {'lat': 34.4482018475607, 'lng': -119.662227630615, 'a
ddress': '955 La Paz Rd., Santa Barbara, CA', 'serial': 'VRT-2207
619790744', 'mac': '02:02:00:64:b7:98', 'lanIp': None, 'networkId
': 'N_641762946900876737', 'name': 'Gymnasium', 'model': 'MR16',
'firmware': 'Not running configured version', 'floorPlanId': None
}, {'lat': 34.4467508605466, 'lng': -119.659395217896, 'address':
'955 La Paz Rd., Santa Barbara, CA', 'serial': 'VRT-220761979074
3', 'mac': '02:02:00:64:b7:97', 'lanIp': None, 'networkId': 'N_64
1762946900876737', 'name': 'Deane Hall, SW', 'model': 'MR16', 'fi
rmware': 'Not running configured version', 'floorPlanId': None},
{'lat': 34.4502278787217, 'lng': -119.662302732468, 'address': '9
55 La Paz Rd., Santa Barbara, CA', 'serial': 'VRT-2207619790742',
'mac': '02:02:00:64:b7:96', 'lanIp': None, 'networkId': 'N_64176
2946900876737', 'name': 'Voskuyl Library, floor 1, NE', 'model':
'MR16', 'firmware': 'Not running configured version', 'floorPlanI
d': None}, {'lat': 34.4473967298302, 'lng': -119.659620523453, 'a
ddress': '955 La Paz Rd., Santa Barbara, CA', 'serial': 'VRT-2207
619790741', 'mac': '02:02:00:64:b7:95', 'lanIp': None, 'networkId
': 'N_641762946900876737', 'name': 'Health Center, NE', 'model':
'MR16', 'firmware': 'Not running configured version', 'floorPlanI
d': None}, {'lat': 34.4500686291437, 'lng': -119.662292003632, 'a
ddress': '955 La Paz Rd., Santa Barbara, CA', 'serial': 'VRT-2207
619790740', 'mac': '02:02:00:64:b7:94', 'lanIp': None, 'networkId
```

Cisco DNA Center

Cisco DNA center is a controller as well as an analytics platform that makes Cisco's intent-based networking possible. It consists of five major components.

- Design
- Policy
- Provision
- Assurance
- Platform

DNA Center Dashboard

DNA Design component allows you to design your network using workflows while allowing for importing existing network designs and device images from APIC-EM (Enterprise Module) and Cisco Prime Infrastructure into DNA Center.

DNA Policy is about user and device profiles that help deliver on secure access as well as segmentation. Application policies ensure consistent network performance based on business requirements.

DNA Provision allows you to use policy-based automation to deliver services to network-based on business priority and simplifies device deployment. It is the module that is responsible for delivering zero-touch deployment.

DNA Assurance enables networking elements to stream telemetry for ensuring application performance and user connectivity in real-time.

DNA Platform allows developers to directly access the DNA through the developer toolkit or SDK. To review APIs, you can click on Platform > Developer Toolkit.

DNA center appliance hosts SDN controller, analytics engine and telemetry storage. At the time of writing, a 44-core DNA appliance (DN2-HW-APL) is listed for USD 88.6K in Cisco's GPL. It has to be installed and run on the bundled bare metal server, as we speak, there is no virtual appliance package available.

DNA center licenses come in three flavors, i.e.

- Essentials (includes basic automation and network visibility)
- Advantage (includes Essentials, plus advanced automation, image lifecycle management, AI/ML analytics and assurance and API/SDK integration)
- Premier (Everything in Advantage, plus encrypted traffic analytics and multi-domain policy segmentation)

Let's now look at the various aspects of DNA dashboard and types of data it provides.

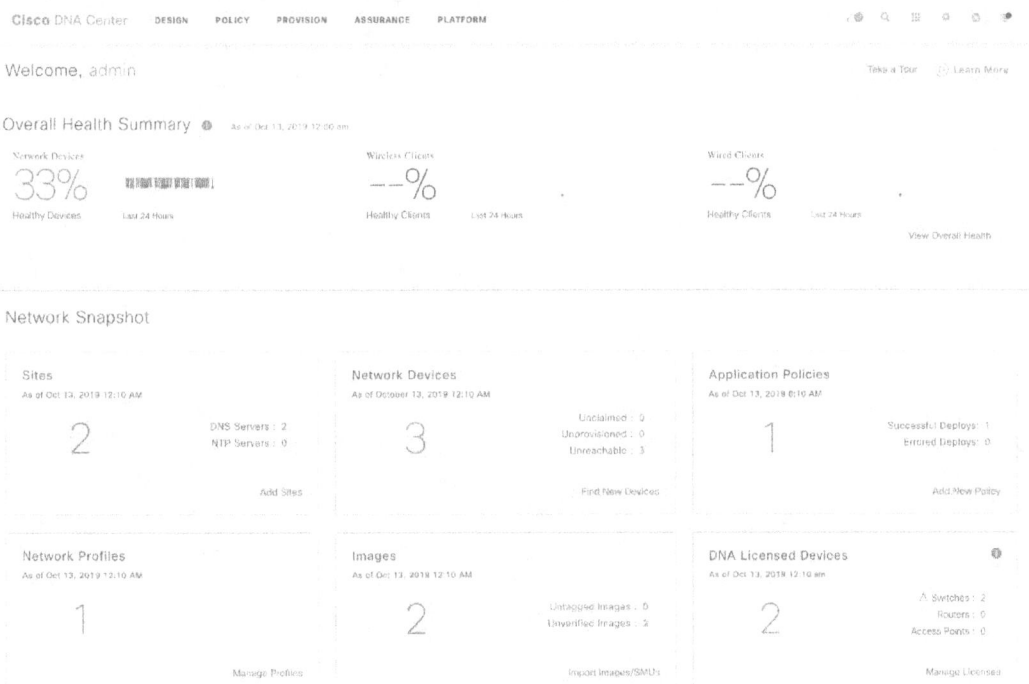

Network Configuration and Operations

 **Design**

Model your entire network, from sites and buildings to devices and links, both physical and virtual, across campus, branch, WAN and cloud.

- Add site locations on the network
- Designate golden images for device families
- Create wireless profiles of SSIDs

 **Policy**

Use policies to automate and simplify network management, reducing cost and risk while speeding rollout of new and enhanced services.

- Segment your network as Virtual Networks
- Create scalable groups to describe your critical assets
- Define segmentation policies to meet your policy goals

 **Provision**

Provide new services to users with ease, speed and security across your enterprise network, regardless of network size and complexity.

- Discover Devices
- Manage Unclaimed Devices
- Set up fabric across sites

 **Assurance**

Use proactive monitoring and insights from the network, devices, and applications to predict problems faster and ensure that policy and configuration changes achieve the business intent and the user experience you want.

- Assurance Health
- Assurance Issues

 **Platform**

Use DNA Center Platform, to programmatically access your network through Intent APIs, integrate with your preferred IT systems to create end-to-end solutions and add support for multi-vendor devices.

- View the API Catalog
- Configure DNA Center - to - Third-Party Integrations
- Schedule and Download - Data and Reports

Tools

Discovery
Automate addition of devices to controller inventory

Inventory
Adds, update or delete devices that are managed by the controller

Topology
Visualize how devices are interconnected and how they communicate

Image Repository
Download and manage physical and virtual software images automatically

Command Runner
Allows you to run diagnostic CLIs against one or more devices

License Manager
Visualize and manage license usage

Template Editor
An interactive editor to author CLI templates

Network Plug and Play
N-PnP functionality has moved to Provision page. Click here to begin.

Telemetry
Telemetry Design and Provision

Data and Reports
Access Data Sets, Schedule Data Extracts for Download in multiple formats like PDF, Reports, CSV, Tableau etc.

Let's now use the DNA center SDK by using the python client module.

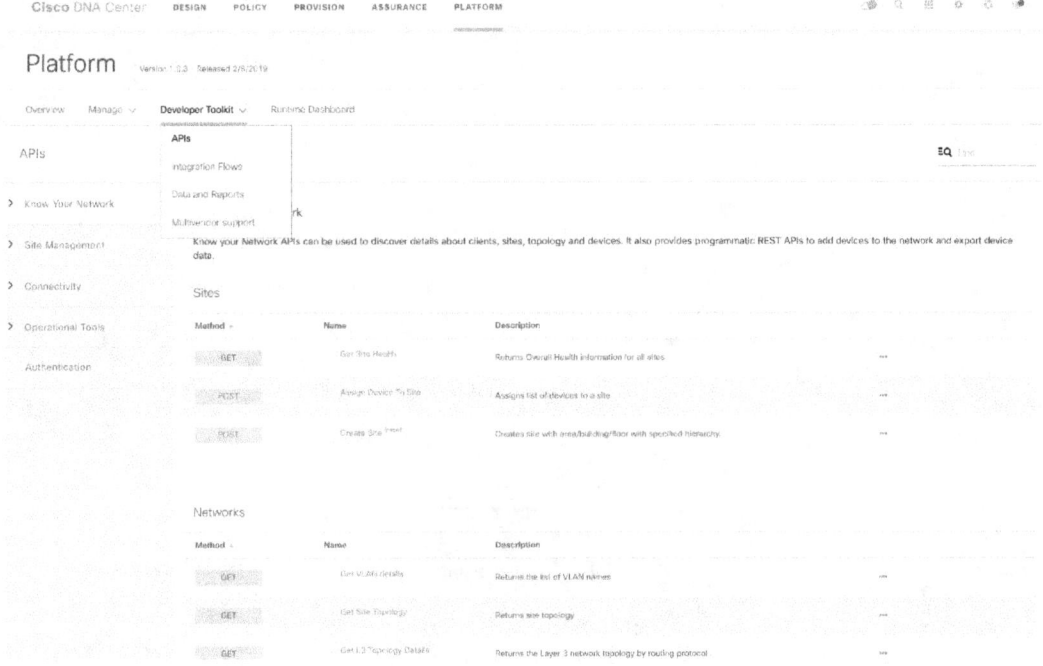

Cisco DNA Center   DESIGN   POLICY   PROVISION   ASSURANCE   PLATFORM

Platform   Version 1.0.0   Released 2/8/2019

Overview   **Manage** ∨   Developer Toolkit ∨   Runtime Dashboard

Bundles

▽ Filter   ≡Q Find

Bundle	Status	Description	
B Basic ITSM (ServiceNow) CMDB synchronization Cisco Systems, Inc. v1.0.1	DNAC 1.2.5 + Version Dated Dec 16, 2018	ACTIVE	You can schedule a synchronization or trigger an update between the DNA Center device inventory and your ITSM(ServiceNow) configuration management database(CMDB). These activities integrate DNA Center processes into the IT System Management processes of incident, change and problem management. Note: If your network devices...	Configure
D DNA Center REST API Cisco Systems, Inc. v1.0.3	DNAC 1.2.5 + Updated May 20, 2019	ACTIVE	This bundle contains the REST API exported by Cisco DNA Center. These REST APIs provide a rich set of capabilities, including the ability to discover network devices, query network health and provision network devices.	
N Network Events for REST API Endpoint Cisco Systems, Inc. v1.0.2	DNAC 1.2.5 + Updated May 20, 2019	ACTIVE	You can use this bundle to publish DNA Center events to any REST API endpoint, as well as to receive updates about the event and its associated artifacts(incident, problem or request for change). The bundle then populates the Runtime Dashboard with this data.	Configure
N Network Issue Monitor and Enrichment for ITSM (ServiceNow) Cisco Systems, Inc. v1.0.1	DNAC 1.2.5 + Updated May 20, 2019	ENABLED	You can use this bundle to monitor your network for assurance and maintenance issues, and then publish the event details about these issues to an ITSM(ServiceNow) system. This bundle also contains APIs that extract rich network context data. Please note that, if your network devices have not yet been synchronized between...	Configure
	SWIM Events for ITSM (ServiceNow)			

Showing 6 of 6

Cisco DNA Center   DESIGN   POLICY   PROVISION   ASSURANCE   PLATFORM

Platform   Version 1.0.0 - Released 2/8/2019

Overview   Manage ∨   Developer Toolkit ∨   **Runtime Dashboard**

Runtime Dashboard

                                                        ⟳ Refresh   Last 6 hours ∨

Event Summary ⓘ

0

API Summary ⓘ

Call Status

Completed Call Performance

API Name	Average	Low		High
Create Site	8.152s			
Get Site Health	0.236s			

View All

Integration Flow Summary ⓘ

REST-Based (0) | 0 new   Schedule-Based (1) | 0 new

▽ Filter   ⟱ Export   ≡Q Find

Domain	Name		Instances				Performance		
		All (6)	⊘	●	●	●	Minimum	Maximum	Average

No data to display

Cisco DNA Center   DESIGN   POLICY   PROVISION   ASSURANCE   PLATFORM

Platform   Version 1.0.2 - Released 2/8/2019

Overview   Manage ⌄   Developer Toolkit ⌄   Runtime Dashboard

Bundles

Configuratio   **Configurations**

Set global settings or across multiple bundles for a custom platform experience.

Event Settings

General Settings

Event Settings

▽ Filter   ≡Q Find

	Event Name ⌃	Domain	Type	Category	Severity	Workflow	Actions
☐	802.11r client roaming slowly	Onboarding	Network	Warn	P3	Incident	Edit
☐	802.11r FT client roaming slowly	Onboarding	Network	Warn	P3	Incident	Edit
☐	AP Anomaly	AP RLM Event	Network	Warn	P3	Incident	Edit
☐	AP Coverage Hole	Availability	Network	Warn	P3	Incident	Edit
☐	AP CPU High Utilization	Utilization	Network	Warn	P3	Incident	Edit
☐	AP Down	Availability	Network	Warn	P2	Incident	Edit
☐	AP Flap	Availability	Network	Warn	P3	Incident	Edit
☐	AP License Exhausted on WLC	Utilization	Network	Warn	P3	Incident	Edit
☐	AP License Utilization on WLC	Utilization	Network	Warn	P3	Incident	Edit
☐	AP Memory High Utilization	Utilization	Network	Warn	P3	Incident	Edit

Showing 225 of 225

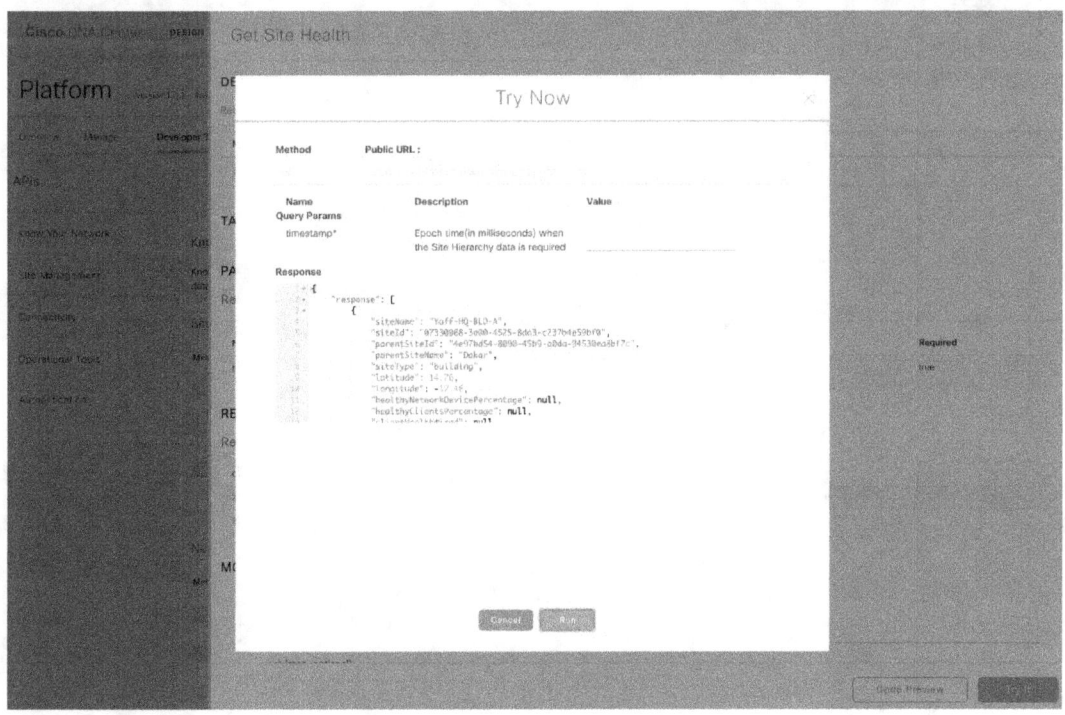

Creating a site.

Toolkit provides information about all of the API calls that are part of the SDK. However, before we proceed further, let me summarize the types of APIs that are available with the DNA Center.

- Northbound APIs
- Southbound APIs
- Eastbound APIs
- Westbound APIs

Northbound APIs, also known as, Intent APIs provide support for policy-based abstraction of business intent, allowing focus on business outcomes as opposed to mechanics of how. It is a RESTful APIs that allows the use of GET, POST, PUT and DELETE HTTP methods with JSON encoding to discover and control the network. All API calls require the use of a security token that identifies the privileges of an authenticated user making the RESTful API calls. You must obtain a security token before you can make use of any of the DNA center APIs.

Southbound APIs allow managing non-Cisco infrastructure by way of SDK that allow the creation of packages for 3rd party devices. Package contains mapping of Cisco DNA center features to other vendors' southbound protocols. In summary, southbound APIs are a gateway to multivendor support within the Cisco DNA center.

Events and Notifications provide the ability to establish a notification handler, so when specific DNA center events are triggered, such as SoftWare Image Management (SWIM) events, 3rd party systems can take actions in response to those events. Notifications can also be generated for internal events such as Assurance event causing an external ITSM system to initiate a ticket.

Westbound APIs, or what's also known as Integration APIs, are provided so that other 3rd party systems such as ITSM can be integrated with Cisco DNA center. Using integration APIs, you can implement change management, and approval and pre-approval chains. They also allow integration for reporting and analytics capabilities such as capacity planning, asset management, compliance control, and auditing. Last but not least, integration APIs allow support for IT4IT reference architecture so if you are using an external system that supports that, you can be sure to optimize your end to end IT value chain.

Further Reading

Cisco DNA Center User Guides[16]
Cisco DNA Center Maintain and Operate Guides[17]
Cisco DNA Center Install and Upgrade Guides[18]

Cisco ACI

[16] https://bit.ly/2w2rWNH

[17] https://bit.ly/2TLz7mB

[18] https://bit.ly/3cOxpbA

Cisco ACI tools help network engineers, network automation engineers and network admins to configure, develop, debug and automate the deployment lifecycle of tenants and applications. Cisco ACI solution offers CLI and GUI-based access as well as REST API access for management purposes that are available from within CLI, GUI, and even SDK. The same REST interface is used to read and write from and to the Management Information Tree (or MIT). The REST API also provides access to statistics, faults and audit events including push-based event notification.

CLI interface into APIC, leaf and spine switches offer the following facilities.

- CLI along with Python-based interpreter with ability to switch between them seamlessly
- Python commands or batch scripting can be used for automation
- VRF-based access to manage lifecycle of monitoring, operation and configuration data
- Utilizes REST API-based access into APIC

APIC GUI-based features provide access to the fabric, leaf and spine switches.

- HTML-based UI
- Access to monitoring, operational and configuration data (much like CLI)
- Access to APIC and switches within the fabric through a single sign-on mechanism
- Utilizes REST API-based access into APIC

It is critical to note that the ACI programmability options go beyond the APIC REST API and include the following options.

- ACI Toolkit (subset of APIC REST API)
- Cobra SDK (complete functions of APIC REST API)
- APIC REST Python Adapter (ARYA)

The ACI toolkit is a set of Python libraries that you can use for basic configuration of a subset of the object model. The Cobra SDK provides you with access to all REST functions using the native Python 3.x bindings. Since it supports full functionality, it is suited for complex queries, managing L4-7 devices, and initial fabric builds, etc. The ARYA is a tool that converts XML/JSON objects to equivalent Python code.

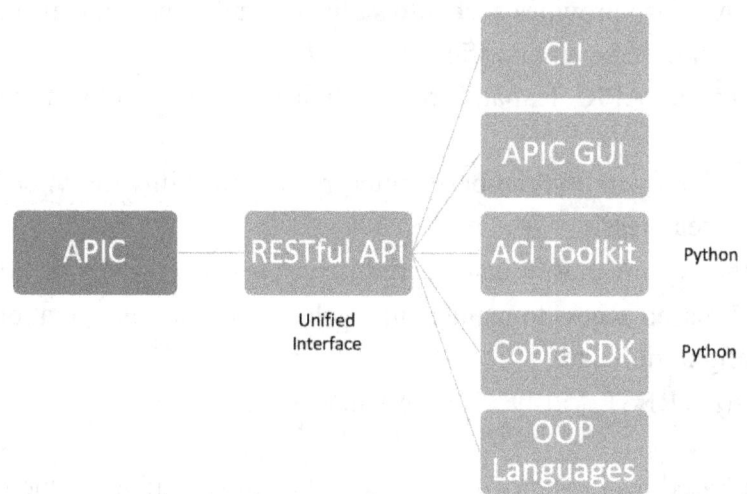

Both APIC and Nexus 9K switches support NX-OS as well as Manage Object (MO) CLI models. Cisco Nexus 9K switches can be configured in NX-OS mode to access the device-level APIs, in that mode switches can be managed much like a Linux machine.

Here object model refers to the logical topology (such as a tenant, EPGs, etc.), whereas the concrete model refers to the physical topology (such as ports, trunks, etc.).

CLI Type	APIC v1.0 to v1.1	APIC v1.2 and later	Nexus 9K
NX-OS	Available	Default Mode	Default Mode
Object Model via Bash	Default Mode	Available, type "bash" to access	n/a

While NX-OS CLI type access is possible into APIC, it doesn't mean that it is the same as traditional NX-OS running on a Nexus 7K switch for example. Let us note down some subtle differences between the two.

CLI Mode	APIC NX-OS	Traditional NX-OS
Entering Global Config Mode	apic#configure	nexus7k#configure terminal
Node or Leaf-level Configuration	Must select the switch using the "leaf" command	n/a

Let's now explore the APIC v4.1(1k) GUI interface with the following topology.

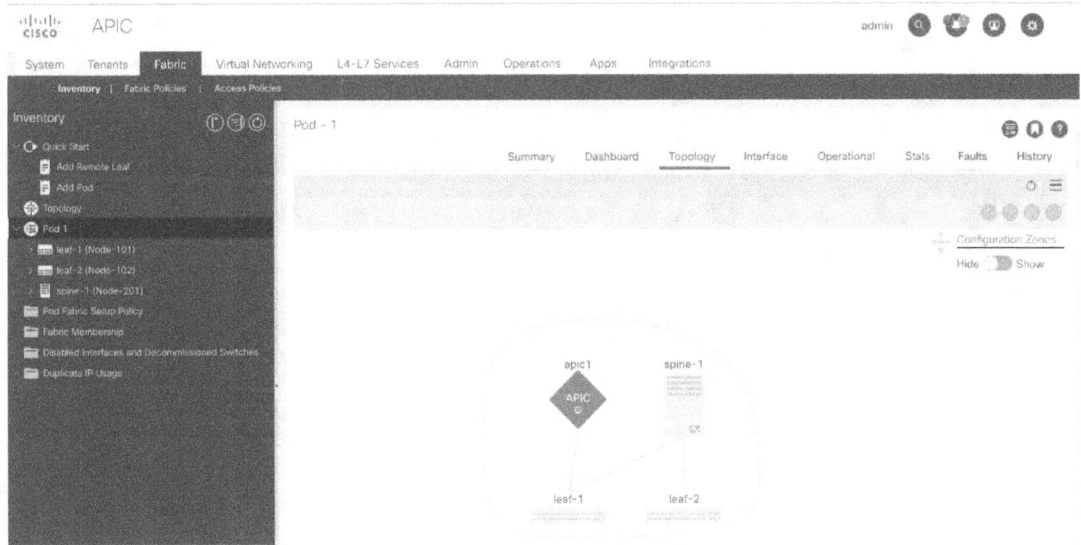

System Tab.

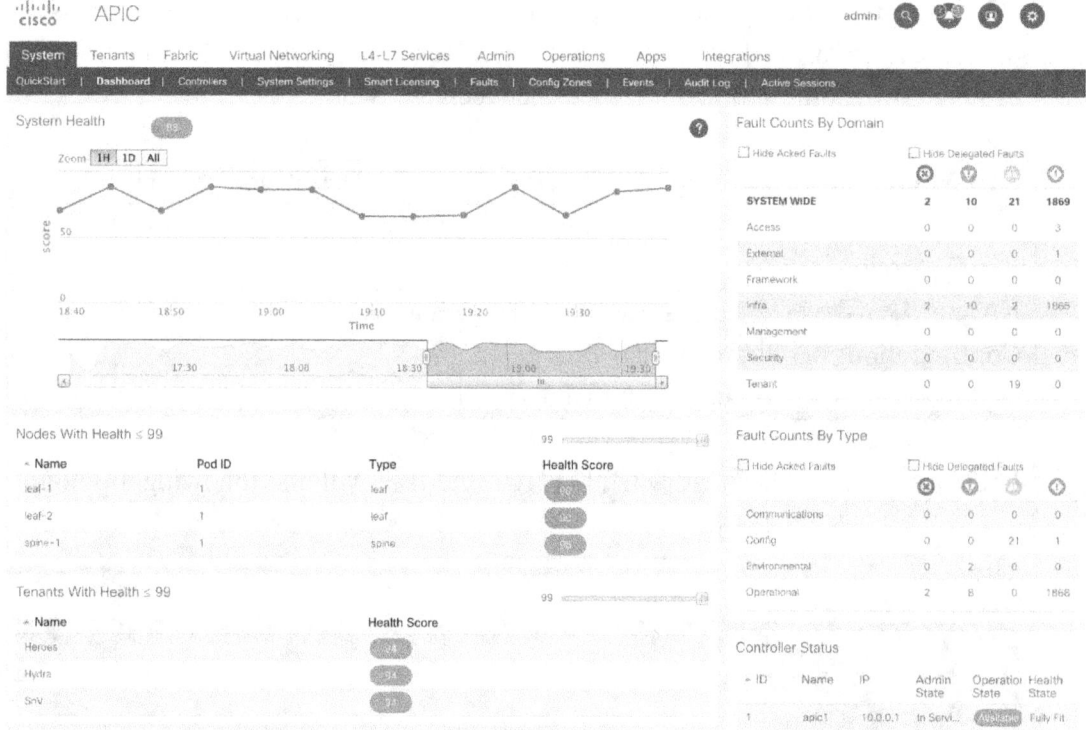

Tenants > Heroes Tab.

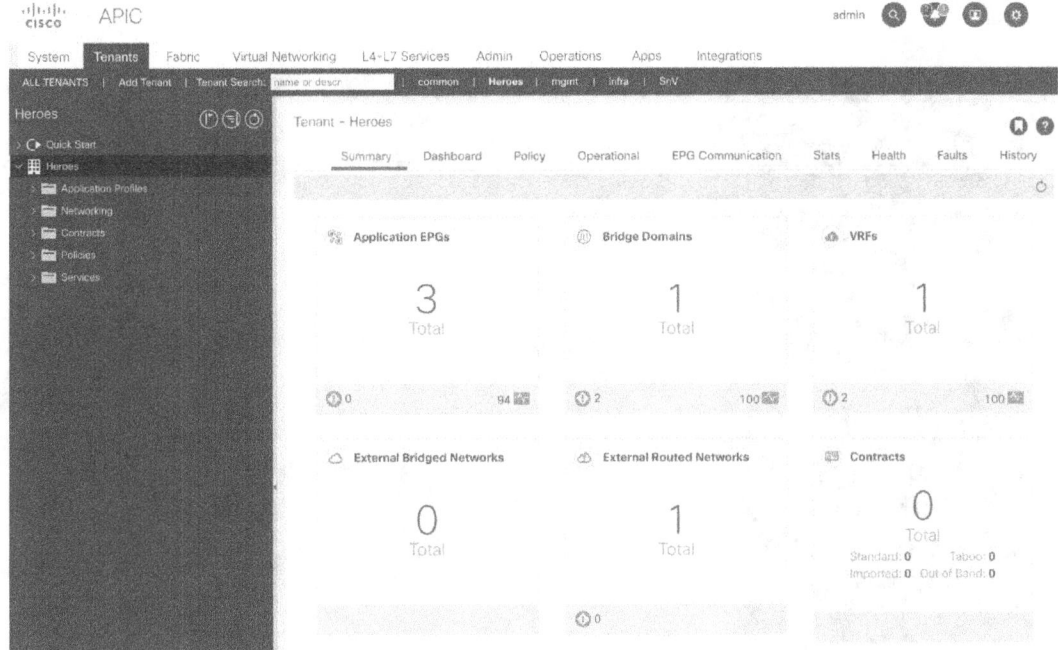

Tenants > Heroes > Policy Tab. As we discussed earlier, everything within the ACI fabric is defined as an object or managed object or MO. Each MO inherits properties and how it is going to function from the class it belongs to. MOs are connected in a parent/child relationship and, as a whole, that's what known as MIT.

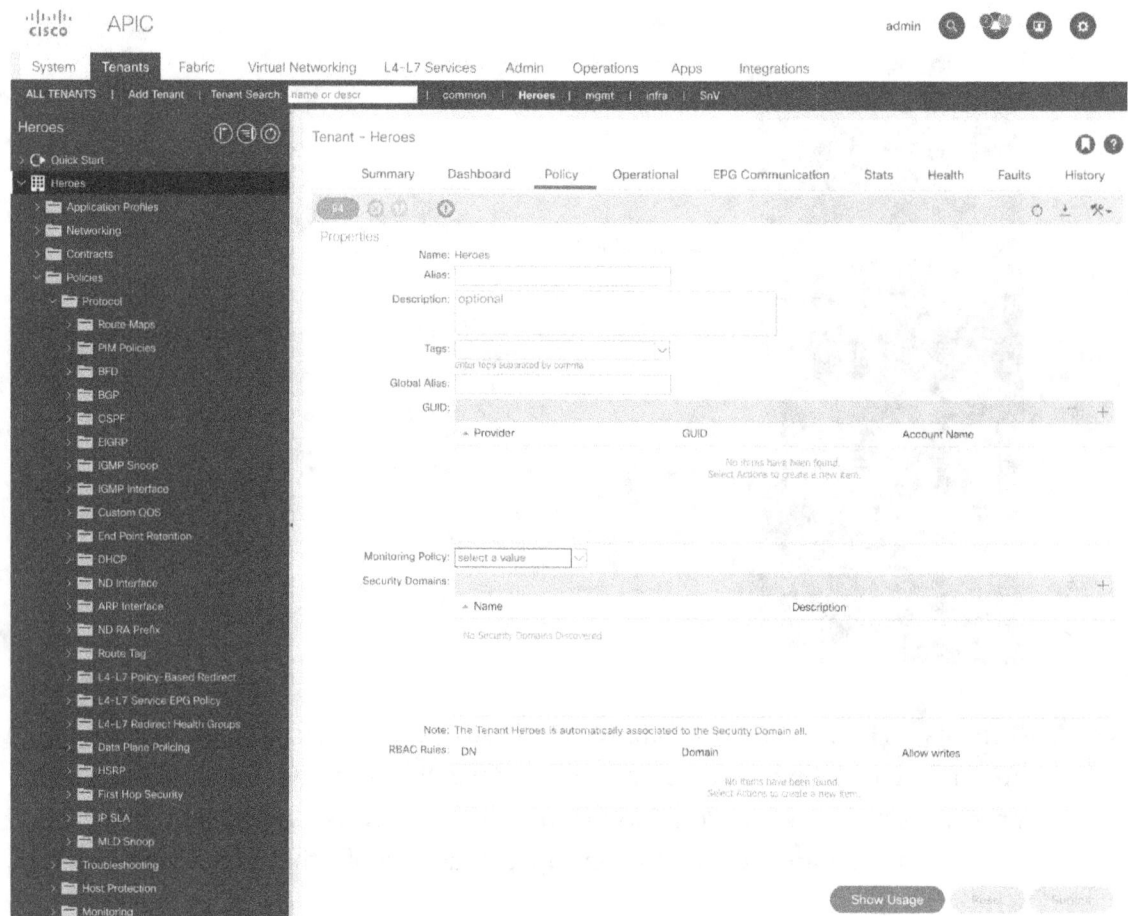

Tenants > Contracts

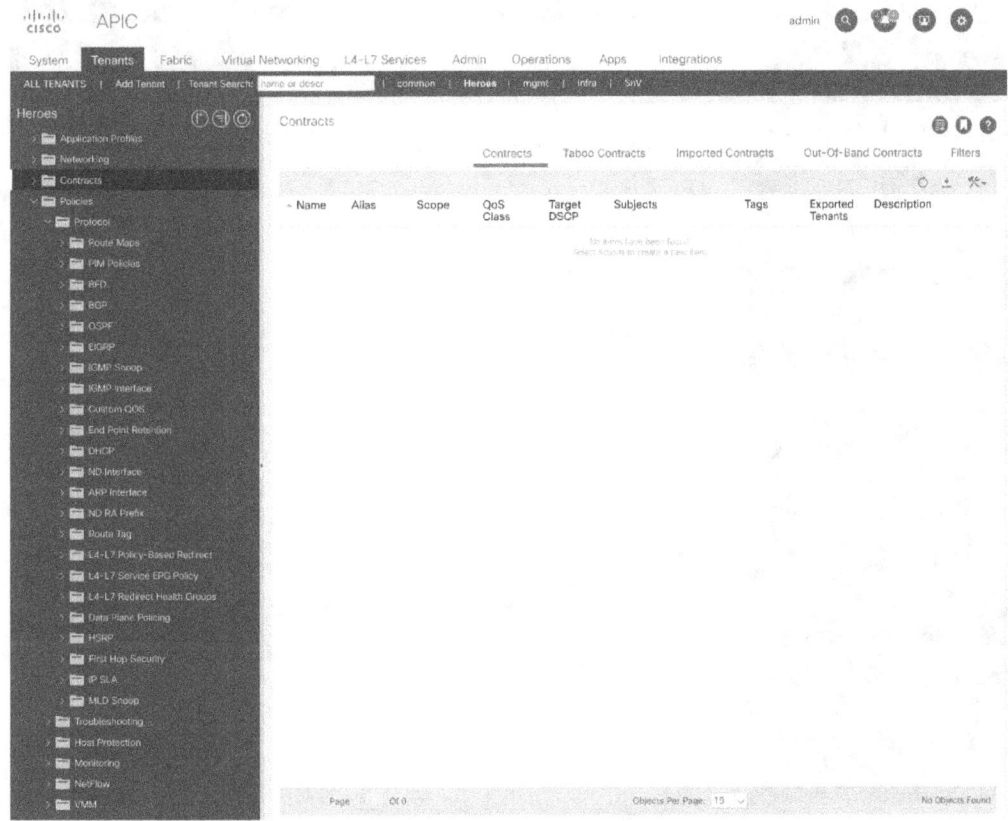

App object is a child of Save_The_Planet Application Profile but also at the same time has relationships with Domains, Contracts, Subnets, etc. These relationships can be 1:1, 1:n or even n:n.

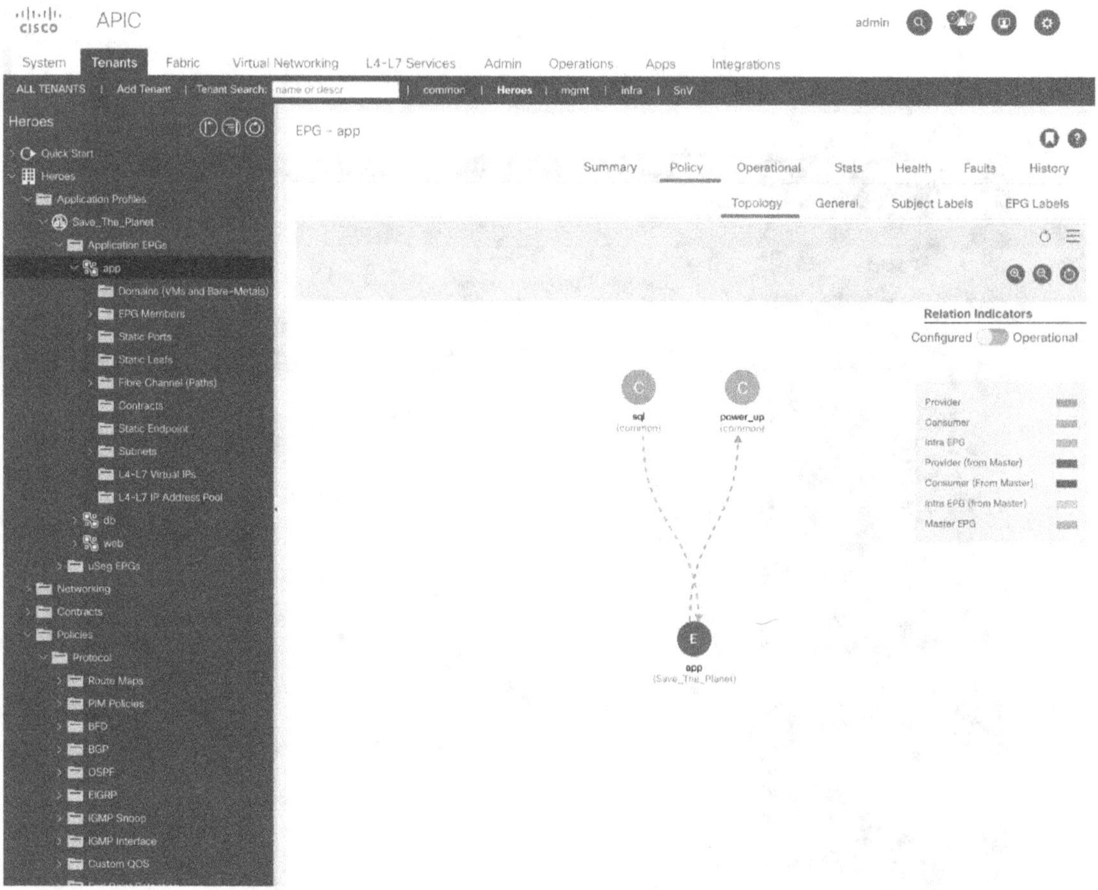

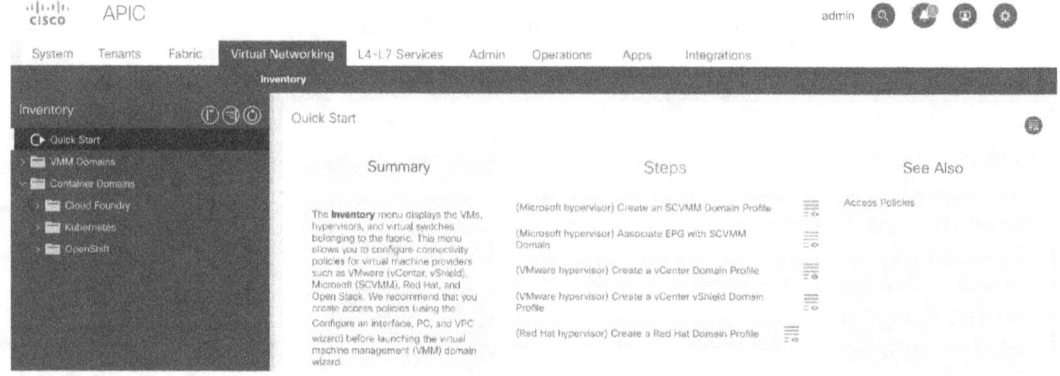

Virtual Networking options.

APIC REST API allows for use of HTTP GET, POST and DELETE methods. It allows data to be encoded either into JSON or XML formats. REST API authentication works with a username and password.

Before you can construct a REST API call, you need to understand Relative Name (or RN) and Distinguished Name (or DN). Each MO has an RN which identifies an object from other child objects of a given parent so what that means is what each RN must be unique within the same parent. RN helps you nail down the most specific objects that you are interested in (e.g., a host identified by an IP address).

ACI Module	ACI Object (Common Name)	Relative Name (RN)
fv (fabric virtualization)	Tenant	tn-name
fv (fabric virtualization)	Context/VRF	ctx-name
fv (fabric virtualization)	Bridge Domain (BD)	BD-name
fv (fabric virtualization)	Subnet	subnet-ip
fv (fabric virtualization)	App Profile	ap-name
fv (fabric virtualization)	EPG	epg-name
fv (fabric virtualization)	Client Endpoint	cep-name
fv (fabric virtualization)	IP Address	ip-addr
l3ext	L3 External	out-name
vz (virtual zone)	Filter	flt-name
vz (virtual zone)	Contract	brc-name
vz (virtual zone)	Contract Subject	subj-name

Now, let's look at some real examples of MOs from our APIC GUI.

tn-heroes

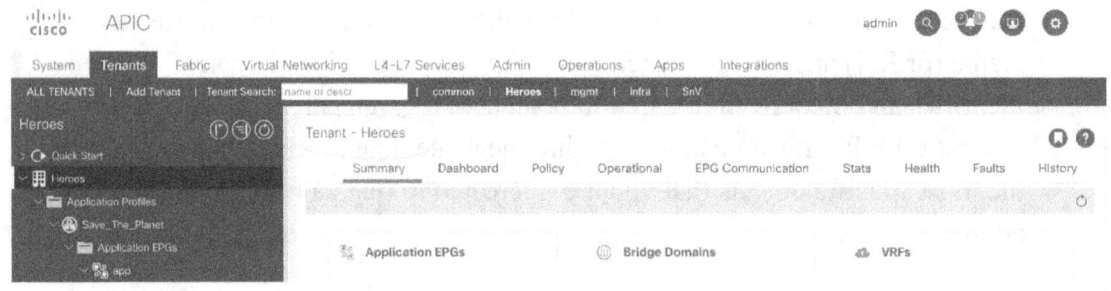

ctx-sql

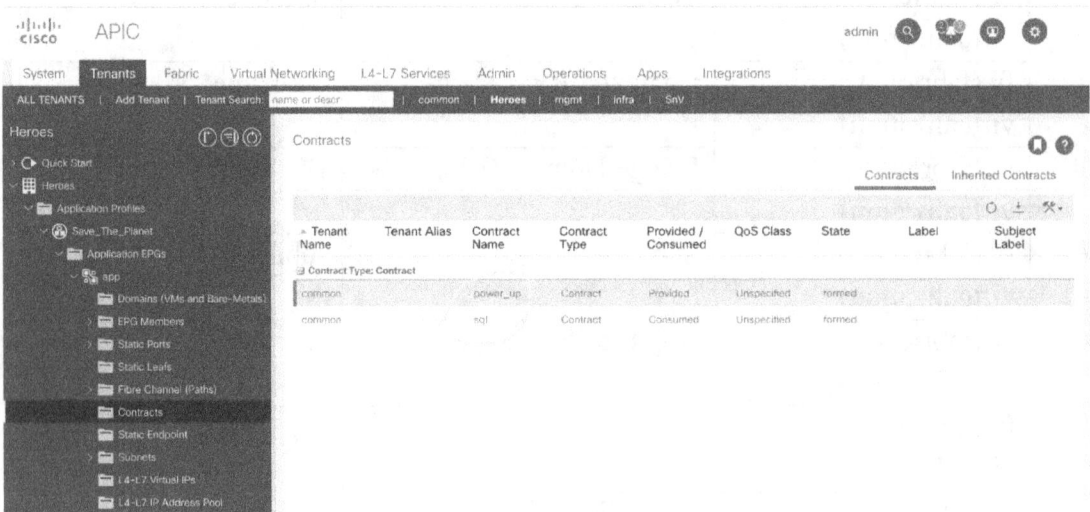

Now, a DN consists of a series of RNs starting with the root and then cascading each child RN to your desired object.

dn = root/{rn1}/{rn2}/{rn3}

Going back to our tenant (tn-heroes) example and corresponding RNs, we can come up with several DNs.

- uni/tn-Heroes/ap-Save_The_Planet/epg-app|fvAEPgContracts
- uni/tn-Heroes/ap-Save_The_Planet/epg-app|fvAEPgVMMBindings
- uni/tn-Heroes/ap-Save_The_Planet/epg-app|fvAEPgMembers

You can also identify the DN by looking at the APIC URLs in the browser.

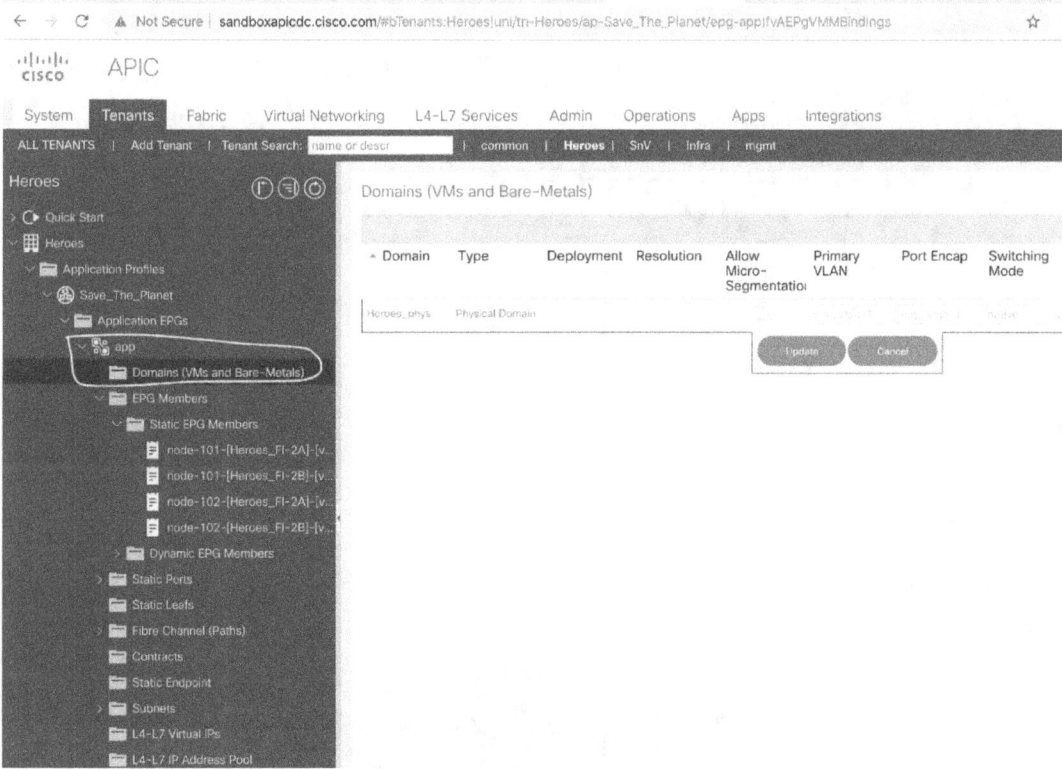

Both RNs and the DNs are super critical when it comes to making the REST API calls, either using the POSTMAN (GUI app) or using the ACI toolkit, Cobra SDK, etc. If you are using an APIC server with a self-signed certificate (such as DevNet sandbox), be sure to turn off "SSL Certificate Verification" within Postman Settings > General tab. Without that, your API requests will simply fail.

174

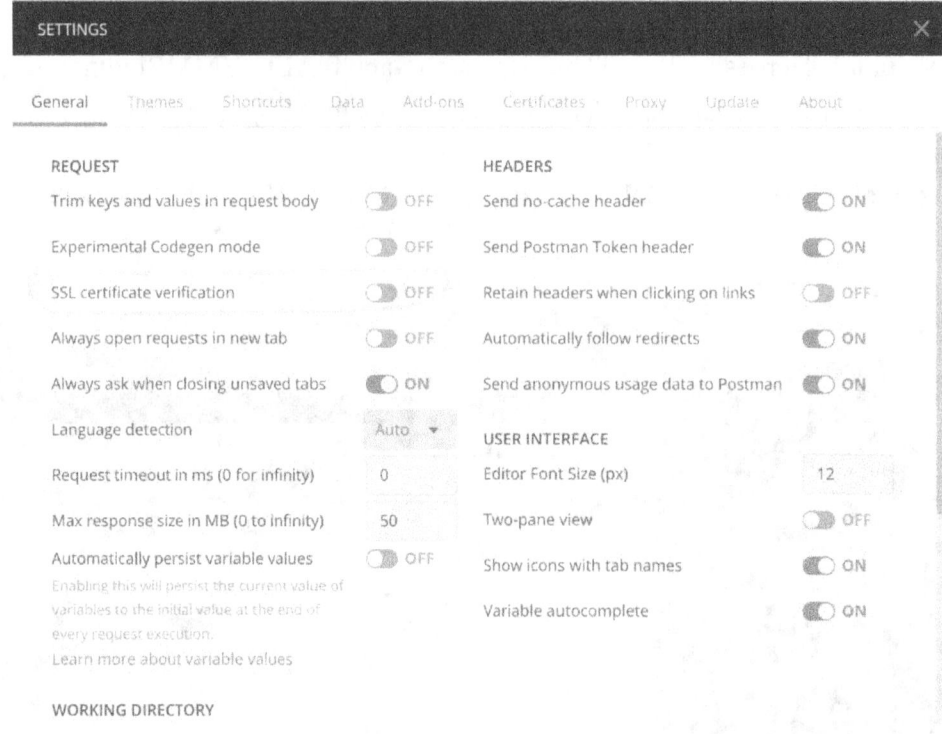

APIC GUI

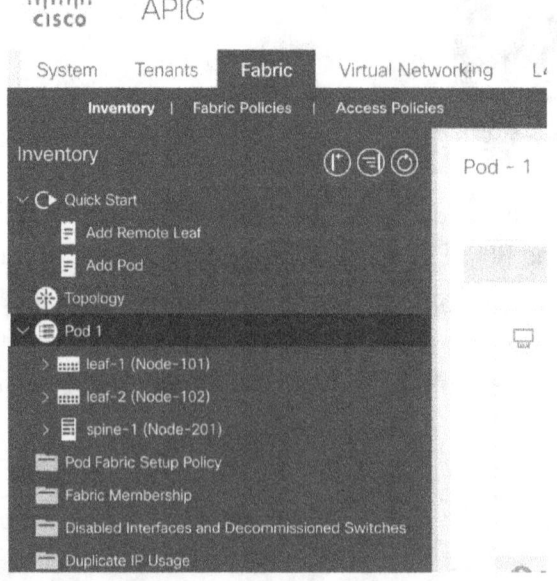

Using REST API with POSTMAN (JSON)

The first and the second half of the POSTMAN GUI show JSON encoded requests and responses. Once you perform a POST, POSTMAN will cache your APIC authorization token (or session cookie) for 600 seconds and will use that to perform subsequent HTTP requests.

For reference, you can see the token and value in the response body below.

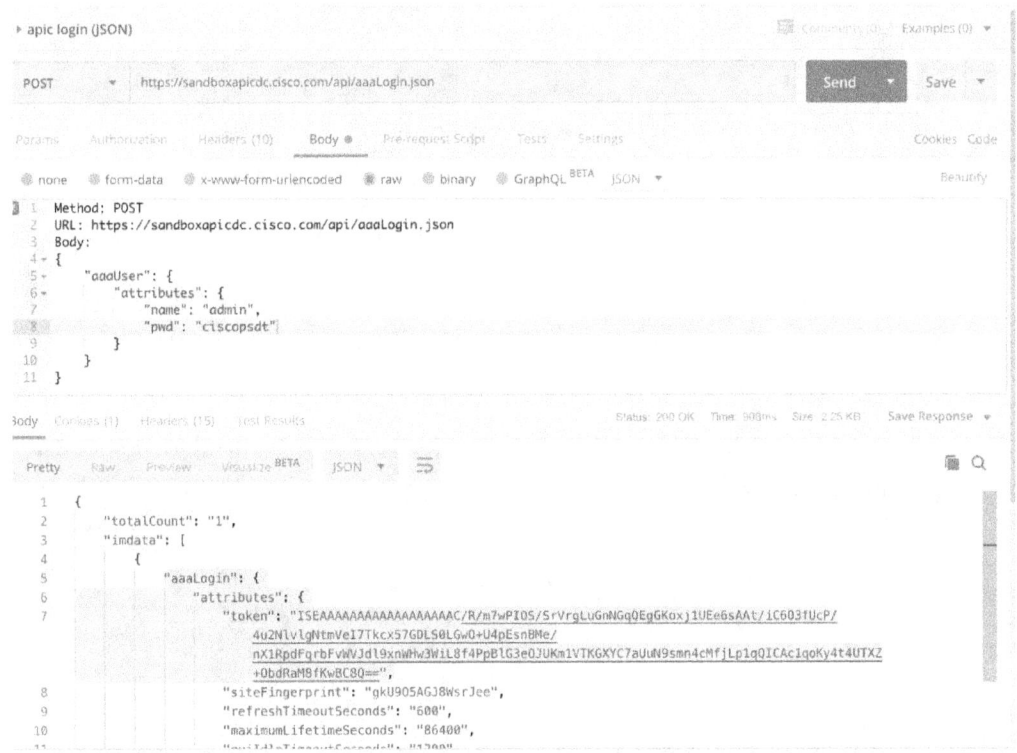

The response is easier to read if you switch to Pretty as opposed to Raw format.

Using REST API with POSTMAN (XML)

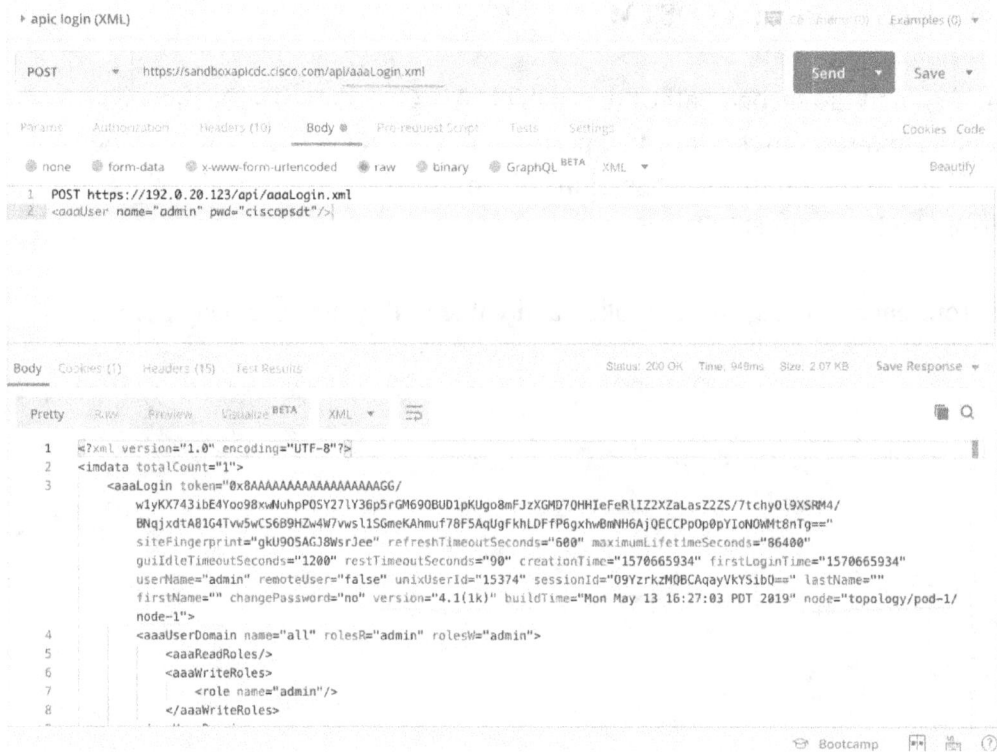

Once you've an authenticated session, you can perform a GET to read a specific DN (e.g., /uni/tn-Heroes/ap-Save_The_Planet).

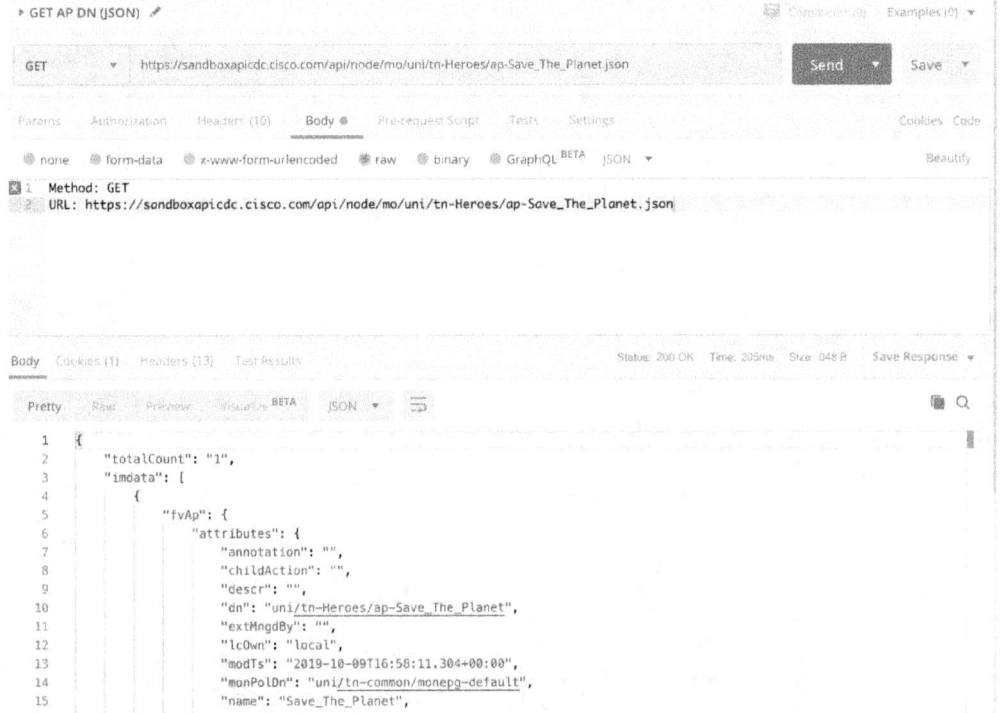

```
1   {
2       "totalCount": "1",
3       "imdata": [
4           {
5               "fvAp": {
6                   "attributes": {
7                       "annotation": "",
8                       "childAction": "",
9                       "descr": "",
10                      "dn": "uni/tn-Heroes/ap-Save_The_Planet",
11                      "extMngdBy": "",
12                      "lcOwn": "local",
13                      "modTs": "2019-10-09T16:58:11.304+00:00",
14                      "monPolDn": "uni/tn-common/monepg-default",
15                      "name": "Save_The_Planet",
```

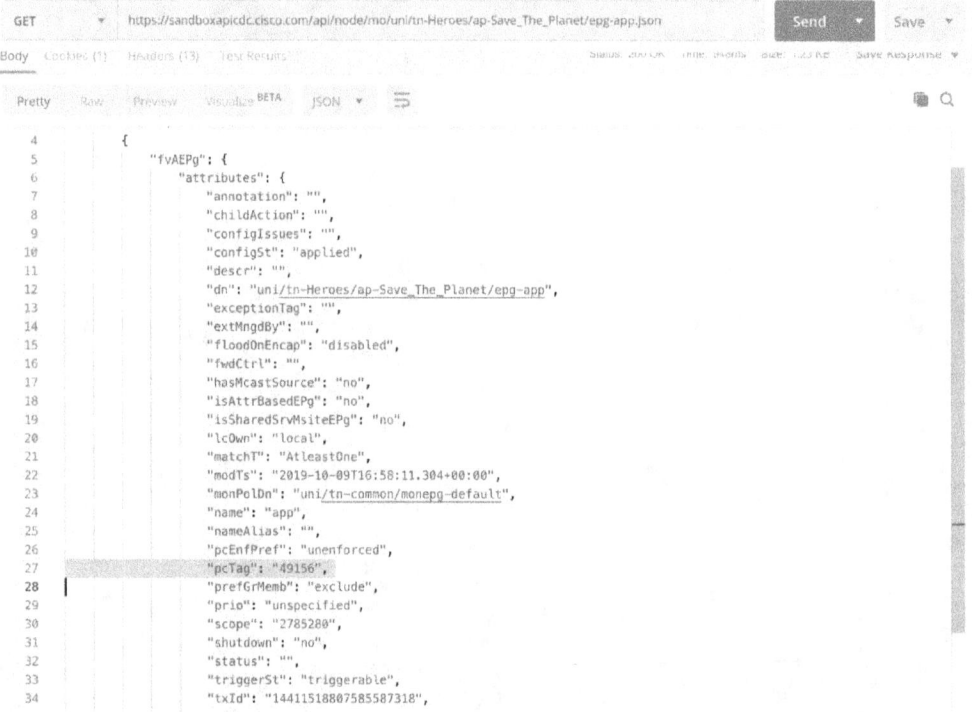

You can also get started with POSTMAN by importing the existing DevNet collections posted on GitHub.

Using REST API with ACI Toolkit

ACI toolkit is nothing but a collection of Python libraries that would allow you to deal with commonly used objects within the ACI MIT. For example, you can create, read, update and delete most of the MIT objects inside the tenant class as well as fabric access policies.

Python Code

```
1   import acitoolkit
2
3   url = 'https://sandboxapicdc.cisco.com'
4   username = 'admin'
5   pwd = 'ciscopsdt'
6   session = acitoolkit.Session(url, username, pwd)
7   print(session.login())
```

Code Output

```
Python 3.7.4 (default, Jul  9 2019, 00:06:43)
[GCC 6.3.0 20170516] on linux
<Response [200]>
```

Now, let's run a query to pull a list of all ACI nodes.

Python Code

```
1   from acitoolkit.acisession import Session
2   from acitoolkit.aciphysobject import Node
3
4   url = 'https://sandboxapicdc.cisco.com'
5   usr_name = 'admin'
6   password = 'ciscopsdt'
7   session = Session(url, usr_name, password)
8   nodes = Node.get(session)
9   for node in nodes:
10      print(node.name)
```

Code Output

```
Python 3.7.4 (default, Jul  9 2019, 00:06:43)
[GCC 6.3.0 20170516] on linux
leaf-1
leaf-2
spine-1
apic1
>
```

Now, let's repeat the query and pull a list of all ACI tenants.

Python Code

```
1  from acitoolkit import *
2
3  url = 'https://sandboxapicdc.cisco.com'
4  usr_name = 'admin'
5  password = 'ciscopsdt'
6  session = Session(url, usr_name, password)
7  nodes = Node.get(session)
8  tenants = Tenant.get(session)
9
10  for tenant in tenants:
11      print(tenant.name)
```

Code Output

```
Python 3.7.4 (default, Jul  9 2019, 00:06:43)
[GCC 6.3.0 20170516] on linux
infra
mgmt
common
Heroes
SnV
AAA_Tenant
Hydra
CCC_Tenant
DDD_Tenant
EEE_Tenant
FFF_Tenant
PROD
GGG_Tenant
BBB_Tenant
>
```

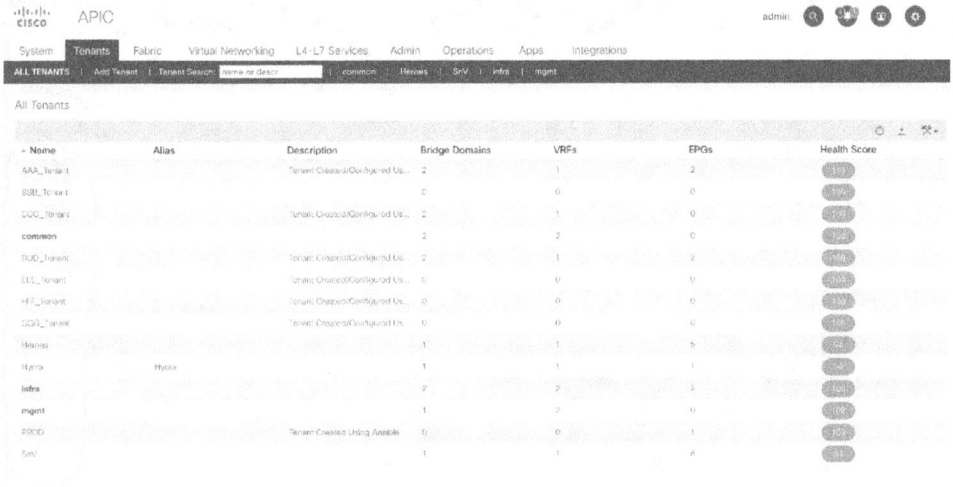

Cisco SD-WAN

vManage is the centralized management platform for configuring, monitoring and maintaining Cisco SD-WAN (formerly Viptela) devices. Once installed, you can access vManage using a web browser. When you log into vManage, the dashboard provides a bird's eye view of the network.

These are the Cisco SD-WAN components.

- vManage (centralized management dashboard). It serves as the management plane of the SD-WAN solution)
- vBond orchestrator (orchestrates connectivity between vEdge routers and vSmart controllers)
- vSmart controller (controls the flow of data traffic by working with vBond orchestrator. It is the control plane of the SD-WAN solution)
- vEdge routers (virtualized routers that help secure virtual overlay network at branch offices, campuses, etc. It is the data plane of the SD-WAN)

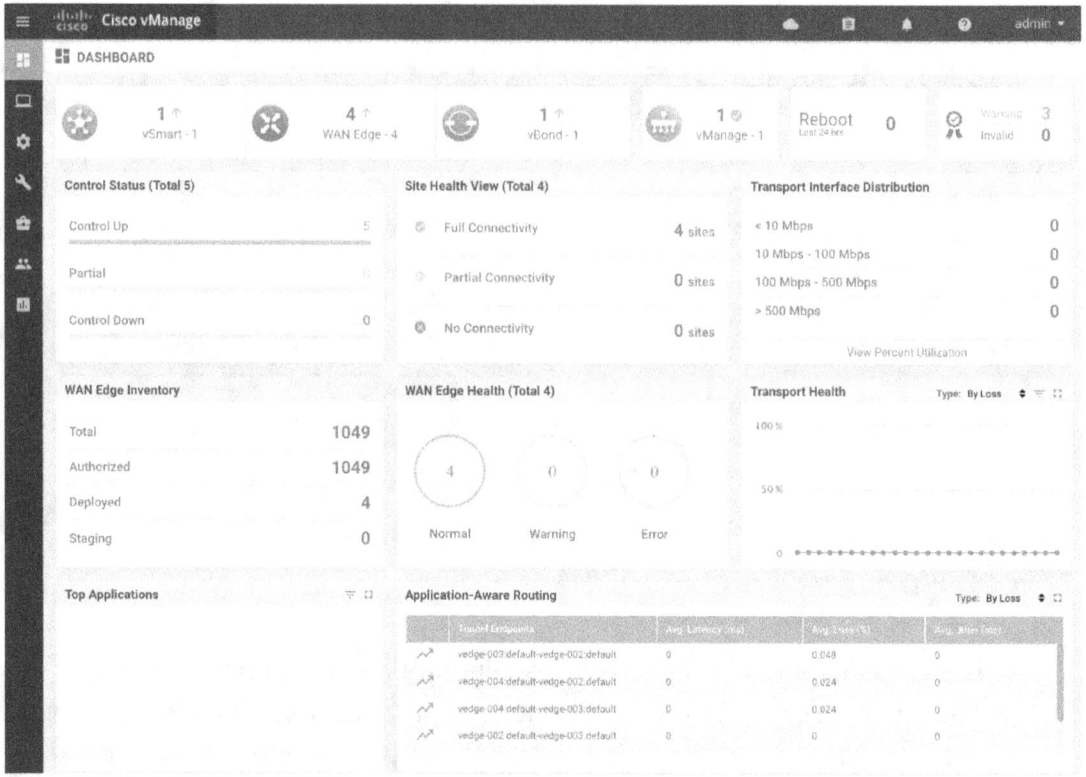

vManage provides REST API access for retrieving real-time and configuration state information about the SD-WAN overlay. vManage REST APIs support the following categories of operations.

- Administration
- Certificate Management
- Configuration
- Device and Inventory
- Monitoring including Real-Time
- Troubleshooting

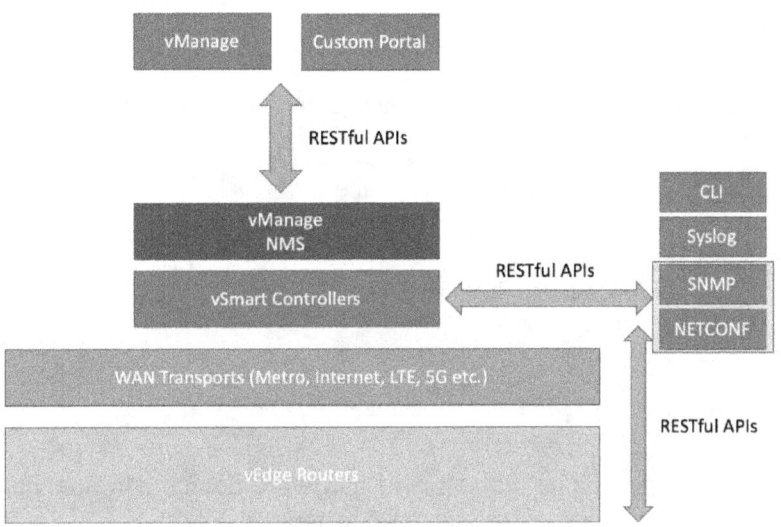

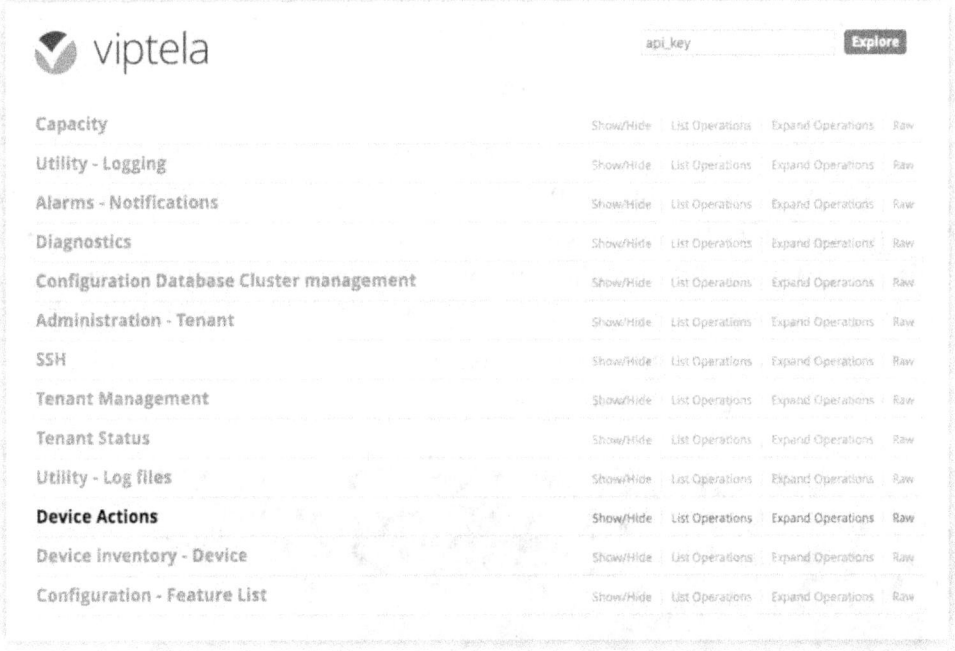

You can access the vManage RESTful API documentation by going to the server itself.

https://vManage-ip-address:8443/apidocs

You can construct your API call URLs using the following format.

https://vmanage-ip-address:8443/dataservice/blah

For example, you could list all network devices attached to your SD-WAN overlay.

https://vmanage-ip-address:8443/dataservice/device

Likewise, you can get the health status of hardware device components such as CPU or memory by sending in the following URL.

https://vmanage-ip-address:8443/dataservice/device/hardware/environment?deviceId=system-ip-address

Much like APIC, you can send in your REST API calls either via Postman, Python or another OOP language of your choice. Again, if you use Postman, and your vManage server is using a self-signed certificate, you need to disable "SSL certificate verification". For Python, if you use requests library for sending in your HTTP methods, you can add on "verify=False" in your POST or GET requests. Even if you provide verify=False, then you will notice a warning message like below that you can ignore.

```
Python 3.7.4 (default, Jul  9 2019, 00:06:43)
[GCC 6.3.0 20170516] on linux
/home/runner/.local/share/virtualenvs/python3/lib/python3
.7/site-packages/urllib3/connectionpool.py:1004: Insecure
RequestWarning: Unverified HTTPS request is being made. A
dding certificate verification is strongly advised. See:
https://urllib3.readthedocs.io/en/latest/advanced-usage.h
tml#ssl-warnings
  InsecureRequestWarning,
```

Another thing to keep in mind is that every time you successfully authenticate using the vManage admin username and password, the server issues a session token or cookie that you can use to send in more requests.

Let me share examples from Postman and Python connecting to vManage servers via REST API calls.

Postman

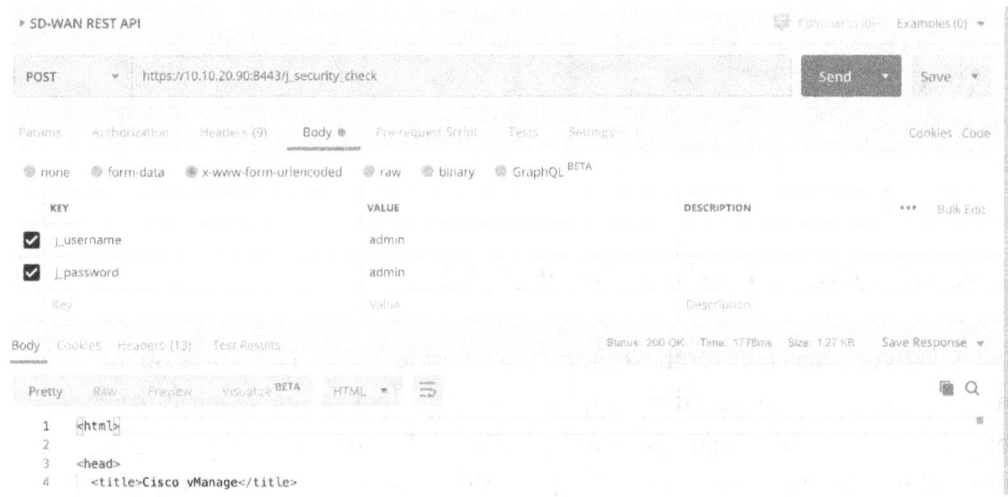

Python Code

```
1   import requests
2   import json
3
4   url = 'https://sandboxsdwan.cisco.com:8443/j_security_check/'
5 - data = {
6     'j_username': 'devnetuser',
7     'j_password': 'Cisco123!'
8   }
9   response = requests.post(url, data, verify = False)
10  print(response)
11  r = requests.get('https://sandboxsdwan.cisco.com:8443/dataservice
        /device', verify = False)
12  print(r.json())
```

Code Output

```
{
  "header": {
    "generatedOn": 1540335618852,
    "viewKeys": {
      "uniqueKey": [
        "system-ip"
      ],
      "preferenceKey": "grid-Device"
    },
    "columns": [
      {
        "title": "Hostname",
        "property": "host-name",
        "display": "iconAndText",
        "iconProperty": "device-type",
        "hideable": false,
        "icon": [
          {
            "key": "vmanage",
            "value": "images/vmanage_table.png"
```

Cisco Network Services Orchestrator (NSO)

Cisco Network Services Orchestrator (NSO, formerly tail-f) enables operators to adopt the service configuration solution and helps them achieve a multi-vendor network while keeping management centralized. It provides lifecycle service automation with the YANG model-driven platform. Thanks to YANG, it supports multi-vendor networks through Network Element Drivers (or NEDs).

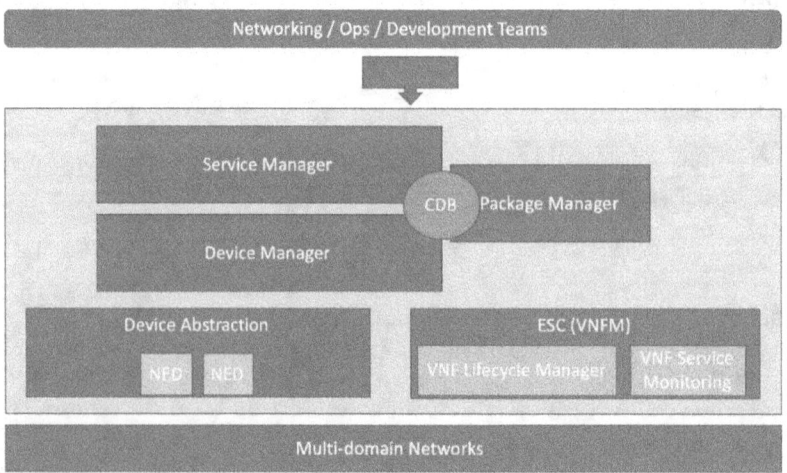

Historically, YANG started with NETCONF, however as RESTCONF became a popular interface, it was added to the YANG model, giving network managers two choices to access the model-driven interface.

Configuration Database (or CDB) is a tree-like database that is controlled by the YANG schema. The CDB holds NSO's view of the complete network configuration whether you are reading or writing to NSO.

NSO device manager keeps a list of all managed devices and stores a master copy of the configuration for each managed device inside CDB. Whenever a change occurs, the device manager passes on the requirement changes to the NEDs, so you need to install a NED for every type of device, e.g., one for IOS XE, one for IOS XR, likewise one for Juniper Junos, etc.

The NEDs communicate through the native device's southbound protocol. Here are a few use cases that you can use NSO for.

- Device bring-up, e.g., simplifying the deployment of a new device such as a router.
- NFV orchestration, e.g., creating, modifying or deleting virtualized services as requested by customers.
- SD-WAN orchestration, e.g., lifecycle management for Cisco iWAN.

There are a bunch of other use cases such as ACL or QoS management, configuration audit, OS upgrade, etc.

Following list outlines the available northbound NSO interfaces.

- CLI (Network-wide CLI that provides transactions across multiple devices and support for the service models)
- RESTCONF API (Standardized REST interface that supports for auto-generating Swagger/OpenAPI documents from YANG)
- NETCONF (For OSS applications that want to interface the devices and services managed by NSO)

- Java (Interface used to build applications and clients for NSO)
- JavaScript (Interface used to build custom web interfaces)
- SNMP (Allows NSO to present operational data over SNMP to upper layer management systems)
- MAAPI (Available as CLI utilities such as C-API, Java API, and a Python API)
- REST API (Complete model via HTTP, can exchange data using XML and JSON)

Let's now try out a minimal NSO install and see what we can do with it. "netsim" is just a network simulator to create two IOS devices before we fire up the NSO itself ("ncs" command).

```
$
$ncs-netsim create-network cisco-ios 2 ios
DEVICE ios0 CREATED
DEVICE ios1 CREATED
$ncs-setup --dest . --netsim-dir netsim
Using netsim dir netsim
$ls
README.ncs  README.netsim  logs  ncs-cdb  ncs.conf  netsim  packages  scripts  state
$ncs-netsim start
DEVICE ios0 OK STARTED
DEVICE ios1 OK STARTED
$
```

```
$ncs-netsim start
DEVICE ios0 OK STARTED
DEVICE ios1 OK STARTED
$ncs
$
```

NSO (or Tail-f NCS) CLI comes in two flavors, Cisco (-C option) or Juniper. For this exercise, we will stick with Cisco's style. As shown in the output below, we first choose our NCS CLI and then synchronize NSO with our simulated two IOS devices.

```
$ncs_cli -u admin -C

admin connected from 127.0.0.1 using console on e2dea4937861
admin@ncs# devices sync-from
sync-result {
    device ios0
    result true
}
sync-result {
    device ios1
    result true
}
admin@ncs# 
```

Now, we can verify if the two IOS configurations are in sync or not (i.e., into CDB).

```
admin@ncs# devices device ios1 check-sync
result in-sync
admin@ncs# 
```

Now, we enter into NCS configuration mode and then examine the configuration for ios1. Please note that the output below is truncated, however, you can use spacebar to continue to the end of the configuration much like how you do it on the router with more.

```
admin@ncs# config
Entering configuration mode terminal
admin@ncs(config)# show full-configuration devices device ios1 config
devices device ios1
 config
  no ios:service pad
  ios:ip vrf my-forward
   bgp next-hop Loopback 1
  !
  ios:ip community-list 1 permit
  ios:ip community-list 2 deny
  ios:ip community-list standard s permit
  no ios:ip domain-lookup
  no ios:ip http server
  no ios:ip http secure-server
  ios:ip routing
  ios:ip source-route
  ios:interface FastEthernet1/0
  exit
  ios:interface Loopback0
  exit
  ios:class-map match-all a
  !
  ios:class-map match-all cmap1
   match mpls experimental topmost 1
   match packet length max 255
   match packet length min 2
   match qos-group 1
  !
  ios:policy-map a
  !
  ios:policy-map map1
   class c1
    drop
    estimate bandwidth delay-one-in 500 milliseconds 100
    priority percent 33
   !
  !
  no ios:spanning-tree optimize bpdu transmission
```

Let's now execute one more configuration command to display BGP configuration.

```
admin@ncs(config)# show full-configuration devices device ios1 config | context-match bgp
devices device ios1
 config
  ios:ip vrf my-forward
   bgp next-hop Loopback 1
devices device ios1
  ios:router bgp 64512
devices device ios1
 config
  ios:router bgp 64512
   neighbor 1.2.3.4 ebgp-multihop 3
admin@ncs(config)# []
```

Now, let's try to make a small configuration change on device ios1.

```
admin@ncs(config)# devices device ios0 config
admin@ncs(config-config)# ios:hostname nso.cisco.com
admin@ncs(config-config)# top
admin@ncs(config)# show configuration
devices device ios0
 config
  ios:hostname nso.cisco.com
 !
!
admin@ncs(config)# []
```

Now, let's try to make a small change (i.e., enable password) across both IOS devices.

```
admin@ncs(config)# devices device * config ios:enable password magic
admin@ncs(config-config)# show configuration
devices device ios0
 config
  ios:hostname nso.cisco.com
  ios:enable password magic
 !
!
devices device ios1
 config
  ios:enable password magic
 !
!
admin@ncs(config-config)# []
```

Let's view our changes by doing a "dry-run", before we actually commit or revert them.

```
admin@ncs(config-config)# commit dry-run outformat native
native {
    device {
        name ios0
        data hostname nso.cisco.com
             enable password magic
    }
    device {
        name ios1
        data enable password magic
    }
}
admin@ncs(config-config)# []
```

Now, that all looks good, we commit our changes and exit out.

```
admin@ncs(config-config)# commit
Commit complete.
admin@ncs(config-config)# end
admin@ncs# []
```

You can also add newer services and take automation further by way of packages.

```
admin@ncs# >>> System upgrade has completed successfully.
show packages package oper-status
packages package cisco-ios
 oper-status up
packages package simple-service
 oper-status up
admin@ncs# ▯
```

```
admin@ncs# config
Entering configuration mode terminal
admin@ncs(config)# simple-service test1 device ios0 secret mypasswd
admin@ncs(config-simple-service-test1)# show configuration
simple-service test1
 device ios0
 secret mypasswd
!
admin@ncs(config-simple-service-test1)# commit dry-run
cli {
    local-node {
        data +simple-service test1 {
            +    device ios0;
            +    secret mypasswd;
            +}
             devices {
                device ios0 {
                    config {
                        ios:enable {
                            password {
            -                    secret magic;
            +                    secret mypasswd;
                            }
                        }
                    }
                }
            }
    }
}
admin@ncs(config-simple-service-test1)# ▯
```

Before performing a commit, you can always go and make changes. For example, we just modified our enable secret password from "mypasswd" to "securepasswd". You can notice that both the outgoing (older) and incoming (newer) line items are prefaced by "-" and "+" signs respectively.

```
admin@ncs(config-simple-service-test1)# secret securepasswd
admin@ncs(config-simple-service-test1)# commit dry-run
cli {
    local-node {
        data  simple-service test1 {
        -       secret mypasswd;
        +       secret securepasswd;
         }
         devices {
            device ios0 {
                config {
                    ios:enable {
                        password {
        -                   secret mypasswd;
        +                   secret securepasswd;
                        }
                    }
                }
            }
        }
    }
}
```

Last but not least, we can also peek inside the service code so we can enhance or build our own service by using either templates, Java or even Python.

```
admin@ncs# exit
$cd packages/simple-service
$ls -R
.:
load-dir  package-meta-data.xml  src  templates  test

./load-dir:
simple-service.fxs

./src:
Makefile  yang

./src/yang:
simple-service.yang

./templates:
simple-service-template.xml

./test:
Makefile  internal

./test/internal:
Makefile  lux

./test/internal/lux:
Makefile  basic

./test/internal/lux/basic:
Makefile  run.lux
$
```

Let's now look at the contents of two files, i.e., simple-service.yang and simple-service-template.xml. YANG file describes the interface to the service and a bunch of other stuff (such as constraints etc.), whereas XML file shows the mapping between the service model as per the YANG file and intended device configuration.

```
module simple-service {
        namespace "http://com/example/simpleservice";
        prefix simple-service;

        import tailf-ncs { prefix ncs; }
        import tailf-common { prefix tailf; }

        list simple-service {
                key name;

                uses ncs:service-data;
                ncs:servicepoint simple-service;

                leaf name {
                        type string;
                }

                leaf device {
                        type leafref {
                                path "/ncs:devices/ncs:device/ncs:name";
                        }
                        tailf:info "The device to configure";
                }

                leaf secret {
                        type string;
                        tailf:info "Enable secret for this device";
                }
        }
}
src/yang/simple-service.yang (END)
```

```
<config-template xmlns="http://tail-f.com/ns/config/1.0"
                  servicepoint="simple-service">
  <devices xmlns="http://tail-f.com/ns/ncs">
      <device>
      <name>{./device}</name>
      <config>
        <enable xmlns="urn:ios">
          <password>
            <secret>{./secret}</secret>
          </password>
        </enable>
      </config>
      </device>
  </devices>
</config-template>
templates/simple-service-template.xml (END)
```

NSO/NCS is also accessible via NETCONF or RESTCONF APIs via Python PyNSO library. Actual southbound communication protocol, i.e., NETCONF or REST, or XML depends on the device itself.

Python Code

```
1  from pprint import pprint
2
3  from pynso.client import NSOClient
4  from pynso.datastores import DatastoreType
5
6  client = NSOClient('<ip-address>', 'admin', 'admin')
7  pprint(client.info()['version'])
8  pprint(client.get_datastore(DatastoreType.RUNNING))
```

Once you install NSO, you can access it via web as well as SSH.

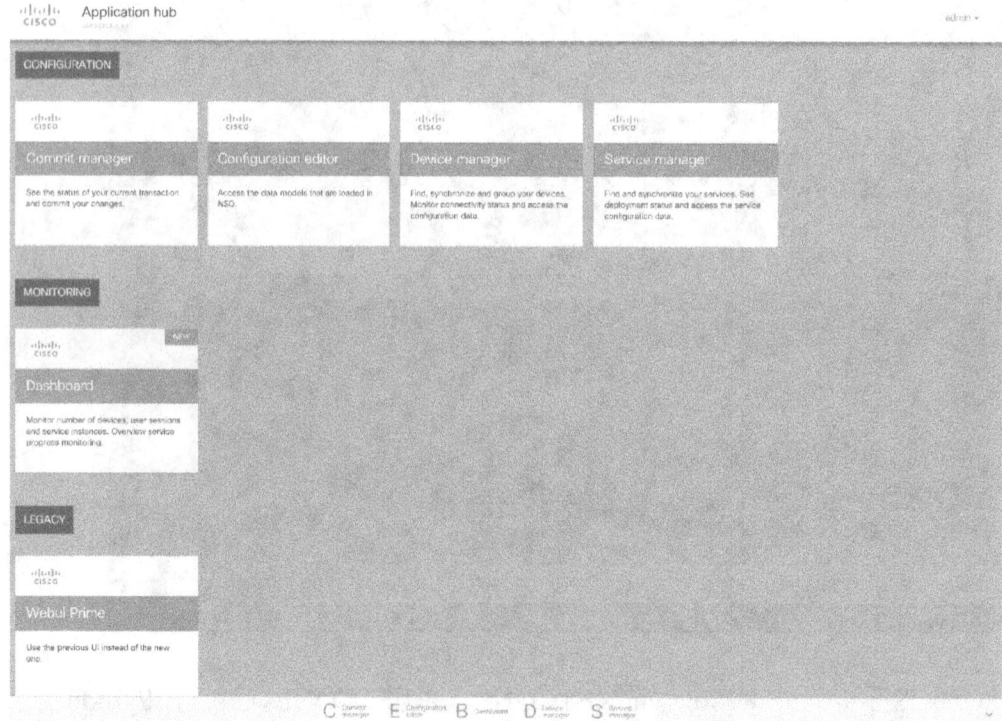

Alternatively, you can also use REST API via Postman or Python to configure or monitor your devices. In the example below, we will use Postman to create an L3 VPN named "ford".

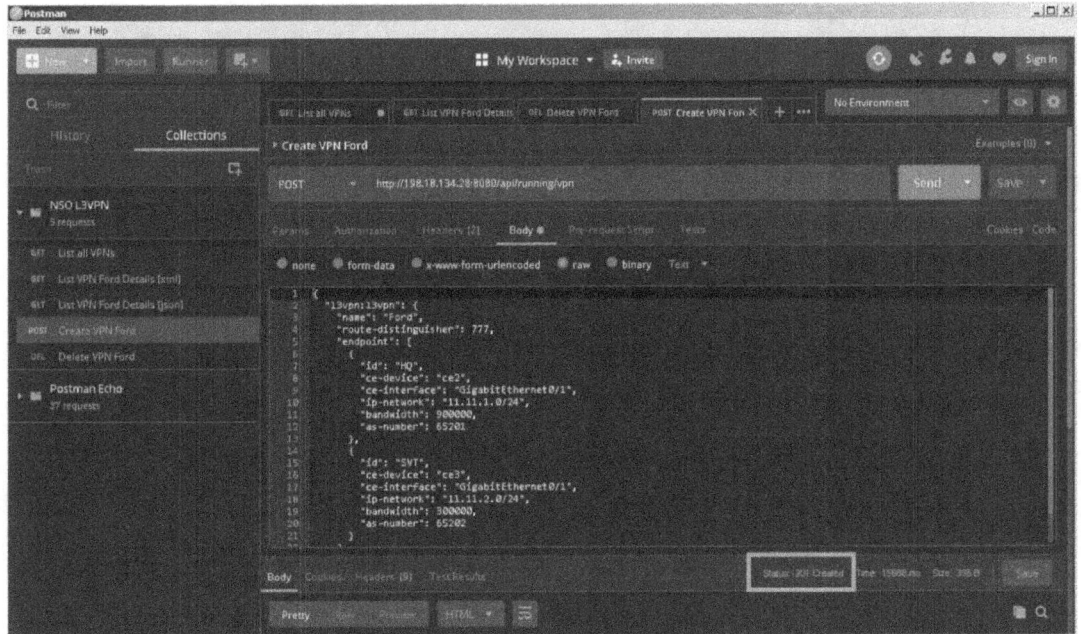

In the example below, Postman is showing two L3 VPNs, named ford and volvo, when queried for the list.

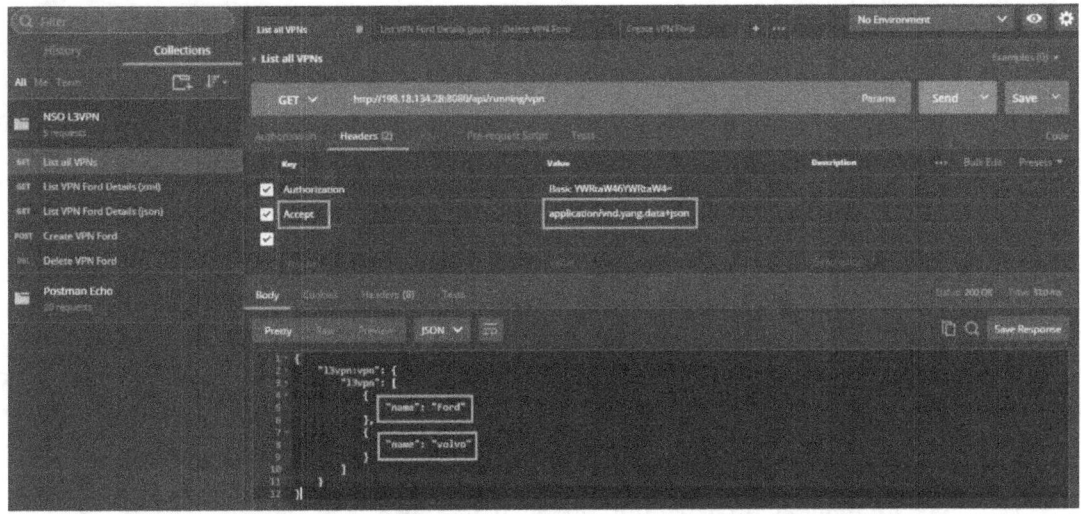

In summary, you can use either of the following options to configure or monitor your networking devices via NSO.

- NSO GUI
- NSO CLI
- NSO REST APIs

Describe the capabilities of Cisco compute management platforms and APIs (UCS Manager, UCS Director, and Intersight)

The Cisco Unified Computing System (UCS) was introduced in 2009 to improve flexibility and manageability of rack and blade servers. Here are a few reasons from historical point of view.

- Optimize compute, storage and network configurations
- Improve efficiency of virtualization, cloud computing, PaaS and other frameworks that abstract compute, storage and network resources
- Enable end-users to provision arbitrary configurations of virtualized infrastructure that can be mapped to underlying physical infrastructure capabilities
- Apply "Infrastructure as Code" disciplines to physical infrastructure

UCS Manager

Cisco UCS Manager or UCSM is an all-in-one platform for managing all UCS components. It can be used to access, configure, administer and monitor the networking, compute and storage resources inside the UCS chassis and all chassis when connected to a fabric interconnect. UCSM runs within the fabric interconnect.

Cisco UCSM can manage up to 160 physical servers whereas UCS Central (UCSC) can manage up to 10,000 physical servers.

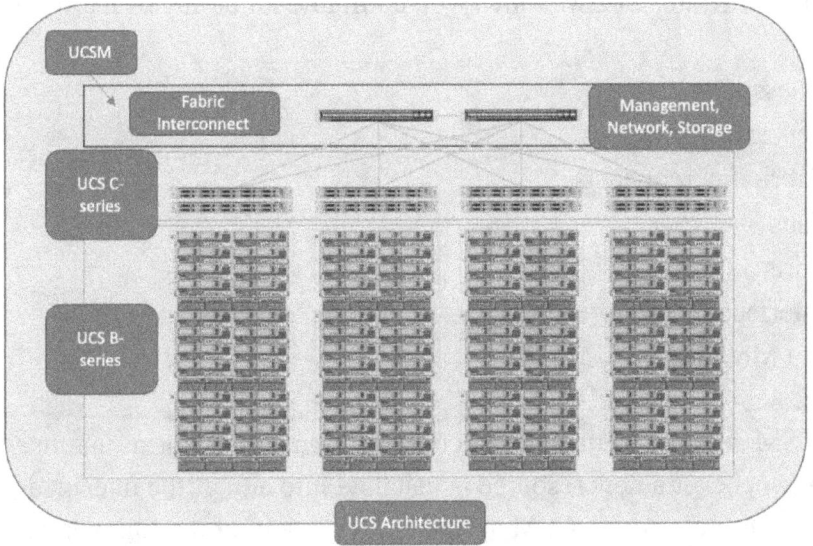

A UCS domain can consists of up to 2 UCS Fabric Interconnects and a minimum of one Cisco chassis with one blade or rack-mounted server. A single UCSM can control a mix of up to 40 chassis with a mix of blade and rack-mounted servers. You can also manage single UCS server using the Cisco Integrated Management Controller (CIMC).

As indicated in the UCS architecture, UCSM runs on the primary Fabric Interconnect (FI) and is assigned a virtual IP which allows failover to the secondary FI should there be a failure.

The UCSM, UCS Central, and CIMC all use the same unified API. There are five different ways you can interface with UCSM. Cisco UCSM mediates all communication within the system and no direct user access to the UCS components is required.

- UCSM GUI
- UCSM CLI
- XML API
- KVM
- IPMI

In terms of hardware, UCSM allows you configure all or any of the following.

- Chassis
- Servers
- Fabric Interconnects
- Fans
- Ports
- Interface Cards
- I/O Modules

Cisco UCSM is aware of the current configuration and performs automated discovery whenever a new resource is installed into any of the managed UCS servers. You can also use UCSM to manage all or any of the following resources in a UCS domain.

- Servers
- WWN addresses
- MAC addresses
- UUIDs
- Bandwidth

Likewise, it allows you to manage server pools, service profiles, monitor faults, configure network ports, create VLANs, create VSANs and fibre channel adapter profiles among other things. However, it is worth noting that UCSM cannot perform cross-system management i.e., any device that's outside the UCS domain. In terms of software stack, you obviously cannot use UCSM to manage OS or perform any kind of application provisioning or management.

Cisco UCSM uses a concept of service profiles to assign identity to a server when a service profile is associated with the server. Service profile is a container that includes all server configuration even including the burned-in characteristics such as BIOS or MAC addresses, WWN, etc. You can define hundreds of service profiles if you want however only one can be associated to a server at a time. As soon as a service profile is applied, the new server assumes all of the characteristics as defined in the service profile.

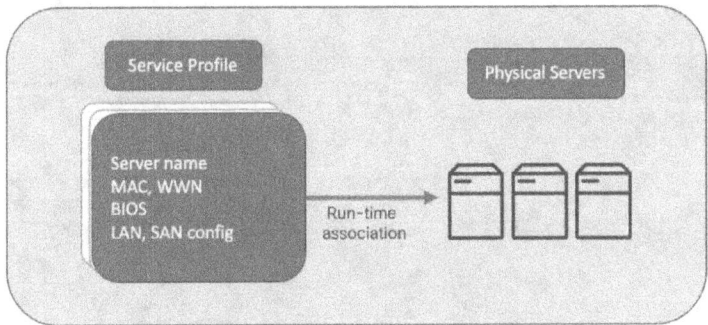

A UCS domain is scoped by the following parameters.

- Up to two fabric interconnects
- Minimum of one chassis with one blade or rack-mounted server
- Up to a maximum of 20 UCS-5100 blade servers or up to 160 servers (subject to change by Cisco)

Cisco UCS Manager GUI

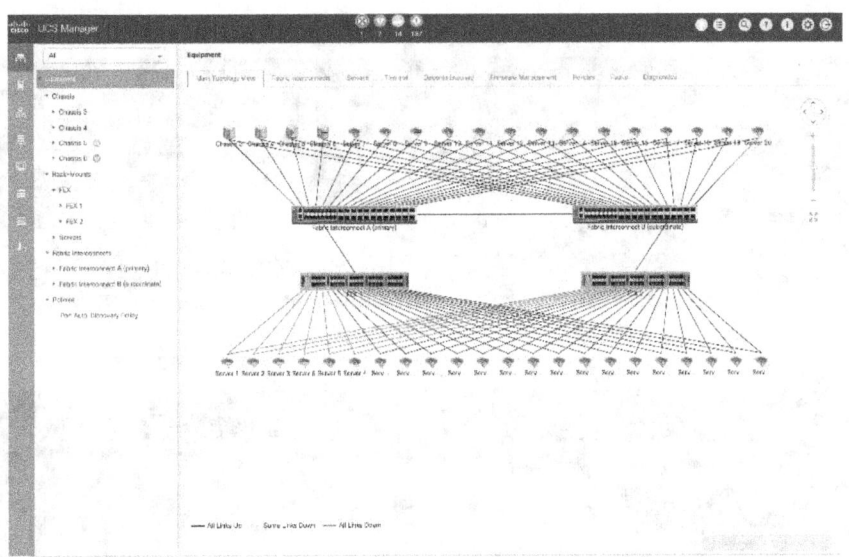

Cisco UCS Central GUI

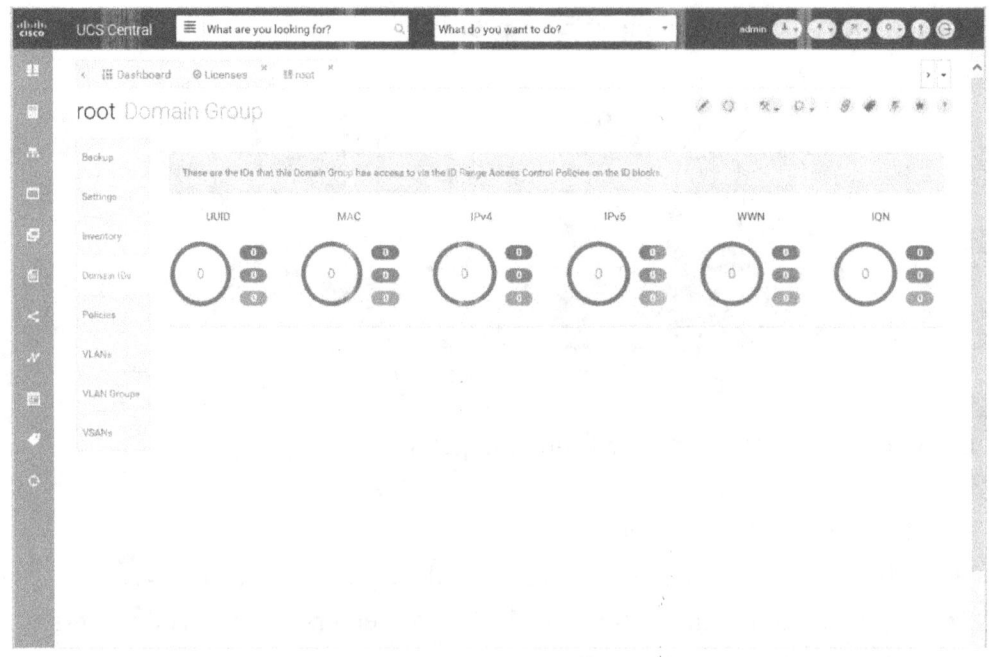

UCSM, UCS Central and IMC also come with several PowerTool variants for those who prefer PowerShell CLIs over GUI or API access.

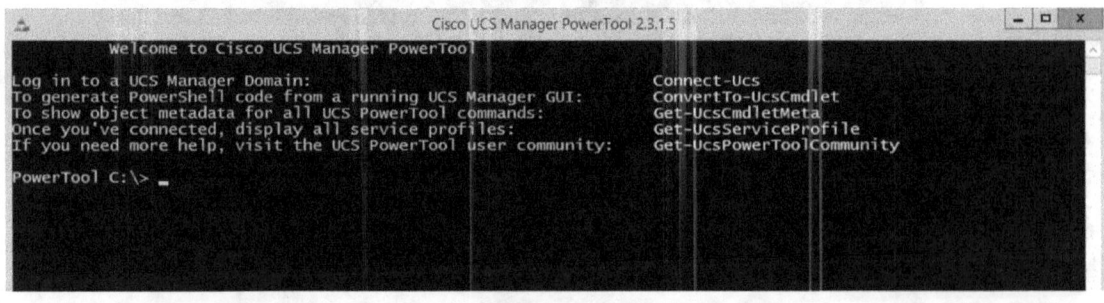

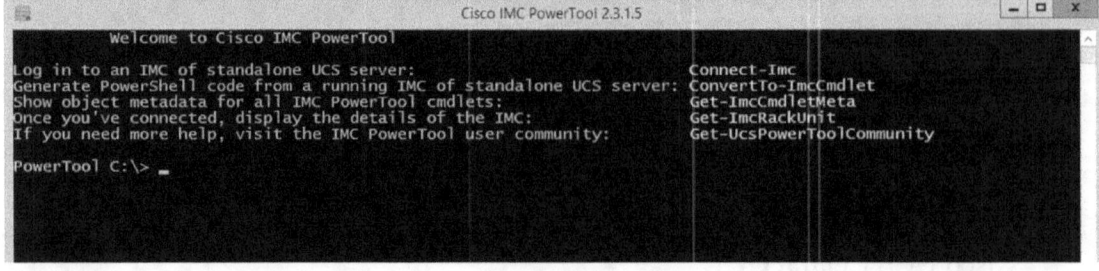

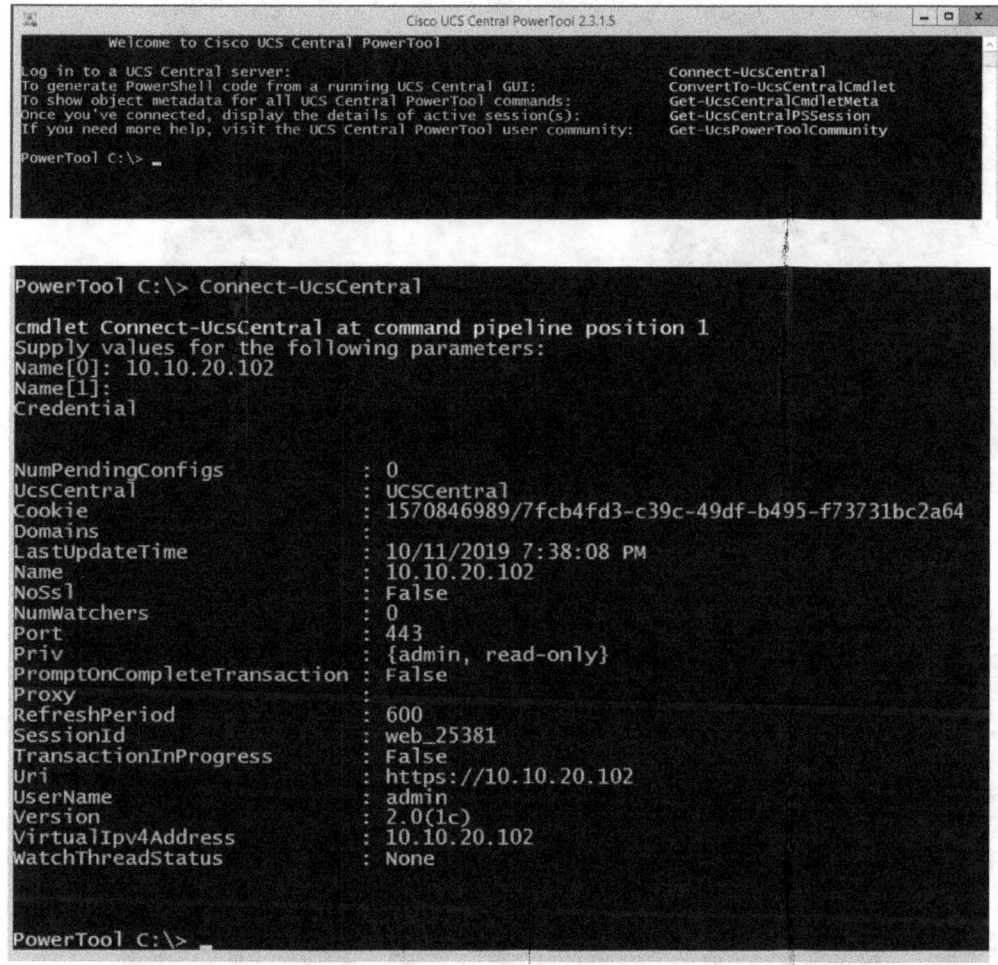

In order to log into any of the PowerTools, e.g., UCSM, you need to provide the UCSM IP address and credentials as shown below.

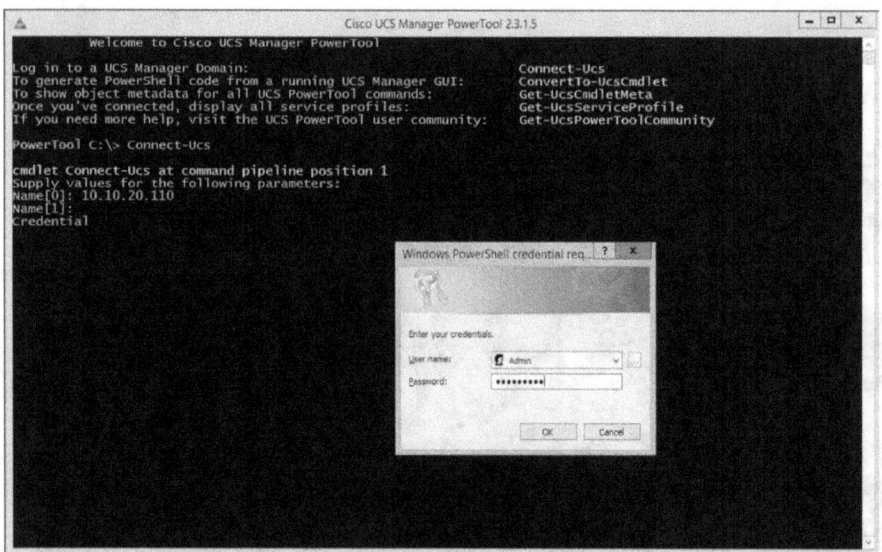

Once your credentials are accepted, you will see a response like below.

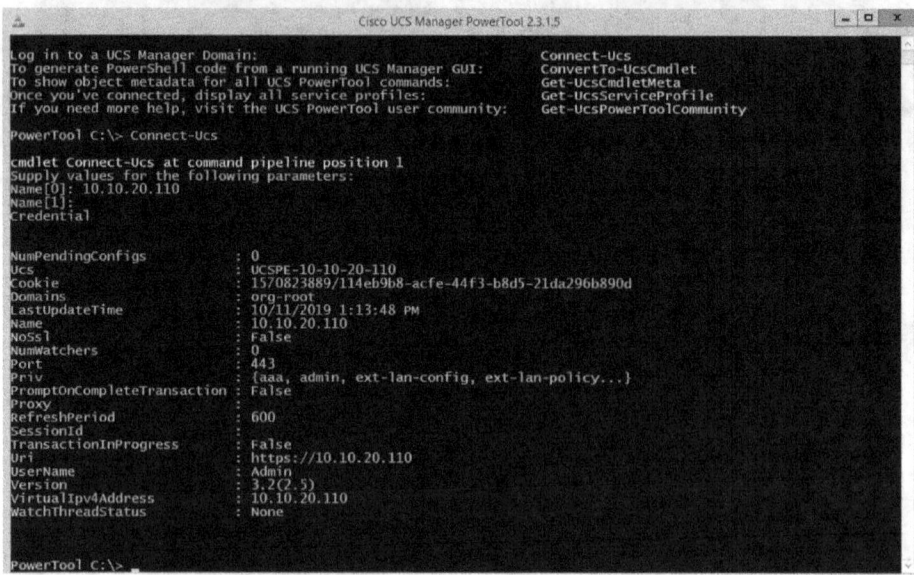

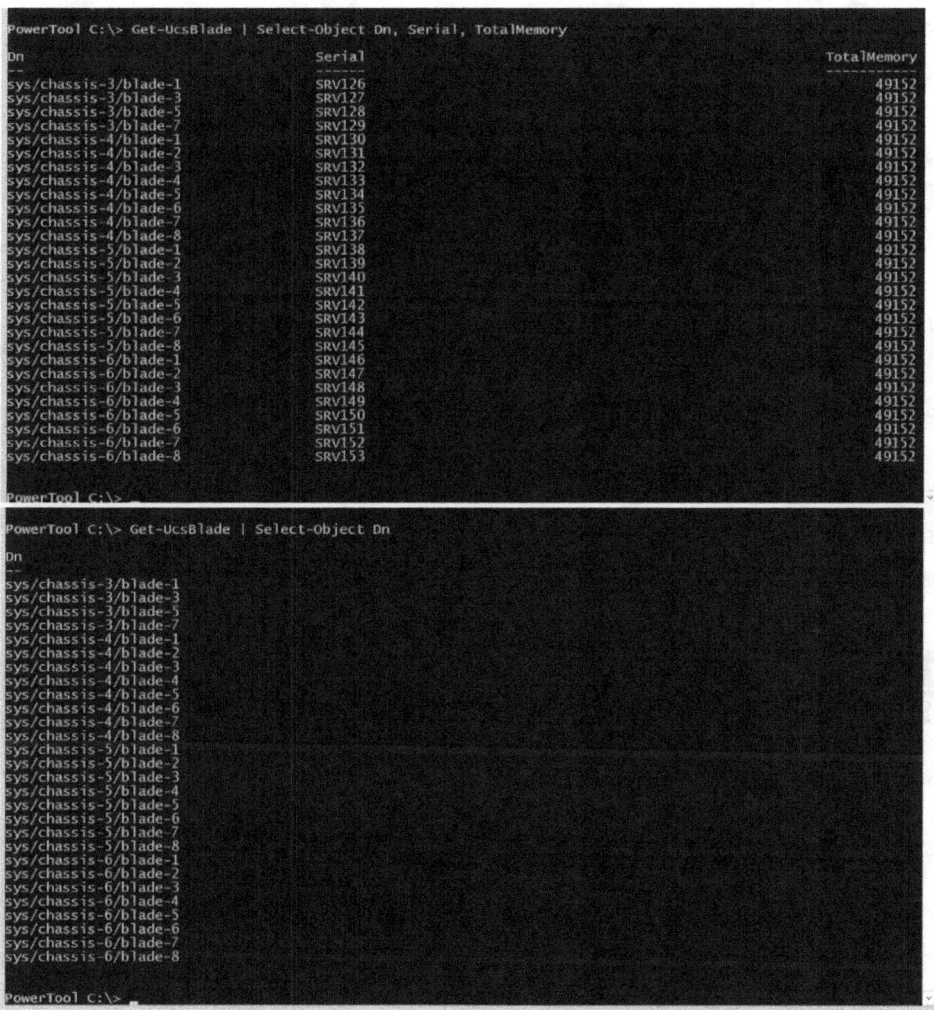

Now, let's try to retrieve some UCSM information using Python.

XML APIs are natively available from the UCSM API server, whereas RESTful APIs are available via UCS Integrated Management Controller (or IMC) Redfish. You'd use IMC when you are not using a fabric interconnect or what's known as running UCS unmanaged.

While you can use JSON to encode your HTTP requests with UCS IMC, it doesn't change the fact that behind-the-scenes UCS organizes all of the managed objects in an MIT, where each node in the tree represents an MO or group of objects that contains its administrative and operational states. The hierarchy starts at the top with "sys" and then contains parent and child nodes. Object naming with UCSM is similar to what we have seen with Cisco ACI, i.e., relative (RN) and distinguished names (DN). Last but not least, it is important to note that API access via IMC doesn't contain access to all MOs as opposed to XML APIs.

dn = {rn}/{rn}/{rn}/…

You can send in those API requests, XML or REST, via Python SDK or Postman. Again, much like ACI, you will need to login first via aaaLogin method, get your session cookie and then send in subsequent API requests. You can refresh your session cookie by using the aaaRefresh method and logout using aaaLogout.

UCSM Python API Example

Query for Blades and display the Dn, Serial, and TotalMemory Attributes using UCS Python SDK.

```
Windows PowerShell                                    _  □  x

PS C:\Users\developer> python
Python 2.7.14 (v2.7.14:84471935ed, Sep 16 2017, 20:19:30) [MSC v.1500 32 bit (Intel)] on win32
Type "help", "copyright", "credits" or "license" for more information.
>>>
>>>
>>> from ucsmsdk.ucshandle import UcsHandle
>>> handle = UcsHandle("10.10.20.110","admin","ciscopsdt")
>>> handle.login()
True
>>> blades = handle.query_classid("ComputeBlade")
>>> for blade in blades:
... print (blade.dn,blade.serial,blade.total_memory)
  File "<stdin>", line 2
    print (blade.dn,blade.serial,blade.total_memory)
        ^
IndentationError: expected an indented block
>>> for blade in blades:
...        print(blade.dn,blade.serial,blade.total_memory)
...
('sys/chassis-3/blade-1', 'SRV126', '49152')
('sys/chassis-3/blade-3', 'SRV127', '49152')
('sys/chassis-3/blade-5', 'SRV128', '49152')
('sys/chassis-3/blade-7', 'SRV129', '49152')
('sys/chassis-4/blade-1', 'SRV130', '49152')
('sys/chassis-4/blade-2', 'SRV131', '49152')
('sys/chassis-4/blade-3', 'SRV132', '49152')
('sys/chassis-4/blade-4', 'SRV133', '49152')
('sys/chassis-4/blade-5', 'SRV134', '49152')
('sys/chassis-4/blade-6', 'SRV135', '49152')
('sys/chassis-4/blade-7', 'SRV136', '49152')
('sys/chassis-4/blade-8', 'SRV137', '49152')
('sys/chassis-5/blade-1', 'SRV138', '49152')
('sys/chassis-5/blade-2', 'SRV139', '49152')
('sys/chassis-5/blade-3', 'SRV140', '49152')
('sys/chassis-5/blade-4', 'SRV141', '49152')
('sys/chassis-5/blade-5', 'SRV142', '49152')
('sys/chassis-5/blade-6', 'SRV143', '49152')
('sys/chassis-5/blade-7', 'SRV144', '49152')
('sys/chassis-5/blade-8', 'SRV145', '49152')
('sys/chassis-6/blade-1', 'SRV146', '49152')
('sys/chassis-6/blade-2', 'SRV147', '49152')
('sys/chassis-6/blade-3', 'SRV148', '49152')
('sys/chassis-6/blade-4', 'SRV149', '49152')
('sys/chassis-6/blade-5', 'SRV150', '49152')
('sys/chassis-6/blade-6', 'SRV151', '49152')
('sys/chassis-6/blade-7', 'SRV152', '49152')
('sys/chassis-6/blade-8', 'SRV153', '49152')
>>>
```

UCS Ansible

Cisco UCS Ansible is available for UCSM as well as for CIMC. Much like
Python SDK, UCS Ansible combines the UCSM authentication with the object
query. UCS Ansible modules are known as tasks in an Ansible playbook.

Below is an example Ansible playbook that configures a new VLAN (#2) on a
Cisco UCSM.

```
1 ▾ -
2        name: 'Configure a VLAN'
3 ▾     ucs_vlans:
4            hostname: 10.10.10.1
5            username: admin
6            password: password
7            name: vlan200
8            id: '200'
9            native: yes
10
```

Cisco UCS Director

UCS Director (or UCSD) is a powerful model-based and multi-vendor data center management platform that can help you run your local data center including UCS much like a private IaaS cloud. Cisco UCSD is a 64-bit appliance that uses the following templates.

- OVF for VMware vSphere
- VHD for Microsoft Hyper-V

UCS Director includes the following salient features.

- Orchestration engine: It allows you to deploy infra components such as bare-metal servers, virtualized resources etc.
- Intersight led CI/CD for UCSD: It helps you to manage on-premise UCSD install much like a SaaS software which includes automated software updates that include bug fixes, enhancements, etc. (much like cloud based Intersight)
- Self-service portal: It allows end-users to deploy new infra with approval workflows and lifecycle management
- ACI support: It integrates with Cisco ACI so UCSD workflows can include APIC configuration and management tasks

- Programmatic access: It allows automation via Java libraries, PowerShell, and SDK

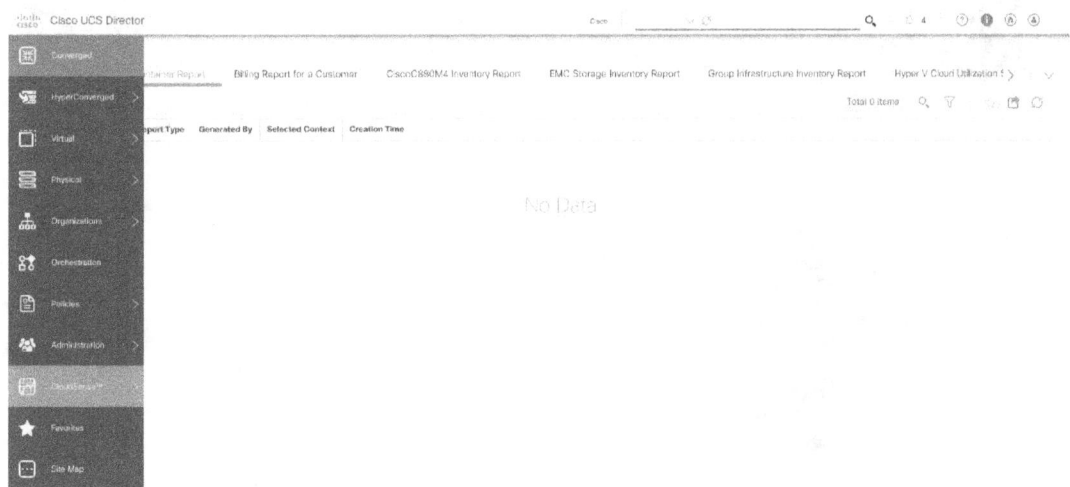

Cisco UCSD provides the following programmability and automation options.

- REST API (The API and the API browser)
- Tasks (atomic or monolithic tasks that are written in CloupiaScript[19])
- Script Libraries (CloupiaScript methods, Java jar files, etc.)
- PowerShell Host (PowerShell Cmdlets via PowerShell Host)

Before you are able to make REST API calls, you need to retrieve your API key. You can get your key by going to UCSD GUI and Edit My Profile > Show Advanced Settings > REST API Access Key. You can, optionally, also "Enable Developer Menu" to see REST API Browser.

When making REST API requests, regardless of the method, you must pass the REST API key within the HTTP header.

```
X-Cloupia-Request-Key: <key value>
```

---

[19] Cloupia was acquired by Cisco in 2012 and the product was eventually branded into the Cisco UCS Director.

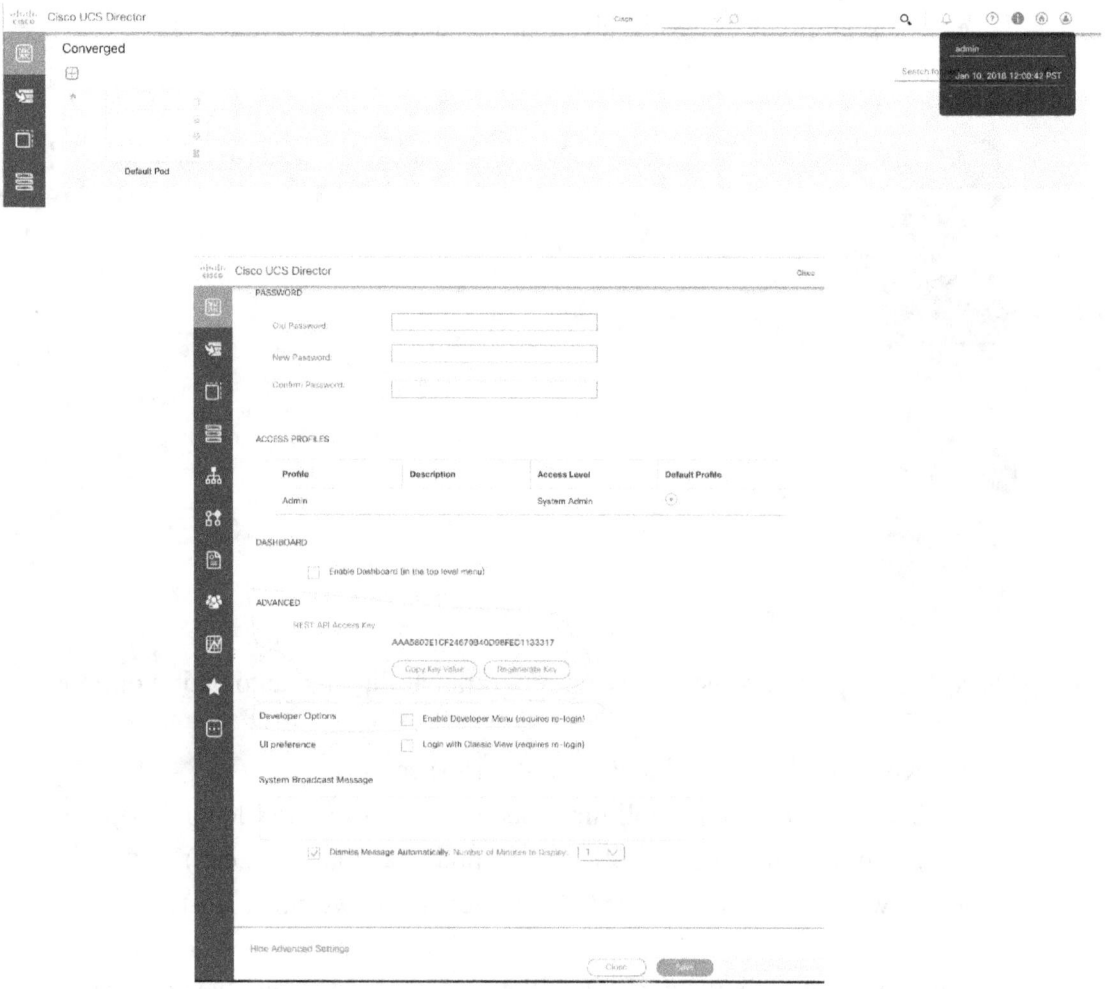

You can also use Postman to retrieve it as shown below.

Now, let's retrieve logged-in user information in JSON.

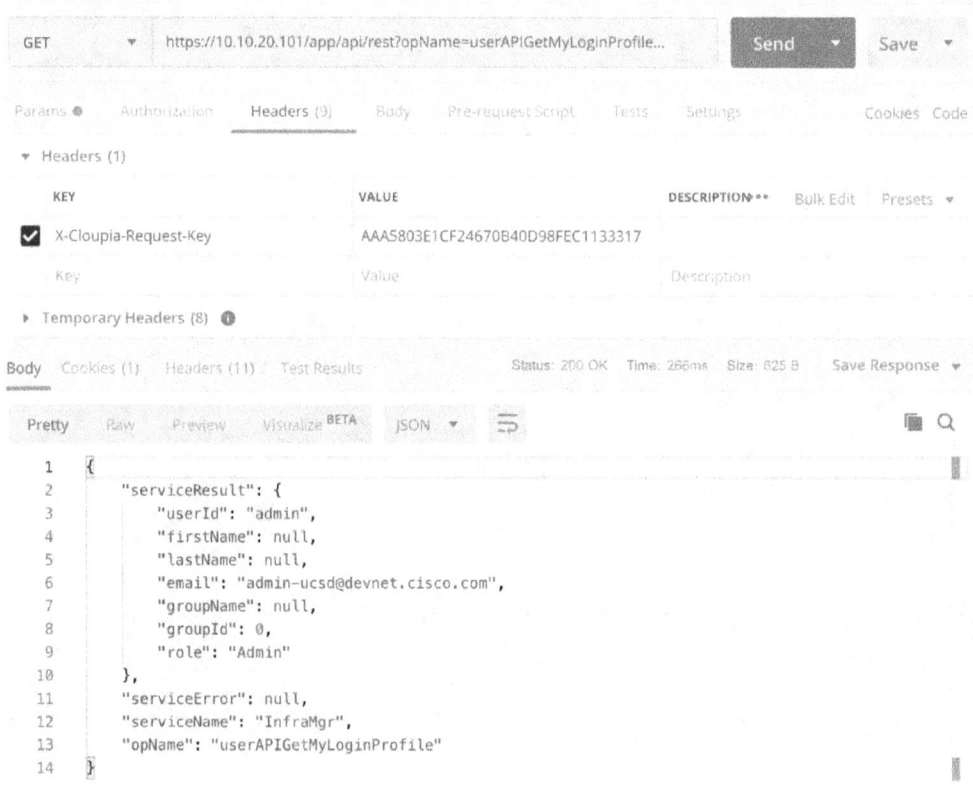

Now, let's retrieve logged-in user information in XML.

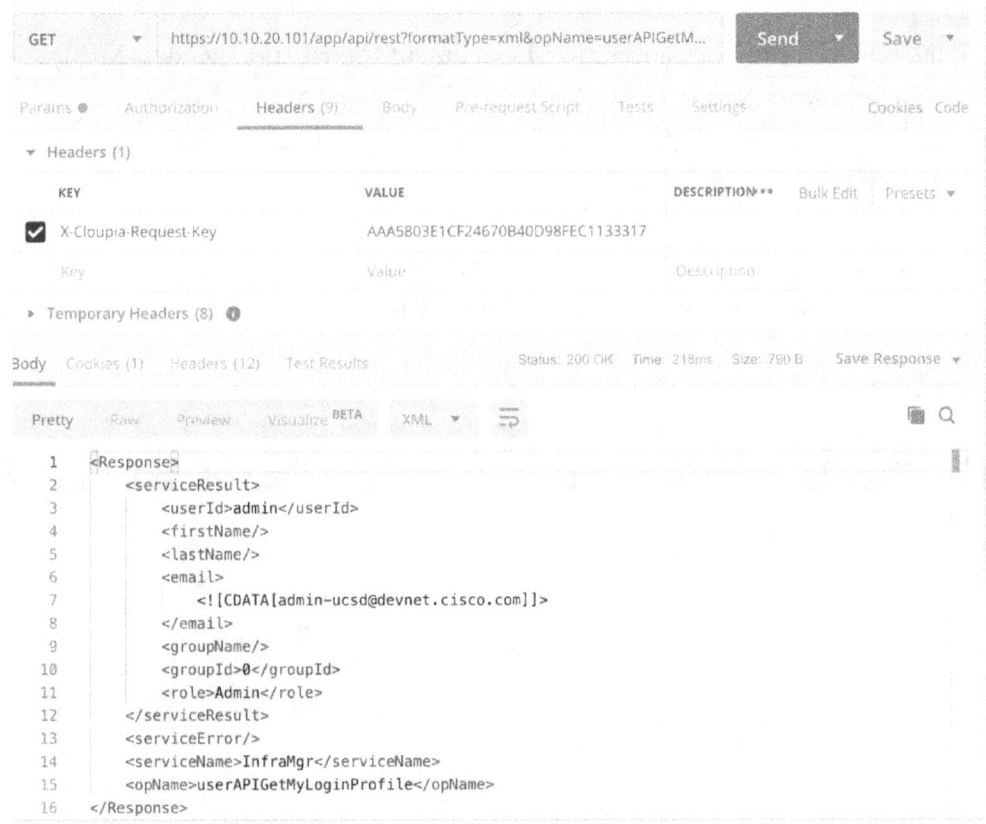

You can also go to Users and Groups and see those Postman requests coming in.

Cisco Intersight

Intersight is a cloud-based solution for Cisco UCS management which also includes HyperFlex. You can think of Intersight as a UCS Director as-a-service and some more. You can access Intersight using the web, PowerShell (via PowerTool) or the Python SDK.

The Intersight API provides access to Management Information Model (MIM) and exchanges messages using JSON over HTTPS transport. Intersight also supports Ansible for the purposes of device inventory collection and configuration management of resources.

To integrate your UCSM instances into Intersight, first, you need to log in to each instance by navigating to Admin > Device Connector.

UCSM-1

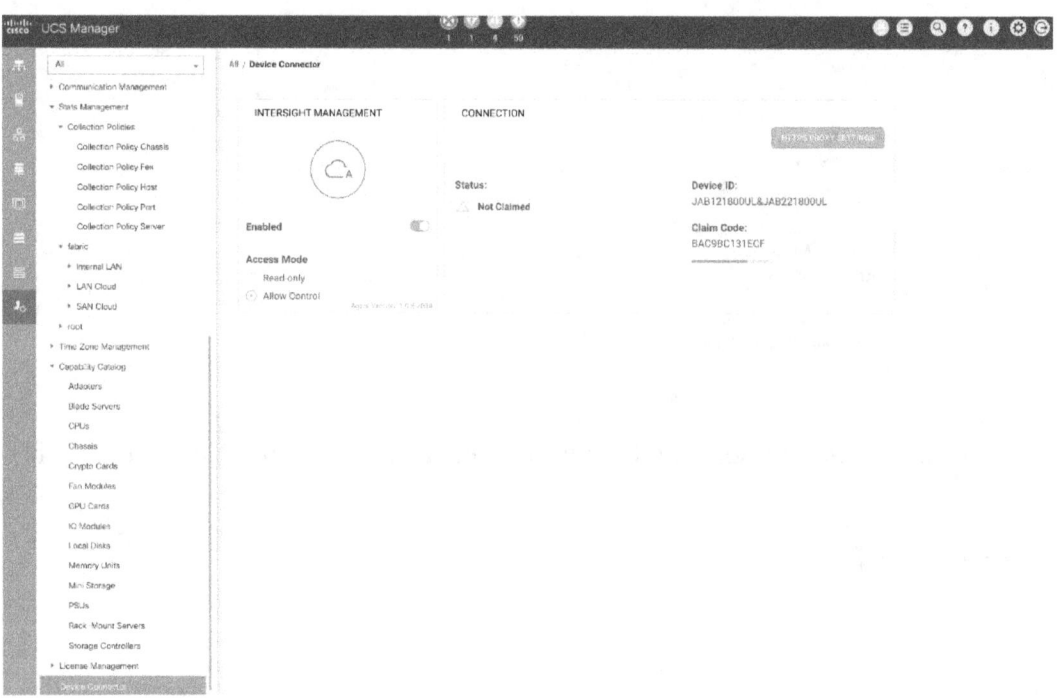

UCSM-2

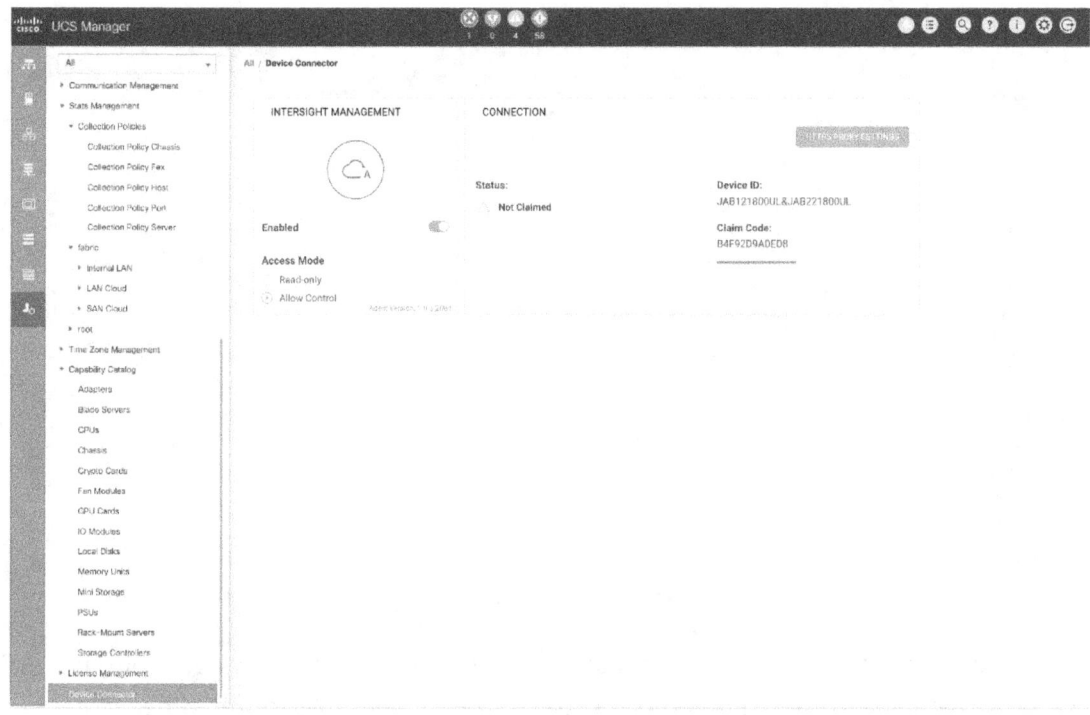

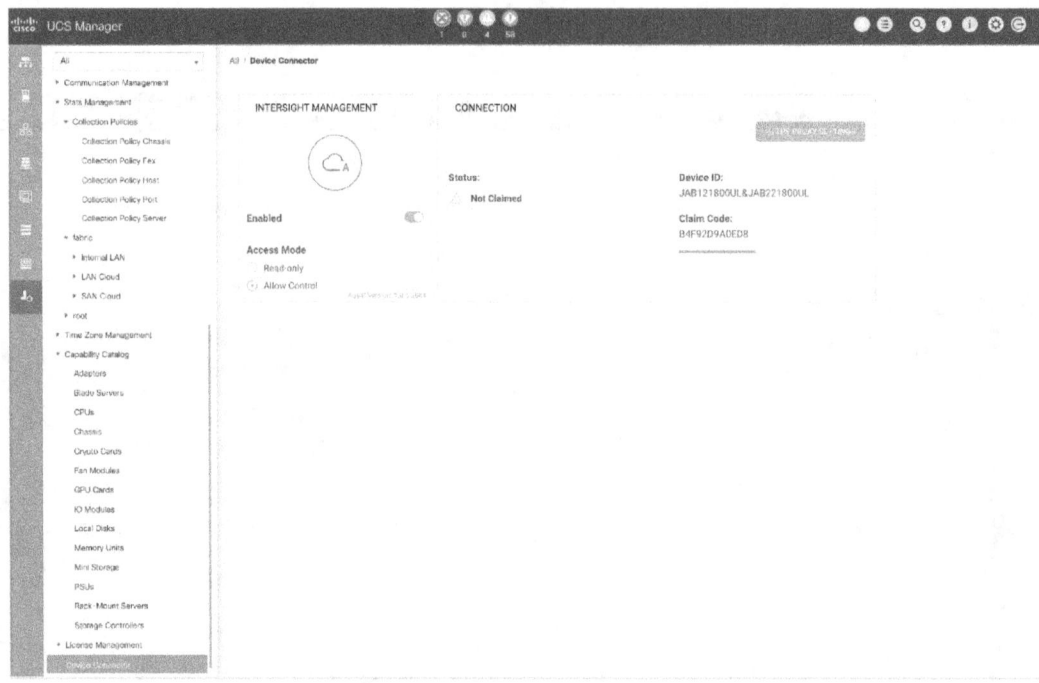

Once you have that information handy, you can go back to Intersight.com, log in and add those device IDs and claim codes one by one. Just for reference, the device ID is the serial number of the primary and subordinate fabric interconnects and claim codes are time-based tokens and they do expire after a short duration (in minutes). If you enter an expired claim code, you will see the following error message.

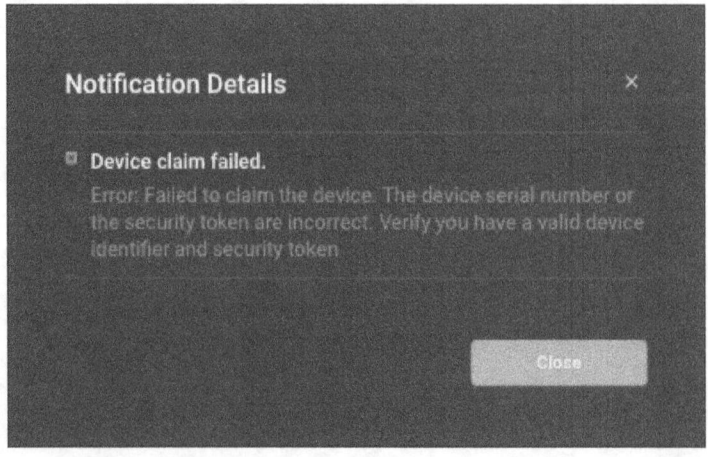

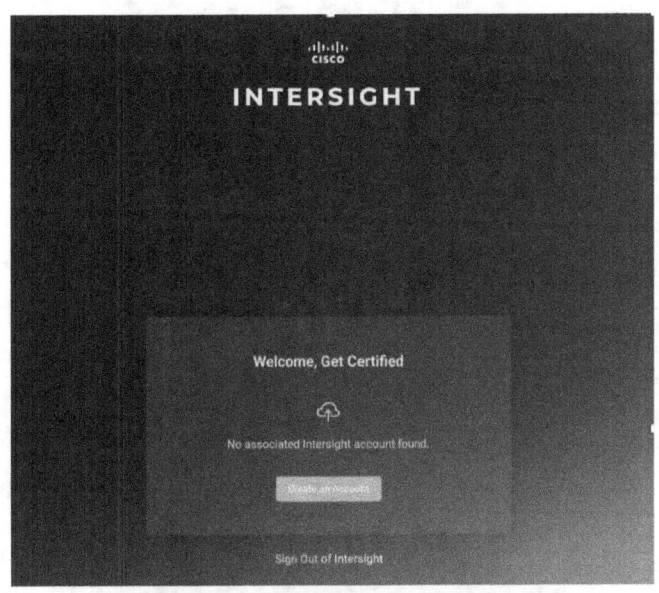

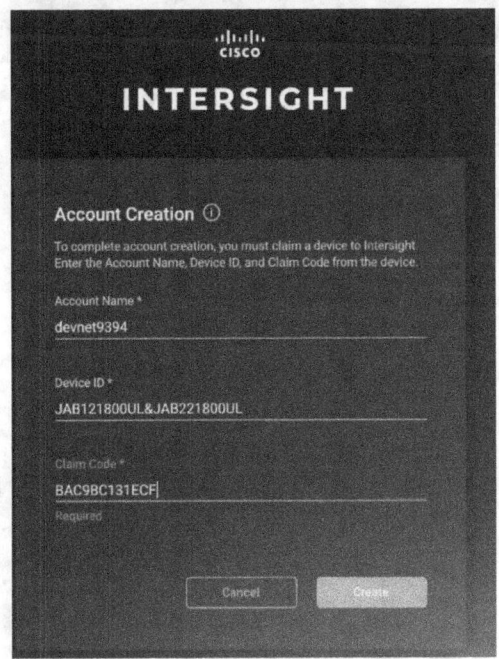

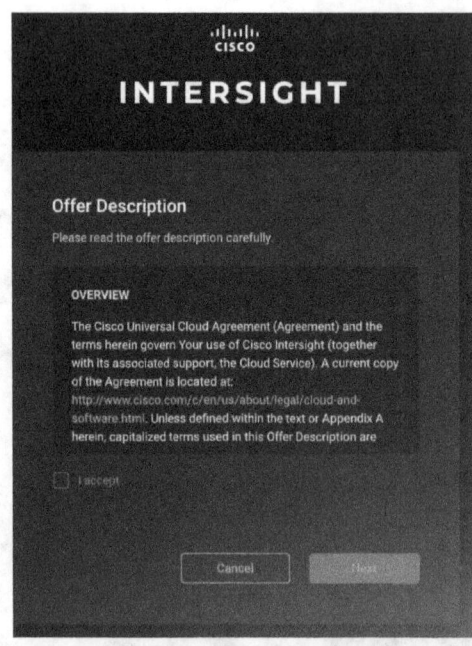

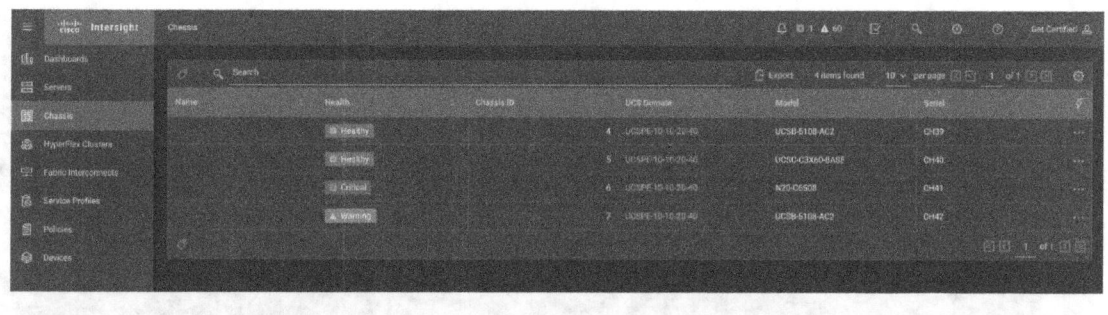

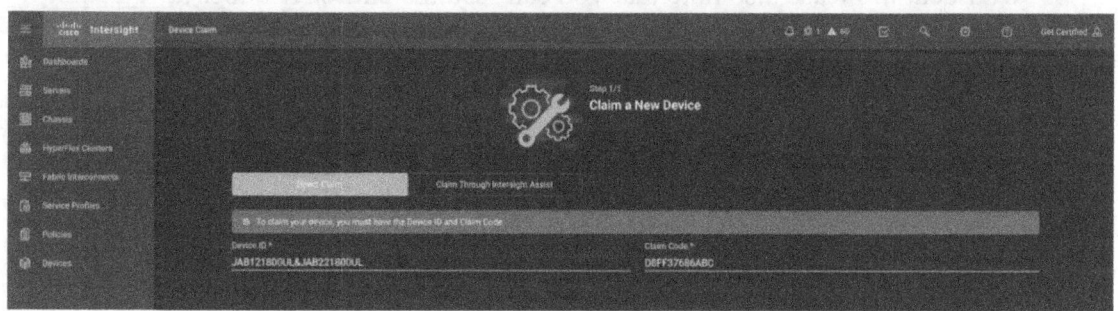

Let's now add UCSM-2 into Intersight to complete your integration.

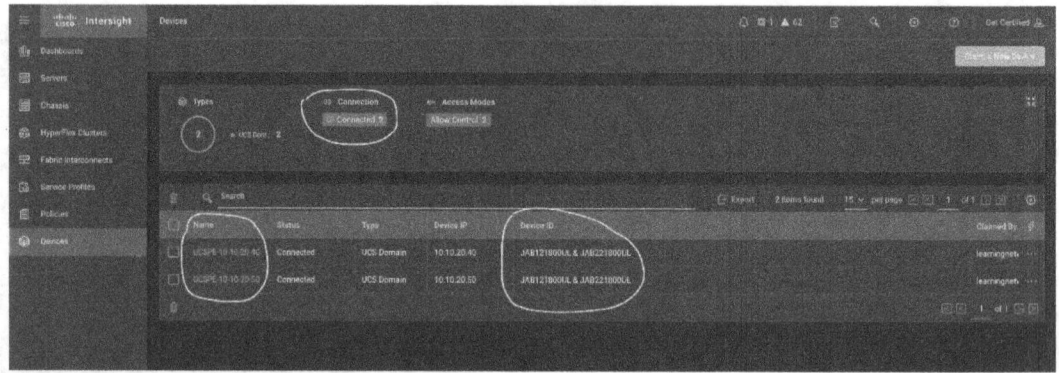

Now, that we're done with UCSM to Intersight integration, let's now review the information that Intersight can display through its various GUI options.

REST API access into Intersight

Any API access into Intersight requires Essentials license, i.e., Base license won't cut it. Please also note that you can read the entire API docs at Intersight Developer Center[20]. You can also download Python SDK, PowerShell SDK and ITSM plugin for ServiceNow using the Downloads tab.

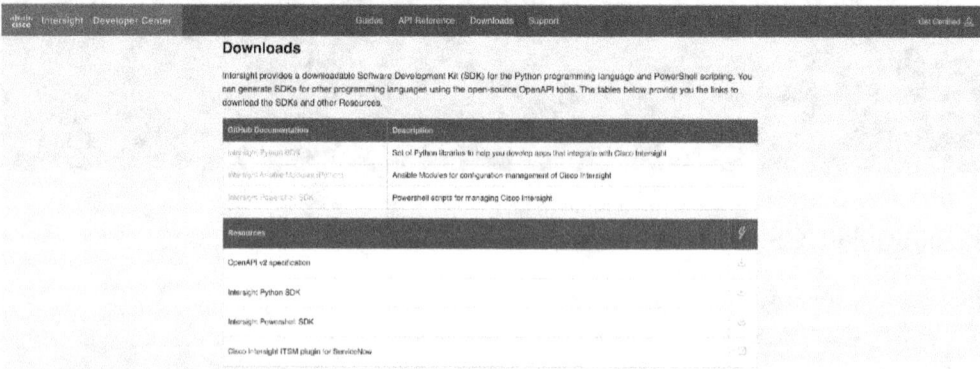

---

[20] https://bit.ly/2GOaoXw

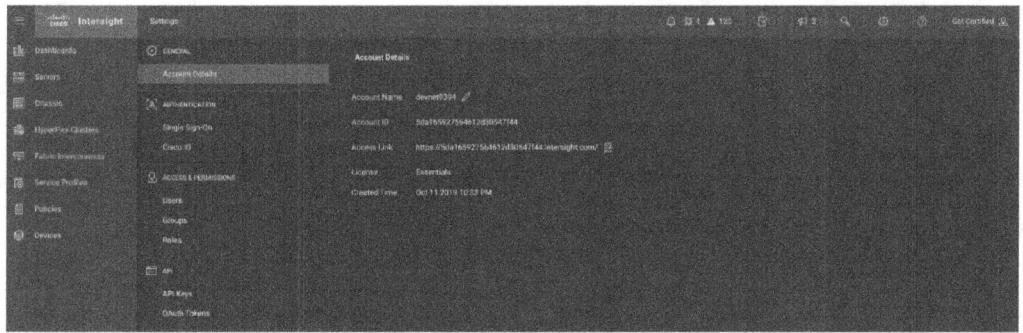

Click on the gear icon on the top-right, choose Settings > API Keys to get started. You can generate and copy/download your API key and private (secret key text) on this screen.

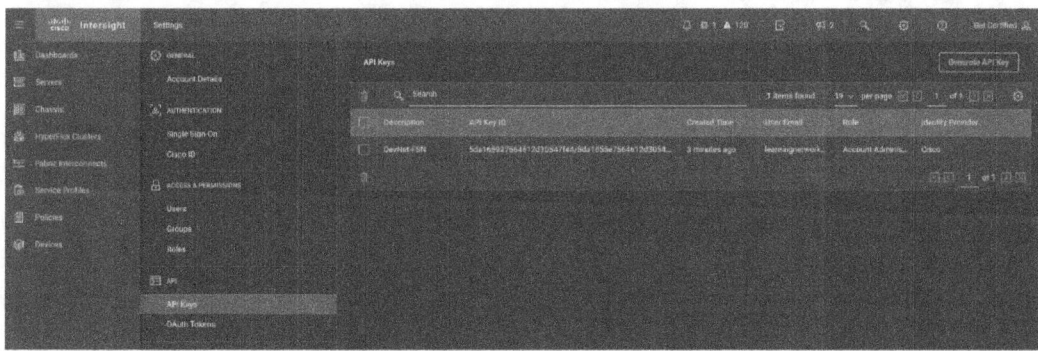

In order to send API requests, you need to configure Postman Collection or use Python SDK. In either case, you need to use both API keys and contents of the file with the RSA secret key.

Postman Collection > Pre-request Script

EDIT COLLECTION ✕

Name

InterSight

Description   Authorization   Pre-request Scripts ●   Tests   Variables

This script will execute before every request in this collection. Learn more about Postman's execution order.

```javascript
 1  function doHttpSig() {
 2
 3      var navigator = {}; //fake a navigator object for the lib
 4      var window = {}; //fake a window object for the lib
 5      eval(postman.getGlobalVariable("jsrsasign-js")); //import javascript jsrsasign
 6
 7
 8      function computeHttpSignature(config, headerHash) {
 9        var template = 'keyId="${keyId}",algorithm="${algorithm}",headers="${headers}",signature
              ="${signature}"',
10            sig = template;
11
12        // compute sig here
13        var signingBase = '';
14        config.headers.forEach(function(h){
15          if (signingBase !== '') { signingBase += '\n'; }
16          signingBase += h.toLowerCase() + ": " + headerHash[h];
17        });
18
19        var kjursig = new KJUR.crypto.Signature({"alg": "SHA256withRSA"});
20        kjursig.init(config.secretkey);
21        kjursig.updateString(signingBase);
22        var hash = kjursig.sign();
23
```

Cancel   Update

```
1 ▾ function doHttpSig() {
2
3     var navigator = {}; //fake a navigator object for the lib
4     var window = {}; //fake a window object for the lib
5     eval(postman.getGlobalVariable("jsrsasign-js")); //import
          javascript jsrsasign
6
7 ▾   function computeHttpSignature(config, headerHash) {
8       var template = 'keyId="${keyId}",algorithm="${algorithm}"
            ,headers="${headers}",signature="${signature}"',
9         sig = template;
10
11      // compute sig here
12      var signingBase = '';
13 ▾    config.headers.forEach(function (h) {
14 ▾      if (signingBase !== '') {
15          signingBase += '\n'
16          a;
17        }
18        signingBase += h.toLowerCase() + ": " + headerHash[h];
19      });
20
21 ▾    var kjursig = new KJUR.crypto.Signature({
22        "alg": "SHA256withRSA"
23      });
24      kjursig.init(config.secretkey);
25      kjursig.updateString(signingBase);
26      var hash = kjursig.sign();
27
28 ▾    var signatureOptions = {
29        keyId: config.keyId,
30        algorithm: config.algorithm,
31        headers: config.headers,
32        signature: hextob64(hash)
33      };
34
35      // build sig string here
36 ▾    Object.keys(signatureOptions).forEach(function (key) {
37        var pattern = "${" + key + "}",
38          value = (typeof signatureOptions[key] != 'string') ?
                signatureOptions[key].join(' ') : signatureOptions[key]
                ;
39        sig = sig.replace(pattern, value);
40      });
41
42      return sig;
43    }
44
45    var curDate = new Date().toGMTString();
46    var targetUrl = request.url.trim(); // there may be surrounding
         ws
47    targetUrl = targetUrl.replace(new RegExp('^https?://[^/]+/'), '/'
         ); // strip hostname
48    var host = request.url.trim();
```

```
49    host = host.replace(new RegExp('^https?://'), '');
50    host = host.replace(new RegExp('/.*$'), '');
51    var method = request.method.toLowerCase();
52    var body = request.data;
53 ▾  if (method == "get") {
54      body = "";
55    }
56    var sha256digest = CryptoJS.SHA256(body);
57    var base64sha256 = CryptoJS.enc.Base64.stringify(sha256digest);
58    var computedDigest = 'SHA-256=' + base64sha256;
59
60 ▾  var headerHash = {
61      date: curDate,
62      digest: computedDigest,
63      host: host,
64      '(request-target)': method + ' ' + targetUrl.toLowerCase()
65    };
66
67 ▾  var config = {
68      algorithm: 'rsa-sha256',
69      keyId: environment['key-id'],
70      secretkey: environment['shared-secret'],
71      headers: ['(request-target)', 'date', 'digest', 'host']
72    };
73    var sig = computeHttpSignature(config, headerHash);
74
75    postman.setEnvironmentVariable('httpsig', sig);
76    postman.setEnvironmentVariable('computed-digest', computedDigest
          );
77    postman.setEnvironmentVariable("current-date", curDate);
78    postman.setEnvironmentVariable("target-url", targetUrl);
79  }
80
81 ▾ if (globals['jsrsasign-js'] === undefined) {
82    console.log("jsrasign library not already downloaded. Downloading
          now. ")
```

Postman Environment

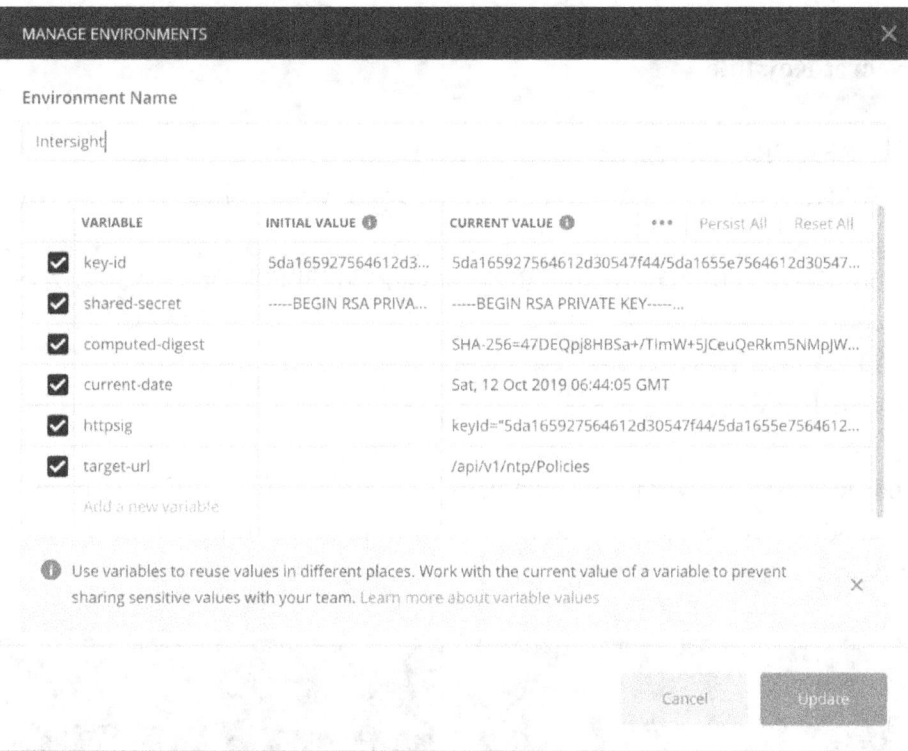

Postman Request (must be saved within the Collection)

Please note that the GET URL in the above screenshot can also be https://intersight.com/api/v1/asset/ManagedDevices.

Sample Secret Key File

-----BEGIN RSA PRIVATE KEY-----
NIIEowIBAAKCAQEAws4ufVP6i+pe8SkN3uDMBhwSzjPbTyRxotmDHeN/u BGPx+7z
T5FUAgq669HqoVbxJPQDBqK6thBBfxsgP+GJPj0d7PhP9hiBrU+xha0dZ2de4 BvH
--TRUNCATED FOR BREVITY--
-----END RSA PRIVATE KEY-----

Last but not least, if you ever need to unclaim or unattach your UCSM(s) from within Intersight, then all you need to do is to remove those from within Devices as shown below.

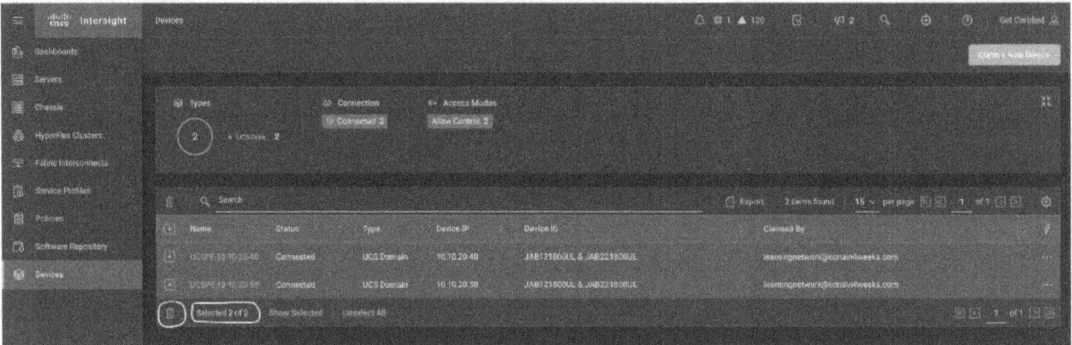

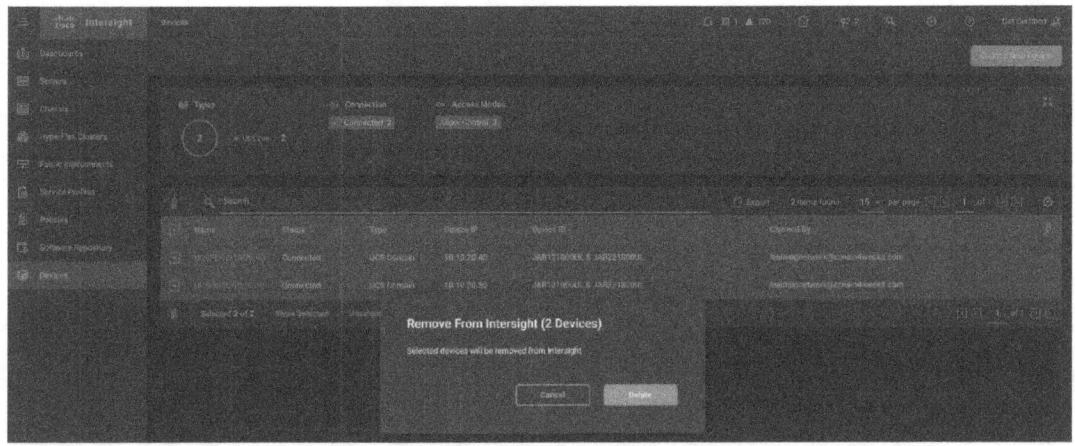

You can hit Delete to confirm and remove your UCSM(s).

Further Reading

Cisco Intersight API Reference[21]

Describe the capabilities of Cisco collaboration platforms and APIs (WebEx Teams, WebEx devices, Cisco Unified Communication Manager including AXL and UDS interfaces, and Finesse)

Cisco Unified Communications Manager (or CUCM) supports AXL and UDS APIs. These APIs allow developers and partners a simpler way to automate and manage UC devices, user profiles and calls.

WebEx Teams

Cisco WebEx teams is a collaboration solution that allows teams to connect and collaborate regardless of their location, device or even network transport. Users or teams can share messages and files, make voice calls and conduct video

---

[21] https://bit.ly/2W7LNWo

conferencing that includes support for whiteboarding. The target audience for WebEx teams comprises of enterprise functions such as sales, marketing, and finance.

With Teams, Cisco is now directly competing with Microsoft Teams and Slack. Cisco has a leg up when it comes to integration with on-premise UC resources when competing with Slack and even Microsoft however those remain formidable competitors.

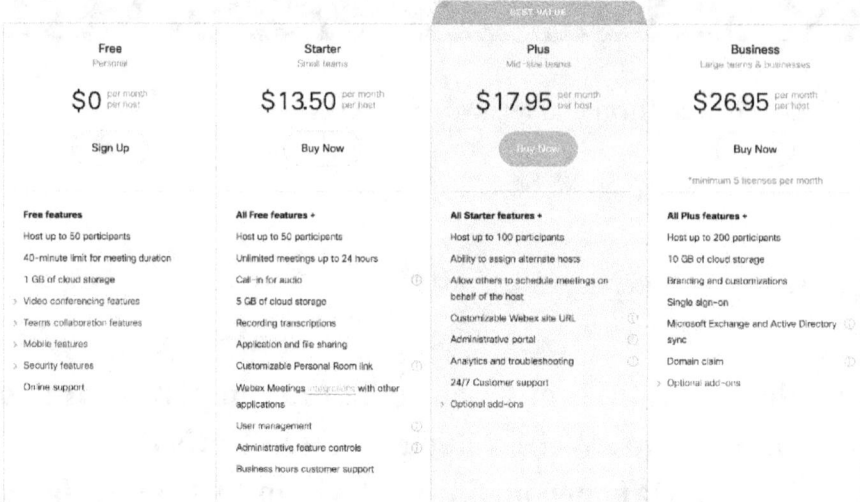

WebEx Teams API allows you to do any of the following.

- Create webhooks to enable fine-grained communication with applications and services in response to WebEx Teams events
- Create bots that emulate WebEx users and mediate with external applications
- Use WebEx embedding APIs for Java, node.JS, browsers, mobile OS platforms such as iOS and Android.

You can access and manipulate any of the following resources using the WebEx Teams REST APIs.
- Organizations

- Teams
- People
- Rooms (Spaces)
- Memberships (relationships to a room) / Team Memberships (relationships to a team)
- Messages

WebEx Devices

Cisco WebEx devices include WebEx board, WebEx Room and WebEx Desk devices.

Meet Webex Devices.

Get the most out of Cisco Webex Meetings and Cisco Webex Teams
with tools designed for better team collaboration.

Cisco Webex Board
All-in-one whiteboard, wireless presentation screen, and video conferencing system for smarter team collaboration.

Cisco Webex Room Devices
Intelligent video conferencing devices for meeting rooms of all sizes.

Cisco Webex Desk Devices
Simple-to-use and compact video conferencing devices designed for desktops.

WebEx Meetings REST API

It can be used to access the WebEx platform to build interactive bots, integration with other apps or even giving guests or outside users the right to reach out to users inside your organization. If you have a WebEx teams account, you are all set to use API access.

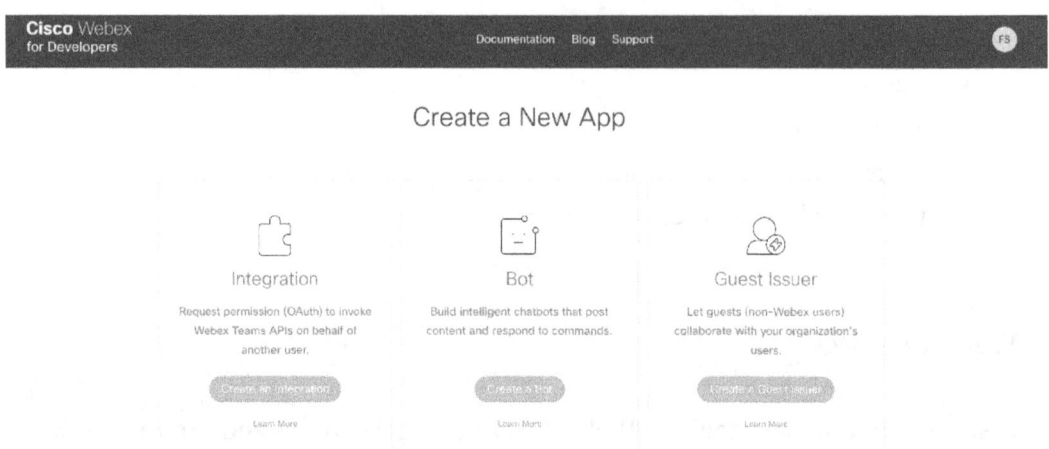

Once you select integration and fill up the app form, you will be shown the API credentials that you can use to make API calls.

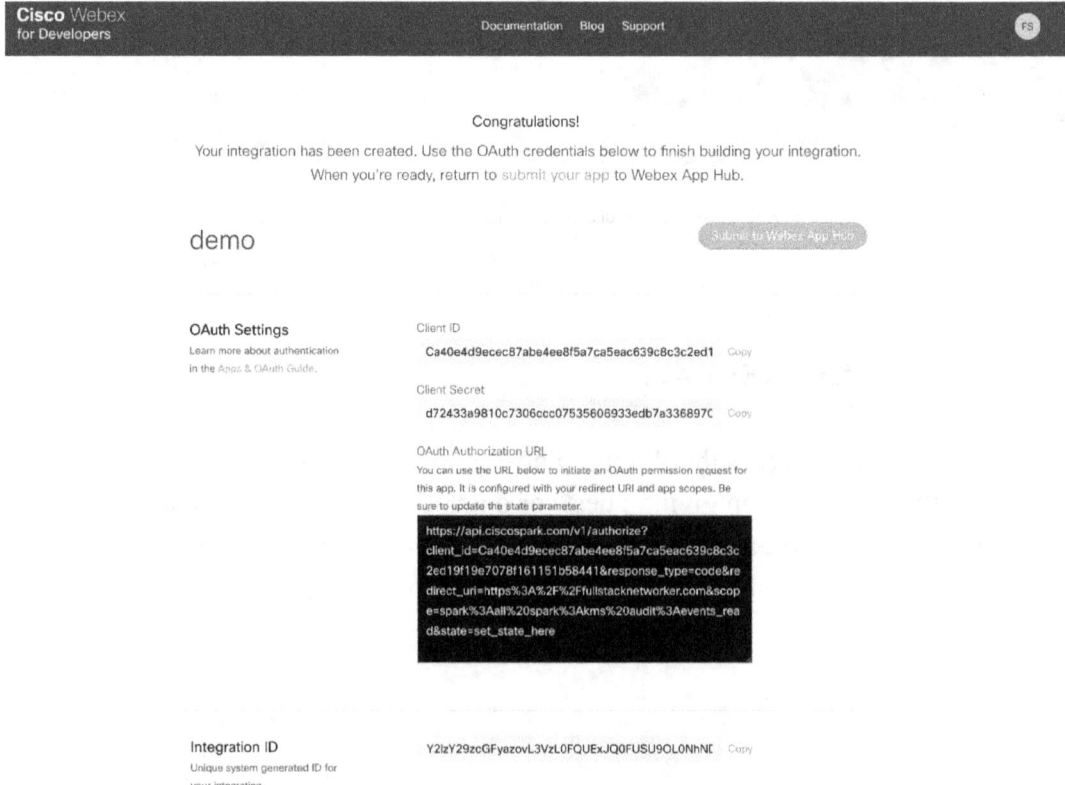

The most fun part about WebEx APIs is that you can simply follow the API docs and corresponding documentation. As long as you're signed in, you don't even need Postman or Curl, etc. to invoke the API commands.

Let's run through a few of them. Our account is FSN, and we have a team named FSN-SJC with a Space named "Space-1".

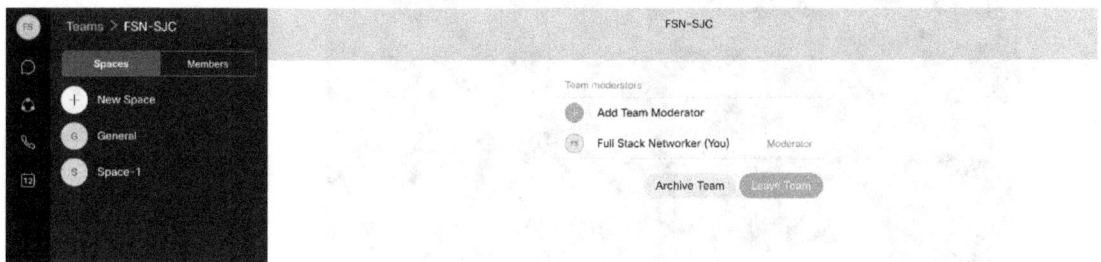

Now, let's look at the API request screen from within the API docs (note that we're signed into WebEx already).

https://api.ciscospark.com/v1/rooms?teamId=Y2lzY29zcGFyazovL3VzL1RFQU 0vMjQ3ZWMyYzAtZWQyOS0xMWU5LTlmOWYtYjMwODk1OTQzOWRk &max=1

```
{
  "items": [
    {
      "id": "Y2lzY29zcGFyazovL3VzL1JPT00vNzcsZGNkNzAtZWQyOS0xMWU5LWI4NmYtODE2MjlhNGRkYTRz",
      "title": "Space-1",
      "type": "group",
      "isLocked": false,
      "lastActivity": "2019-10-12T19:48:08.781Z",
      "teamId": "Y2lzY29zcGFyazovL3VzL1RFQU0vMjQ3ZWMyYzAtZWQyOS0xMWU5LTlmOWYtYjMwODk1OTQzOWRk",
      "creatorId": "Y2lzY29zcGFyazovL3VzL1BFT1BMRS9kNWY3OWV1OC0xZWVmLTQ0YTctODDYWES00Nj2hYTgxNDclYjg",
      "created": "2019-10-12T19:48:08.781Z",
      "ownerId": "0d609cde-0645-45B3-8fe9-b00c0b6f42f3"
    }
  ]
}
```

Let's now create a Space named "Unicorn" using the REST API call.

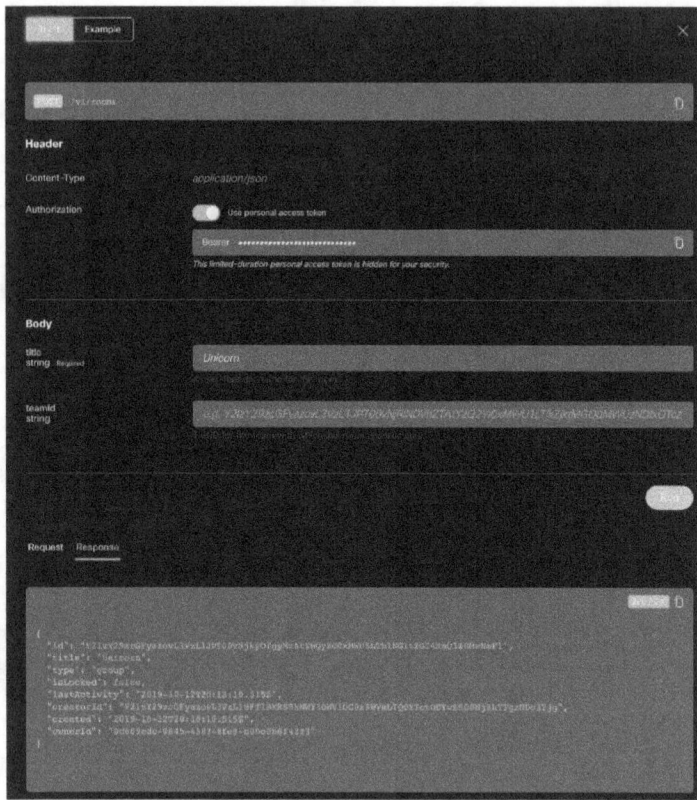

Now, let's verify via the WebEx Teams GUI that we indeed have the new "Unicorn" Space added.

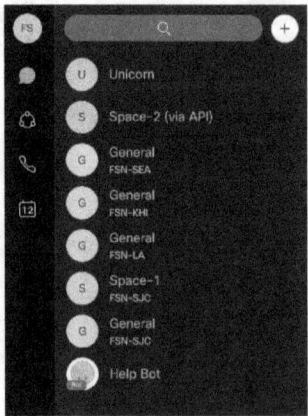

You can also execute API calls using the Cisco Spark Python APIs (formerly known as WebEx Team SDK).

CUCM (AXL, UDS Interfaces, and Finesse)

Cisco Unified Communication Manager (CallManager or CUCM) is an Enterprise unified communication and collaboration platform that allows for voice and video calling as well as messaging and mobility. The guts of CUCM include reliable, secure and scalable call control and session management features.

Today, you can deploy CUCM as part of all-in-one business solution (e.g., Business edition 6K or 7K series) or install it and run from Cisco UCS and Cisco HyperFlex infra in the form of pre-tested and validated designs, and you can also get it in the form of a service either from WebEx or through private or public cloud provider or Cisco partner.

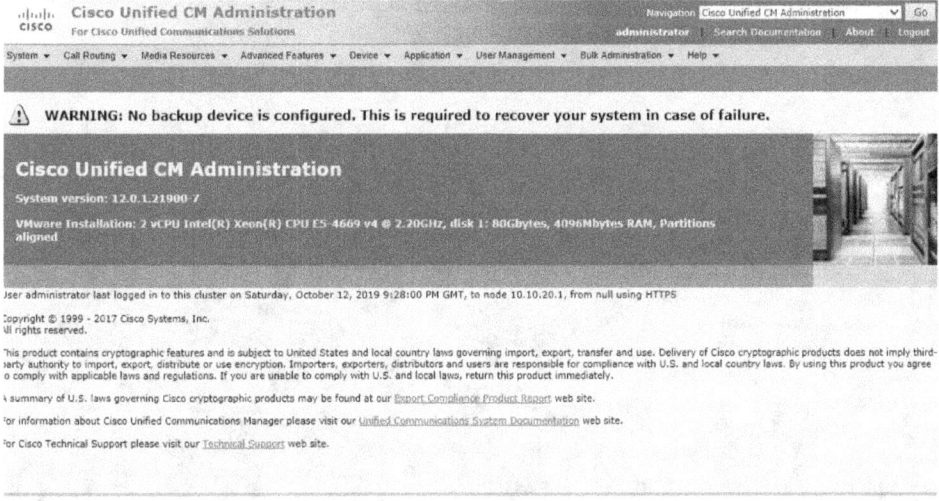

AXL

AXL is a Simple Object Access Protocol (or SOAP) based API that enables CUCM provisioning. You can access the APIs in a variety of ways including Java, PHP, AXL WSDL toolkit and cURL.

With AXL, you need to instantiate a SOAP client by using the AXAPI.wsdl file along with your PHP or Python code. You can get the necessary .xsd files from CUCM > Application > Plugins as part of the AXL toolkit.

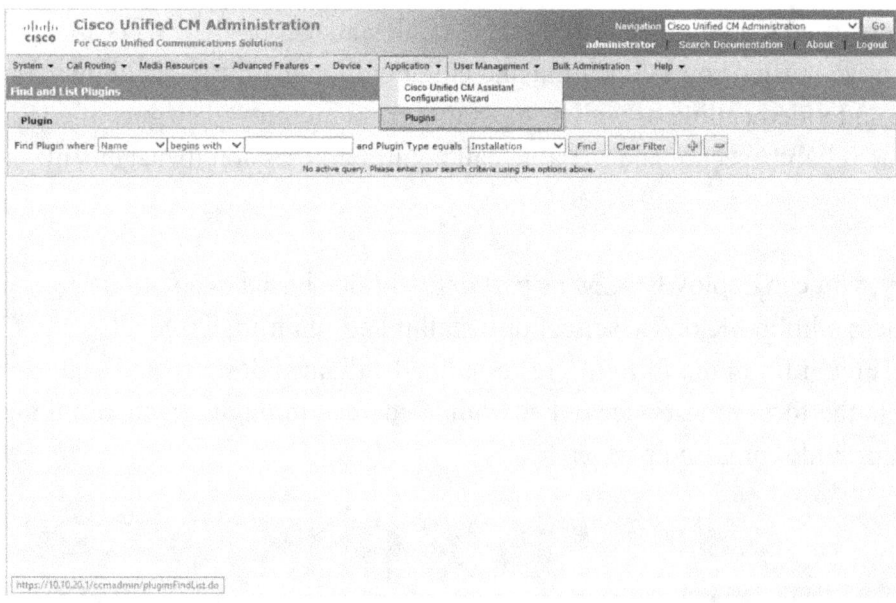

PHP Code

```php
<?php
 $host="10.10.20.100";
 $username="administrator";
 $password="ciscopsdt";

 $context =
  stream_context_create(array('ssl'=>array('verify_peer_name'=>true,
  'allow_self_signed'=>true,
  'cafile'=>"/var/www/html/PHP-Sample/10.10.20.100"
  )));
```

```php
$client = new SoapClient("/var/www/html/PHP-Sample/AXLAPI.wsdl",
    array('trace'=>true,
    'exceptions'=>true,
    'location'=>"https://".$host.":8443/axl",
    'login'=>$username,
    'password'=>$password,
    'stream_context'=>$context
    ));
?>
```

Once you've done that, you need to secure the connection by authenticating it.

```php
<?php
    $context =
stream_context_create(array('ssl'=>array('verify_peer_name'=>true,
    'allow_self_signed'=>true,
    'cafile'=>"/var/www/html/PHP-Sample/UCM-blah.cisco.com"
    )));
?>
```

You're set to execute your first API call at this point. Let's now use name (you could also use UUID) and query the list of elements that are attached to this phone.

```php
<?php
    $response = $client->getPhone(array("name"=>"SEP010101010199"));
?>
```

UDS Interfaces

The User Data Services (or UDS) is a REST API interface into various resources and entities into CUCM. For example, you can manage user's devices, subscribed services, and speed dials.

You can perform any of the following actions using the UDS APIs. This is a non-exhaustive list.

- Directory search for users
- Manage Call forward, DND, Speed dials, etc.
- Set language and locale
- Subscribe to IP Phone Service Apps
- Reset PIN or password credentials

To send in an API call, you can simply use basic auth that only requires username and password. You can execute your API call via Postman.

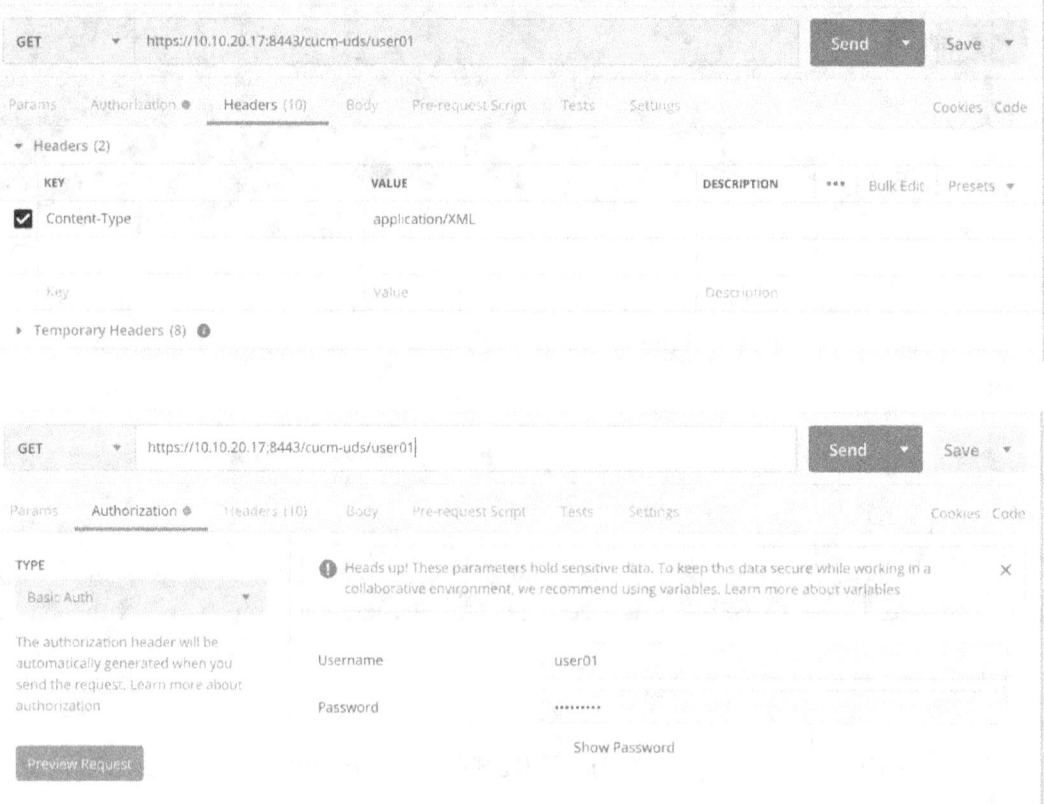

Further Reading

UDS API Documentation[22]

Cisco Finesse

Cisco Finesse is a collaborative customer care software that provides agent and supervisor desktop for the entire ecosystem that interacts with your customer service organization. It offers transparent integration for contact center functions, e.g., agent call history, desktop chat, team messaging, agent to agent call transfer, silent monitoring, etc.

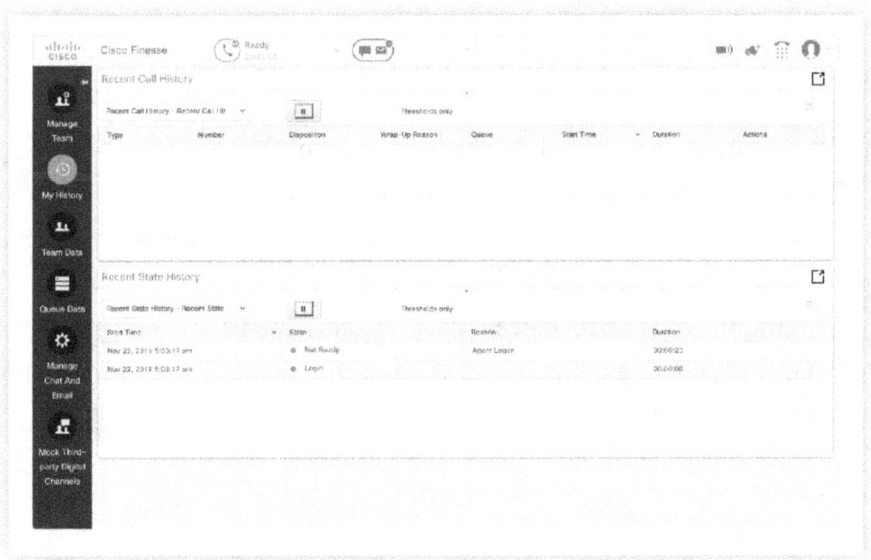

A contact center, aka call center, is a central location where an organization handles the customer service for their business. The actual delivery of customer service can happen in the form of text, calls, and chat. The contact center has two categories of tasks, inbound and the outbound. When a customer initiates the communication with the customer service team, it is considered an inbound task.

---

[22] https://bit.ly/2Q7Ogwo

When a customer service agent initiates the conversation with a customer, it is termed as the outbound task.

Cisco Finesses can be deployed in two different ways.

- Standalone Finesse (Finesse sits on top of Contact Center Enterprise/Unified Contact Center Express software)
- Co-resident Finesse (Finesse is used with Unified Contact Center Express software)

Finesse supports REST APIs and provides an SDK that you can use to perform agent and supervisor actions programmatically such as user sign-in/out, agent states, call control, task routing, desktop chat, etc.

At a high-level, Finesses REST APIs provide the following functionality.

- User (represents an agent, supervisor or admin)
- Dialog (represents a call and the participants)
- Media (represents a user's state in a non-voice Media Routing Domain)
- Team (represents a team of users)
- Systeminfo (represents current state of the system)
- ClientLogs (enables you to access and send client-side logging to the Finesses server)

You can use Postman to send in Finesse API requests in as long as you've had the following information handy.

- Finesse server FQDN or IP
- Agent name
- Agent ID (e.g., 9876)
- Agent password
- Agent extension
- requestId (e.g., "blah")

If you are using Finesse in a unified CCX deployment, be sure to include the port number in the URL as well i.e., blah.examle.com:8443 or 10.10.20.100:8443.

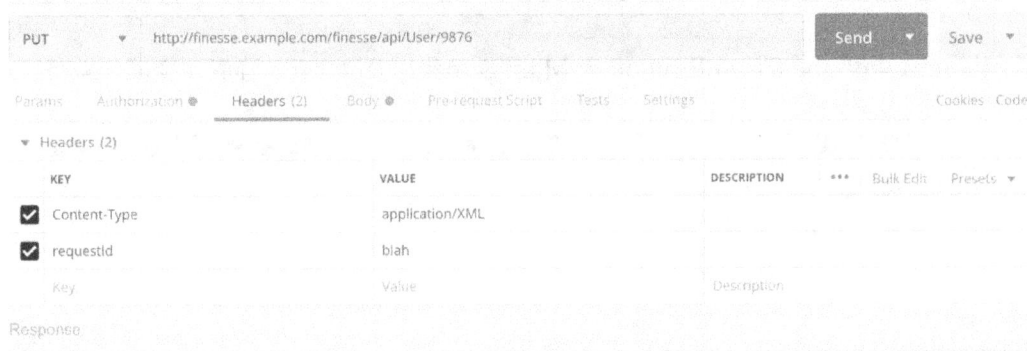

PUT on http://finesse.example.com/finesse/api/User/9876
Status 202: Accepted

Further Reading

Finesse and DevNet[23]
Finesse Developers Guide[24]
Finesse JavaScript Library[25]

Describe the capabilities of Cisco security platforms and APIs (Firepower, Umbrella, AMP, ISE, and Threat Grid)

Cisco's security portfolio includes products and solutions such as:

- Advanced Malware Protection (AMP) for endpoints
- Cisco Firepower Management Center (FMC)
- Cisco Firepower Threat Defense (FTD)

---

[23] https://bit.ly/339nkld

[24] https://bit.ly/2wRixbM

[25] https://bit.ly/2W7LXgs

- Cisco Identity Services Engine (ISE)
- Cisco Threat Grid
- Cisco Umbrella (formerly OpenDNS)

Let's start with the Cisco Firepower Management Center (or FMC) Dashboard.

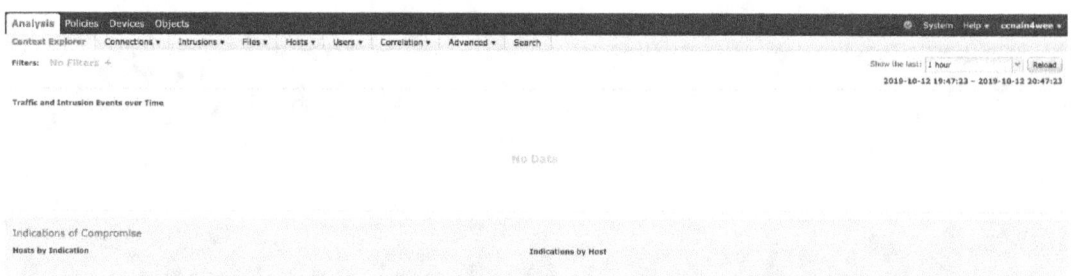

You can enable REST API by going to System > Configurations > REST API Preferences.

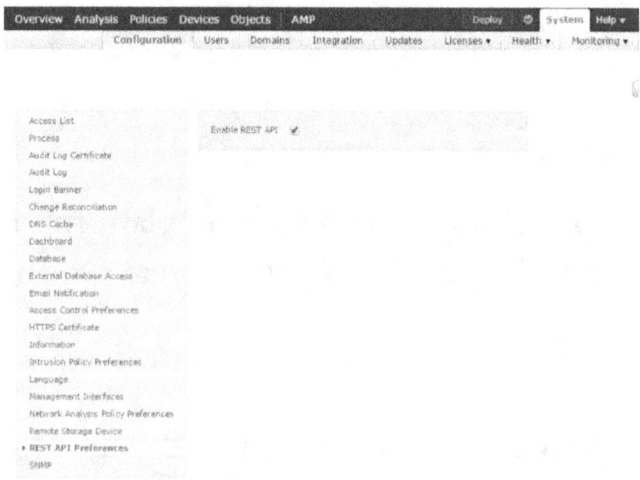

Once it is enabled, you can head over to API Browser to make your API calls. API Browser takes care of authentication token behind the scenes since it is already an authenticated session.

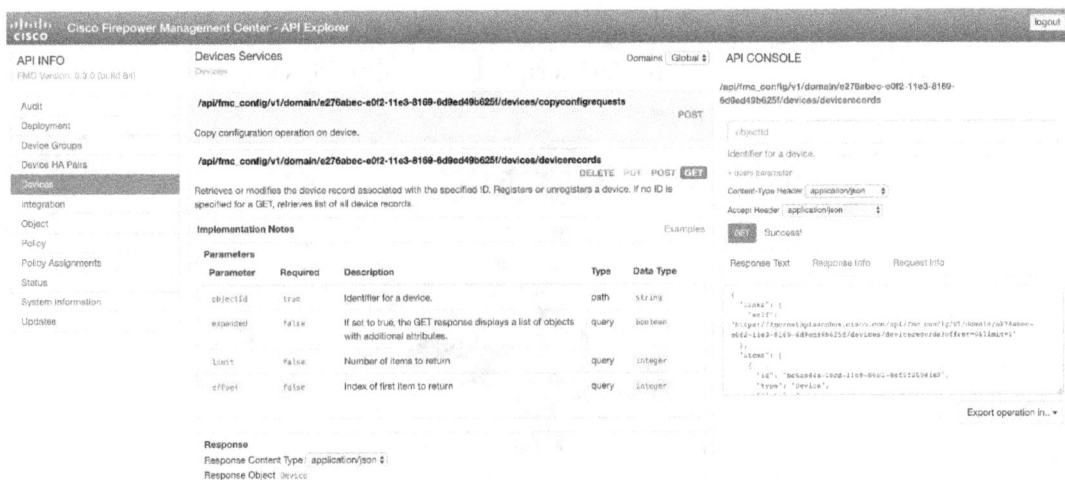

If you look at the top-right, we made an API call to the following URL.

/api/fmc_config/v1/domain/e276abec-e0f2-11e3-8169-6d9ed49b625f/devices/devicerecords

Now, the cool thing is that, if you click on the export drop-down menu, you can download either Python and/or Perl scripts to perform the same query.

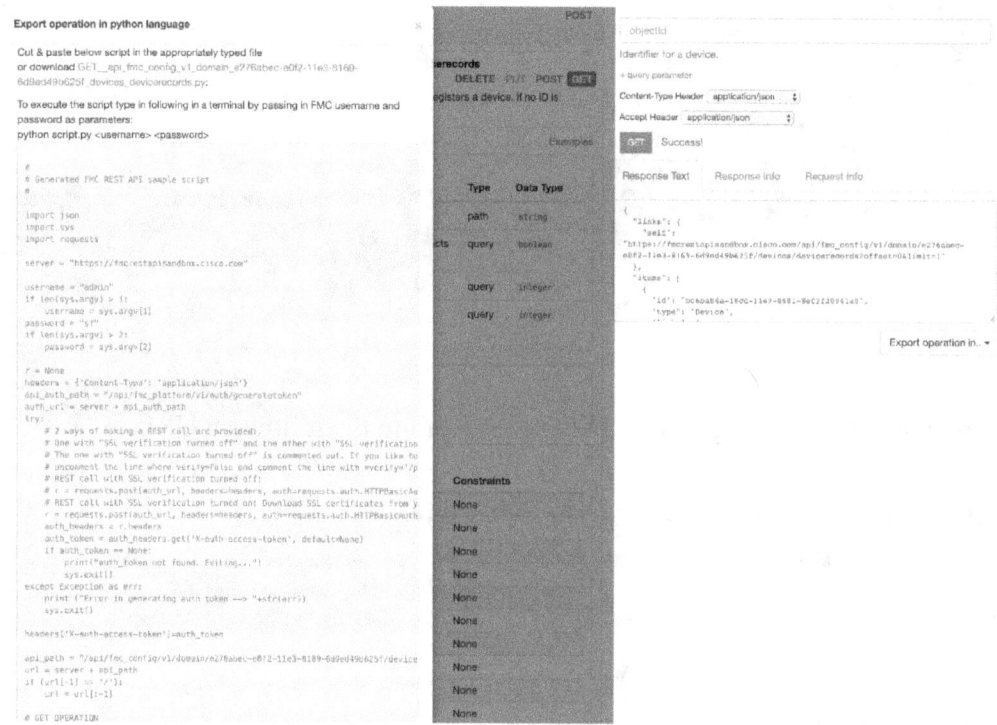

When you use Python code, you obviously would need a session token which we can obtain using the basic username and password auth.

Python Code (simplified version)

```
 1   import json
 2   import sys
 3   import requests
 4
 5   server = "https://fmcrestapisandbox.cisco.com"
 6
 7   username = "ccnain4wee"
 8   password = "Fq3L8GVG"
 9
10   r = None
11   headers = {
12     'Content-Type': 'application/json'
13   }
14   api_auth_path = "/api/fmc_platform/v1/auth/generatetoken"
15   auth_url = server + api_auth_path
16
17   r = requests.post(auth_url, headers = headers, auth = requests.auth
         .HTTPBasicAuth(username, password), verify = False)
18   auth_headers = r.headers
19   auth_token = auth_headers.get('X-auth-access-token',
20     default = None)
21
22   headers['X-auth-access-token'] = auth_token
23
24   api_path = "/api/fmc_config/v1/domain/e276abec-e0f2-11e3-8169
         -6d9ed49b625f/devices/devicerecords"#
25   param
26   url = server + api_path
27   if (url[-1] == '/'):
28     url = url[: -1]
29
30   # GET OPERATION
31   r = requests.get(url, headers = headers, verify = False)
32
33   status_code = r.status_code
34   resp = r.text
35   json_resp = json.loads(resp)
36   print(json.dumps(json_resp, sort_keys = True, indent = 4,
         separators = (',', ': ')))
```

Code Output

```
{
    "items": [
        {
            "id": "bc6ba84a-18cd-11e9-8681-8ef2f20941a0",
            "links": {
                "self": "https://fmcrestapisandbox.cisco.com/api/f
mc_config/v1/domain/e276abec-e0f2-11e3-8169-6d9ed49b625f/devices/d
evicerecords/bc6ba84a-18cd-11e9-8681-8ef2f20941a0"
            },
            "name": "VFTD",
            "type": "Device"
        }
    ],
    "links": {
        "self": "https://fmcrestapisandbox.cisco.com/api/fmc_confi
g/v1/domain/e276abec-e0f2-11e3-8169-6d9ed49b625f/devices/devicerec
ords?offset=0&limit=1"
    },
    "paging": {
        "count": 1,
        "limit": 1,
        "offset": 0,
        "pages": 1
    }
}
>
```

Another example where we query the server version.

Cisco Umbrella

Cisco Umbrella (formerly OpenDNS) is an anti-malware solution that uses DNS requests to perform malware inspection and content filtering. Umbrella provides four groups of APIs.

- Enforcement API (integrates security events)
- Network Devices API (integrates hardware devices)
- Investigate API (provides you data about security incidents)
- Reporting API (enables organizations to run reports)

Cisco Umbrella solution also provides integrations such as Meraki MR for wireless protection and security use cases.

- Wi-Fi protection when guests are on your network
- Per-app blocking
- Endpoint security for off-network devices
- Web filtering

You can get started with Cisco Umbrella in three steps.

Register your network public IP address or what Umbrella calls network identity by going to Deployments > Core Identities > Networks > Add from within the Umbrella dashboard. IPv4 addresses can even be dynamic, however, IPv6 addresses have to be static for Umbrella solution to work. IPv4 dynamic IP address works by downloading and installing a piece of software known as Dynamic IP updater.

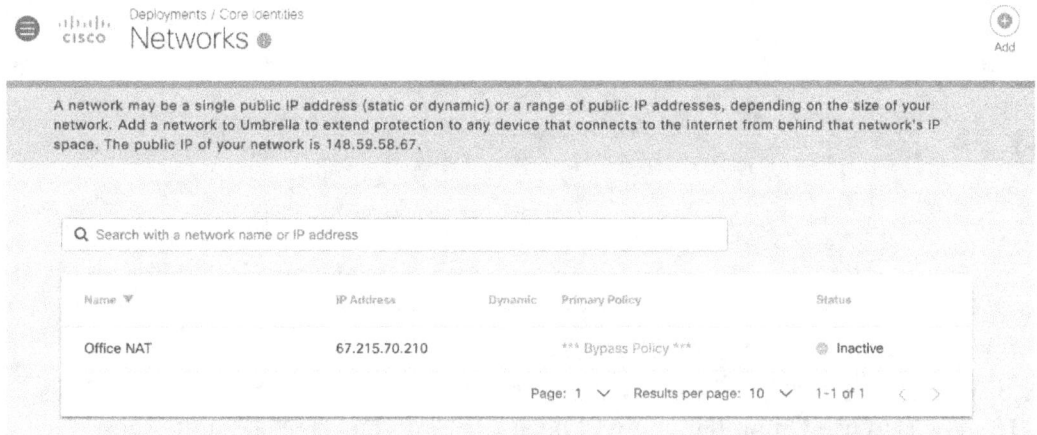

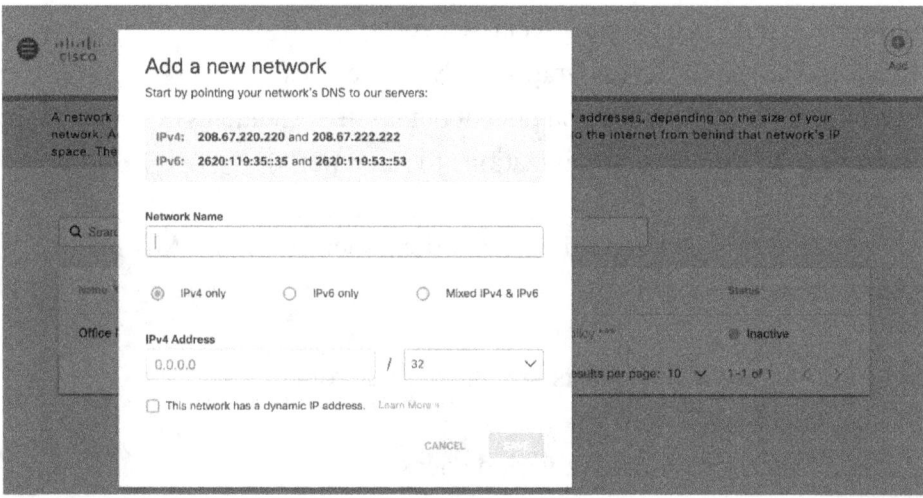

When you log in the very first time, you may be prompted to download Umbrella roaming client.

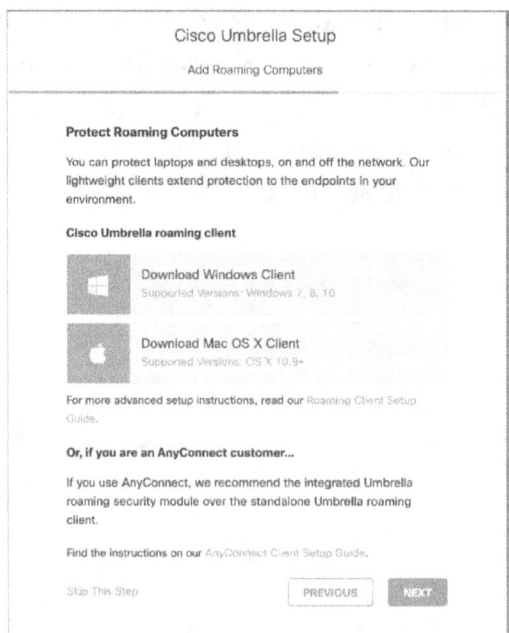

Now, typically your DNS server IP addresses point to your ISP's addresses. However, to use Umbrella, you will need to point your DNS IPs to Cisco

Umbrella DNS servers. If you are using an edge router or a firewall, you will need to log in and update the DNS IP addresses to the following.

The Umbrella IPv4 addresses are:

208.67.222.222
208.67.220.220

The Umbrella IPv6 addresses are:

2620:119:35::35
2620:119:53::53

The last and final step is to add a policy. You will define your security and access controls for your network, i.e., what traffic is inspected, and what's allowed or blocked.

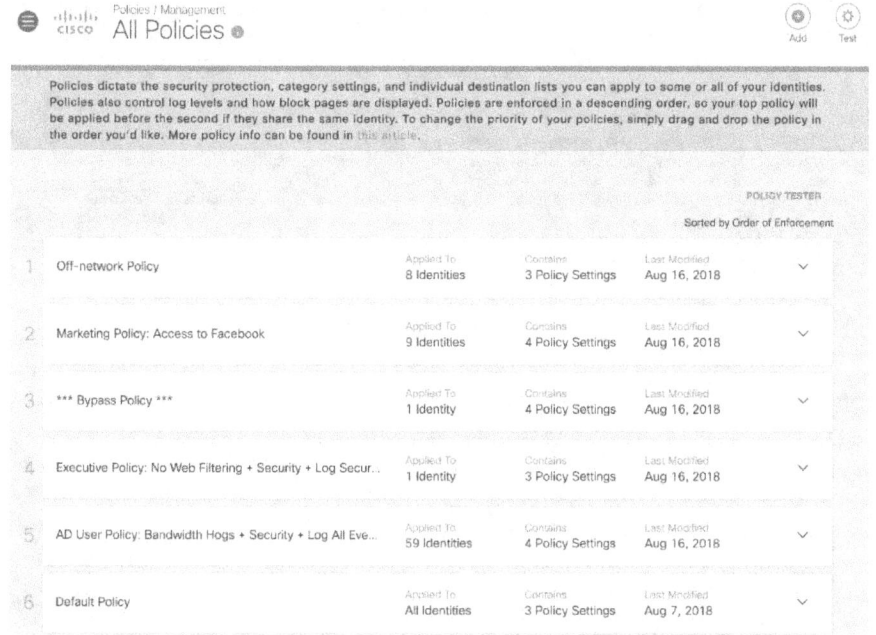

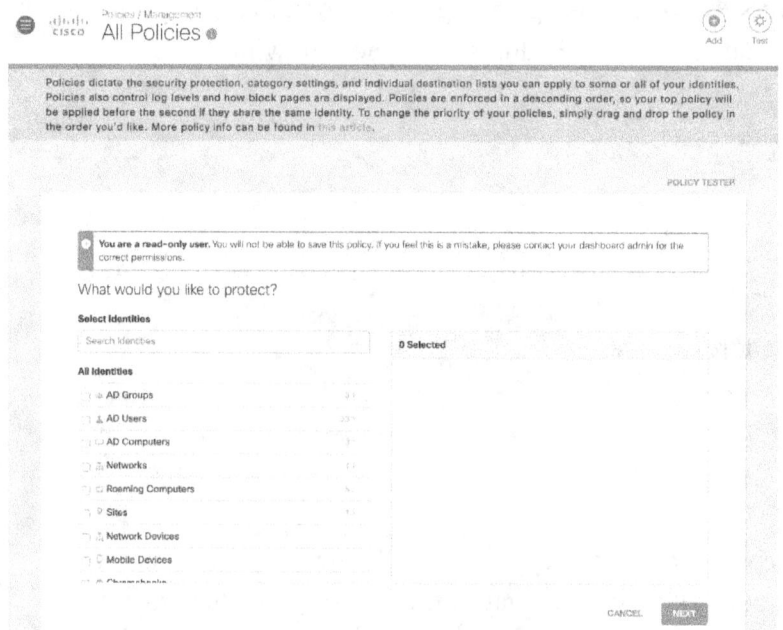

Optionally, you can also test your policies using the same interface.

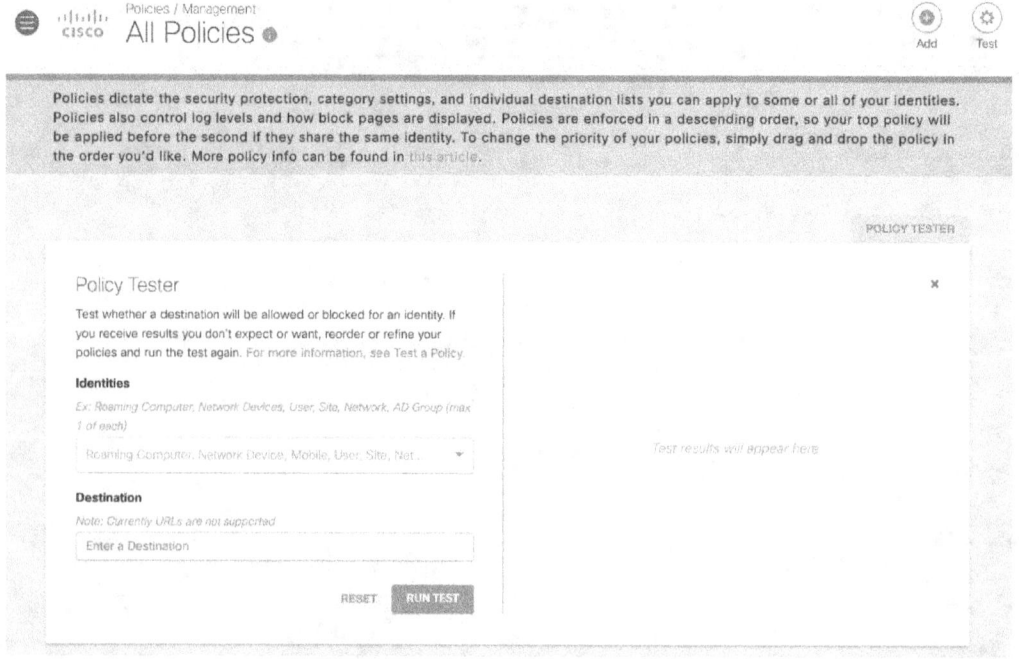

Let's now look at an example policy.

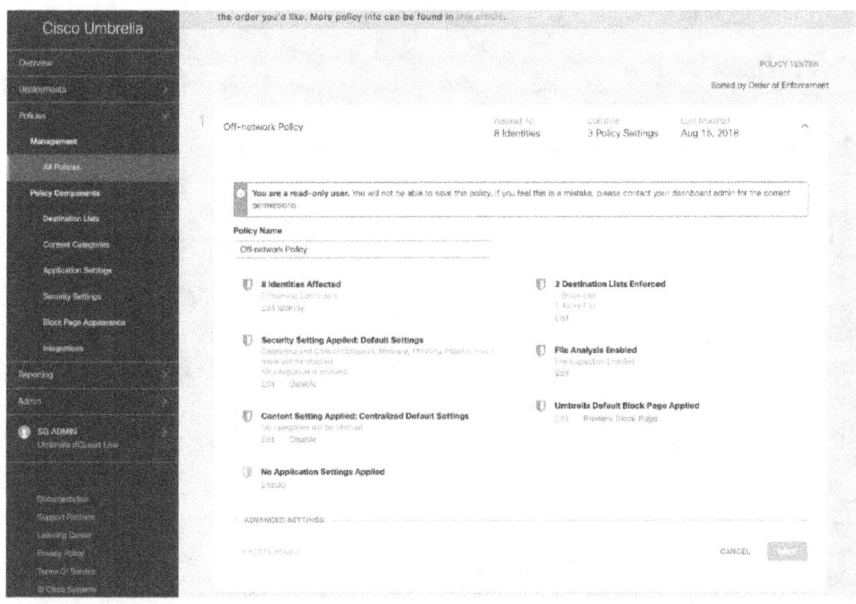

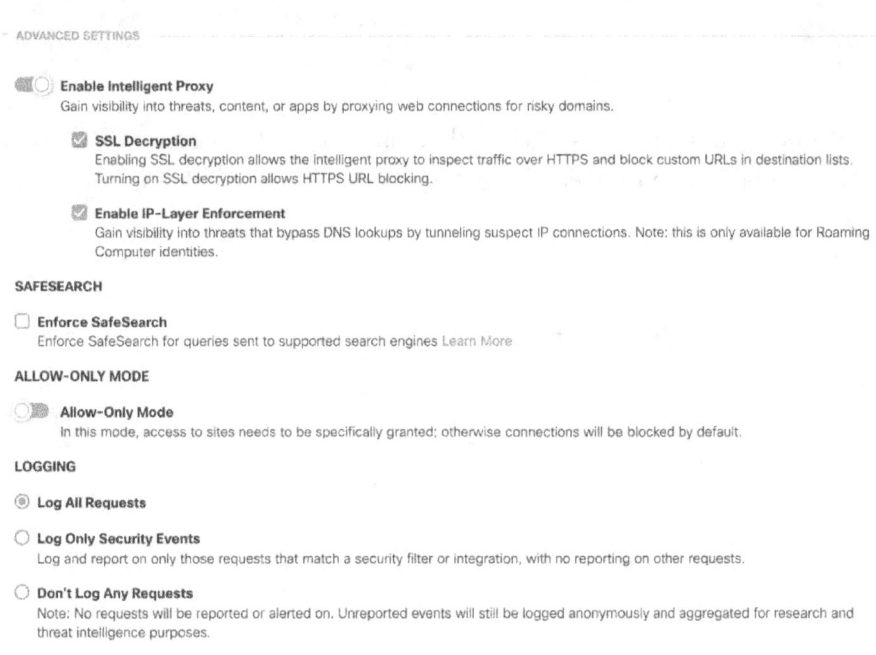

Umbrella dashboard offers a bird's eye view of the network, such as details around deployments, policies, reporting and administration as shown below.

Dashboard Overview

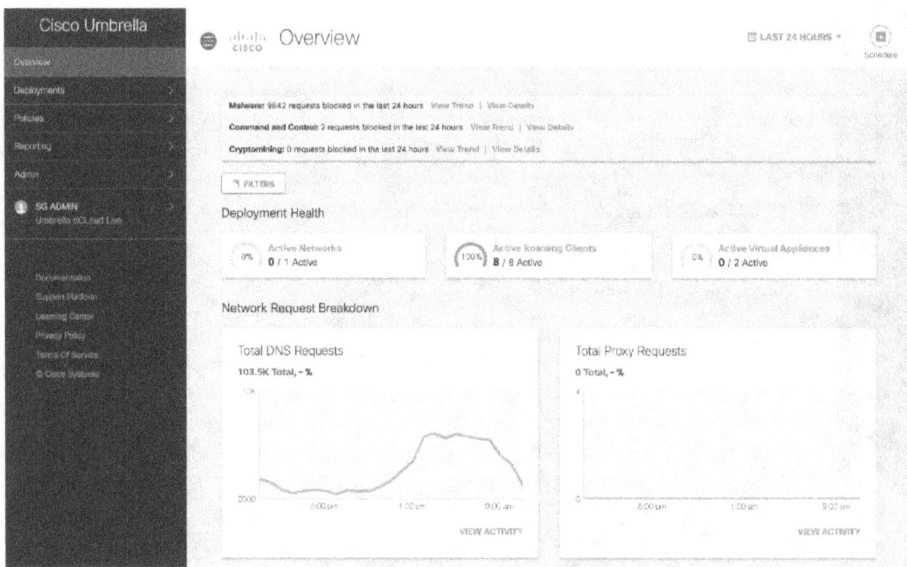

Umbrella offers comprehensive REST APIs to access deployment, policies, and reporting functions. You will need to create your API key before you can make remote API calls.

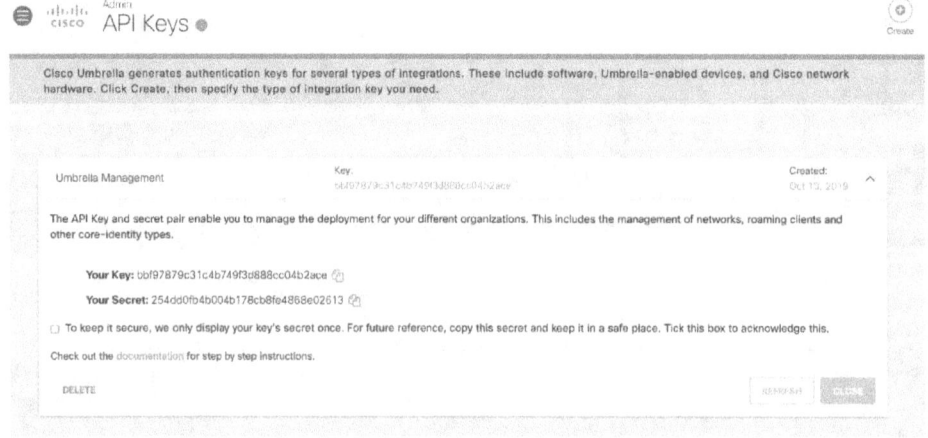

REST API responses are in JSON. You can make API calls using cURL, Postman or umbr-api Python library. You can also make those calls live from within the API docs hosted on Umbrella API Reference[26].

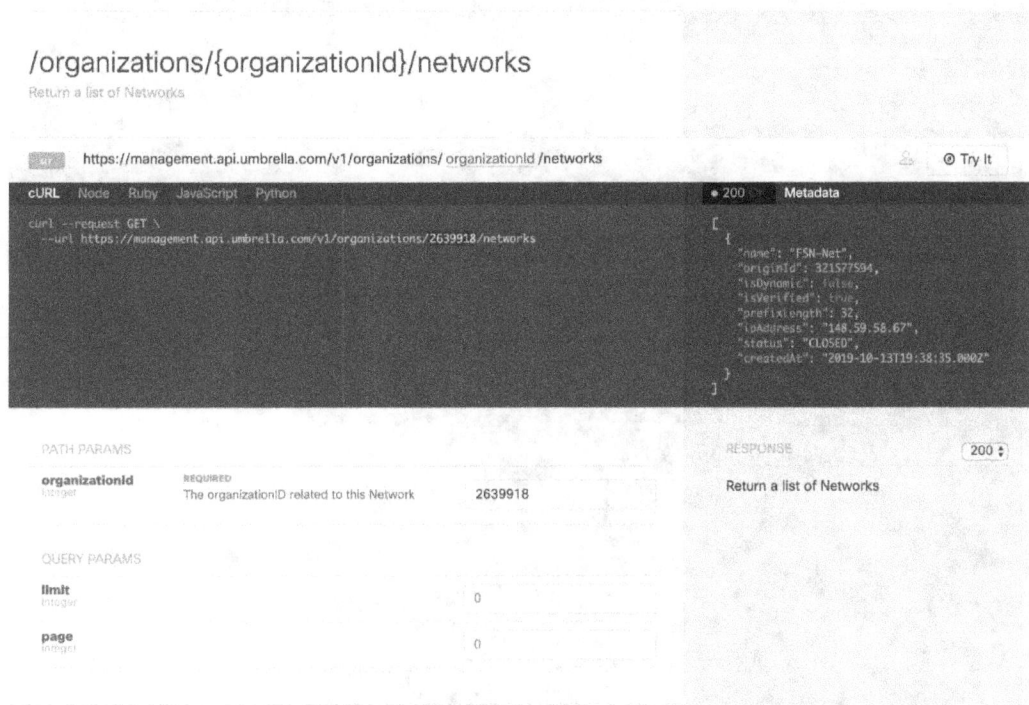

Last but not least, every time you make an API call using API reference docs, it will ask you for some required parameters (such as an organizationid) and a username/password to authenticate. Organizationid can be found in the dashboard URL whereas the username and password mean your API key and your API secret respectively.

cisco https://dashboard.umbrella.com/o/2639918/#/deployments/core/networks

You can also use Python to make the same API call.

26 https://bit.ly/3b7i45a

Python Code (GET request is using a pre-existing session cookie)

```python
import requests

url = "https://management.api.umbrella.com/v1/organizations/2639918/networks"

response = requests.request("GET", url)

print(response.text)
```

Code Output

```
● 200 OK    Metadata
[
  {
    "name": "FSN-Net",
    "originId": 321577594,
    "isDynamic": false,
    "isVerified": true,
    "prefixLength": 32,
    "ipAddress": "148.59.58.67",
    "status": "CLOSED",
    "createdAt": "2019-10-13T19:38:35.000Z"
  }
]
```

Cisco AMP

Cisco Antimalware Protection (or AMP) provides antimalware protection in a variety of deployment scenarios, before/during and after an attack takes place once necessary integration with Threat Grid is in place.

Cisco AMP solution includes uses the following capabilities to achieve antimalware protection.

- File reputation
- Static and dynamic analysis
- Retrospective detection
- File trajectory
- Endpoint Indication of Compromise (IoC)
- Outbreak control
- Antivirus engine

Cisco AMP solution can be deployed in a variety of ways, including the following.

- AMP for endpoints, such as windows or Macs or Linux machines using AnyConnect client
- AMP for networks, as part of Firepower NGIPS appliance
- AMP on Firewalls and ASA with Firepower services
- AMP on ESA or WSA, pretty much like adding antimalware protection as an add-on to ESA and WSA appliances
- AMP with Threat Grid, where Threat Grid enhances AMP's malware analysis. This can be deployed as a standalone (on-premise with 504 or 5504 appliances) or a cloud-based solution. Threat Grid combines sandboxing with threat intelligence into one unified antimalware solution.

AMP uses REST APIs which require HTTP Basic Auth. First, you need to log into your https://console.amp.cisco.com account (North American domain), hop over to Accounts > Business Page, Click on Edit. Under features, click on Regenerate where it says "3rd party API access" to generate the client ID and secure key. All responses are encoded in JSON.

https://api.amp.cisco.com/v1/<your_client_id>:<your_api_key>@<api_endpoint
>

Cisco ISE

Cisco Identity Services Engine (or ISE) provides a network-based approach for security posture and trusted access everywhere based on identity context. It offers enterprise users the access they need along with the automated device onboarding. It provides complete contextual endpoint visibility and profiles for users, devices and even applications for both IT and Operational Technology (OT) networks. It reduces attack surface with threat protection and streamlines network management and compliance.

Cisco ISE offers automation and integration via External RESTful Services (or ERS) API. ERS can interface with external clients to perform CRUD operations on ISE resources. ERS uses HTTPS on TCP 9060.

The ERS APIs are disabled by default, but you can enable them by logging into your ISE Policy Administration Node (or PAN). Once you're logged in, you need to navigate to Administration > System > Settings and select ERS Settings from the left sidebar and Enable the ERS APIs by selecting "Enable ERS for Read/Write" and click on Save.

Once ERS is enabled, you can perform CRUD operations on ISE PAN (RW) and Read-only (i.e., GET) operation on any of the ISE Policy Service Node (or PSN). You can access ERS documentation using the following URL on your ISE install.

https://ise.yourdomain.com:9060/ers/sdk

You can send in ERS API requests using either Postman, cURL, or Python SDK. There are three mandatory Request headers that you need to send in, i.e.

- ACCEPT (application/xml or application/json)
- AUTHORIZATION (basic and username/password)
- CONTENT-TYPE (application/xml or application/json)

Once APIs are set up, the simplest request that you can send in could be to GET a list of all ISE nodes.

URL: https://ise.yourdomain.com:9060/ers/config/node

API credentials: ers-user / *******
Headers: Content-type: application/json, Accept-type: application/json

Please note that ERS API user could be either default ISE admin account or you can opt to create separate ERS admin (R/W) or ERS user (R) privileges, the latter approach is recommended by Cisco since it allows for easy auditing and tracking of API related activities.

Cisco Threat Grid

Threat Grid also offers REST API access and you can configure it by going to https://blah.threatgrid.com dashboard. If you're already logged in, you can directly execute your API queries without needing an API key. For Python or Postman, you're going to need the API key.

https://blah.threatgrid.com/api/v2/iocs/feeds/domains?after=2018-01-08T21%3A39%3A13Z&before=2019-10-13T22:39:13Z&api_key=<your-key-value>

Threat Grid offers three different kinds of API versions, for example, IOC and curated feeds in the form of v1/v2, and v3 respectively. Curated feeds are the simplest to make. All responses are encoded in JSON format by default, however, v3 APIs are also optionally supported response encoding in CSV or STIX.

In real-world scenarios, you could use API automation and harvest the data feeds for the following purposes.

- Use curated feeds to craft Snort rules on-the-fly
- Import feeds into Cisco Threat Intelligence Director (or CTID) which is part of Firepower devices
- Import CSV format data into a SIEM platform such as Splunk

Describe the device level APIs and dynamic interfaces for IOS XE and NX-OS

IOS XE

Starting with 16.3 and 16.6 versions (which are now EOS), IOS XE can support YANG-based data modeling exposed from the devices with RESTCONF and NETCONF APIs respectively. Modeled data offers multiple advantages over unstructured CLI or SNMP interfaces.

Model-based Data Modeling Benefits
- Structured configuration and operational data access (no screen scraping)
- Data object definition (such as range checking, values etc.)
- Easier automation via Python or another scripting language of your choice
- Multiple data operations within a single message
- Atomic configuration application, fully or none applied with automatic rollback in case of failure

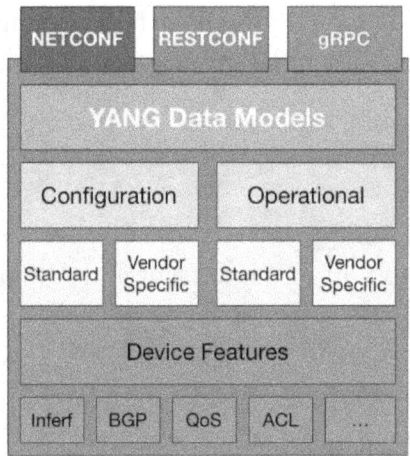

Please note that YANG, NETCONF, and RESTCONF (RFC 8040) are all IETF standards whereas gRPC is not an IETF standard but rather an open source standard protocol.

IOS XE supports two types of data models, i.e., open and native models.

Open YANG models are created by open standard bodies such as IETF or OpenConfig group and their goal is to harmonize the configuration across vendors.

Native models, on the other hand, are vendor-specific and closely follow the vendor's OS and CLI to facilitate the transition to automation.

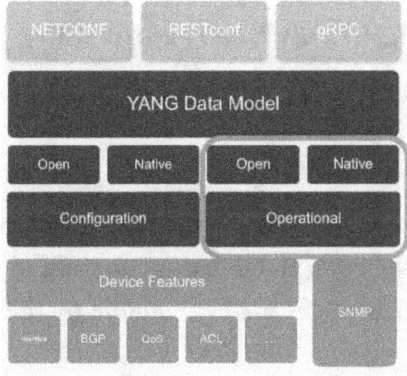

So, what happens to SNMP? Well, SNMP will likely linger on but mostly utilized for monitoring use case, configuration management never caught on with SNMP.

NX-OS

Nexus OS has a long history of API interfaces and automation related features.

- POAP / PXE
- RPM
- Python and Guest Shell
- NX-API
- NETCONF, RESTCONG, gRPC
- Embedded Event Manager (EEM)

NX-API REST uses HTTP/HTTPS for transport, and you can either JSON or XML for data encoding.

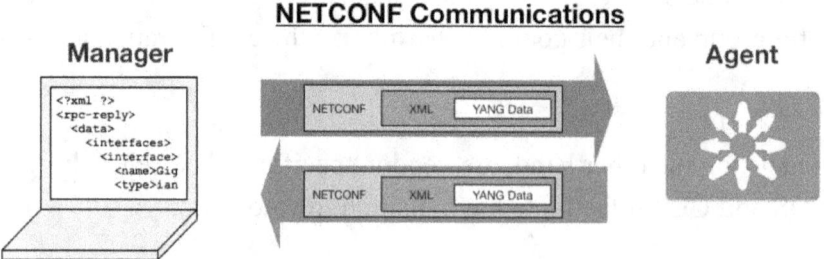

Identify the appropriate DevNet resource for a given scenario (Sandbox, Code Exchange, support, forums, Learning Labs, and API documentation)

DevNet provides developers a starting point for everything related to the Cisco Platform APIs, API documentation, education, including developer support. It is crucial to understand the resources made available by the Cisco DevNet.

Your DevNet starting point is the developer.cisco.com which contains the following resources.

- Learning Tracks
- Video Course
- Sandbox
- Code Exchange
- Ecosystem Exchange

You can explore those resource by your area of interest, e.g., IoT, Cloud, Networking, Data Center, Security, and Collaboration.

Sandbox

Cisco Sandboxes are bare metal servers, real routers or switches, emulators and simulators running their respective software stacks pre-configured and pre-tested that are available to you at no cost. Cisco IOS XE, IOS XR, NX-OS, etc. are all available as sandboxes at Cisco DevNet.

Cisco provides some of the sandboxes as always-on which means they are available without prior reservation, however, that also means that they are shared and thus read-only so you can't make any changes to them. However, at the time of writing, the majority of sandboxes do require a reservation, and you can book them in chunks of hours (default) or even up to seven days at a time.

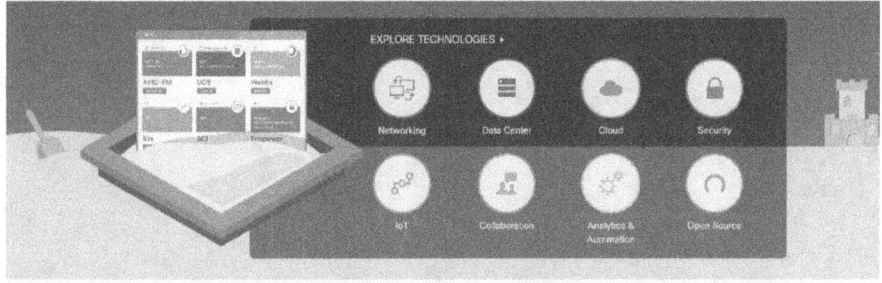

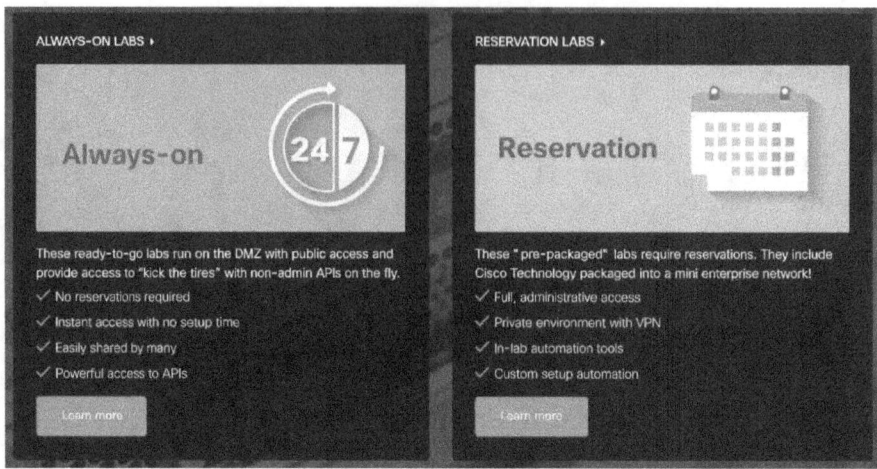

You can only use or reserve one sandbox at a time but all you need is a Cisco account to access them. Sandbox access depends on the type of resource that's inside the sandbox, however, most are accessible via HTTP/HTTPS, SSH, and Remote Desktop (RDP). You'd need to download and install the Cisco AnyConnect client beforehand, as accessing a reserved sandbox i.e., where you can make changes for testing, is only possible after connecting into your target private sandbox network via VPN.

Cisco provides a free download[27] of the VPN client for connecting into a Sandbox, however with one exception. For those of you using macOS Catalina, you'd need to download Cisco AnyConnect version 4.8.00175 or higher in order to install and use it on Catalina. At the time of writing, it is NOT provided by Cisco free of cost.

---

[27] https://developer.cisco.com/site/sandbox/anyconnect/

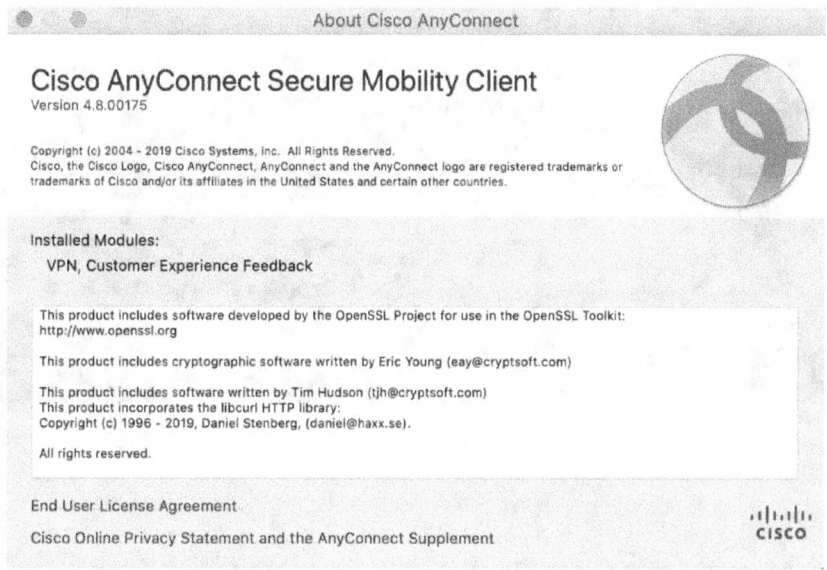

Code Exchange

DevNet provides multiple ways for the community members to share information and code with each other. Those community forums or portals are known as Exchanges. At the time of writing, DevNet hosts Code, Automation and Ecosystem Exchanges.

Code exchange features Repos from DevNet GitHub users. You can explore the existing repos using the site search function. You can also explore repos by their ranks or by the language they were written (e.g., Go or Python) and technology category such as networking, data center, and security, etc.

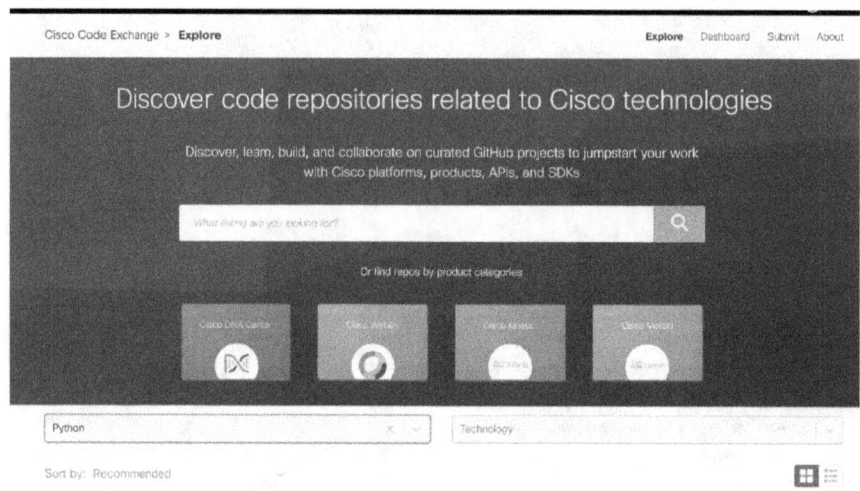

After you're logged into Cisco DevNet, you can submit your GitHub repo using a simple form.

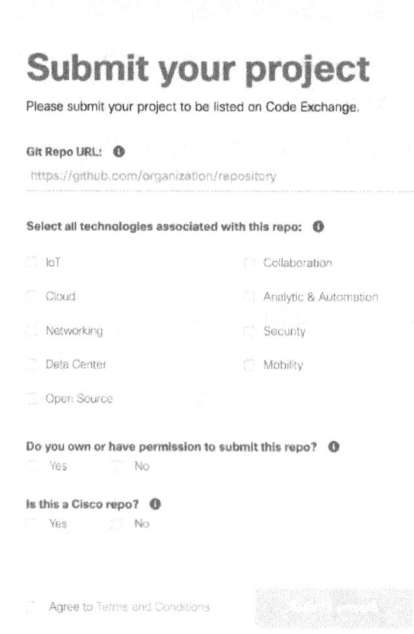

The Automation Exchange provides a collection of network automation related solutions and toolkits. Unlike Code and Automation exchanges, the Ecosystem Exchange caters to solution providers or partners and currently contains about

1500 solutions across different technologies to help you jump start your solution development.

Support Forums

DevNet offers a knowledge base, community-supported forums, live chat and case-based ticket system (paid with a subscription) where you can post your queries about either the sandboxes or published API docs.

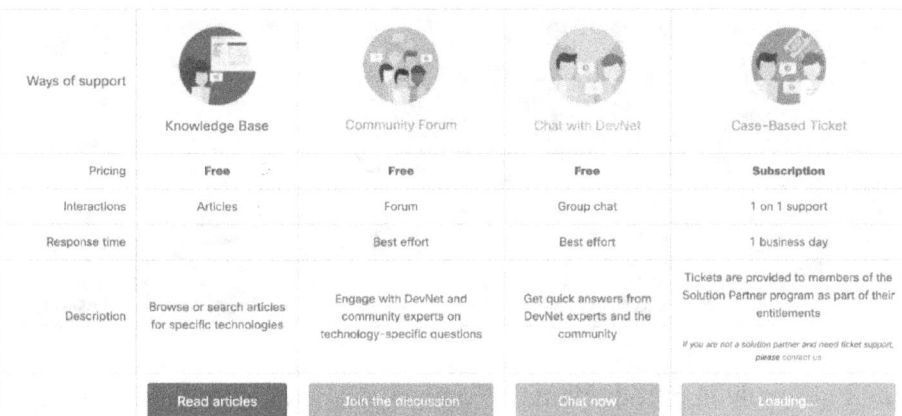

DevNet case-based support is geared for solution partners who would like to get one-on-one support and a response time of one business day. If you have a Cisco TAC contract for your organization, you can also use that to escalate a case to DevNet support.

Learning Labs

Learning labs allow you to learn the infrastructure and application concepts with the help of hands-on in the form of DevNet sandboxes. Learning Labs include topics from Enterprise Infrastructure, Security, Data Center, Collaboration, Cloud, SDN, and IoT.

Learning Labs feature online tutorials for concepts such as model-driven programmability, REST APIs, Python, and instructions and exercises for Cisco platforms.

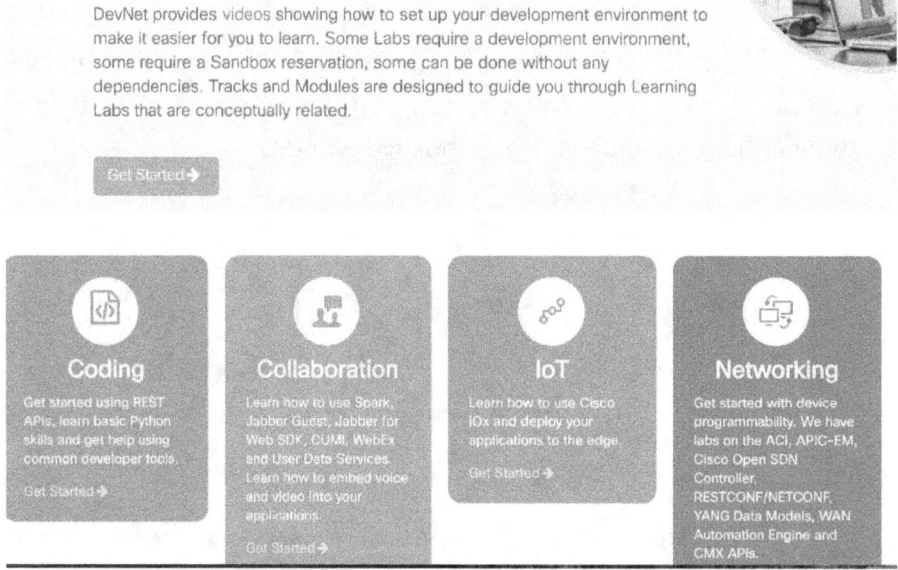

Learning Labs include introduction, lab objectives, perquisites, and cloning the GitHub repo to your local machine. Lab curriculum includes examples with python scripts (mostly supporting Python 2.7.x as opposed to 3.7.x), REST APIs, SDKs, etc.

API Documentation

Cisco DevNet developer documentation provides ready reference information for Cisco infrastructure and application APIs. These APIs are used for networking, services, cloud, security, collaboration, and networking as witnessed in the automation examples earlier in this section.

Cisco Developer Documentation

Find Cisco developer documentation such as API references, getting started guides, and examples

Cisco developer documentation provides in-depth reference information for Cisco product APIs. These APIs are used for networking, automation, mobility and location services, IoT, cloud, security, and collaboration products. Browse the developer documentation for API reference, how-to information, and sample code.

Network Controller APIs

Application Centric Infrastructure (ACI) - Define and enforce policies on application deployment lifecycles in your data center.

Data Center Network Manager (DCNM) - Provision, monitor, route, switch, and administer your data center's Cisco Fabric.

Cisco DNA Center - Automate and operate your network to configure and observe at scale, using the Cisco DNA Center REST API.

Meraki - Leverage the Dashboard APIs to build custom networking solutions for secure, zero-touch provisioning.

Network Services Orchestrator (NSO) - Automate your network services lifecycle and configure programmatically.

Network Device APIs

IOS XE - Provide standards-based, consistent, programmable interfaces for Cisco network devices.

IOS XR - Use model-driven interfaces for structured configuration and operational data.

IOx - Host applications on Cisco hardware, including container-based deployments.

DevNet Events

DevNet not only brings community together online but also offline in the form of various in-person events. There are DevNet events that you can attend, i.e.

- DevNet Zone
- DevNet Express
- DevNet Create

The DevNet Zone is an educational event for developers held at yearly Cisco Live events. It consists of hands-on workshops, demos, presentations and Learning Lab stations that you can use even if you have no prior experience with APIs or a programming language such as Python.

The DevNet Express is a two-day event hosted by Cisco Sales Engineers. It consists of multiple learning tracks and an agenda that includes both presentations and hands-on activities. For example, you can learn about automation with Cisco DNA Center, Collaboration, DC, Security or even Meraki solution.

The DevNet Create is yet another two-day event that showcases innovation in the areas of network automation, performance monitoring, and APIs. At this event, there is another track that's known as Camp Create which offers the opportunity to work with others, use Cisco's latest platforms and technologies and come up with a demo to share with everyone at the end of the two days.

Further Reading

Setting up your local development environment[28]
REST API Basics[29]
Introduction to Git[30]
Google's Python Class[31]
Learn Python[32]

Apply concepts of model driven programmability (YANG, RESTCONF, and NETCONF) in a Cisco environment

Model driven programmability harnesses the power of models, i.e., matching the devices' capabilities to standardized models making it easier to configure networking devices. A data model is a structured method to describe any object, e.g., our driving licenses describe us in an individual way.
There are numerous benefits of using model-driven programming approach.

- It provides configuration language that is human-readable and machine friendly

---

[28] https://bit.ly/3cSac8A

[29] https://bit.ly/2IFbrtF

[30] https://bit.ly/2wUDjHx

[31] https://bit.ly/2vZQdnl

[32] https://bit.ly/2wMcFRp

- It provides support for multiple model types, including native, OpenConfig and IETF.
- It decouples configuration language from transport and encoding formats.
- It uses model-driven APIs for abstraction and simplification
- It leverages open source for wider support

The most common data models today, is Yet Another Next Generation (YANG). YANG is also the modeling language which is defined in RFC 6020 and RFC7950. It uses protocols such as NETCONF and RESTCONF for data model programmable interfaces.

NETCONF uses remote procedure calls and notifications. YANG module defines the hierarchies of data that can be used for NETCONF operations. There are two main YANG data models.

- Open YANG models (developed by the vendors and standards bodies such as IETF or OpenConfig. They are created to be independent of the underlying platform)
- Native models (developed by the vendors such as Cisco or Juniper. They can only be used on the devices they are created for)

The terms used in YANG model are defined in the RFC. Here are some commonly used terms.

- Anyxml (a data node that can contain an unknown chunk of XML data)
- Augment (adds new scheme nodes to an existing schema node)
- Container (an interior data node that only contains child nodes)
- Data model, node, and tree (model defines how data such as a node in the schema tree is instantiated. The data tree contains the instantiated tree of configuration and state data)
- Leaf (node with no child nodes)
- Leaf-list (like leaf node but defines a set of nodes rather than one)
- Module (defines the hierarchy of nodes that can be used for NETCONF operations)

- State data (non-configuration data, such as status or statistics)

YANG defines four nodes for data modeling.

- Leaf nodes
- Leaf-list nodes
- Container nodes
- List nodes

YANG module contains a sequence of statements and each statement starts with a keyword, followed by an optional argument, and then a semicolon or a block of sub-statements enclosed within braces.

statement = keyword [argument] (";" / "{" *statement "}")

There are four main statements in a YANG module, i.e., container, list, leaf and leaf-list.

NETCONF

The NETCONF protocol uses XML-based data encoding for both the configuration and the protocol messages. It provides a small set of operations to both manage device configurations and get device state information. The basic protocol provides the following configuration related operations.

- Retrieve
- Configure
- Copy
- Delete

Following list includes operations that you can accomplish using NETCONF protocol.

- Get

- Get-config
- Edit-config
- Copy-config (create/replace an entire configuration datastore)
- Delete-config (delete a configuration datastore)
- Lock (lock the configuration datastore)
- Unlock (release a configuration lock)
- Close-session (graceful session closure)
- Kill-session (force termination of a session)

There are some similarities and some big differences between NETCONF and SNMP protocols.

SNMP

- Defined to remotely configure and monitor devices
- Uses pull model to retrieve data which doesn't scale well
- Doesn't have discovery process for finding MIBs
- No concept of a transaction
- Lacks backup and restore of device configuration
- Limited industry support for configuration MIBs (but plenty of monitoring)

NETCONF

- Defined to remotely configure and monitor devices
- Multiple configuration stores (candidate, running and startup)
- Configuration testing and validation
- Built-in distinction between configuration and operational data
- Built-in capability exchange
- Selective data retrieval
- Streaming and playback of event notifications

Protocol Use Cases	NETCONF	SNMP

Get Collection of status fields	Yes	Yes
Get Collection of configuration fields	Yes	Yes
Protocol security	Yes	Yes (v3)
Set configuration fields in transaction	Yes	No
Transactions that go across multiple network elements	Yes	No
Send event notifications	Yes	No
Test configuration before commit	Yes	No

NETCONF service uses SSH for transport and the default SSH port is TCP 830. You can use terminal to log into a NETCONF server or device and issue NETCONF commands directly (or use a Python script, something we'll discuss shortly).

$ ssh developer@devasc-iosxe-mgmt-1.cisco.com -p 830

When the login is completed, the NETCONF server will respond with a <hello> message listing capabilities for the device. The NETCONF session remains open after the initial response.

```xml
<?xml version="1.0" encoding="UTF-8"?>
<hello xmlns="urn:ietf:params:xml:ns:netconf:base:1.0">
<capabilities>
<capability>urn:ietf:params:netconf:base:1.0</capability>
<capability>urn:ietf:params:netconf:base:1.1</capability>
<capability>urn:ietf:params:netconf:capability:writable-running:1.0</capability>
<capability>urn:ietf:params:netconf:capability:xpath:1.0</capability>
<capability>urn:ietf:params:netconf:capability:validate:1.0</capability>
<capability>urn:ietf:params:netconf:capability:validate:1.1</capability>
......truncated for brevity.......
<capability>
    urn:ietf:params:netconf:capability:notification:1.1
   </capability>
</capabilities>
```

```
<session-id>1315</session-id></hello>]]>]]>
```

You can continue here with NETCONF commands, such as get-config.

```
<?xml version="1.0"?>
  <rpc xmlns="urn:ietf:params:xml:ns:netconf:base:1.0"
  message-id="1331">
  <get-config>
    <source>
      <running/>
    </source>
  </get-config>
  </rpc>]]>]]>
```

RESTCONF

RESTCONF is defined in RFC8040 and provides a REST like interface to configuration information and control. The operations are similar to NETCONF however encapsulated within the HTTP messages. There is difference in how YANG language is used, i.e., it is still used to define the command structure syntax so the semantics of the configuration datastore configuration, state and events remain as-is.

RESTCONF can use XML or JSON encoding format for data structured data. HTTP verbs such as GET, POST, PUT, PATCH and DELETE are directed to a RESTCONF API to access data resources within the YANG data models. A network device can serve both NETCONF and RESTCONF at the same time.

It is worth noting the differences between the two protocols.

RESTCONF	NETCONF
supports running datastore (edits of	Supports running and candidate data

candidate data store are immediately committed)	stores
Doesn't support obtaining and releasing data store lock	Supports obtaining and releasing data store lock
Doesn't support transactions across multiple devices	Doesn't support transactions across multiple devices
Implicit validation for edit operations	Explicit validation for edit operations

You can access RESTCONF APIs using the following syntax.

https://<host>/restconf/<resource-type>/<yang-module:resource>

When you do an initial GET, you receive the following.

Request

```
GET /restconf HTTP/1.1
Host: device.fullstacknetworker.com
Accept: application/yang-data+json
```

Response

```
HTTP/1.1 200 OK
Date: Thu, 26 Mar 2020 20:56:30 GMT
Server: device.fullstacknetworker.com
Content-Type: application/yang-data+json
    {
      "ietf-restconf:restconf" : {
        "data" : {},
        "operations" : {},
        "yang-library-version" : "2020-01-10"
      }
    }
```

As noted earlier, the RESTCONF protocol supports two media types, i.e., application/yang-data+xml and application/yang-data+json.

If you're using a Python script, you can construct your headers as follows.

```
headers = {
    'Content-Type': 'application/yang-data+json',
    'Accept': 'application/yang-data+json'
    }
```

Besides RESTCONF/NETCONF APIs, IOS XE also offers Guest Shell access on or off box. For Guest Shell, you need to use a 16.5 or later version, and you can configure it using three CLIs.

- iox
- If you're running IOS XE 16.8 or later, you'd need to configure Guest shell virtual interface.

  App-hosting appid guestshell
          Vnic management guest-interface 0
- guestshell enable, wait until you see "Guestshell enabled successfully" message.

```
csr1000v-1#conf terminal
Enter configuration commands, one per line.  End with CNTL/Z.
csr1000v-1(config)#iox
csr1000v-1(config)#gues
csr1000v-1(config)#guest
csr1000v-1(config)#app
csr1000v-1(config)#app-
csr1000v-1(config)#app-hosting app
csr1000v-1(config)#app-hosting appid gu
csr1000v-1(config)#app-hosting appid gues
csr1000v-1(config)#app-hosting appid ?
  WORD  no description

csr1000v-1(config)#app-hosting appid guestshell
csr1000v-1(config-app-hosting)#vnic mana
csr1000v-1(config-app-hosting)#vnic management gues
csr1000v-1(config-app-hosting)#vnic management guest-interface 0
csr1000v-1(config-app-hosting)#ex
csr1000v-1(config)#ex
% Ambiguous command:  "ex"
csr1000v-1(config)#exit
csr1000v-1#guestsh
csr1000v-1#guestshell en
csr1000v-1#guestshell enable
Interface will be selected if configured in app-hosting
Please wait for completion
```

```
csr1000v-1#show iox-service

IOx Infrastructure Summary:
---------------------------
IOx service (CAF)    : Running
IOx service (HA)     : Not Supported
IOx service (IOxman) : Running
Libvirtd             : Running
```

However, Guest Shell is something that we've discussed earlier, and it is outside the scope of this section.

YANG and NETCONF Example

For this exercise, we will use IOS XE 16.11 on Cisco CSR1000v.

Enabling YANG and API access on Cisco IOS XE devices boils down to two CLIs, so it couldn't be simpler.

- Privilege level 15 for NETCONF communication (we're using a local user, but you can also use AAA RADIUS):
  o username admin privilege 15 secret fsn123
- Enabling YANG with NETCONF
  o netconf-yang

First things first, we log into our devnet IOS XE sandbox.

```
MAK1-MBP:~ afaqkhan$ ssh -l developer -p 8181  ios-xe-mgmt-latest.cisco.com
The authenticity of host '[ios-xe-mgmt-latest.cisco.com]:8181 ([64.103.37.8]:8181)' can't be established.
RSA key fingerprint is SHA256:+ChihJ4vSUJteAzP9X8IfXIXmvEBPcvGMtSLTT+sGCU.
Are you sure you want to continue connecting (yes/no)? yes
Warning: Permanently added '[ios-xe-mgmt-latest.cisco.com]:8181,[64.103.37.8]:8181' (RSA) to the list of known hosts.
Password:
Password:

Welcome to the DevNet Sandbox for CSR1000v and IOS XE

The following programmability features are already enabled:
  - NETCONF
  - RESTCONF

Thanks for stopping by.
```

Now, let's configure our priv 15 user and YANG/NETCONF. SSH is enabled automatically when you enable NETCONF. NETCONF uses SSH port 830 for transport.

```
csr1000v-1(config)#username admin privilege 15 secret fsn123
csr1000v-1(config)#net
csr1000v-1(config)#netc
csr1000v-1(config)#netconf-
csr1000v-1(config)#netconf-yang ?
  cisco-ia   Configure cisco-ia parameters
  cisco-odm  Configure cisco-odm parameters
  feature    Configure netconf-yang features
  ssh        Configure ssh options
  <cr>       <cr>

csr1000v-1(config)#netconf-yang
csr1000v-1(config)#
```

```
csr1000v-1#show netconf ?
  counters  Show NETCONF statistics counters
  schema    Show NETCONF schema
  session   Show NETCONF session information

csr1000v-1#show netconf sess
csr1000v-1#show netconf session
Netconf Sessions: 0 open, maximum is 4
csr1000v-1#show netconf c
csr1000v-1#show netconf counters
NETCONF Counters
Connection Attempts:0: rejected:0 no-hello:0 success:0
Transactions
      total:0, success:0, errors:0
detailed errors:
      in-use 0           invalid-value 0          too-big 0
      missing-attribute 0      bad-attribute 0          unknown-attribute 0
      missing-element 0        bad-element 0   unknown-element 0
      unknown-namespace 0      access-denied 0          lock-denied 0
      resource-denied 0        rollback-failed 0        data-exists 0
      data-missing 0  operation-not-supported 0        operation-failed 0
      partial-operation 0
csr1000v-1#
```

In order to connect and execute our NETCONF API calls, we can use ncclient and minidom python libraries.

- ncclient (for NETCONF get etc.)
- minidom (for XML)

Let's now write a Python script that uses NETCONF to fetch the router's hostname.

Python Code

```
 1   #import the ncclient library
 2   from ncclient import manager
 3   import sys
 4   import xml.dom.minidom
 5
 6   # use the IP address or hostname of your CSR1000V device
 7   HOST = 'ios-xe-mgmt-latest.cisco.com'#
 8   use the NETCONF port
 9   for your IOS - XE device
10   PORT = 10000# use the user credentials
11   for your IOS - XE device
12   USER = 'developer'
13   PASS = 'C1sco12345'
14
15   with manager.connect(host = HOST, port = PORT, username = USER,
16       password = PASS, hostkey_verify = False,
17       device_params = {
18         'name': 'default'
19       },
20       allow_agent = False, look_for_keys = False) as m:
21
22     hostname_filter = ''
23   ' <
24   filter >
25     <
26     native xmlns = "http://cisco.com/ns/yang/Cisco-IOS-XE-native" >
27     <
28     hostname > < /hostname> <
29     /native> <
30     /filter>
31   ''
32   '
33   result = m.get_config('running', hostname_filter)
34   xml_doc = xml.dom.minidom.parseString(result.xml)
35   hostname = xml_doc.getElementsByTagName("hostname")
36   print("Hostname: " + hostname[0].firstChild.nodeValue)
```

Code Output

```
Hostname: csr1000v-1
>
```

Now, let's display router's NETCONF capabilities.

Python Code

```python
1   from ncclient import manager
2
3   HOST = 'ios-xe-mgmt-latest.cisco.com'
4   PORT = '10000'
5   USER = 'developer'
6   PASS = 'C1sco12345'
7
8   with manager.connect(host = HOST, port = PORT, username = USER,
9       password = PASS, hostkey_verify = False,
10      device_params = {
11         'name': 'default'
12      },
13      look_for_keys = False, allow_agent = False) as m:
14
15      #print all NETCONF capabilities
16   print('***Full List of Capabilities***')
17   for capability in m.server_capabilities:
18      print(capability.split('?')[0])
```

Code Output (truncated)

```
***Here are the Remote Devices Capabilities***
urn:ietf:params:netconf:base:1.0
urn:ietf:params:netconf:base:1.1
urn:ietf:params:netconf:capability:writable-running:1.0
urn:ietf:params:netconf:capability:xpath:1.0
urn:ietf:params:netconf:capability:validate:1.0
urn:ietf:params:netconf:capability:validate:1.1
urn:ietf:params:netconf:capability:rollback-on-error:1.0
urn:ietf:params:netconf:capability:notification:1.0
urn:ietf:params:netconf:capability:interleave:1.0
urn:ietf:params:netconf:capability:with-defaults:1.0
urn:ietf:params:netconf:capability:yang-library:1.0
http://tail-f.com/ns/netconf/actions/1.0
http://tail-f.com/ns/netconf/extensions
http://cisco.com/ns/cisco-xe-ietf-ip-deviation
http://cisco.com/ns/cisco-xe-ietf-ipv4-unicast-routing-deviation
http://cisco.com/ns/cisco-xe-ietf-ipv6-unicast-routing-deviation
http://cisco.com/ns/cisco-xe-ietf-ospf-deviation
http://cisco.com/ns/cisco-xe-ietf-routing-deviation
http://cisco.com/ns/cisco-xe-openconfig-acl-deviation
http://cisco.com/ns/cisco-xe-openconfig-lldp-deviation
http://cisco.com/ns/mpls-static/devs
```

Now, let's try to download the running configuration using NETCONF API call. The output is natively in XML form, so let's convert it to JSON and display.

Python Code (XML)

```
1   import xmltodict from ncclient
2   import manager
3   import json
4   import xml.dom.minidom
5
6   HOST = 'ios-xe-mgmt-latest.cisco.com'
7   PORT = '10000'
8   USER = 'developer'
9   PASS = 'C1sco12345'
10
11  m = manager.connect(host = HOST, port = PORT, username = USER,
12      password = PASS, hostkey_verify = False,
13▾     device_params = {
14          'name': 'default'
15      },
16      look_for_keys = False, allow_agent = False)
17
18  running_config_xml = m.get_config('running')
19  running_config_json = xmltodict.parse(str(running_config_xml))#
        printing running - config in XML
20  print(xml.dom.minidom.parseString(str(running_config_xml
        )).toprettyxml())
```

Code Output (truncated)

```
            </console>
        <vty>
            <first>0</first>
            <last>4</last>
            <login>
                <local/>
            </login>
            <transport>
                <input>
                    <input>ssh</input>
                </input>
            </transport>
        </vty>
    </line>
        <diagnostic xmlns="http://cisco.com/ns/yang/Cisco-IOS-XE
-diagnostics">
            <bootup>
                <level>minimal</level>
            </bootup>
        </diagnostic>
    </native>
    <licensing xmlns="http://cisco.com/ns/yang/cisco-smart-licen
se">
        <config>
            <enable>false</enable>
            <privacy>
                <hostname>false</hostname>
                <version>false</version>
            </privacy>
            <utility>
                <utility-enable>false</utility-enable>
            </utility>
```

Python Code (JSON)

```python
1  import xmltodict from ncclient
2  import manager
3  import json
4  import xml.dom.minidom
5
6  HOST = 'ios-xe-mgmt-latest.cisco.com'
7  PORT = '10000'
8  USER = 'developer'
9  PASS = 'C1sco12345'
10
11  m = manager.connect(host = HOST, port = PORT, username = USER,
12    password = PASS, hostkey_verify = False,
13    device_params = {
14      'name': 'default'
15    },
16    look_for_keys = False, allow_agent = False)
17
18  running_config_xml = m.get_config('running')
19  running_config_json = xmltodict.parse(str(running_config_xml))#
        printing running - config in XML
20  print(xml.dom.minidom.parseString(str(running_config_xml
        )).toprettyxml())
```

Code Output (Truncated)

Before we move on from NETCONF examples, let us go over the device handlers that are supported by the ncclient. You can notice, in all our code, we used the 'default' device handler which is the same as "csr" for the Cisco CSR1000v device.

Juniper: device_params={'name':'junos'}
Cisco CSR: device_params={'name':'csr'}
Cisco Nexus: device_params={'name':'nexus'}
Huawei: device_params={'name':'huawei'}
Alcatel Lucent: device_params={'name':'alu'}
H3C: device_params={'name':'h3c'}
HP Comware: device_params={'name':'hpcomware'}

Let me note down some code choices that we have made when using ncclient and why.

- <u>Manager</u> object is used to lookup operations, e.g., get_config etc.

```
ncclient.manager.OPERATIONS
= {'delete_config': <class 'ncclient.operations.edit.DeleteConfig'>, 'get_schema': <class
'ncclient.operations.retrieve.GetSchema'>, 'get': <class 'ncclient.operations.retrieve.Get'>, 'lock': <class
'ncclient.operations.lock.Lock'>, 'copy_config': <class 'ncclient.operations.edit.CopyConfig'>, 'close_session':
<class 'ncclient.operations.session.CloseSession'>, 'dispatch': <class 'ncclient.operations.retrieve.Dispatch'>,
'poweroff_machine': <class 'ncclient.operations.flowmon.PoweroffMachine'>, 'unlock': <class
'ncclient.operations.lock.Unlock'>, 'get_config': <class 'ncclient.operations.retrieve.GetConfig'>, 'kill_session':
<class 'ncclient.operations.session.KillSession'>, 'discard_changes': <class
'ncclient.operations.edit.DiscardChanges'>, 'commit': <class 'ncclient.operations.edit.Commit'>, 'edit_config':
<class 'ncclient.operations.edit.EditConfig'>, 'validate': <class 'ncclient.operations.edit.Validate'>,
'reboot_machine': <class 'ncclient.operations.flowmon.RebootMachine'>}
```

- Mostly, we're using the following template to connect into the device via NETCONF

```
1  m = manager.connect(
2    host = env_lab.IOS_XE_1["host"],
3    port = env_lab.IOS_XE_1["netconf_port"],
4    username = env_lab.IOS_XE_1["username"],
5    password = env_lab.IOS_XE_1["password"],
6    hostkey_verify = False
7  )
```

- close_session() method is used to close the NETCONF session, i.e., m.close_session(). However, when you use "with manage.connect <> as blah:", it automatically closes the connection once the transaction is done.
- xmltodict comes handy to parse XML to dictionary and thus making it compatible with JSON encoding for further processing. Remember, JSON is a serialization construct thus making it easier to sort and transmit between systems, whereas dictionary is a data structure to use inside your code. However, they both represent objects as name/value pairs.
- We've already discussed xml.dom.minidom library, which is one of the two popular methods to process XML format.
- XML to dictionary conversion can be done with a single line of code. "xml_data" below represents raw XML data.

```
1  Netconf_info = xmltodict.parse(str(xml_data))["rpc - reply"]["data"]
```

- You can also add or delete IOS XE configuration using Manager object, however in both cases, you need to first construct an XML configuration template.

YANG and RESTCONF Example

RESTCONF uses REST APIs and HTTPS port 443 for transport. To configure RESTCONF, you also need to enable HTTPS server and restconf and add a priv 15 user.

Enabling HTTPS server and RESTCONF

```
[csr1000v-1(config)#ip http sec
[csr1000v-1(config)#ip http secure-ser
 csr1000v-1(config)#ip http secure-server ?
  <cr>  <cr>

[csr1000v-1(config)#ip http secure-server
[csr1000v-1(config)#
[csr1000v-1(config)#restconf
[csr1000v-1(config)#
 csr1000v-1(config)#
```

To connect and execute our RESTCONF API calls, we can use various python libraries.

- netmiko
- requests (REST get/post call etc.)
- json (encoding support)

```
 1   import json
 2   import requests
 3   import sys
 4   from argparse import ArgumentParser
 5   from collections import OrderedDict
 6   import urllib3
 7
 8   # Disable SSL Warnings, optional.
 9   urllib3.disable_warnings(urllib3.exceptions.InsecureRequestWarning
        )
10
11   # These variables target the RESTCONF Always - On Sandbox hosted
        by Cisco DevNet
12   HOST = 'ios-xe-mgmt-latest.cisco.com'
13   PORT = '9443'
14   USER = 'developer'
15   PASS = 'C1sco12345'
16
17   # Identifies the interface on the device used
18   for management access# Used to ensure the script isn 't used to
        update the IP leveraged to manage device
19   MANAGEMENT_INTERFACE = "GigabitEthernet1"
20
21   # Create the base URL
22   for RESTCONF calls
23   url_base = "https://{h}:{p}/restconf".format(h = HOST, p = PORT)
24
25   # Identify yang + json as the data formats
26   headers = {
27     'Content-Type': 'application/yang-data+json',
28     'Accept': 'application/yang-data+json'
29   }
30
31   # Define our 5 functions
32
33   # Function to retrieve the list of interfaces on a device
34   def get_configured_interfaces():
35     url = url_base + "/data/ietf-interfaces:interfaces"
36
37   # this statement performs a GET on the specified url
38   response = requests.get(url,
39     auth = (USER, PASS),
40     headers = headers,
41     verify = False
42   )
43
44   #
45   return the json as text
46   return response.json()["ietf-interfaces:interfaces"]["interface"]
47
48   # Used to configure the IP address on an interface
49   def configure_ip_address(interface, ip): #RESTCONF URL
50   for specific interface
```

```python
51   url = url_base + "/data/ietf-interfaces:interfaces/interface={i}"
        .format(i = interface)
52
53   # Create the data payload to reconfigure IP address# Need to use
        OrderedDicts to maintain the order of elements
54   data = OrderedDict([('ietf-interfaces:interface',
55     OrderedDict([
56       ('name', interface),
57       ('type', 'iana-if-type:ethernetCsmacd'),
58       ('ietf-ip:ipv4',
59         OrderedDict([
60           ('address', [OrderedDict([
61             ('ip', ip["address"]),
62             ('netmask', ip["mask"])
63           ])])
64         ])
65       ),
66     ])
67   )])
68
69   # Use PUT request to update data
70   response = requests.put(url,
71     auth = (USER, PASS),
72     headers = headers,
73     verify = False,
74     json = data
75   )
76   print(response.text)
77
78   # Retrieve and print the current configuration of an interface
79   def print_interface_details(interface):
80     url = url_base + "/data/ietf-interfaces:interfaces/interface
          ={i}".format(i = interface)
81
82   # this statement performs a GET on the specified url
83   response = requests.get(url,
84     auth = (USER, PASS),
85     headers = headers,
86     verify = False
87   )
88
89   intf = response.json()["ietf-interfaces:interface"]#
90   return the json as text
91   print("Name: ", intf["name"])
92   try:
93   print("IP Address: ", intf["ietf-ip:ipv4"]["address"][0]["ip"], "
        /",
94     intf["ietf-ip:ipv4"]["address"][0]["netmask"])
95   except KeyError:
96     print("IP Address: UNCONFIGURED")
97   print()
98
99   return (intf)
100
```

```
101  # Ask the user to select an interface to configure.Ensures input
         is valid
102 ▾ def interface_selection(interfaces): #Ask User which interface to
         configure
103  sel = input("Which Interface do you want to configure? ")
104
105  # Validate interface input# Must be an interface on the device AND
         NOT be the Management Interface
106  while sel == MANAGEMENT_INTERFACE or not sel in [intf["name"]
107      for intf in interfaces
108 ▾ ]:
109    print("INVALID:  Select an available interface.")
110  print("          " + MANAGEMENT_INTERFACE + " is used for
         management.")
111  print("          Choose another Interface")
112  sel = input("Which Interface do you want to configure? ")
113
114  return (sel)
115
116  # Asks the user to provide an IP address and Mask.Data is NOT
         validated.
117 ▾ def get_ip_info(): #Ask User
118  for IP and Mask
119  ip = {}
120  ip["address"] = input("What IP address do you want to set? ")
121  ip["mask"] = input("What Subnet Mask do you want to set? ")
122  return (ip)
123
124  # try out functions with user input# Get a List of Interfaces
125  interfaces = get_configured_interfaces()
126
127  print("The router has the following interfaces: \n")
128 ▾ for interface in interfaces:
129    print("  * {name:25}".format(name = interface["name"]))
130
131  print("")
132
133  # Ask User which interface to configure
134  selected_interface = interface_selection(interfaces)
135  print(selected_interface)
136
137  # Print Starting Interface Details
138  print("Starting Interface Configuration")
139  print_interface_details(selected_interface)
140
141  # As User
142  for IP Address to set
143  ip = get_ip_info()
144
145  # Configure interface
146  configure_ip_address(selected_interface, ip)
147
148  # Print Ending Interface Details
149  print("Ending Interface Configuration")
```

```
150  print_interface_details(selected_interface)
151
152  # Get a List of Interfaces
153  interfaces = get_configured_interfaces()
154
155  print("The router has the following interfaces: \n")
156  for interface in interfaces:
157    print("  * {name:25}".format(name = interface["name"]))
158  print("")# Ask User which interface to configure
159  selected_interface = interface_selection(interfaces)
160  print(selected_interface)
161
162  # Print Starting Interface Details
163  print("Starting Interface Configuration")
164  print_interface_details(selected_interface)
165
166  # As User
167  for IP Address to set
168  ip = get_ip_info()
169
170  # Configure interface
171  configure_ip_address(selected_interface, ip)
172
173  # Print Ending Interface Details
174  print("Ending Interface Configuration")
175  print_interface_details(selected_interface)
```

Code Output

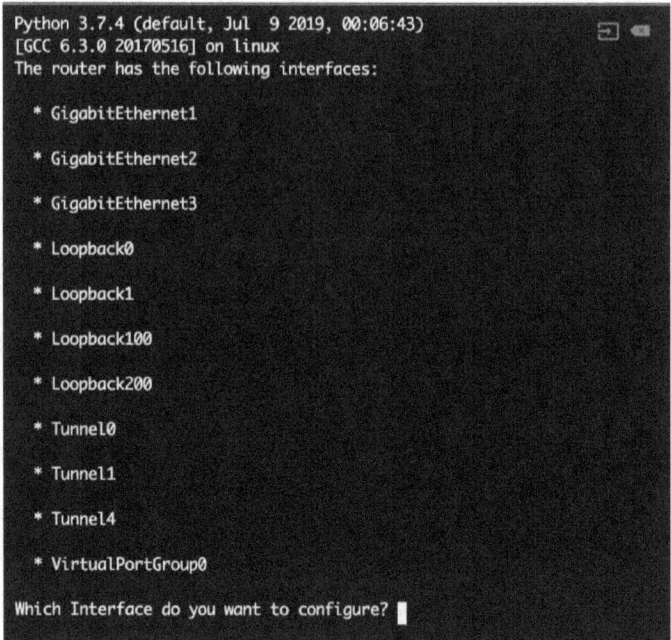

```
Python 3.7.4 (default, Jul  9 2019, 00:06:43)
[GCC 6.3.0 20170516] on linux
The router has the following interfaces:

 * GigabitEthernet1

 * GigabitEthernet2

 * GigabitEthernet3

 * Loopback0

 * Loopback1

 * Loopback100

 * Loopback200

 * Tunnel0

 * Tunnel1

 * Tunnel4

 * VirtualPortGroup0

Which Interface do you want to configure?
```

Here, we modify the IP address on the GigabitEthernet3 interface using a HTTP PUT method.

```
Which Interface do you want to configure? GigabitEthernet3
GigabitEthernet3
Starting Interface Configuration
Name:  GigabitEthernet3
IP Address:  10.100.2.1 / 255.255.255.0

What IP address do you want to set? 172.16.1.1
What Subnet Mask do you want to set? 255.255.255.0

Ending Interface Configuration
Name:  GigabitEthernet3
IP Address:  172.16.1.1 / 255.255.255.0

>
```

First, we import necessary libraries and then set our variables for authentication into our target CSR1000v instance. We set our HTTP request header to be application/yang-data+json and define our functions. Finally, we call our functions or methods, take user input and change IP address on the interface as requested. 9443/HTTPS port is being used for RESTCONF.

Construct code to perform a specific operation based on a set of requirements and given API reference documentation

Obtain a list of network devices by using Meraki, Cisco DNA Center, ACI, Cisco SD-WAN, or NSO.

List of Devices using Meraki API

Python Code

```
1   from meraki import meraki
2
3   apikey = "448e00b44c40d9b3087b5b20f78cb7c12772ea37"
4   myOrgs = meraki.myorgaccess(apikey)# print(myOrgs)
5   orgid = "641762946900403561"
6   myNetworks = meraki.getnetworklist(apikey, orgid)# print(myNetworks
        )
7   networkid = "N_641762946900876741"
8   deviceList = meraki.getnetworkdevices(apikey, networkid)
9   print(deviceList)
10  serialnum = "VRT-2207619790753"
11  clientList = meraki.getclients(apikey, serialnum)# print(clientList
        )
```

Code Output

```
Python 3.7.4 (default, Jul  9 2019, 00:06:43)
[GCC 6.3.0 20170516] on linux
Organization Operation Successful - See returned data for results

Network Operation Successful - See returned data for results

Network Operation Successful - See returned data for results

[{'lat': 30.2668049218999, 'lng': -97.7437949180603, 'address': None, 'seria
l': 'VRT-2207619790755', 'mac': '02:02:00:64:b7:a3', 'lanIp': '10.1.250.41',
 'networkId': 'N_641762946900876741', 'name': 'Office POE switch #2', 'model
': 'MS22P', 'switchProfileId': None, 'firmware': 'switch-11-22', 'floorPlanI
d': None}, {'lat': 30.2668280878068, 'lng': -97.7438807487488, 'address': No
ne, 'serial': 'VRT-2207619790754', 'mac': '02:02:00:64:b7:a2', 'lanIp': None
, 'networkId': 'N_641762946900876741', 'name': 'Office POE switch #3', 'mode
l': 'MS22P', 'switchProfileId': None, 'firmware': 'Not running configured ve
rsion', 'floorPlanId': None}, {'lat': 30.2668002887179, 'lng': -97.743730545
0439, 'address': None, 'serial': 'VRT-2207619790753', 'mac': '02:02:00:64:b7
:a1', 'lanIp': '10.2.250.26', 'networkId': 'N_641762946900876741', 'name': '
Office POE switch #1', 'model': 'MS22P', 'switchProfileId': None, 'firmware'
: 'switch-11-22', 'floorPlanId': None}]
HTTP Status Code: 404 - No returned data

None
> []
```

Manage spaces, participants, and messages in WebEx Teams

List of Spaces using WebEx Teams API

GET https://api.ciscospark.com/v1/rooms
Bearer <access-token>

There are total of seven spaces and the response below includes all of them. The output below has been truncated for brevity.

```
{
  "items": [
    {
      "id": "Y2lzY29zcGFyazovL3VzL1JPT00vNjkyOTgyMzAtZWQyZC0xMWU5LThlNGItZGI4NmQ3ZGMwNmFl",
      "title": "Unicorn",
      "type": "group",
      "isLocked": false,
```

    "lastActivity": "2019-10-12T20:18:10.515Z",

    "creatorId":
"Y2lzY29zcGFyazovL3VzL1BFT1BMRS9kNWY3OWVlOC0xZWVmLTQ0YTctODYwZS00
NjZhYTgzNDc3Yjg",

    "created": "2019-10-12T20:18:10.515Z",

    "ownerId": "0d609cde-0645-4583-8fe9-b00c0b6f42f3"

  },

  {

    "id":
"Y2lzY29zcGFyazovL3VzL1JPT00vZTViMTU5YTAtZWQyYy0xMWU5LTk1MTQtZTMzY
WIwZjFlMTQw",

    "title": "Space-2 (via API)",

    "type": "group",

    "isLocked": false,

    "lastActivity": "2019-10-12T20:14:29.946Z",

    "creatorId":
"Y2lzY29zcGFyazovL3VzL1BFT1BMRS9kNWY3OWVlOC0xZWVmLTQ0YTctODYwZS00
NjZhYTgzNDc3Yjg",

    "created": "2019-10-12T20:14:29.946Z",

    "ownerId": "0d609cde-0645-4583-8fe9-b00c0b6f42f3"

  },

  {

    "id":
"Y2lzY29zcGFyazovL3VzL1JPT00vNzExNWFhNjAtZWQyYy0xMWU5LWI5NTYtOTk3YT
A5NWYxNTUw",

    "title": "FSN-SEA",

  }

]

}

Posting a message into a Room or Space

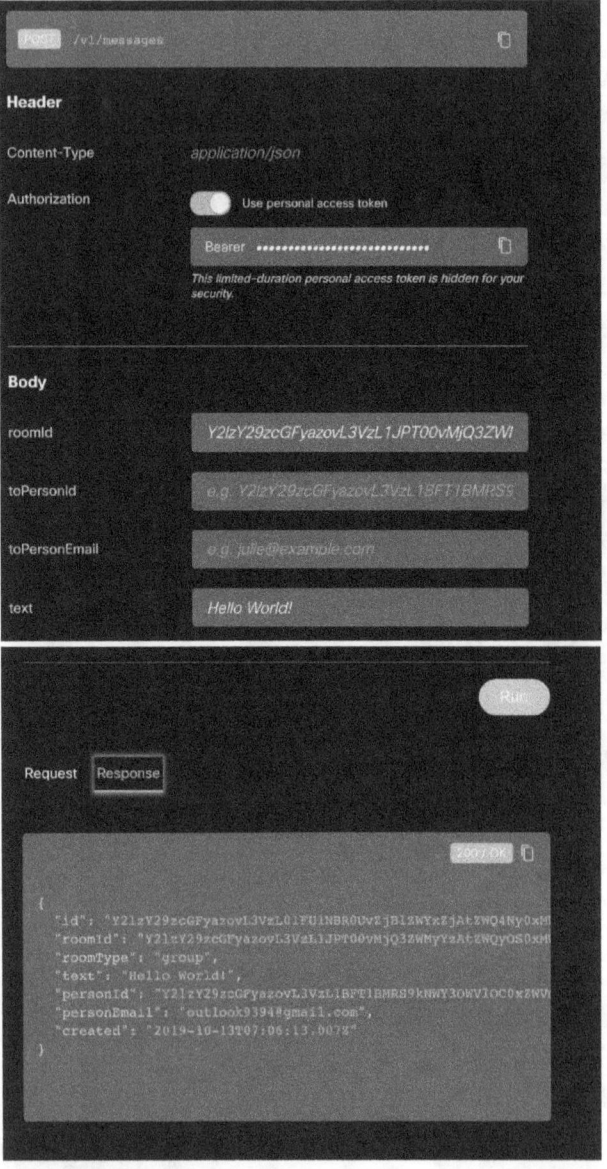

As you can see below, our message "Hello World!" was posted to FSN-SJC General Space.

Obtain a list of clients / hosts seen on a network using Cisco DNA Center

Get network device list using DNA Center

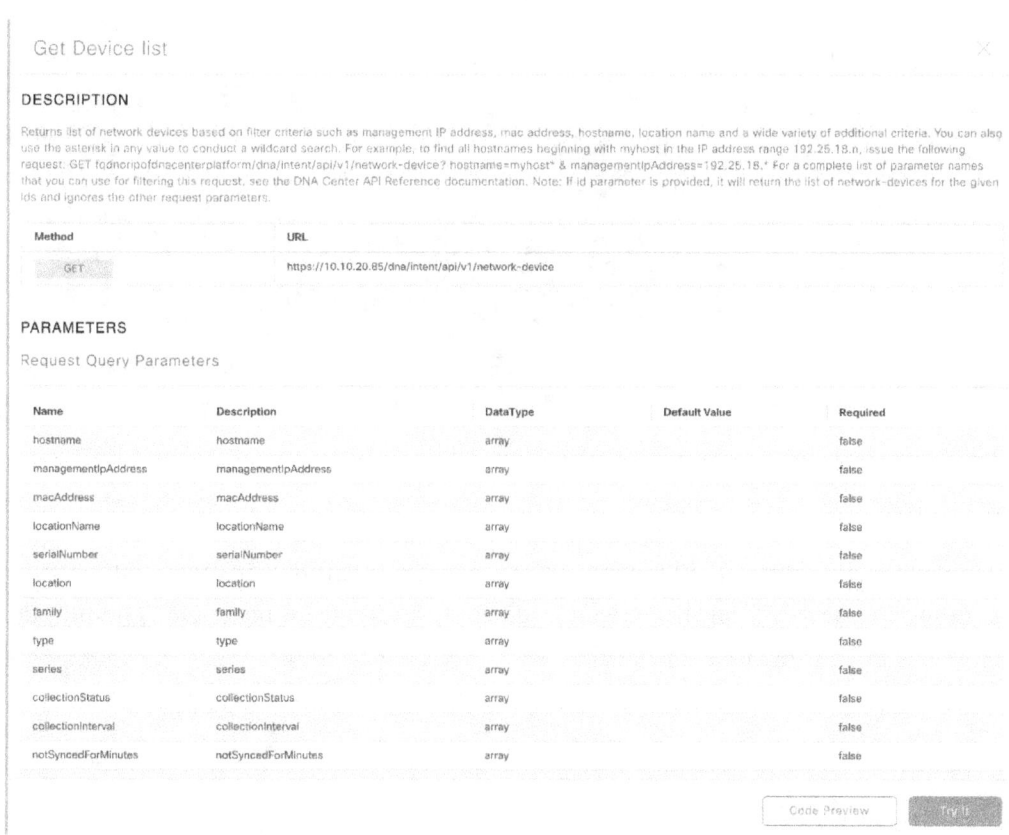

Get Device list

DESCRIPTION

Returns list of network devices based on filter criteria such as management IP address, mac address, hostname, location name and a wide variety of additional criteria. You can also use the asterisk in any value to conduct a wildcard search. For example, to find all hostnames beginning with myhost in the IP address range 192.25.18.n, issue the following request: GET fqdnoripofdnacenterplatform/dna/intent/api/v1/network-device? hostname=myhost* & managementIpAddress=192.25.18.* For a complete list of parameter names that you can use for filtering this request, see the DNA Center API Reference documentation. Note: If id parameter is provided, it will return the list of network-devices for the given ids and ignores the other request parameters.

Method	URL
GET	https://10.10.20.85/dna/intent/api/v1/network-device

PARAMETERS

Request Query Parameters

Name	Description	DataType	Default Value	Required
hostname	hostname	array		false
managementIpAddress	managementIpAddress	array		false
macAddress	macAddress	array		false
locationName	locationName	array		false
serialNumber	serialNumber	array		false
location	location	array		false
family	family	array		false
type	type	array		false
series	series	array		false
collectionStatus	collectionStatus	array		false
collectionInterval	collectionInterval	array		false
notSyncedForMinutes	notSyncedForMinutes	array		false

Code Preview   Try It

Try Now   ✕

license.status	licenseStatus
module+name	moduleName
module+equpimenttype	moduleEqupimentType
module+servicestate	moduleServiceState
module+vendorequipmenttype	moduleVendorEquipmentType
module+partnumber	modulePartNumber
module+operationstatecode	moduleOperationStateCode
id	Accepts comma separated id's and return list of network-devices for the given id's. If invalid or not-found id's are provided, null entry will be returned in the list.

Response

```
 1  {
 2      "response": [
 3          {
 4              "family": "Switches and Hubs",
 5              "errorCode": "DEV-UNREACHED",
 6              "type": "Cisco Catalyst38xx stack-able ethernet switch",
 7              "macAddress": "f8:b7:e2:bf:eb:80",
 8              "location": null,
 9              "hostname": "C3850-SW01.testlab.com",
10              "softwareType": "IOS-XE",
11              "softwareVersion": "16.9.4",
12              "serialNumber": "FCW2137C0HL",
13              "collectionInterval": "Global Default"
```

Cancel   Run

Below is the JSON encoded response that shows the complete device list including the device's family, host name, MAC address, up time, etc. The output below has been truncated for brevity.

```
{
  "response": [
    {
```

"family": "Switches and Hubs",

"errorCode": "DEV-UNREACHED",

"type": "Cisco Catalyst38xx stack-able ethernet switch",

"macAddress": "f8:b7:e2:bf:eb:80",

"location": null,

"hostname": "C3850-SW01.testlab.com",

"softwareType": "IOS-XE",

"softwareVersion": "16.9.4",

"serialNumber": "FCW2137C0HL",

"collectionInterval": "Global Default",

"inventoryStatusDetail": "<status><general code=\"DEV_UNREACHED\"/></status>",

"lastUpdateTime": 1570950332462,

"upTime": "4 days, 5:21:49.34",

"role": "CORE",

"roleSource": "MANUAL",

"apManagerInterfaceIp": "",

"associatedWlcIp": "",

"bootDateTime": "2019-09-25 19:08:48",

"collectionStatus": "Partial Collection Failure",

"errorDescription": "SNMP timeouts are occurring with this device. Either the SNMP credentials are not correctly provided to controller or the device is responding slow and snmp timeout is low. If its a timeout issue, controller will attempt to progressively adjust the timeout in subsequent collection cycles to get device to managed state. User can also run discovery again only for this device using the discovery feature after adjusting the timeout and snmp credentials as required. Or user can update the timeout and snmp credentials as required using update credentials.",

"interfaceCount": "65",

"lastUpdated": "2019-10-13 07:05:32",

"lineCardCount": "2",

    "lineCardId": "a45a013d-1b33-4470-bf98-8287035b76f3, 5ff5f4ff-bf33-4096-ac54-d37878cbcb99",

    "locationName": null,

    "managementIpAddress": "10.10.20.80",

    "memorySize": "852280752",

    "platformId": "WS-C3850-48P-E",

    "reachabilityFailureReason": "SNMP Connectivity Failed",

    "reachabilityStatus": "Unreachable",

    "series": "Cisco Catalyst 3850 Series Ethernet Stackable Switch",

    "snmpContact": "",

    "snmpLocation": "",

    "tagCount": "0",

    "tunnelUdpPort": null,

    "waasDeviceMode": null,

    "instanceUuid": "25f64f9d-4e35-4e9f-baae-849240072be5",

    "instanceTenantId": "SYS0",

    "id": "25f64f9d-4e35-4e9f-baae-849240072be5"

  },

  {

    "family": "Switches and Hubs",

    "errorCode": "DEV-UNREACHED",

    "type": "Cisco Catalyst 9300 Switch",

    "macAddress": "f8:7b:20:71:64:00",

    "location": null,

    "hostname": "C9300-SW01.testlab.com",

    "softwareType": "IOS-XE",

    "softwareVersion": "16.9.4",

    "serialNumber": "FCW2141L001",

"collectionInterval": "Global Default",

"inventoryStatusDetail": "<status><general code=\"DEV_UNREACHED\"/></status>",

"lastUpdateTime": 1570951206171,

"upTime": "2:24:23.77",

"role": "ACCESS",

"roleSource": "AUTO",

"apManagerInterfaceIp": "",

],

"version": "1.0"

Get Overall Network Health using DNA Center

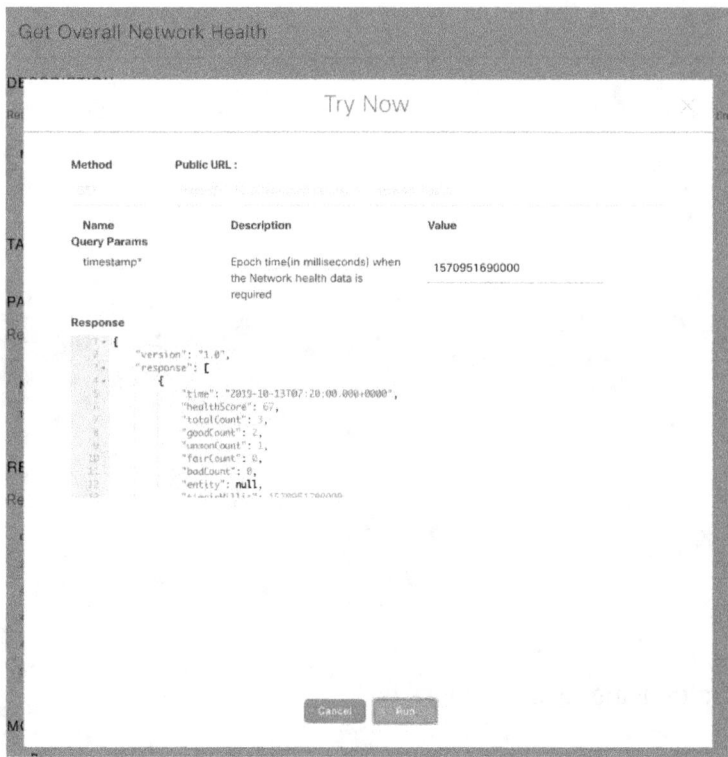

Below is the complete response that shows the overall network health including health scores.

```json
{
  "version": "1.0",
  "response": [
    {
      "time": "2019-10-13T07:20:00.000+0000",
      "healthScore": 67,
      "totalCount": 3,
      "goodCount": 2,
      "unmonCount": 1,
      "fairCount": 0,
      "badCount": 0,
      "entity": null,
      "timeinMillis": 1570951200000
    }
  ],
  "measuredBy": "global",
  "latestMeasuredByEntity": null,
  "latestHealthScore": 67,
  "monitoredDevices": 2,
  "monitoredHealthyDevices": 2,
  "monitoredUnHealthyDevices": 0,
  "unMonitoredDevices": 1,
  "healthDistirubution": [
    {
      "category": "Core",
      "totalCount": 1,
```

```
    "healthScore": 100,
    "goodPercentage": 100,
    "badPercentage": 0,
    "fairPercentage": 0,
    "unmonPercentage": 0,
    "goodCount": 1,
    "badCount": 0,
    "fairCount": 0,
    "unmonCount": 0,
    "kpiMetrics": []
  },
  {
    "category": "Access",
    "totalCount": 2,
    "healthScore": 50,
    "goodPercentage": 50,
    "badPercentage": 0,
    "fairPercentage": 0,
    "unmonPercentage": 50,
    "goodCount": 1,
    "badCount": 0,
    "fairCount": 0,
    "unmonCount": 1,
    "kpiMetrics": []
  }
]
```

```
}
```

Get Site topology details using Cisco DNA

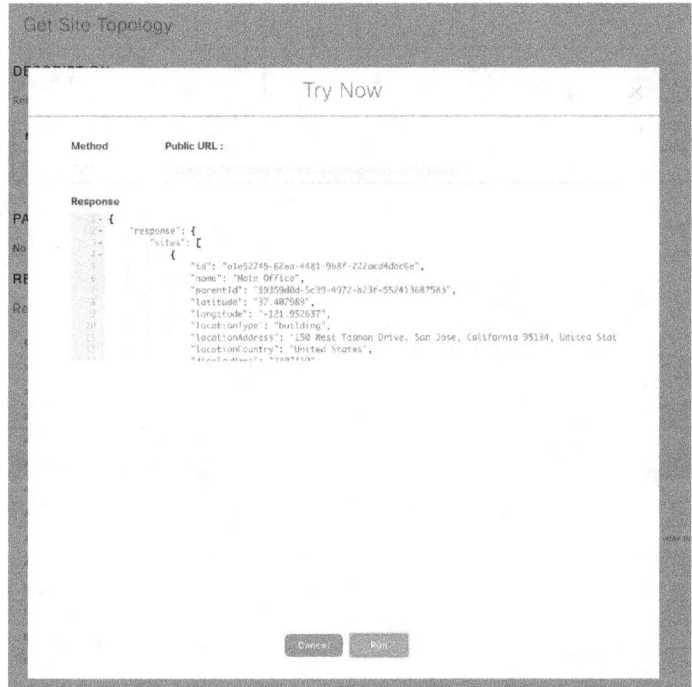

Below is the response that shows the topology details from all sites with information such as name, location, latitude, longitude, etc. The output has been truncated for brevity.

```
{
  "response": {
    "sites": [
      {
        "id": "e1c52245-62ca-4481-9b8f-222acd4dbc6e",
```

"name": "Main Office",

"parentId": "89359d0d-5c39-4972-b23f-552413687583",

"latitude": "37.407989",

"longitude": "-121.952637",

"locationType": "building",

"locationAddress": "150 West Tasman Drive, San Jose, California 95134, United States",

"locationCountry": "United States",

"displayName": "2407419",

"groupNameHierarchy": "Global/Testlab/Main Office"
},
{

"id": "89359d0d-5c39-4972-b23f-552413687583",

"name": "Testlab",

"parentId": "8b820681-a903-4b7b-b803-e32c1f5c0c7e",

"latitude": "",

"longitude": "",

"locationType": "area",

"locationAddress": "",

"locationCountry": "",

"displayName": "2407417",

"groupNameHierarchy": "Global/Testlab"
},
{

"id": "4e3e7a6c-b41a-49a6-b7a1-6663facf4b62",

"name": "San Jose",

```
            "parentId": "8b820681-a903-4b7b-b803-e32c1f5c0c7e",

            "latitude": "",

            "longitude": "",

            "locationType": "area",

            "locationAddress": "",

            "locationCountry": "",

            "displayName": "2407421",

            "groupNameHierarchy": "Global/San Jose"
        },

        {

            "id": "700b0be0-7291-4b6f-91b2-d32763ca2020",

            "name": "Aurangabad",

            "parentId": "8b820681-a903-4b7b-b803-e32c1f5c0c7e",

            "latitude": "",

            "longitude": "",

            "locationType": "area",

            "locationAddress": "",

            "locationCountry": "",

            "displayName": "2407422",

            "groupNameHierarchy": "Global/Aurangabad"

        }

    ]

},

"version": "1.0"

}
```

Further Reading

Introduction to Cisco DNA Center Northbound APIs[33]
Cisco DNA Center API Overview[34]
Cisco DNA Center Northbound API Modules[35]
What and Why of Model Driven Programmability[36]
Introducing YANG Data Modeling for the Network[37]
Exploring IOS XE YANG Data Models with NETCONF[38]
Exploring IOS XE YANG Data Models with RESTCONF[39]
Invoke WebEx REST APIs from the interactive documentation[40]
Building Python Requests to Read and Create WebEx Teams API Items[41]
Understanding ACI[42]
ACI Programmability Options[43]
Introduction to ACI Toolkit[44]
Introduction to Cisco SD-WAN REST APIs[45]
Cisco SD-WAN CLI application developed using the vManage REST API[46]

---

[33] https://bit.ly/2II9pZX

[34] https://bit.ly/2Q9VnEn

[35] https://bit.ly/39M83cj

[36] https://bit.ly/2TXRJ1D

[37] https://bit.ly/2w3BvvZ

[38] https://bit.ly/3b0cTmP

[39] https://bit.ly/2W7S2tw

[40] https://bit.ly/2TZibb9

[41] https://bit.ly/2U38WH7

[42] https://bit.ly/2TSuXlg

[43] https://bit.ly/2TGUJ3o

[44] https://bit.ly/39NgXXk

[45] https://bit.ly/33e1aOQ

Using Postman to interact with the Cisco SD-WAN REST API[47]
NSO as a provisioning tool[48]
Nexus OS Programmability and Automation Overview[49]
Using the Meraki Dashboard API with postman[50]
Meraki Location Scanning API Python[51]
Meraki External Captive Portal[52]
Meraki Wireless Health[53]

---

[46] https://bit.ly/3aPEt61

[47] https://bit.ly/39Llj10

[48] https://bit.ly/38Kkcxp

[49] https://bit.ly/2TJZsS0

[50] https://bit.ly/33cbCpO

[51] https://bit.ly/3aOlQiH

[52] https://bit.ly/3aQ2RVa

[53] https://bit.ly/2Q6uQYQ

Chapter Summary

- The ACI policy model is based on promise theory which is about scalable control of objects rather than using the top-down paradigm.
- NX Toolkit is a bunch of python libraries that allow configuration of Cisco Nexus 9K and 3K series switches.
- ACI toolkit is a collection of python libraries that allow the configuration of the APIC controller
- YANG Development Kit (or YDK) is an SDK that provides APIs that are modeled in YANG to reduce the complexity with the help of APIs, by abstracting out the protocol or encoding details
- Guest Shell is a virtualized Linux-based (LXC) container environment that runs side by side the IOS XE, that separation allows secure execution of various scripts (such as Python) and other software packages
- Every Meraki device, i.e., APs, ethernet switches and security appliances connect over the internet to the Cisco Meraki cloud-based management platform.
- You can use Organization > Configure > Settings to enable REST API access to Meraki cloud platform.
- Once you've generated the Meraki cloud platform access REST API key, you can use either a Python script (with request module) or use Postman to access various Meraki information
- Cisco DNA Center is controller as well as an analytics platform that makes Cisco's intent-based networking possible. It consists of five major components.
  - Design
  - Policy
  - Provision
  - Assurance
  - Platform
- Northbound APIs, also known as, Intent APIs provide support for policy-based abstraction of business intent, allowing focus on business outcomes as opposed to mechanics of how
- vManage is the centralized management platform for configuring, monitoring and maintaining Cisco SD-WAN (formerly Viptela) devices

- vManage provides REST API access for retrieving real-time and configuration state information about the SD-WAN overlay.
- Cisco Network Services Orchestrator (or NSO, formerly Tail-f) provides lifecycle service automation with the YANG model-driven platform
- NSO (or Tail-f NCS) CLI comes in two flavors, Cisco (-C option) or Juniper.
- UCS Manager or UCSM is an all-in-one platform for managing all UCS components
- XML APIs are natively available from the UCSM API server, whereas RESTful APIs are available via UCS Integrated Management Controller (or IMC) Redfish
- UCS Director (or UCSD) is a powerful and multi-vendor data center management platform that can help you run your local data center including UCS much like a private IaaS cloud.
- Intersight is a cloud-based solution for Cisco UCS management which also includes HyperFlex. You can think of Intersight as a UCS Director as-a-service and some more.
- You can access Intersight using the web, PowerShell (via PowerTool) or Python SDK.
- AXL is a Simple Object Access Protocol (or SOAP) based API that enables CUCM provisioning.
- The User Data Services (or UDS) is a REST API interface into various resources and entities into CUCM. For example, you can manage user's devices, subscribed services, and speed dials.
- Cisco Finesse is a collaborative customer care software that provides agent and supervisor desktop for the entire ecosystem that interacts with your customer service organization.
- Cisco Finesse supports REST APIs and provides an SDK that you can use to perform user sign-in/out, agent states, call control, task routing, desktop chat, etc.
- Cisco Umbrella (formerly OpenDNS) is an anti-malware solution that uses DNS requests to perform malware inspection and content filtering.

- Cisco Identity Services Engine (or ISE) provides a network-based approach for security posture and trusted access everywhere based on identity context
- Cisco ISE offers automation and integration via External RESTful Services (or ERS) API.
- Cisco Threat Grid also offers REST API access
- NX-API REST uses HTTP/HTTPS for transport, and you can either JSON or XML for data encoding.
- Cisco Sandboxes are bare metal servers, real routers or switches, emulators and simulators running their respective software stacks pre-configured and pre-tested that are available to you at no cost.
- Code exchange features Repos from DevNet GitHub users.

CHAPTER 4 APPLICATION DEPLOYMENT AND SECURITY

This chapter covers the following exam topics from Cisco's official 200-901 V1.0 DevNet Associate exam blueprint.

- Describe benefits of edge computing
- Identify attributes of different application deployment models (private cloud, public cloud, hybrid cloud, and edge)
- Identify the attributes of these application deployment types
    - Virtual machines
    - Bare metal
    - Containers
- Describe components for a CI/CD pipeline in application deployments
- Construct a Python unit test
- Interpret contents of a Dockerfile
- Utilize Docker images in local developer environment
- Identify application security issues related to secret protection, encryption (storage and transport), and data handling
- Explain how firewall, DNS, load balancers, and reverse proxy in application deployment
- Describe top OWASP threats (such as XSS, SQL injections, and CSRF)
- Utilize Bash commands (file management, directory navigation, and environmental variables)
- Identify the principles of DevOps practices

Describe benefits of edge computing

Edge computing is a distributed data processing model where data is crunched and stored closer to the location of the end device, for example, an Internet of Things device such as network-based sensors, or connected cars or smart grid, etc. This is in contrast to the model where all traffic all the time is taken to the cloud or data center-based for data processing.

So, you may ask, why bother when you already have or can have virtually unlimited pools of computing storage in a data center? Well, edge computing provides a few critical service delivery benefits when compared to the cloud-based model.

- Quicker response times or real-time data processing, i.e., less service latency
- Network bandwidth savings, since not all data need to be backhauled to centralized data center from the endpoint
- Edge layer acts as computing offload for centralized or cloud-based data center resources

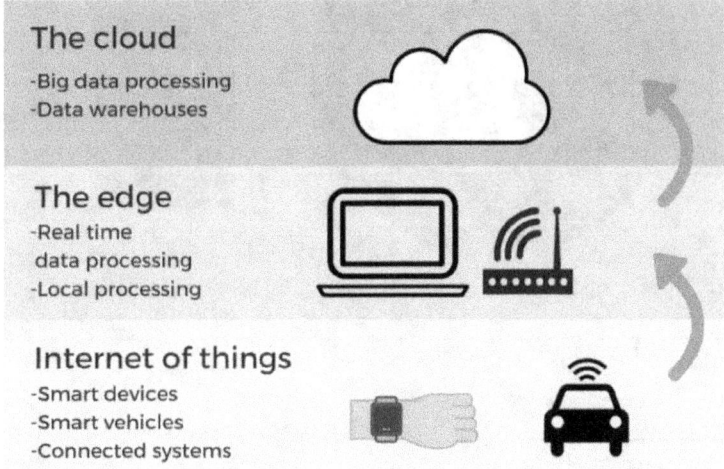

Another way to think about it is that cloud computing is for operating on big data whereas edge computing is for instantaneous or real-time data generated by sensors or endpoints.

Identify attributes of different application deployment models (private cloud, public cloud, hybrid cloud, and edge)

As per the RightScale Cloud Survey[54], the percentage of enterprises that have a multi-cloud strategy grew to 84 percent vs. 81 percent in 2018, which is no surprise given the cloud rise of cloud adoption over the last 8 years or so. The worldwide public cloud services market is projected to grow 17.5 percent in 2019 to an impressive total of $214.3 billion, up from $182.4 billion in 2018, according to the Gartner cloud forecast[55].

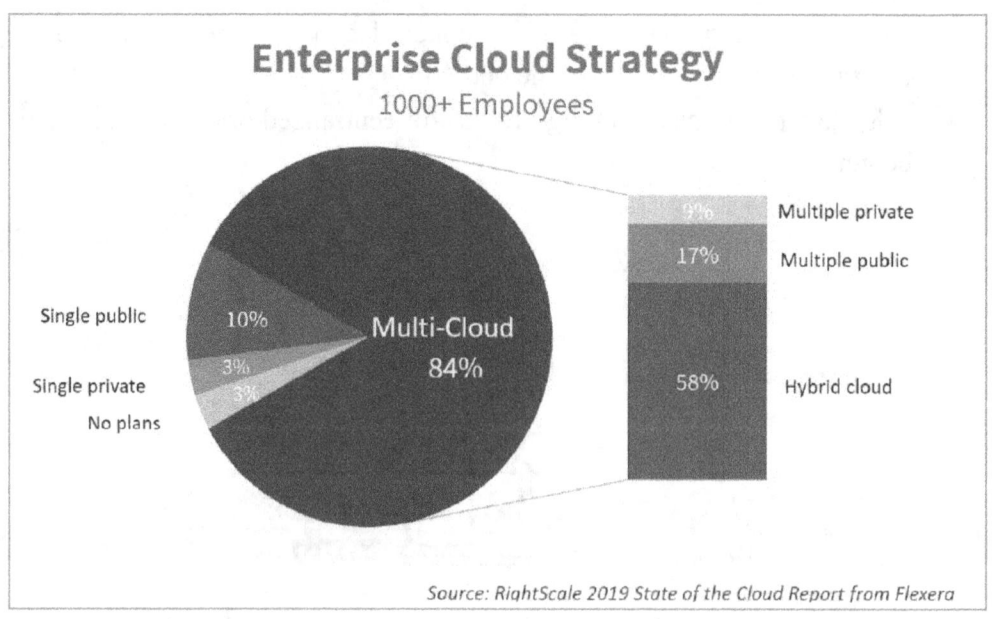

Source: RightScale 2019 State of the Cloud Report from Flexera

---

54 https://bit.ly/2OnGr4H

55 https://gtnr.it/38XA9k0

As cloud adoption picked up, purchasing and maintaining on-premise infrastructure went from an investment to a liability. While cloud and on-premise are two different deployment models, but behind the scene, enterprises still have a singular goal of implementing a lean and agile IT infrastructure that meets or exceeds a company's needs while optimizing the cost. There are three major types of infrastructure, or raw material if you like, that can be deployed on-premise or used in the cloud, i.e.

- Networking infrastructure (routers, switches, firewalls, load balancers what have you)
- Computing (x86 or ARM)
- Data Storage (traditional arrays or HCI)

Likewise, there are four popular cloud deployment and service models respectively.

Cloud Deployment Models

- Private cloud (run by a third-party provider in their own DC or within on-premise DC)
- Public cloud (run by a third-party provider in their own DC)
- Hybrid cloud (mix of public and private cloud)
- Multi-cloud (mix of various public clouds, private cloud is not mandatory)

Private Cloud

The private cloud is about offering computing services either over the Internet or a private internal network, such as WAN. In terms of service offering, private cloud is no different than public cloud but dedicated to the needs and goals of a single enterprise as opposed to being shared and multi-tenant. It is worth mentioning that the private cloud is not to be confused with its location, because it can be located on-premise (internal) or off-premise (hosted).

Due to single-tenant provisioning and dedicated use of resources, private clouds deliver a higher degree of control and customization, as well as a higher level of security and privacy. Private cloud also provides better service SLAs and data security when hosted on-premise or what is known as an internal cloud.

One drawback of an internal cloud is that the company's central IT department is held responsible for the cost and accountability of managing the cloud leading to similar staffing, management, and maintenance expenses as traditional data center ownership. Private clouds can be either self or provider-managed such as Rackspace.

Private Cloud
(On-premise or internal)

Private Cloud
(Off-premise or hosted)

Virtual Private Cloud (VPC)

Virtual private cloud (or VPC) is a private cloud carved out inside a public cloud for the sole purpose of being used by a single tenant. It provides isolation of data both in transit and at-rest resulting in enhanced security and data control.

Cloud provider will let you provision a cloud router and a firewall, so you can connect remote or on-premise resources to a VPC. AWS provides features such as security groups, ACLs and flow logs that capture information about the IP traffic going to and from network interfaces within your VPC.

Public Cloud

The public cloud is defined as computing services offered by third-party providers, such as AWS, over the public Internet, making them available to anyone who wants to use or purchase them. Cloud services may be free or sold on-demand i.e., pay-as-you-go, allowing customers to pay only per usage for the CPU cycles, storage, or bandwidth they use. Public cloud users simply sign up for a service, use the resources made available to them, and pay for what they used within a given amount of time.

As per the CLOUD VISION 2020 survey, digital transformation, IT agility and DevOps are the top drivers for public cloud adoption.

Public Cloud Drivers

How much is each of these trends or factors driving public cloud engagement?
Today vs 2020
(Somewhat/Extremely significant)

	Today	2020
Digital Transformation	Today, 63%	2020, 62%
IT Agility	Today, 62%	2020, 64%
DevOps	Today, 58%	2020, 57%
Mobility	Today, 55%	2020, 59%
AI/Machine Learning	Today, 50%	2020, 66%
IoT	Today, 45%	2020, 58%

Technically speaking, a public cloud is a pool of virtual resources that include computing, storage and networking, all developed from commodity hardware owned and managed by a third-party provider such as AWS or Azure, that is automatically provisioned and allocated among multiple customers in a multi-tenant fashion through a self-service interface. It's an economically compelling way to scale out workloads that experience unexpected demand fluctuations.

A public cloud is the simplest form of all cloud deployments: A customer that needs more resources and platforms such as servers or storage, or services simply pays a public cloud vendor by the hour or the minute, to get access to what's needed when it's needed. Infrastructure, computing power, storage, or cloud applications are decoupled from underlying hardware with the help of virtualization by the vendor, orchestrated mostly by open source management and automation software. Connectivity to a public cloud generally happens via the internet (obviously, encrypted) but also through dedicated low latency network connections available at large colocation data centers, much like AWS Direct Connect.

Hybrid Cloud

A hybrid cloud combines the benefits of public and private clouds by allowing data and applications to be shared between them. When workload demand changes, hybrid cloud computing allows businesses the ability to seamlessly scale using public cloud and thus handle overflow or demand bursts without giving third-party service providers access to the totality of their data.

Hybrid cloud architecture is the best of both worlds approach and that is what allows enterprises to run critical workloads in the private cloud and lower risk workloads in the public cloud and allocate resources from either environment as desired in an automated fashion via APIs. It's a setup that minimizes data exposure and allows medium to large enterprises to maintain a scalable, elastic, and secure portfolio of IT resources and services.

Using a hybrid cloud helps companies eliminate the need to make CAPEX investment to handle short-term or seasonal spikes in demand as well as when the business needs to free up on-premise resources for more sensitive data or applications. In summary, hybrid cloud computing delivers flexibility, scalability, elasticity and cost efficiencies with the lowest possible risk of data exposure.

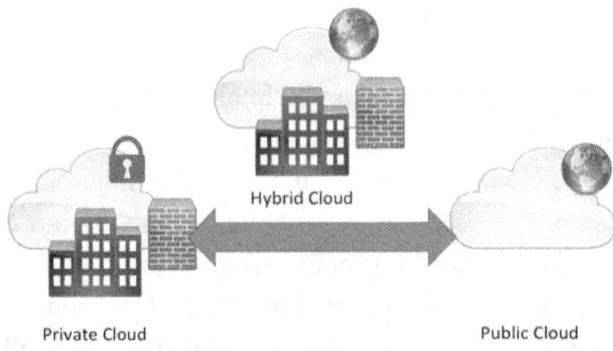

As per Cisco, there are five major challenges involved with deploying and managing a hybrid cloud, i.e.

- Cloud management
- OPEX
- Security
- No common ground
- Lack of expertise within IT

Multi-cloud

Multi-cloud is not yet another cloud model per se, but a cloud deployment approach made up of multiple cloud services, from multiple cloud service providers, public or private.

By definition, a "multi" cloud refers to the presence of more than one cloud deployment of the same type. Unlike hybrid clouds, multi-cloud refers to the presence of multiple clouds of the same type, e.g., two private clouds or two public clouds. The drivers behind the trends are avoiding vendor lock-in, cost savings, performance, better defenses against Distributed Denial of Service (DDoS) attacks, improved reliability and the existence of shadow IT.

IDC predicted that more than 85% of Enterprise IT organizations will chalk up a plan to use multi-cloud architectures by 2018. Cisco also said that a small number of gigantic hyper-scale data centers would hold just over half of all data center servers, and account for 69% of all data center processing power, and 65% of all data stored in data centers. Primarily on the basis of multi-cloud, Gartner also expects 80% of enterprises will have shut down their traditional data centers by 2025, up from just 10 percent today.

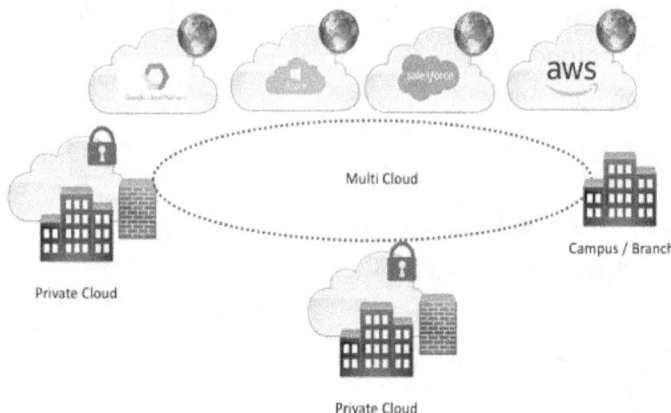

Let us compare the two major cloud models' side by side in the critical areas of capacity, control, cost, service SLAs, security and customization.

	Public	**Private**
Capacity	Multi-tenant, virtually unlimited resources	Single-tenant, limited resources (matched to demand)
Control	Shared with cloud service provider	Complete control to configure and manage resources
TCO	Shared resources, highest return on investment with no upfront costs Everything is OPEX	Non-shared resources with upfront costs, but predictable CAPEX + OPEX
Reliability or Service SLA	>= 99.99% (AWS) >= 99.99% (GCE)	Up to 99.999%
Security	Shared resources, lower	Non-shared

		resources, highest
Customization	Shared resources, limited	Non-shared resources, unlimited

Cloud Service Models

- Infrastructure as a Service (IaaS, e.g., AWS EC2/S3)
- Platform as a Service (PaaS, e.g., Salesforce Lightning Platform)
- Software as a Service (SaaS, e.g., Salesforce)

There is no one size fits all model to help you figure out whether on-premise or cloud is better for your organization, so you'll need to perform the due diligence to determine what works best. There are many different ways we can slice and dice the two models, so let's start with some of the key design components that are relevant to all enterprise deployments.

- Cost
- Security
- Agility and Scalability
- HA and Fault-tolerance
- Customization
- Compliance

	On-Premise	**Cloud**
Cost	CAPEX, lots of upfront costs	OPEX, Pay-as-you-go
Data Security	DC single-tenancy and full control over data	Shared, but superior data controls
Agility and Scalability	Long TTM and MTTR	Faster TTM and Elastic (scale up / scale down)
HA and Fault-tolerance	Can be multi-site, GEO redundant but cost	Multi-site, GEO redundant out of the box

	prohibitive	
Customization (HW + SW)	DC single-tenancy, highly customizable	IaaS: Shared, may be limited SaaS/PaaS: highly customizable
Compliance	DC single-tenancy, superior compliance due to span of control	Shared, meeting emergence compliance landscape can be difficult

In a nutshell, the cloud is here to stay (and grow), however, on-premise is not going away anytime soon either! Let's go over the core cloud concepts in a little more detail.

Cloud computing is the result of a well thought out infrastructure by the providers, in the same way, that electricity, water, and gas are the result of decades of infrastructural development by the utility providers. Cloud computing is made available through network connections in the same way that public utilities have been made available through networks of pipes and wires. By definition, all clouds are scalable (resources are added as demand rises) and elastic (resources grow or shrink as demand rises or falls).

As per Gartner[56], AWS, Azure, and GCE have about 47%, 22% and 8% public cloud market share respectively.

[56] https://bit.ly/37SKIVE

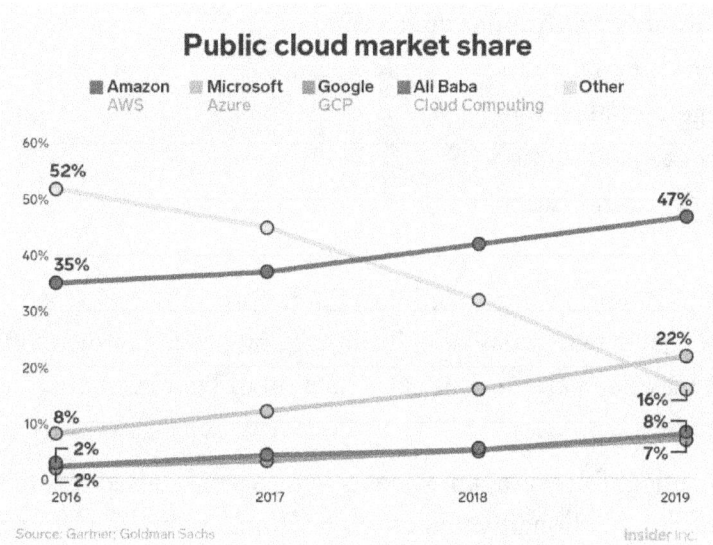

Cisco's definition of cloud outlines the following four aspects as must-have for a cloud service, i.e.

- On-demand means resources follow demand pattern, they are provisioned and deprovisioned with increasing and decreasing demands respectively
- At-scale, means cloud provider has enough supply of resources to meet demands from all its customers, i.e., providing cloud services at-scale.
- Multitenant, means cloud services are inherently multi-tenant out of the box
- Elastic means that corresponding cloud services will grow or shrink based on customer's demand patterns

Identify the attributes of these application deployment types

Virtualization is the process of creating a virtual representation of servers, storage, virtual applications, and networks, using software. The purpose of virtualization is to reduce IT expenses while boosting efficiency, flexibility, and scalability for any business. While virtualization has been around for a long time, it was VMware who pioneered x86 server virtualization.

Different types of virtualizations are as follows:
- Server virtualization
- Storage virtualization
- Network virtualization
- Desktop virtualization

Without virtualization, IT organizations will be forced to deploy a lot more servers to keep pace with today's high storage and processor demands. Each of these servers may be operating only at a fraction of their capacity, thus wasting precious resources.

Enter virtualization. Software, known as a hypervisor, is used to simulate hardware devices' functionality and create a virtual computing environment. Hypervisor allows you to split one system into separate virtual environments known as virtual machines (VMs). Hypervisor is simply a layer between the guest VMs and the underlying physical server hardware. Virtual Machines rely on the ability of the hypervisor to separate the machine's resources and distribute them as per the requirement.

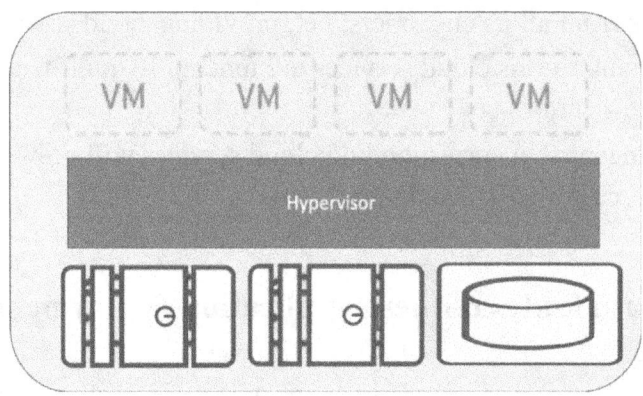

This enables IT organizations to run multiple applications across different operating systems, on a single server. This results in economies of scale and better efficiency.

Some of the additional benefits of virtualization are the following:

- Minimize or reduce downtime.
- Reduced capital and operating costs.
- Increased IT productivity, agility, efficiency and responsiveness.
- Faster provisioning of resources and applications.
- Greater business continuity and disaster recovery.
- Ease of data center management using Software.

Disadvantages of virtualization are the following:

- Increased upfront costs (investing in virtualization software).
- Need to license software.
- There may be a learning curve if IT managers are not experienced.
- Not every application and server will work in a virtualized environment.
- Availability can be an issue if an organization can't connect to their virtualized data.

Hypervisor Type 1 and Type 2

There are two types of hypervisors, i.e., Type-1 and Type-2.

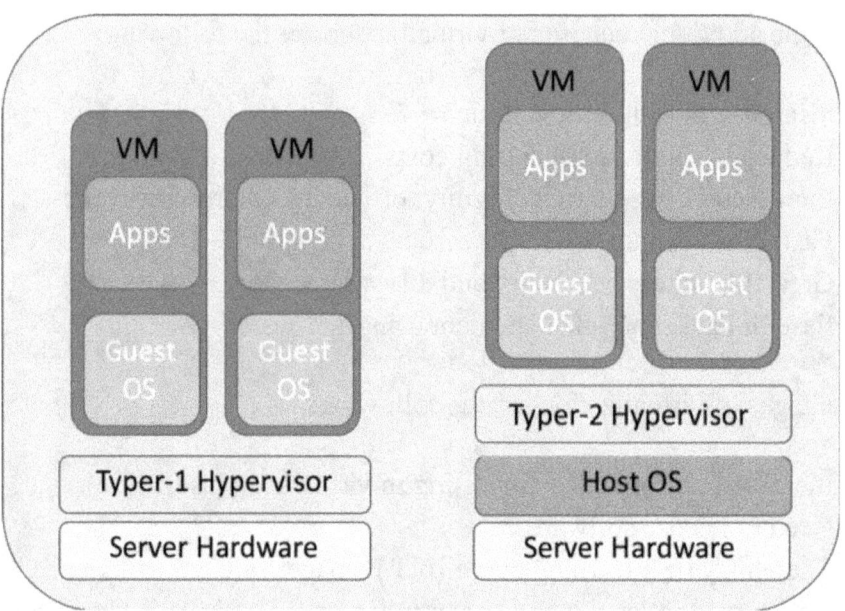

Type-1 hypervisor runs on the physical hardware of the host machine. It doesn't have to load an underlying operating system first. With direct access to the underlying hardware and no other software, these hypervisors are the most efficient hypervisors by running directly atop bare metal.

A Type-2 hypervisor is typically installed on top of an existing operating system and also known as a hosted hypervisor. Type-2 hypervisors are generally not used for data center computing and are reserved for client or end-user, where performance and security are of lesser concern.

Before we move on, it is worth noting that terms hypervisor and Virtual Machine Monitor (or VMM) are often used interchangeably, but in reality, they do not exactly refer to the same piece of software. Hypervisor (or more precisely Type-1 hypervisor) includes VMM as well as the device model. You can think of VMM as software responsible for setting up VMs and handling I/O access for guest OS. VMM ensures that guest OS execution has pretty much identical behavior while running on top of VMM versus bare metal. It is also responsible for efficient program execution as well as managing all hardware resources. The device model is the other part of the hypervisor which provides I/O interfaces for

VMs by way of I/O virtualization. VMM delegates I/O requests to the correct device model. You can think of vNICs and vHBAs as examples of various device models. Device model can be either software-based (e.g., virtIO drivers) or hardware-based or hardware-assisted (e.g., SR-IOV which allows a physical PCIe function to be partitioned into multiple virtual PCIe functions). With software-based solutions, I/O virtualization techniques simply use virtualized CPUs (or vCPUs) alongside the VMs.

Virtual Machine

The virtual machine (or VM) is comprised of a set of configuration and specification files. It comes to life using the physical resources of the underlying host. Each VM is self-contained and is completely independent of other VMs. Multiple VMs can be installed on the same physical server, which enables several operating systems and applications to run on one physical server or host. A thin layer of hypervisor software decouples the virtual machines from the host. It also takes care of dynamically allocating the required resources to each virtual machine.

A virtual machine consists of several types of files that are stored on the supported storage device. The key files that are part of any virtual machine are the virtual disk file, NVRAM setting file, configuration file, and the log file. You can configure a virtual machine using the given virtualization software. You do not need to edit any of the key files, manually.
A virtual machine may contain extra files, if you add Raw Device Mappings (RDMs) or if one or more snapshots exist.

Every virtual machine has virtual devices that provide the same functionality as physical devices. It has additional benefits in terms of portability, manageability, and security.

Key Properties of Virtual Machines are as follows

- Encapsulation
- Hardware Independence
- Isolation
- Partitioning

Compute virtualization is a simplification of legacy architecture to reduce the total number of physical servers. Server virtualization allows us to run multiple operating systems on a single physical machine, where each OS can run inside a separate virtual machine or VM. x86 server virtualization was pioneered by VMware in the late 1990s.

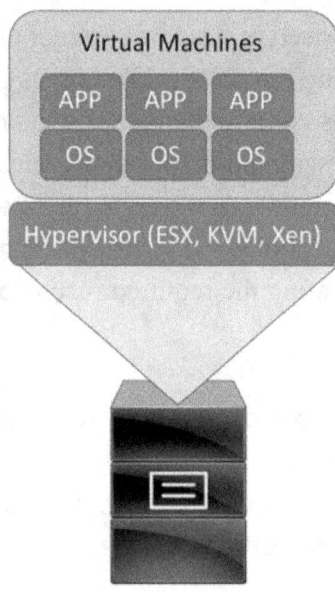

Physical Server

There are numerous benefits of compute virtualization including but not limited to the following.

- Improved security
- Easier administration
- Cost savings
- Consolidation and centralization of physical servers
- Faster TTM

Containers

A container image is a lightweight, portable and executable package of software that consists of code, runtime libraries, system tools, and libraries, etc. Containers are available for both Linux and Windows-based apps.

There are a variety of container technologies that exist today.

- Docker containers
- Java containers
- Unikernels
- LXD (LXD is based on liblxc, its purpose is to control some lxc with added capabilities, like snapshots or live migration)
- OpenVZ
- Rkt
- Windows server containers
- Hyper-V container

It is worth noting that LXCs (Linux Containers) are an OS-level virtualization mechanism for running multiple isolated Linux systems (or containers) on a control host using a single Linux kernel. LXD isn't a repackaging of LXC, in fact, it was built on top of LXC to provide a new, better user experience. Technically speaking, LXD uses LXC through liblxc and its Go binding to create and manage the containers.

Docker Containers

The most popular way to containerize an application is to deploy it as a docker container. Docker is an open platform for developers and sysadmins to build, ship, and run distributed applications, whether on laptops, data center VMs, or the cloud. Docker can build images automatically by reading the instructions from a Dockerfile. A Dockerfile is a text file that contains all the commands a user could call on the command line to assemble an image. In Docker, everything is based on Images. An image is a combination of a file system and parameters. A container is a runtime instance of an image. It lays out the steps the "docker build' command needs to take in order to create an image that can be used to create the actual container.

You can get a list of Docker images on your local by using "docker images" command. By default, docker related files are located under /var/lib/docker folder. It is a simple text file, named Dockerfile.

```
netdevops@netdevops-VirtualBox:/var/lib/docker$ sudo ls
builder      containers  network    plugins    swarm   trust
containerd   image       overlay2   runtimes   tmp     volumes
```

Container image contains executable package of a piece of software that includes everything needed to run it: code, runtime, system tools, system libraries, settings.

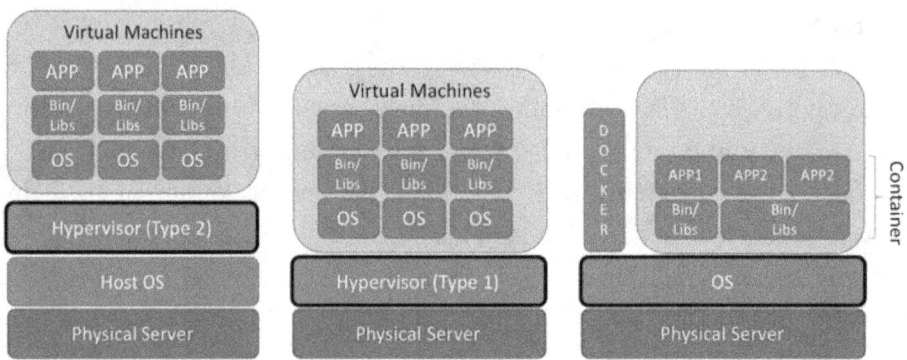

It is crucial to understand the difference between a VM and a container. Containers are an abstraction at the app layer that packages code and dependencies together whereas VMs are an abstraction of physical hardware, turning one server into many virtual ones.

	Virtual Machine (VM)	Docker Container
Host OS	Yes	N/A

Hypervisor	Yes	N/A
Guest OS	Yes	N/A
Bins/Libraries	Yes	Yes
Application	Yes	Yes
Typical Size (bytes)	Tens of GBs	Tens of MBs
Startup time	Slower	Faster

There are three fundamental technologies, when put together, provide us the overall container technology.

- Namespaces (helps isolate different parts of the running container, e.g., pid, mnt and net namespaces for process, filesystem and networking)
- Control groups (cgroups, a standard Linux concept that allows a system to limit the resources)
- Union File systems (or UnionFS are file systems that are built layer by layer)

A simplified version of the docker container workflow looks like the following.

- Create or copy a new image using "docker build"
- Run a container ("docker run" or "docker container create")
- The docker daemon checks if it has a local copy of the image, else pulls the image from registry
- The docker daemon creates a container based on the image. If "docker run" command was used, it will log into it and execute the requested command.

Here is a list of commands that can be used inside a Dockerfile.

- FROM

- MAINTAINER
- RUN
- CMD
- EXPOSE
- ENV
- COPY
- ENTRYPOINT
- VOLUME
- USER
- WORKDIR
- ARG
- ONBUILD
- STOPSIGNAL
- LABEL

You can start a docker container locally by using the following command. The "-d" parameter is short for --detach and means that we want to run it in the background whereas the "-P" tells Docker to publish it on the ports that we exposed.

```
sudo docker run -d -P my-app-image
```

You can see your container by listing the Linux processes.

```
sudo docker ps
```

If you want to make your Docker images available to others, you need to store it in an image registry. By default, Docker uses the Docker Hub registry however you can also create and use your own. A registry stores a collection of repositories, i.e., where you store one or more versions of a specific Docker image. You can publish your image into repo but first committing your container "sudo docker commit" and then push the image to the repo using "sudo docker push" command. You can't help but notice that this process looks similar to how version control systems such as Git work

Kubernetes

Kubernetes is an open-source platform for orchestrating container-based workloads and microservices. It facilitates declarative configuration as well as automation. Kubernetes services, support, and tools are widely available, thanks to its large, rapidly growing ecosystem. Google open sourced Kubernetes in 2014, something they have been using internally for quite some time. It is important to understand that Kubernetes is not a legacy all-inclusive PaaS system.

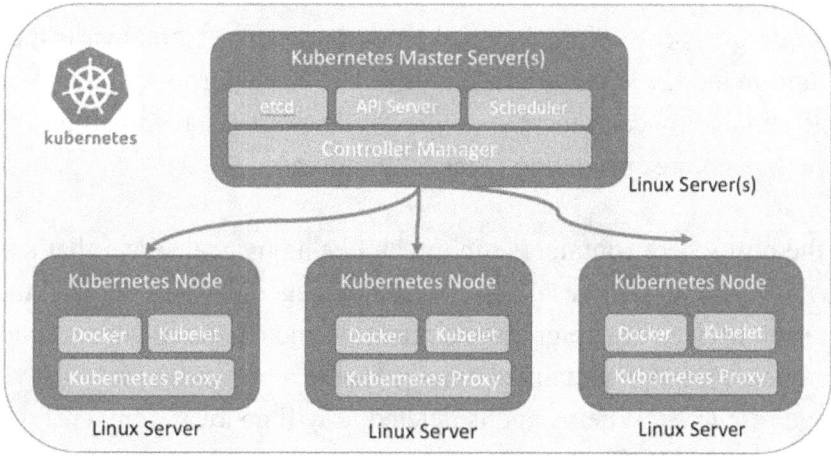

Kubernetes has three major features, i.e., it can be used as
- a container platform
- a microservices platform
- a portable cloud platform

The Legacy way to deploy applications is to install the applications on a host using the operating-system package manager. This had the disadvantage of mixing the applications' executables, configuration, libraries, and lifecycles with each other and the underlying host OS.

Now, technically you could repurpose virtual-machine images in an immutable manner to achieve predictable rollouts and rollbacks, but VMs don't share the inherent benefits of containers in the areas of portability and faster startup times. Immutable refers to replacing components as opposed to changing them, enterprise IT services and software are updated (or changed) in an incremental way making them mutable.

With containers, it is possible to deploy applications based on operating-system-level virtualization rather than using a hypervisor or hardware virtualization. Containers are isolated individually from each other as well as from the underlying host. They are easier to build and portable across clouds and OSs as opposed to VMs.

Let's now go over some of the key Kubernetes concepts. Container is the smallest unit in the Kubernetes terminology. The main purpose of Kubernetes is to manage and deploy containers. It is also worth noting that Kubernetes management is not just limited to Docker containers.

Node is the host where containers run, much like a physical server that's also known as host where VMs reside. A pod is a management unit in the Kubernetes world. It is comprised of one or more containers and has its IP address and storage namespaces. All containers running inside a pod share those networking and storage resources. When a pod is deleted, it will go away forever. Pod is defined using a YAML file.

```
1   apiVersion: v1
2   kind: Pod
3 ▾ metadata:
4     name: nginx-pod
5 ▾  labels:
6       app: nginx
7 ▾ spec:
8     containers:
9 ▾   - name: nginx
10      image: nginx:1.15.2
```

Deployment is how you handle HA in Kubernetes. While a pod by itself is mortal, but with "deployment", Kubernetes can ensure that desired number of pods are always up and running. Again, "deployment" is defined using a YAML file.

```
 1   apiVersion: extensions/v1beta1
 2   kind: Deployment
 3 ▾ metadata:
 4     name: nginx-deployment
 5 ▾ spec:
 6     replicas: 2
 7 ▾  template:
 8 ▾   metadata:
 9 ▾    labels:
10        app: nginx
11 ▾   spec:
12      containers:
13 ▾     - name: nginx
14         image: nginx:1.15.2
15
```

Kubernetes service, also known as micro-service, is an abstraction which defines a logical set of pods and policy which dictates how to access them. Kubernetes architecture also includes something known as label. This isn't your MPLS label. Here, label refers to a semantic tag which can be attached to Kubernetes objects to mark them as part of a group. Labels are assigned as key/value pairs.

Kubernetes annotations are similar to labels, but they allow you to attach an arbitrary key-value information to an object. Unlike labels, annotations are free form and can contain less structured data, you can think them as a way of attaching rich meta-data to an object.

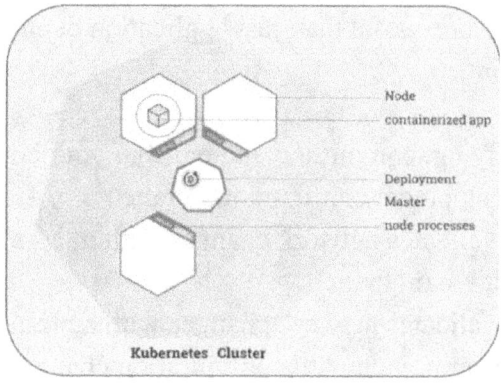

Before we wrap up this discussion, let's take a peek at the popularity of three of these fundamental virtualization technologies.

It is no secret that, over the past five years, containers have become way more popular than VMs.

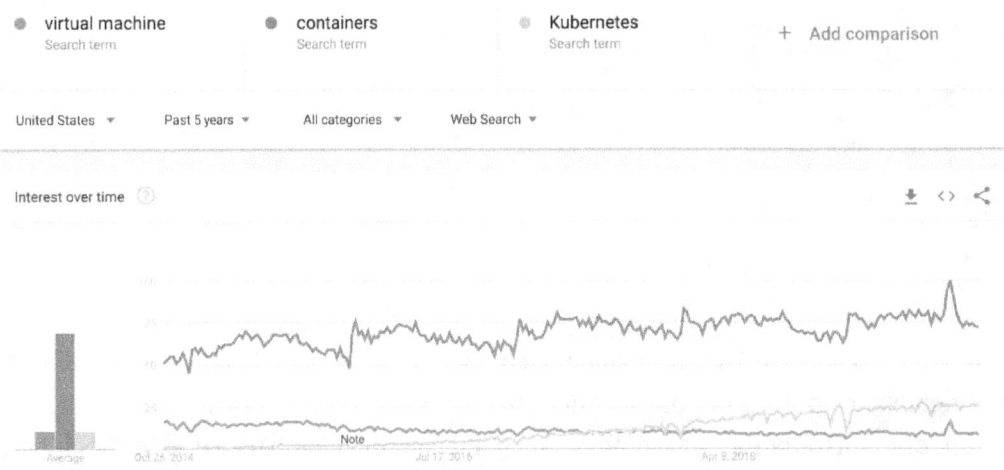

Describe components for a CI/CD pipeline in application deployments

There are four crucial components of a CI/CD pipeline, whether that's for application deployment (aka software) or network deployments (aka NetDevOps). In this section, we will address both software and network CICD together which is far more useful than just application deployments as mentioned in the DevNet blueprint.

1. Creating, verifying, committing and pushing your configuration change within the development configuration branch
2. Build system validates network changes with integration testing and merges dev into main branch
3. Build system validates network changes with a production test network and builds master branch with configuration changes

4. Build system deploys final configuration using Ansible deployment playbook

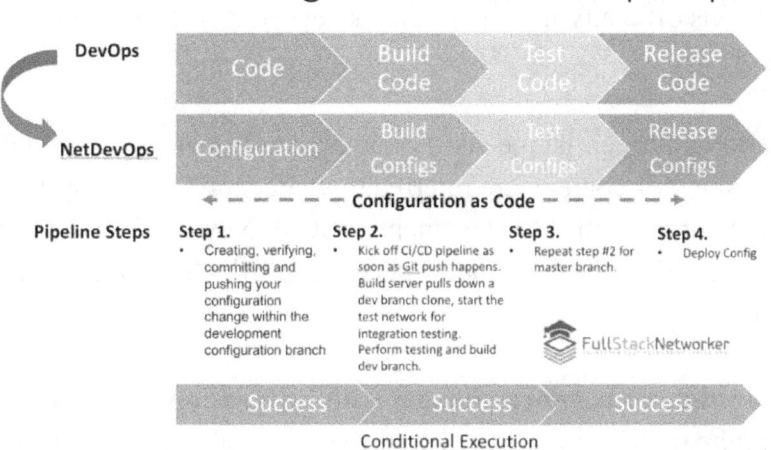

Creating, verifying, committing and pushing your configuration change within the development configuration branch

It consists of creating, verifying, committing and pushing your configuration change within the development configuration branch. What do I mean by a development branch? Within an organization, where developers are writing new features or fixing bugs, they do so by cloning or pulling down a main or a master branch as a development or dev branch. Then, they make all their changes first into that dev branch, as opposed to adding them directly to main or master code.

Now, let's revisit DevOps toolchain. During this step, your toolchain would include GitHub, Ansible, and a tool to help you build the topology for unit testing, for example using Vagrant or Cisco VIRL in case if the device or unit is from Cisco. Let me clarify unit testing here. In this context, unit testing means verifying and validating the configuration change that you just made as a NetDevOps. This kind of unit testing is also known as white box testing.

Once unit testing is successfully completed, you will need to merge and commit your validated configuration into dev configuration branch, again using GitHub or another similar tool. When you do a push, say you use "git push" command, then your configuration is pushed into your build tool such as Jenkins or Drone which is another open source CICD platform. Once you "push" your configuration, this officially initiates and kicks off your NetDevOps CICD pipeline.

Before we proceed further, let me clarify one of many DevOps jargon. Git or GitHub, as used in this context, are referred to as Version Control System or VCS and also Source Control Management or SCM. Now, SCM is NOT be confused with Software Configuration Management which is a much bigger and a separate topic.

Build system validates network changes with integration testing and merges dev into main branch

During step #1, as soon as you performed the "git push", git will reach out to your build tool using the same dev branch. Your build tool will pull down a clone of your dev branch and start executing the pipeline that you configured it with. First step, in your CICD pipeline, will likely be to start your simulated test network topology. How does that happen? You will be using a virtual topology, so your build tool will need to use Vagrant or Cisco VIRL to perform that action. Once that is completed, depending on the pipeline configuration, your build server may use Ansible to configure your virtual test network that you just built.

To conduct effective integration testing, you will need a testing strategy, let's say in the form of an Ansible playbook, that allows you to validate that your test network is working as expected with the modified network configuration. Let me clarify. The purpose of integration testing, as opposed to unit testing, is to ensure that entire existing network continues to work without any hiccups after your configuration changes are committed. Now, before you say, wow I need to write test plans too! Listen, in a medium to large organization, you can expect integration testing playbooks to be written by dedicated QA or Test engineers.

Once test validation is completed, your build tool should take down the integration test network topology and merge the validated dev branch into your master or main branch.

Build system validates network changes with a production test network and builds master branch with configuration changes

Your build system builds the master branch and repeats all the steps carried out in step #2. Let's revisit the steps.

Your build server will kick off CICD pipeline by creating a simulated version of your production network, validate your network change as part of master branch using the test topology, if everything goes fine, it will take down the test topology and complete building the master configuration branch.

Build system deploys final configuration using Ansible deployment playbook

Once master branch build is successfully done, depending on your pipeline configuration, your build server should push your configuration into your production network using perhaps yet another Ansible playbook.

While all of this may sound overwhelming but let me assure you that once you have configured a pipeline and corresponding ansible playbooks a few times, it will all come as second nature to you. Beyond the very first step where you create, verify, commit and push your network change as part of dev branch, everything else is handled automatically by your build system, as part of CICD pipeline, and that is where you see real value in both speed and accuracy of network change deployment.

Network Changes with NetDevOps Pipeline

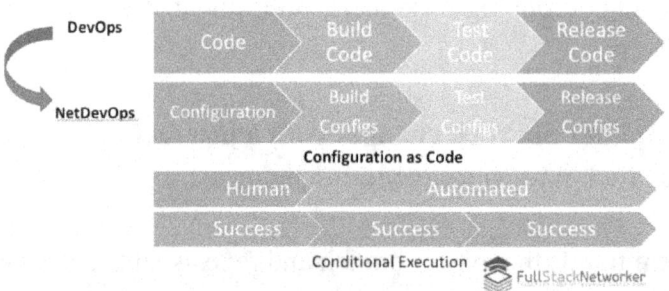

The CI process provides a way to automate the build and test processes so that developers working on the same codebase can integrate their code into a shared main code, typically several times a day. The build pipeline looks like the following.

- Code compilation
- Unit test
- Static code analysis
- Integration testing
- Packaging and versioning
- Publishing the version package to docker hub etc.

The CD means that those changes are engineered to be self-contained so at any given time, you could deploy a working application software. The Continuous Delivery doesn't mean that you actually "deploy" several times a day, that actually known as Continuous Deployment. CD just means that you have a version that you could deploy, if you wanted to.

The Continuous Deployment is the ultimate and final piece of CI/CD paradigm, so once changes are made, built, tested and integrated with the main branch, and perhaps tested again (product testbed), they are deployed into production in an automated fashion.

Now, obviously there is no magic, and some bad things can still pass through the CI/CD gate, so there are some deployment best practices that can be adopted to limit the impact.

- Rolling upgrade (minor releases that don't require complete re-installation)
- Canary pipeline (new version of software is rolled out to a subset of users)
- Blue-green deployment (new code goes into an entirely new deployment while holding onto the old code in reserve, if users on new code/service face issues, user traffic is diverted back to old servers. If no issues, new environment becomes the production environment and the old one is retired.)

Construct a Python unit test

We have discussed unit testing in Python earlier in "Describe the concepts of test-driven development" lesson as part of Section 1.0.

Interpret contents of a Dockerfile

Before we get into Dockerfile, we need to understand what Docker is. It is an open-source project that automates the deployment of applications that are run inside containers.

Docker can build images based on the content (or the commands) of a docker text file or Dockerfile. When you issue a "docker build" command, docker will create an automated build based on commands contained in the docker file as well as the context which is nothing but the set of files at PATH or URL folders in your local filesystem. You can find Dockerfile in the root of the context.

Docker Architecture

Docker architecture consists of the following key components.

- Docker Engine
- Docker Client

- Docker Registries
- Docker Objects
    - Images
    - Containers
    - Volumes
    - Networks

Docker Engine is at the core of the Docker system. It is installed on the host server and consists of client/server architecture. Three key components live inside the engine, i.e.

- Server: It is dockerd or the daemon that creates and manages images, containers, networks, what have you.
- REST API: RESTful API interface into the Docker daemon.
- CLI: client interface into docker daemon which accepts commands.

Docker Client is the client-side user interface that is used to send CLIs to dockerd. Docker commands utilize REST APIs behind the scenes. Docker client can interface with multiple daemons.

Docker Registries is where docker images are stored, so when you run "docker pull" or "docker run" commands, the docker image that is being pulled or run, comes out of the configured registry. Likewise, "docker push" causes an image to be stored in the registry.

Docker Objects are images, containers, volumes, networks, etc. Please note that Docker images are part read-only templates to create a docker container and partly read/write, so when you edit your Dockerfile you rebuild your docker image. Docker rebuild is your way of creating your own docker images.

Docker image is run inside a docker container.

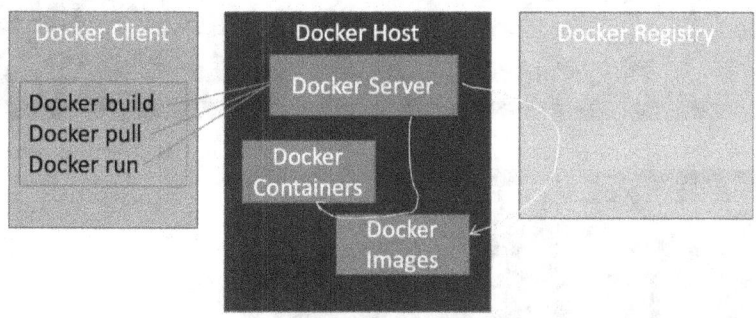

Installing Docker

Installing docker on Ubuntu, Linux flavor that we've been using throughout this book, is pretty straightforward and a two-step process.

```
netdevops@netdevops-VirtualBox:~$ lsb_release -a
No LSB modules are available.
Distributor ID: Ubuntu
Description:    Ubuntu 18.04.1 LTS
Release:        18.04
Codename:       bionic
netdevops@netdevops-VirtualBox:~$
```

First you install docker.

sudo apt install docker.io

Then you start and automate docker so it can on subsequent startup as a service.

sudo systemctl start docker
sudo systemctl enable docker

```
Synchronizing state of docker.service with SysV service script with /lib/systemd
/systemd-sysv-install.
Executing: /lib/systemd/systemd-sysv-install enable docker
```

```
netdevops@netdevops-VirtualBox:~$ docker --version
Docker version 18.09.0-beta3, build 7718f80
netdevops@netdevops-VirtualBox:~$ ▊
```

```
Management Commands:
  builder     Manage builds
  config      Manage Docker configs
  container   Manage containers
  engine      Manage the docker engine
  image       Manage images
  network     Manage networks
  node        Manage Swarm nodes
  plugin      Manage plugins
  secret      Manage Docker secrets
  service     Manage services
  stack       Manage Docker stacks
  swarm       Manage Swarm
  system      Manage Docker
  trust       Manage trust on Docker images
  volume      Manage volumes
```

```
Commands:
  attach      Attach local standard input, output, and error streams to a running container
  build       Build an image from a Dockerfile
  commit      Create a new image from a container's changes
  cp          Copy files/folders between a container and the local filesystem
  create      Create a new container
  diff        Inspect changes to files or directories on a container's filesystem
  events      Get real time events from the server
  exec        Run a command in a running container
  export      Export a container's filesystem as a tar archive
  history     Show the history of an image
  images      List images
  import      Import the contents from a tarball to create a filesystem image
  info        Display system-wide information
  inspect     Return low-level information on Docker objects
  kill        Kill one or more running containers
  load        Load an image from a tar archive or STDIN
  login       Log in to a Docker registry
  logout      Log out from a Docker registry
  logs        Fetch the logs of a container
  pause       Pause all processes within one or more containers
  port        List port mappings or a specific mapping for the container
  ps          List containers
  pull        Pull an image or a repository from a registry
  push        Push an image or a repository to a registry
  rename      Rename a container
  restart     Restart one or more containers
  rm          Remove one or more containers
  rmi         Remove one or more images
  run         Run a command in a new container
  save        Save one or more images to a tar archive (streamed to STDOUT by default)
  search      Search the Docker Hub for images
  start       Start one or more stopped containers
  stats       Display a live stream of container(s) resource usage statistics
  stop        Stop one or more running containers
  tag         Create a tag TARGET_IMAGE that refers to SOURCE_IMAGE
  top         Display the running processes of a container
  unpause     Unpause all processes within one or more containers
  update      Update configuration of one or more containers
  version     Show the Docker version information
  wait        Block until one or more containers stop, then print their exit codes

Run 'docker COMMAND --help' for more information on a command.
```

Utilize Docker images in local developer environment

Once you've docker installed, you can build a Dockerfile, and then build, pull or run your image.

```
root@netdevops-VirtualBox:~/ansible image# docker images
REPOSITORY          TAG        IMAGE ID        CREATED          SIZE
ansible_python3     latest     ada329553150    16 months ago    783MB
gitea/gitea         latest     b8e82a9f73cc    16 months ago    75.2MB
plugins/slack       latest     3745b6f596be    18 months ago    9.24MB
drone/agent         0.8        036235ad8b05    19 months ago    13.4MB
drone/drone         0.8        deca91a2f909    19 months ago    30.5MB
plugins/git         latest     272b4de1492a    23 months ago    66.8MB
```

Let's zoom into ansible_python3 docker image. You can see that our Dockerfile is contained inside the ansible image folder.

```
root@netdevops-VirtualBox:~/ansible image# pwd
/home/netdevops/ansible image
root@netdevops-VirtualBox:~/ansible image# ls
Dockerfile  requirements.txt
root@netdevops-VirtualBox:~/ansible image# cat Dockerfile
#Docker container with Python 3.6.5 and Ansible 2.5.4
FROM python:3.6-jessie

RUN mkdir -p /usr/src/app
WORKDIR /usr/src/app

ONBUILD COPY requirements.txt /usr/src/app/
ONBUILD RUN pip install --no-cache-dir -r requirements.txt

ONBUILD COPY . /usr/src/app
root@netdevops-VirtualBox:~/ansible image#
```

If you can't locate your Dockerfile(s), you can try the following.

cd /
find . -name Dockerfile

Identify application security issues related to secret protection, encryption (storage and transport), and data handling

Application security is about protecting any sensitive data (or secret) that your application creates, uses and accesses to carry out its various intended use cases. The scope of sensitive information can vary from state to state and country to country. There is also a number of regulatory and compliance requirements for how to handle some types of data such as PCI (financial information) and HIPAA (patient health records, etc.).

Application related secrets and sensitive data come in many shapes and forms.

- Passwords
- Passphrases
- Encryption keys
- API keys
- OAuth tokens
- Payment information
- Any kind of personally identifiable information such as names, physical or email addresses, usernames etc.
- Demographic information such as gender or income or level of education
- Machine specific information such as IP or MAC addresses

Encryption is a key enabler of data confidentiality, whether we're talking about data at rest or data in transit as data is vulnerable in either state. Data at rest is data stored on a hard drive, flash drive, or in some sort of archived format. Modern enterprises must secure both data at rest and in transit. Data at rest is considered relatively more secure than data in transit, however, hackers often find data at rest to be more valuable than data in motion.

Protocols such as HTTPS, SSL, TLS, FTPS are used to protect data in transit, whereas encryption algorithms such as AES are used to encrypt data at rest. VPNs are also used to secure data in motion with various encryption algorithms both at OSI layer 3 (IPSec) and layer 2 (MACsec). Both macOS and windows offer OS-level full disk or volume encryption for data at rest. Both operating systems allow the use of AES-XTS 128 or 256-bit encryption as recommended by NIST.

Best Practices for Application Data Protection

Commonly used best practices for data encryption at rest and in-motion include the following measures.

- First and foremost, you need to classify your data based on what's customary to your business vertical and regions where your customers are located (e.g., US versus EU)
- Use of network-based security solutions such as FW, IPS, DLP
- Use of proactive vs. reactive approaches to data protection
- Use of data protection solutions that allow policies which prompt, block or encryption data in transit
- Use of encrypted transport protocols, such as SSH, TLS and IPsec VPNs

Data Handling

Secure data handling relies on data marking if you don't know what and where your sensitive data is located, chances are that your data is already hacked. Managing your sensitive data is the first step towards putting together a data breach prevention policy. In addition to data controls, you also need to put in place a security clearance system that would govern necessary controls over data access.

Data marking means classifying and labeling your data. During this process, each dataset is assigned a label to identify its classification. For example, the federal government uses top-secret, secret and confidential classifications to guard data that of national interest.

Once data is classified or marked, then you can define your data security requirements. As we discussed, encryption is the first and foremost tool to safeguard data security. Trusted Platform Module (or TPM) chip is a cryptographic hardware that provides greater security by way of a system of attestation and also improved form of encryption that includes hash values based on system firmware, configuration, or even operation system (OS).

Data marking can be in physical forms such as physical assigning labels, or virtual where digital marks or labels are embedded inside the documents, e.g., in the form of watermarks, headers, footers, annotations, etc.

Data handling requires that datasets are remarked and reclassified over their lifecycle, much like the US government that parodically declassifies older secret and top-secret information.

Software Vulnerabilities

Software vulnerabilities are as old as the software itself as most developers are focused on getting the job done and by no means are security experts. Today, there is hardly any codebase that doesn't utilize some kind of libraries from the open source which only expands the exposure to vulnerabilities. The most recent example of this stark reality came along in the form of Heartbleed bug (buffer over-read situation) discovered in OpenSSL library.

There are a number of tools that can be used to scan for known code vulnerabilities.

- Bandit
- Brakeman
- VisualCodeGrepper

There are a couple other best practices, when followed, can help reduce the scope of unknown software vulnerabilities.

- Storing only as much data as needed (if you don't need a piece of information for some essential function, simply don't store it)
- Limit storing unencrypted data in the cloud (with so much flash-based media in use today, it is virtually impossible to truly wipe every sector so ensure that your cloud data is encrypted at-rest)
- Roaming devices (with the rise of mobile workforce and the mobile devices, your attack surface is much wider than it used to be)

Explain how firewall, DNS, load balancers, and reverse proxy work in application deployment

A firewall is generally a network-based system that separates the trusted network (often private) from an untrusted network (often public internet). To accomplish this separation, it controls and monitors the flow of traffic to/from those two networks.

Firewalls are mostly network-based. However, they can also be host-based. Host-based firewalls run on host computers such as servers or PCs but perform same function of traffic control and monitoring as their network-based counterparts do.

There are a few things to keep in mind when it comes to application software deployment with regard to firewalls.

- Firewalls should not allow any outside access to the untested applications
- Firewalls need to allow any provisions needed to test an application (e.g., access to database or another server, etc.)
- The development environment should be replica of the production environment

Today, there are many different types of firewalls out there.

- Stateless firewalls or packet filters (e.g., Cisco IOS Access Control Lists or ACLs)
- Stateful firewalls that maintain OSI layer 3 and 4 state to perform the firewalling function (e.g., Cisco PIX or even baseline ASA firewall)
- Application firewalls that maintain state information for application-level protocols such as HTTP, FTP, DNS etc.
- Proxy server firewalls that could use either general-purpose x86 or bespoke hardware and act as gateway between from one network to another but for a specific application, thus acting as a proxy to initiate connection on the behalf of users behind it. There are two types of proxy servers out there, forward or reverse.
  - Forward Proxy: In most cases when you hear the words "proxy server", people are referring to forward proxy. Forward proxies forward traffic to external websites on behalf of the internal clients.
  - Reverse Proxy: This is where a proxy server is placed in front of web servers and thus front ending all client requests coming from the internet and then forwarding or load balancing that traffic to the web servers behind it. Cloud Access Service Broker (or CASB) is another form of application access control that can be configured as forward or reverse proxies.
- Next-generation firewalls that support application layer controls but at the same time provide deep packet inspection capabilities, sandboxing, IPS-like features, identity management (user IDs, or IP and MAC address etc.)

Firewalls can filter and maintain state for both applications using TCP (connection-oriented) and UDP (connectionless) transport protocols. With TCP protocol, a firewall can maintain a complete TCP session state by opening up two half-open TCP sessions (one from host-to-FW and the other from FW-to-target-server), and then eventually stitching them up so traffic can flow seamlessly between the client and the target server. Please note that there are lots of other security features that are provided by the firewall when inspecting TCP traffic. Application protocols that use TCP include HTTP, FTP, SSH.

UDP is a stateless protocol however firewalls still track UDP datagrams in IP packets by using the source/destination addresses and source/destination port numbers. Application protocols that use UDP are TFTP, DNS, NTP, etc.

DNS is used for name resolution so when you browse to www.yahoo.com in your web browser, your host networking stack will first send a cleartext DNS query (likely using your ISP DNS servers) to resolve that name into an IP address (e.g., 98.136.103.24). As soon as an IP address is unknown, your browser can utilize TCP/HTTP protocols to make a web request and start communicating with the yahoo web server(s).

Load balancers are reverse proxies that distribute application traffic across a number of servers, in most cases web traffic to multiple web servers. Load balancers are thus used to increase service capacity (more concurrent users) and also the reliability of the service by mitigating the single point of failure scenario.

Load balance can use a variety of algorithms to perform the task of load balance. Here are a few common approaches.

- Persistent sessions (load balancer maintains the session stickiness as required by the application)
- Round robin (the server sends each request to the next server on the list)
- Least connections (send new requests to a server that's least busy)
- IP hash (load balancing decision is made based on a hash. The hash can take into account various fields such IP address of the incoming connection)
- Blue-green deployment (blue and green refers to new product and old production environments, load balancer sends traffic to blue but switches back to green in case of service issues due to new code in the blue environment)

- Canary deployment (starts out by redirecting small portion of user traffic or load to blue environment, and depending on the presence or lack of issues thereof, keep or switch traffic to the old environment)

Describe top OWASP threats (such as XSS, SQL injections, and CSRF)

Open Web Application Security Project (or OWASP) is an organization and an online community that provides unfiltered, unbiased and practical information on topics related to internet and web application security.

OWASP is focused on providing education, tools and other sources to help developers avoid some of the well-known security vulnerabilities in web software.

- Tools (Zed Attack Proxy, Dependency Check, DefectDojo, etc.)
- Code projects (ModSecurity Core Rule Set)
- Documentation projects (OWASP Application Security Verification Standard, Cheap Sheet Series, and the famous OWASP Top Ten)

As per OWASP, the top 10 application security risks or vulnerabilities in 2019 are the following.

1. Injection
2. Broken Authentication
3. Sensitive data exposure
4. XML External Entities (XXE)
5. Broken Access control
6. Security misconfigurations
7. Cross Site Scripting (XSS)
8. Insecure Deserialization
9. Using Components with known vulnerabilities
10. Insufficient logging and monitoring

In this section, we will discuss XSS, SQL injections and CSRF in more detail.

XSS

Reflected cross-Site Scripting (or XSS) occurs when an attacker injects a malicious piece of code inside a single HTTP response that can be executed by the target browser. Reflection is used as an attack amplification method since client-side scripts are injected into a website so they can be propagated further. It is primarily considered a client-side attack.

In 2019, WordPress (Content Management System or CMS that runs about 34% of websites), has been in the news when several plugins were found to have malicious code that could be used by remote attackers to take over control of the entire website or deface a single blog post. As per OWASP, an XSS can be divided into three broad categories, i.e., stored, reflected and DOM-based.

Type of XSS	Server-Side	Client-Side
Stored	Stored	Stored
Reflected (XSS)	Reflected	Reflected
DOM-Based	N/A	Subset of Client

How to Test for XSS

You can test for XSS by injecting a JavaScript inside a web request (e.g., POST) and see if your script comes back out as part of the server response. Most modern scanners such as Grabber, Zap or Vega have built-in features to detect XSS attacks.

How to Mitigate XSS

You can mitigate XSS attacks by separating the untrusted data from the active browser content.

- Use latest frameworks that natively avoid XSS attack vectors (e.g., React JS, or Ruby on Rails etc.)
- Avoid untrusted HTTP request data based on the HTML output
- Apply context-sensitive data encoding to mitigate against DOM-based attack vectors
- Enable Content Security Policy (or CSP) and mitigate XSS

SQL injection attack

Code injection is when an attacker sends invalid data to a web application with the malicious intention. It is considered as a server-side attack.

Let's understand code injection with the help of the following SQL query.

SELECT * FROM courses WHERE track = 'DevNet' AND version = 1

In this example, SQL query supposed to return all rows where track is set to 'DevNet' and version is equal to 1.

Now, imagine, if we were to send the following HTTP request.

https://example.com/courses?track=DevNet'--

Above would result in the following SQL query.

SELECT * FROM courses WHERE track = 'DevNet'--' AND version = 1

Double dash sequence means comments, so this effectively removes the remainder of the query i.e., the part after it (AND version = 1). This means that all courses will be displayed including the versions that may be unknown to the public. If taken further, a skilled attacker can modify the web request to display all courses in all categories even ones that are hidden.

How to Mitigate SQL Injection Code Attack

This injection could easily be prevented by rewriting the SQL query in a way where user request doesn't directly impact the resulting query. In case of hardening against such attacks, the string used in the query can simply be a hardcoded constant and avoid taking any variable from any possible origin – internal or external.

Cross Site Request Forgery (CSRF)

CSRF is a type of attack that is initiated by a user (via mostly social engineering) where they receive and click on a link sent by an attacker after they have authenticated into the target system.

If successful, CSRF can compromise user data, now if that user happens to be an admin then we're talking about compromising the entire web application. For successful CSRF, the attacker relies on the following tactics.

- Knowledge of web browser operation
- Knowledge of valid web application URLs
- Knowledge of HTML tags that allow access to web assets such as images <img> tag.

How to Mitigate CSRF Attacks

You can either manually test your web links or utilize a tool such as BURP, OWASP also provides a list of recommended tools that can help mitigate against CSRF attacks.

Utilize Bash commands (file management, directory navigation, and environmental variables)

There are three kinds of user interfaces within Linux, i.e., GUI, CLI and Text User Interface or TUI. Vi editor is an example of a text user interface where you convey all of your editing commands using text interface.

Shell is a type of command-line interface that takes user commands and converts them into instructions for the Linux operating system to execute.

There are five shells are available on Linux depending on the distribution.

- Types of SHELL
  - Sh
  - Bash
  - Csh
  - Tcsh
  - ksh

Bash is the default shell on Ubuntu as well as CentOS and RedHat Linux. Let us outline a few characteristics of Bash.

- Prompt $ for user and # for root user
- Supported Features
  - Aliases
  - History
  - File Completion
- Bash startup files
  - Invoked as an interactive login shell, or with `--login'
  - Invoked as an interactive non-login shell
  - Invoked non-interactively
  - Invoked with the sh command
  - POSIX mode
  - Invoked remotely
  - Invoked when UID is not equal to EUID

Shell scripting is the bedrock of automation. The Bash is the default shell on Linux and macOS operating systems. To ensure the bash scripts are efficient, here are a few best practices you might want to follow.

- Standardize the ordering and presentation of parameters

- Create a code hierarchy that divides tasks
- Create high-level scripts for the entire deployments
- Separate deployment-specific information from the code itself so code can be reused

The ultimate goal of any script is to achieve a desired state in a system regardless of the starting conditions. This quality of software is known as Idempotency as we discussed earlier. It is worth noting a few Idempotency principles.

- Look before you leap (i.e., if ain't broke, don't fix it!)
- Before making changes, get to a known-good state
- Test for idempotency (build automation that is free from side effects)
- One bad apple spoils the bunch (all components of a procedure must be individually idempotent for the procedure as a whole to be idempotent)

F
ile Management Commands

Linux is a file-oriented OS which means that many things that administrator has to do in Linux can be traced down to managing files under Linux operating system. All files or directories appear under the root directory.

Depending on if your hardware runs BIOS with or without UEFI support, you will either have Master Boot Record (MBR) which uses a standard partition table and contains primary and extended partitions.

If your BIOS has UEFI support, then you can utilize GUID Partition Table (or GPT). You can have more than four partitions on each disk. If you have 2 TB+ disks, then that's your option. gdisk utility is used to create GPT partitions.

Linux file system is presented as one hierarchy with the root directory as its starting point. This hierarchy may be distributed over different devices and even computer systems that are mounted on to the root directory.

- Some of the important Linux directories are.

- /   The root directory.
- /bin   Contains executable programs.
- /boot   Contains files needed to boot the system.
- /dev   Contains files used for accessing physical devices.
- /etc   Contains configuration files for programs and services.
- /home   Contains Local users home directories.
- /lib, /lib64   Contains Shared libraries used by programs.
- /root   Home directory for the root user.
- /tmp   Contain Temporary files.
- /usr   Contains subdirectories containing program files, libraries.
- /var   Contains files that may change in size dynamically. E.g., log files.

The vi editor is available on almost all Unix and Linux systems. It can be used from any type of terminal because it uses standard alphabetic keys as navigation commands.

You may use vi to open an already existing file by typing "vi filename". It will create a new file if one doesn't exist. Vi editor has two modes, namely command and insert. All user input within vi is treated as case sensitive much like rest of the Unix/Linux

There are two vi modes of operation. In command mode, the alphabets on the keyboard are used to perform editing functions (like moving the cursor, deleting text, etc.). To enter command mode after you're inside vi, press the escape key. In insert mode, the letters you type become words and sentences much like what happens in Microsoft Word immediately after launching it. vi starts up in command mode.

Linux/Unix operating systems have the ability to multitask in a manner similar to other operating systems. Linux was designed to allow more than one user to have access to the system at the same time. In order for this multiuser design to work properly, there needs to be a method to protect users from each other. This is where permissions come in to play. Permissions are the "rights" to act on a file or directory. The basic rights are read, write, and execute.

The control of users and groups is a core element of CentOS Linux system administration. Users can be a human being, or an account used by specific applications identified by a unique numerical identification number called user ID (or UID). Users within a group can have read-write or execute permissions or any combination of read/write/execute for files owned by that group.

A group is an organization unit tying users together for a common purpose, which can be reading permissions, writing permission, or executing permission for files owned by that group. Similar to UID, each group is associated with a group ID (or GID).

Essential Tools for Managing Text File Contents are the following.

- less   opens the text file in a easy to read format.
- cat   show the contents of the text file on the screen.
- head   show first 10 lines of text file.
- tail   show last 10 lines of text file.
- cut   filter column or character in a text file.
- sort   sort the content of the text file.
- wc   count the number of lines, word and characters in
  text   file.
- grep   to find a specific word or character from a text file.
- find   to find a specific file inside a file system.

In order to copy files and directories, you need to use the cp command. cp command allows you to copy files and directories in a Linux environment. CP syntax is pretty simple, cp /path/to file/path/to/destination. Use cp -R command to copy an entire subdirectory, with its contents and everything within it. Please note that hidden files are not copied by default.

mv is for moving files. It can also be used to rename a file. You can use rm command to remove a file.

While Linux OS is pretty secure out of the box, however, local access can still create a security hole, i.e., where a user does not don't assign correct permissions to files and directories. In Linux, each file and directory have three user-based permission classes:

owner - Owner permissions apply only the owner of the file or directory; they will not impact the actions of other users.
group - Group permissions apply only to the group that has been assigned to the file or directory, they will not affect the actions of other users.
all users - All Users permissions apply to all other users on the system, this is the permission group that you want to watch the most.

There are three basic permissions in Linux which are assigned to the objects. The three basic permissions are read, write, and execute. Linux permission system does not use inheritance, i.e., newly created files or directories don't inherit parent permissions rather they have default permissions. The default file and directory permissions that are set when you create files and directories can be set using the umask command. chmod command is used to change the permission of files and directories. The concept of owner and groups for files is fundamental to Linux.

Every file is associated with an owner and a group. You can use chown and chgrp commands to change the owner or the group of a particular file or directory. You can use "ls –l" to see ownership of the file, and chown command is used to change ownership of file and directory.

Directory Navigation Commands

Regardless of the shell, here are a list of CLIs that you can use to navigate Linux filesystem.

- ls is a Linux shell command that lists directory contents of files and directories.
- ls [options] [file|dir]
    - ls -a   list all files including hidden file starting with '.'
    - ls -d   list directories
    - ls -i   list file's inode index number
    - ls -l   list with long format - show permissions
    - ls -la   list long format including hidden files
    - ls -lh   list long format with readable file size
    - ls -s   list file size
    - ls -S   sort by file size
    - ls -t   sort by time & date
    - ls -X   sort by extension name
- cd
    - cd is a Linux command to change the directory/folder of the terminal's shell
        - $ cd ~   Change to home directory
        - $ cd /   Change to root directory
        - $ cd .. Change to parent directory
- pwd
    - pwd - print working directory OR Present working directory, is a Linux command to get the current working directory.

Environmental Variables

Variables are a very important aspect of Shell scripting; they are very useful in Shell scripting. A variable is a temporary store for a piece of information. A variable in bash can contain several characters, a string of characters. Shell variables are in uppercase characters by convention.

Bash keeps a list of two types of variables: Global variables and Local variables. Global variables are also called Environment variables, which will be available to all Shells. printenv command is used to display all the environment variables.

Local variables are visible only within the block of code. It's not visible to other Shells. That's the major difference between Global and Local variables, which can be justified from the name. Local is a keyword which is used to declare the local variable.

You can also set your variables in shell scripting. It can be useful for keeping track of results of commands and being able to refer to and process them later. To set values within variables, use 'variable', and then the 'value'.

Bash is a case sensitive environment so whenever you are creating your variable you must be consistent in your use of uppercase and lowercase letters.

Shell Script

```
1  #!/bin/bash
2  # A simple two-variable example
3  myvariable=Hello
4  anothervar=World!
5  echo $myvariable $anothervar
6  echo
7  sampledir=/etc
8  ls $sampledir
```

Shell Script Output (Ubuntu)

First, we enter all of the commands into using a text editor and save it as helloworld.sh.

```
netdevops@netdevops-VirtualBox:~$ cat helloworld.sh
#!/bin/bash
myvariable=Hello
anothervar=World!
echo $myvariable $anothervar
echo
sampledir=/etc
ls $sampledir
```

Once that's done, we need to assign execute permission to our shell script using chmod command.

```
netdevops@netdevops-VirtualBox:~$ ls -la helloworld.sh
-rw-r--r-- 1 netdevops netdevops 112 Oct 23 22:33 helloworld.sh
netdevops@netdevops-VirtualBox:~$ chmod u+x helloworld.sh
netdevops@netdevops-VirtualBox:~$ ls -la helloworld.sh
-rwxr--r-- 1 netdevops netdevops 112 Oct 23 22:33 helloworld.sh
```

Now, our script is ready for execution (ls output truncated).

```
netdevops@netdevops-VirtualBox:~$ sudo ./helloworld.sh
Hello World!

acpi                host.conf           popularity-contest.conf
adduser.conf        hostname            ppp
alternatives        hosts               printcap
anacrontab          hosts.allow         profile
ansible             hosts.deny          profile.d
apache2             hp                  protocols
```

/etc contents for reference so you know your script executed correctly.

```
netdevops@netdevops-VirtualBox:~$ ls /etc/
acpi                    host.conf           popularity-contest.conf
adduser.conf            hostname            ppp
alternatives            hosts               printcap
anacrontab              hosts.allow         profile
ansible                 hosts.deny          profile.d
apache2                 hp                  protocols
apg.conf                ifplugd             pulse
apm                     ImageMagick-6       python
apparmor                init                python2.7
apparmor.d              init.d              python3
apport                  initramfs-tools     python3.6
appstream.conf          inputrc             qemu-ifdown
```

Identify the principles of DevOps practices

DevOps was borne out of necessity where two previously siloed groups could no longer remain siloed because of the pace of the software development cycle. Those two siloed groups were application developers and testers and system admins (or IT guys responsible for deployment and integration).

The watershed moment arrived with the Agile model of software development as a legacy waterfall model took backstage. Agile is about short sprints and frequent releases which necessitated that the two teams collaborated and work together. All of the internet shops that we know today, Facebook, Amazon, Google, Netflix all use DevOps because that is how they can continuously develop, integrate, deliver and deploy.

DevOps stands for Development and Operations. It is not a new technology or a tool, as we just learned based on that brief history, that it is about the corporate culture surrounding software development and delivery hence teamwork is the meta point here.

The main principles of DevOps are the following.

- Culture with effective teamwork and open communication, technical processes and toolchain
- Automation of processes
- Measurement of KPIs

- Learning feedback loop, where best practices and knowledge from each cycle is fed into the next one

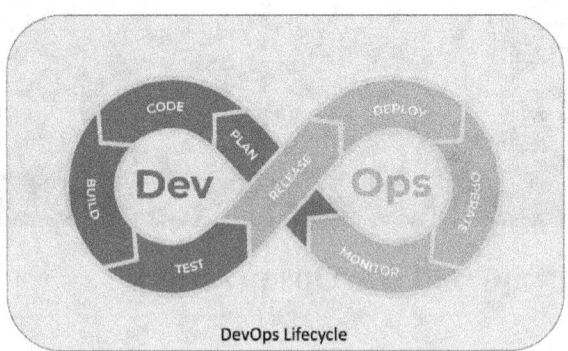

DevOps Lifecycle

Let's beak down each of those processes.

Plan

As opposed to the legacy waterfall model of software development, Agile planning breaks down overall work into smaller sprints and that helps increase the frequency of releases. The downside is that team may not be aware of every detail as they get started. But it is a good trade-off between code velocity versus documentation.

Code

Engineers commit code in smaller bunches several times a day. Git is a commonly used tool for version control or source code management. Jira is another tool frequently used by software and test teams to track bugs, open issues and the overall project management.

Build

Build is the process of merging dev branch or branches and produce integration or master branch that can be tested. Jenkins is your build tool that enables continuous development, integration and delivery (not to be confused with deployment which is a different thing altogether).

Test

There can be several types of tests, i.e., unit, integration and system test etc.

Release

Release is the fit and finished application software that is ready for deployment.

Deploy

This is about making the newly available application software to customers.

Operate

It is about post-deployment optimization, changes to infrastructure security, performance, availability etc.

Monitor

This phase applies to entire DevOps lifecycle where software is monitored, analyzed and measured. This is where continuous feedback makes it back into each new iteration and respective planning phases.

The SRE and DevOps have many core principles and best practices to live by.

- Relentless focus on automation (avoiding toil and retaining talent)
- Failure is normal (software design based on embracing failure and using it to enhance automation)
- Redefining "Availability" (it is what a business can tolerate)

The last idea around availability is codified in the form Service Level Objective (SLO) and Service Level Indicators (SLIs). SLO is the precise numerical internal target for the availability whereas SLI is a measure of a service's behavior, i.e., the frequency of successful probes of the system. SLO is a key element of Service Level Agreement (SLA) between a service provider and a customer. SLOs are agreed as a means of measuring the performance of a service provider and are used to avoid disputes between the two parties.

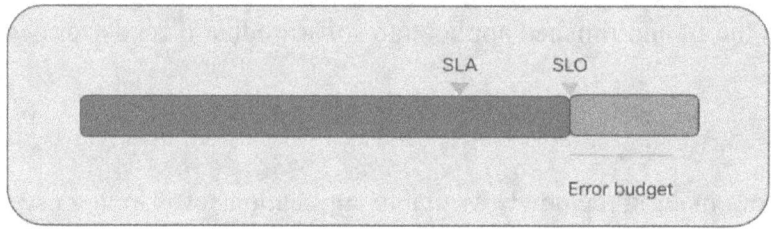

Chapter Summary

- Edge computing is a distributed data processing model where data is crunched and stored closer to the location of the end device, for example an Internet of Things device such as network-based sensors, or connected cars or smart grid, etc.
- The private cloud is about offering computing services either over the Internet or a private internal network, such as WAN
- Virtual private cloud (or VPC) is a private cloud carved out inside a public cloud for the sole purpose of being used by a single tenant
- The public cloud is defined as computing services offered by third-party providers, such as AWS, over the public Internet, making them available to anyone who wants to use or purchase them.
- A hybrid cloud combines the benefits of public and private clouds by allowing data and applications to be shared between them
- Multi-cloud is not yet another cloud model per se, but a cloud deployment approach made up of multiple cloud services, from multiple cloud service providers, public or private.
- Cloud computing is the result of a well thought out infrastructure by the providers, in the same way that electricity, water, and gas are the result of decades of infrastructural development by the utility providers.
- Hypervisor allows you to split one system into separate virtual environments known as virtual machines (VMs).
- A Type-2 hypervisor is typically installed on top of an existing operating system and also known as hosted hypervisor.
- A container image is a lightweight, portable and executable package of software that consists of code, runtime libraries, system tools and libraries, etc.
- By default, docker related files are located under /var/lib/docker folder.
- Container image contains executable package of a piece of software that includes everything needed to run it: code, runtime, system tools, system libraries, settings.
- Kubernetes is an open source platform for orchestrating container-based workloads and microservices

- Docker is an open-source project that automates the deployment of applications that are run inside containers.
- Docker Client is the client-side user interface that is used to send CLIs to dockerd
- Application security is about protecting any sensitive data (or secret) that your application creates, uses and accesses to carry out its various intended use cases.
- Open Web Application Security Project (or OWASP) is an organization and an online community that provides unfiltered, unbiased and practical information on topics related to internet and web application security.
- Reflected cross-Site Scripting (or XSS) occurs when an attacker injects a malicious piece of code inside a single HTTP response that can be executed by the target browser.

λ

CHAPTER 5 INFRASTRUCTURE AND AUTOMATION

This chapter covers the following exam topics from Cisco's official 200-901 V1.0 DevNet Associate exam blueprint.

- Describe the value of model driven programmability for infrastructure automation
- Compare controller-level to device-level management
- Describe the use and roles of network simulation and test tools (such as VIRL and pyATS)
- Describe the components and benefits of CI/CD pipeline in infrastructure automation
- Describe principles of infrastructure as code
- Describe the capabilities of automation tools such as Ansible, Puppet, Chef, and Cisco NSO
- Identify the workflow being automated by a Python script that uses Cisco APIs including ACI, Meraki, Cisco DNA Center, or RESTCONF
- Identify the workflow being automated by an Ansible playbook (management packages, user management related to services, basic service configuration, and start/stop)
- Identify the workflow being automated by a bash script (such as file management, app install, user management, directory navigation)
- Interpret the results of a RESTCONF or NETCONF query
- Interpret basic YANG models
- Interpret a unified diff
- Describe the principles and benefits of a code review process
- Interpret sequence diagram that includes API calls

Describe the value of model driven programmability for infrastructure automation

Using data models, i.e., a programmatic and standard-based way of creating and deploying configurations to any vendor network device, has been much needed and is nowhere in the form of the de-facto YANG model.

YANG is a modeling language that provides the schema. The defining characteristics of a data model are the following.

- Determines the structure
- Determines the syntax
- Determines the data semantics

It does all of the above so that data is externally visible, consistent and complete. It is not be confused with a protocol since the protocol is complementary to a data model since it helps provides remote primitives to view and modify the data and helps encode the data as per the model. SNMP and NETCONF are examples of protocols whereas MIBs and YANG modules are examples of data models.

As a model, YANG was standardized by IETF with the formation of NETMOD WG back in 2008 and subsequently published as RFC 7950 or YANG 1.1.

YANG language is used to model data, the data here refers to configurational data, state data, RPCs, and notifications. While YANG provides the complete description of all data sent between the client and a server (e.g., NETCONF client and server), it is at the same time transport protocol independent. It was conceived with NETCONF as transport protocol and XML as underlying encoding, but it was later on extended to support RESTCONF and JSON as well.

The neat thing about being a data modeling language is that you don't have to fork it to add newer features, you augment it by adding new modules.

Let's understand YANG as a data modeling language by comparing its structure to that of Python.

YANG Element	YANG Element Description	Python Equivalent
Module	Complete YANG file	Module
Data Type	Strings, integers, boolean are pre-defined, you can also define your own.	Data Types
Leaf	Single variable which can hold one value	Data Structure: variable
Leaf-list	Collection of variables of the same data type	Data Structure: Lists
List	Collection of key/value pairs, key is a leaf whereas value can take on any data type (i.e., strings, integers, boolean etc.)	Data Structure: Dictionary
Container	High level hierarchy that groups leaf, leaf-list, list and can group even other containers	Class

Each vendor, such as Cisco or Juniper, has its own YANG modules that describe how to configure their device i.e., configuration state and how to retrieve information from the device i.e., the operational state.

These modules are known as native modules, but they are consistent with the same modeling language and semantics that we described in the table above. This helps short circuit the learning curve and nuances associated with each vendor's CLI by allowing them to publish multiple YANG files for each equipment. Please note that in the YANG world, NMS is the client whereas the device (say a router or a switch) is a server, e.g., in case of NETCONF, they would be NETCONF server and client.

IETF defines the most common parts of network device configuration in the form of IETF modules, let's say things like configuring interfaces a vendor has to still support the module before it can be used for the device.

Beyond native and IETF modules, internet shops like Google and some telcos, have come also come up with some common YANG modules that require all vendors to support to configure features like BGP, or interfaces, or VLANs, etc. Given the heavyweights behind the initiative, vendors have come around to support these YANG modules as well. These are formally known as OpenConfig YANG models.

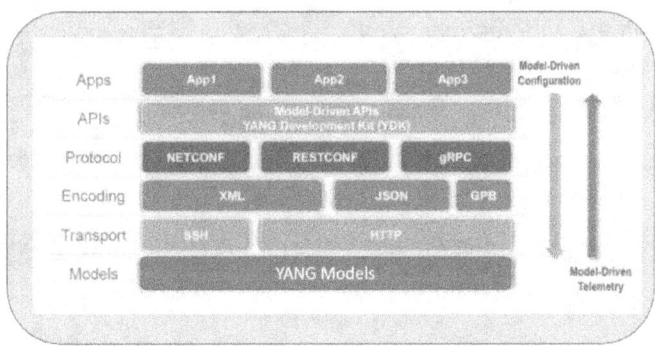

You can refer to the previous section for real-world examples where we used YANG models with both NETCONF and RESTCONF protocols and XML and JSON encodings to pull in data from Cisco CSR1000v.

Compare controller-level to device-level management

While merchant silicon, from the likes of Broadcom, was around long before SDN, what SDN brought to the fore was clear separation of control and data plane in the form of a centralized network provisioning and management architecture that is controller-based with southbound and northbound APIs for integration with hardware and application software respectively.

In the process, SDN helped create software-based network overlays where a large number of individual devices, physical or virtual, that could now be managed using a centralized controller as opposed to managing each device on its own with the help of an NMS.

	Controller-Based Model	**Device-Based Model**
Control Plane	Centralized	Distributed
Data Plane	Distributed	Distributed
Management Framework	Policy or intent-driven	NMS
Network Provisioning	API-driven automation	CLIs, GUIs etc.
Network Monitoring	Streamed Telemetry (publisher/subscriber)	NMS/SNMP
AI/ML-based Operations	Yes	No

Controlled-based management can fully take advantage of software-driven innovation esp. AI and ML in the areas of provisioning, monitoring, and operations. As we speak, all networking vendors are prioritizing API interfaces for newer features over implementing newer CLIs or GUIs.

Describe the use and roles of network simulation and test tools (such as VIRL and pyATS)

A network simulator is simply a piece of software that simulates a network topology that could be composed of any number of network devices. Cisco packet tracer is an example of a simulator.

In contrast to simulators, emulators virtualize real network devices, so they offer more feature richness when compared to simulators. GNS3 and Cisco VIRL are examples of emulators.

The key benefits of simulators as opposed to using real hardware are the following.

- Lightweight software, less resource-intensive

- Flexibility, easy to modify topology and turn on and off simulated devices
- Diversity, choice of routers, switches, firewalls, etc.
- Cost, way cheaper to buy or license (e.g., VIRL) than real hardware

Simulators also come with their downsides, e.g., they can't handle or artificially constrained to take on limited traffic volume and generally they lack feature parity with real software.

Typical use cases for simulated and emulator software are

- Feature testing
- Becoming familiar with CLIs and APIs
- Preparing for certification exams that require hands-on testing such as CCIE labs

	Simulators	**Emulators**
Software	Cisco Packet Tracer	VIRL, GNS3
Feature Richness	Not so much	Yes
Resource Requirements	Lower	Higher
Traffic Handling Ability	Lower	Higher

Cisco VIRL

Virtual Internet Routing Lab or VIRL is Cisco's closed source, virtual network emulator. If you have ever used Cisco Modeling Labs or CML, VIRL is just a limited version of CML. Currently, the VIRL Personal Edition subscription would cost you $199 per year.

There is a big upside to VIRL which none of the other emulators such as GNS3 or EVE-NG offer, and that is access to the near latest IOS XE, IOS XR, NX OS, and ASAv software. You can also save device configurations or entire simulated network topologies as .virl files. VIRL file uses YAML encoding and contains complete descriptions of the IOS routers, interface configurations, login credentials, etc. You can also convert .virl files to "testbed" files for use with pyATS and Genie (to be discussed shortly).

To implement VIRL, all you need is a modern computer, laptop or desktop or a server. Memory and storage requirements start at 8GB DRAM and 100GB of free disk space. You can run the VIRL server as a VM inside VMWare ESXi, Workstation, Workstation Player or even VMWare Fusion Pro for macOS. You can also run VIRL directly on top of a bare-metal server.

Cisco VIRL also offers several other benefits.

- Automatic configuration or bootstrapping of networking nodes via AutoNetkit
- Can be integrated with physical real-world networks
- VIRL server image is available as OVA, VM, and ISO
- Topology portability, you can export your topology and import on another VIRL server

Once the VIRL server is installed, you can interact with it using a client utility VM Maestro.

VIRL Limitations

While VIRL offers tons of awesome benefits over either using another emulator, simulator or physical networking devices, it also comes with some limitations.

- It is not free (whereas GNS3 and EVE-NG are)
- It has higher memory and disk space requirements as you scale up nodes beyond 20 and/or if you use NX-OS or IOS XR images which require 12 and 16GB DRAMs respectively
- It doesn't support any interface type other than Ethernet
- Some nodes running NX-OSv or IOS XRv can take a long time to boot up. VIRL doesn't allow changes to an existing topology, e.g., you can't add/remove nodes or interfaces or modify how they are connected.

Cisco pyATS

Cisco Python Automated Test System (pyATS) bundled with Genie can be used as a test and DevOps automation tool. It provides features, solutions, and system test automation with products including routers, switches, firewalls, etc. It was developed by Cisco for internal use and then Cisco made it available to the public.

Using Cisco pyATS python-based framework, developers can write a small linear test case as well as a complex test suite. Genie builds upon pyATS to provide a simple textual CLI and a suite of the pre-built catalog of test cases that can be used by someone without the knowledge of coding, i.e., most network engineers today.

Out of the box, pyATS-Genie supports Cisco IOS XE, IOS XR, NX-OS, and Cisco ASA products. You can connect to individual devices using CLI or API such as RESTCONF or NETCONF. It can also consume, parse and implement topologies even from sources like Microsoft Excel spreadsheets. It can also be integrated with automation tools such as Ansible for building, provisioning and teardown.

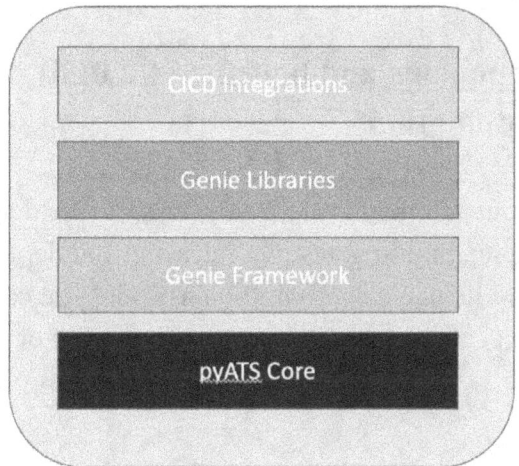

There are a few concepts that you need to understand about how tests are defined in pyATS in the form of Python scripts.

Test Cases

It contains one or more test steps that are to be carried out.

Test Scripts

These are simply a collection of test cases and provide a wrapper where tasks like setting up the test environment or tearing down of it take place.

Job File

It consists of one or more test scripts and define how a test is executed. E.g., a test can take command line arguments, or it could use variables that are applied to test runs.

Easypy

It is the runtime environment for the actual test execution.

Describe the components and benefits of CI/CD pipeline in infrastructure automation

CI/CD pipeline is about automating steps in your software delivery process or components, i.e., coding, building, testing, releasing and deploying your code. If you treat your network device's configuration as code, you can apply the same stages and automation concepts to networking automation or what's also known as NetDevOps.

Network Changes with NetDevOps Pipeline

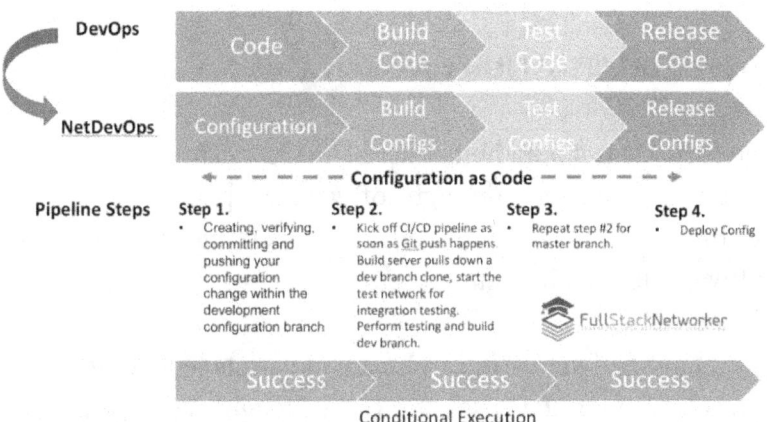

In addition to CI/CD components, let's also understand exactly what CI and CD mean.

Continuous Integration (CI) is about merging all working code from all developers working on the shared mainline code multiple times a day. CI attempts to enhance code quality by testing, reviewing, and running test cases automatically with the help of DevOps tools. CI cycles are run at regular intervals throughout a day. It also enhances quality by reporting failure and success rates each day in real-time.

Continuous Delivery (CD) is a software release approach using which development teams can produce and test code in short cycles with the help of DevOps automation tools. CD enhances code quality by shortening the feedback loop. It is not to be confused with continuous deployment when a delivered code is deployed to end customers.

The benefits of CI/CD pipeline are well known and include the following, i.e.

- Faster software builds
- Faster Time to Market (TTM)
- Code quality improvements

- Higher development productivity

Describe principles of infrastructure as code (IaC)

Infrastructure as Code (or IaC) is a paradigm where DevOps team provision and manage a given stack for an application through software as opposed to using a manual process to configure various server hardware or operating systems. It is also referred to as software-defined infrastructure.

On the surface, it may sound like just writing a bunch of scripts to automate a manual process, but it is far from it. IaC uses descriptive languages to code provisioning and deployment processes. For example, with Ansible, you can install an application, verify that the application is running properly, create a user with proper credentials and then set up your new application.

This code-based infrastructure automation treats configuration as code in theory and then applies software design practices much like what developers do with code, i.e., version control (via Git), run automated tests (with Jenkins or Drone or another build server) and provision networking infrastructure throughout development, testing, integration and deployment stages using Ansible, YAML and some kind of templates such as Jinja2.

In Chapter 4, we discussed a term immutability which means the state of being unchangeable, but in DevOps circles it means treating infrastructure or systems as code and performing no manual operations whatsoever. Immutability brings tremendously more value to IaC.

Benefits of IaC

With infrastructure setup or configuration as code, you can reap the following benefits.

- Configuration version control where all changes are tracked
- Use of CI/CD pipeline tools (such as a build server etc.)

- Use of complementary technologies (such as using Containers or Kubernetes)

Like with any approach, IaC also has its pitfalls if not managed properly, i.e.

- New configuration management toolchain and associated learning curve
- Lack of prerelease testing can lead to errors that spread through infrastructure, could be servers or networking hardware
- Manual changes, aka configuration drift, made outside configuration management toolchain can wreak havoc

Examples of IaC tools include AWS CloudFormation, Red Hat Ansible, Chef, Puppet, SaltStack, and Terraform. Most of these tools can function with standard template formats such as JSON and YAML.

GitOps, or operations by pull request, is a form of modern IaC. With GitOps, each branch is deployed to segregated infrastructure.

- Development
- Test
- Production

During Development, developers make changes in the Development branch, filing commits and making pull requests. These requests are automatically queued for testing. The operators analyze results and developers have to iterate until tests pass. Once that happens, the changes are merged into the Test branch.

During Test, when changes are merged from Development into Test, the code is deployed to a test environment and is subjected to a more extensive set of automated tests.

During Production, tested changes are again reviewed and merged to Production.

Describe the capabilities of automation tools such as Ansible, Puppet, Chef, and Cisco NSO

Before we discuss the automation tools, it is crucial to revisit some of the core concepts related to automation.

Idempotency is about producing desired results each time an automation is run. It enables convergence and composability. It enables you to both gather collections and deploy collections to perform incremental upgrades. For example, if you have a Docker cluster and there is a misconfiguration, you can roll back the most recent change and then rebuild the entire cluster.

As we discussed earlier, procedural code can achieve idempotency but most of the infrastructure automation tools use declarative or static model that represents the desired outcome. Ansible and Puppet use declarative Domain-Specific Languages (or DSLs), whereas Chef uses procedural approach to infrastructure automation.

It is also important to understand the various operations terms such as provisioning, configuration, deployment and orchestration.

Provisioning means obtaining a resource, enabling communications and putting it into service. For example, installing an operating system. It is generally about the lower-level platform readiness. Configuration means installing applications and services on top of the lower-level platform that has already been provisioned. Deployment is about building, arranging and integrating applications such as database or Kubernetes clusters often across multiple nodes. Orchestration has to do with managing workload and lifecycles and reacting to changes in real-time such as autoscaling. In the abstract form, it refers to workflow automation that carries out tasks to deliver business results.

Ansible is an open source automation tool or platform that is easy to setup and can help you with the following tasks.

- Configuration management
- Application deployment
- Task automation or Orchestration

Ansible architecture is simple and lightweight.

- Control node (can run on any Linux machine that has Python installed). It connects to managed devices using SSH to execute shell commands, inject Python scripts, etc.
- Plugins enable Ansible to gather facts from and perform operations on infrastructure that doesn't support running Python locally.

Ansible folder hierarchy includes the following components.

- Inventory files (or hostfiles help organize inventory of resources)
- Variable files (files that describe the variables values related to groups of hosts and individual hosts)
- Library and utility files (Python code for custom modules and utilities)
- Main playbook files (YAML files)
- Role folders and files (role folder that contains a /tasks folder and main.yaml tasks file)

Configuration management tools include Ansible, Puppet, and Chef and they are well known in the DevOps circles. These tools enable you to automate applications, infrastructure, and networks to a high degree without the need to do any manual programming. Puppet is written in Ruby and refers to its automation instruction set as Puppet manifests. The major point to note here is that Puppet is agent-based. Agent-based means a software agent needs to be installed on all devices you want to manage with Puppet. "Devices" here refers to servers, routers, switches, firewalls, and the like. It is often not possible to load an agent on many networking devices. Hence, this requirement limits the number of devices that can be used with Puppet out of the box. The agent requirement raises the barriers to deployment for Puppet as far as networking is concerned. Furthermore, with some investment and cultural change, DevOps virtuous cycle brings with it the benefits of improved scalability, reliability, maintainability, and faster release rollouts with higher quality.

Chef, another popular configuration management tool, follows much of the same model as Puppet. Chef is written in Ruby and uses a declarative model, is also agent-based. Chef refers to its automation instruction as recipes and when they are grouped, they are known as cookbooks.

The two notable differences between Puppet, Chef, and Ansible are that Ansible is written in Python and that it is natively agentless. Being agentless significantly lowers the barrier to deployment from an automation perspective.

Ansible can integrate and automate any device using any API. For example, integrations can use REST APIs, NETCONF, SSH, or even SNMP, if desired. Ansible sets of tasks (instructions) are known as playbooks. Each playbook is made up of one or more plays, where each play consists of individual tasks.

	Chef	**Puppet**	**Ansible**
Who owns it	Chef Labs	Puppet Labs	Red Hat
Agent	Required	Required	Not Required
Language written in	Ruby	Ruby	Python
Tasks are known as	recipes	manifests	plays
Group of tasks known as	cookbooks	modules	playbooks
Config Language	Custom	Custom	YAML
Ease of Use	Steep learning curve	Steep learning curve with	Easier

		DSL/Ruby	
Pricing	Free (Chef Basics), $72/node afterwards	Free (Open Source) up to 10 nodes, $120/node afterwards	Free (CLI), unlimited nodes Free (Ansible Tower) up to 10 nodes, paid afterwards with or without support. Tower pricing ranges from $50-$175 per managed node per year. Ansible Engine and Tower provide essentially same functionalities except with the difference that Engine comes with CLI whereas Tower is a web-based.

When using the configuration management tools, from a RESTful service standpoint, for an operation (or service call) to be idempotent, clients can make that same call repeatedly while producing the same result.

Puppet comprises of a little more complex architecture than Ansible. It consists of the following components.

- Designated server to host main application components such as puppet server (formerly puppet master), facter, and puppetDB. It can run on a

VM or a container. Puppet server requires a Network Time Protocol (NTP) client.
- Secure client (Puppet agent, it needs to be installed and configured on the target devices)
- Puppet modules (for targets that can't run Puppet agent)

Puppet is heavier than Ansible and thus requires more hardware resource to run. Like Ansible, Puppet provides a host of resources that can be executed to define configuration actions to be performed on target hosts. A single Puppet server can manage up to 4,000 hosts. You can find plenty of Puppet modules for Cisco ISO and Cisco UCS (via UCSM).

Chef provides a complete system for working with IaC. There are three main Chef components.

- Chef workstation (standalone operator workstation)
- Chef Infra client (the host agent, it runs on hosts and retrieve configuration templates. Cookbooks enable control of hardware devices such as Cisco routers and switches since you can't run Chef client locally)
- Chef Infra server (It replies to queries from Chef infra agents on validated hosts and responds with configuration updates, etc.)

Cisco provides modified Chef Infra agents that run in the guest shell of NX-OS. Cisco also maintains Chef Cookbook for NX-OS infrastructure. Cisco UCS infrastructure is easily managed with Chef via a cookbook that enables integration with Cisco IMC (via UCSM). You can also integrate with Intersight via Python or PowerShell SDKs.

NSO and Ansible can be used integrated. Ansible tasks use modules (as Clients) to perform their activities whereas NSO uses JSON RPC API perform operations on NSO. NSO can use YANG modules to describe the schema of the data can be modified using JSON RPC.

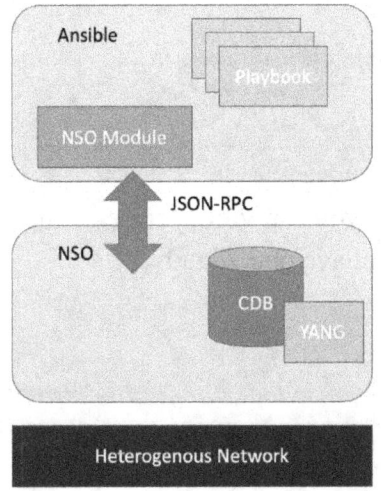

Identify the workflow being automated by a Python script that uses Cisco APIs including ACI, Meraki, Cisco DNA Center, or RESTCONF

Python-based Workflow Automation with Cisco Meraki

Let's say we want to create a script that helps us automate the following workflow.

- Get the existing Inventory
- Create a network
- Get the inventory again
- Claiming an Unused Device and adding it into a Network
- Change some properties for the device

To get started, we need to make sure that access to our Meraki Dashboard API is enabled. You can go to Organization > Configure > Settings > Dashboard API access section.

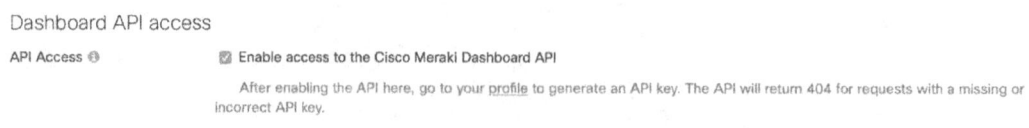

If you click on profile link, you can view your existing API keys, make sure that you create one if you don't have one already.

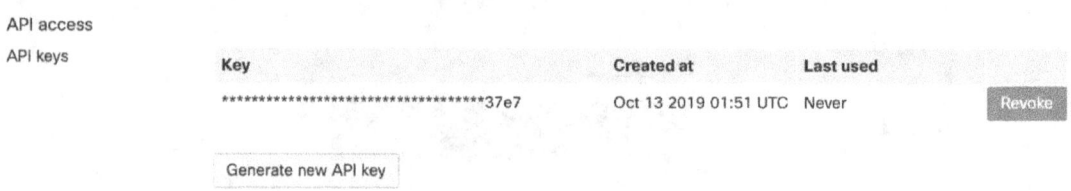

If you don't have one already, click on "Generate new API key" to get started.

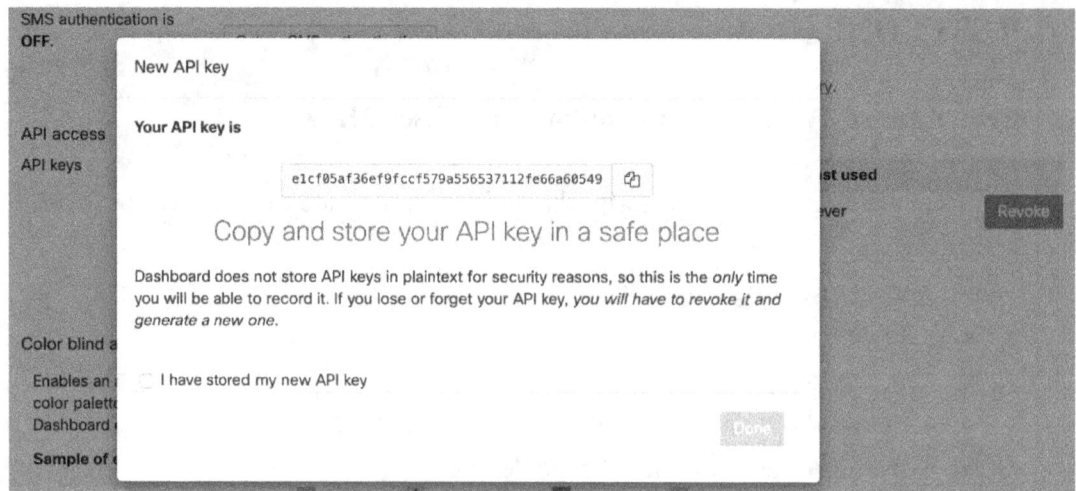

Our API key is "e1cf05af36ef9fccf579a556537112fe66a60549".

Now, before we can proceed to implementing the actual workflow, we need to get our Meraki Organization ID.

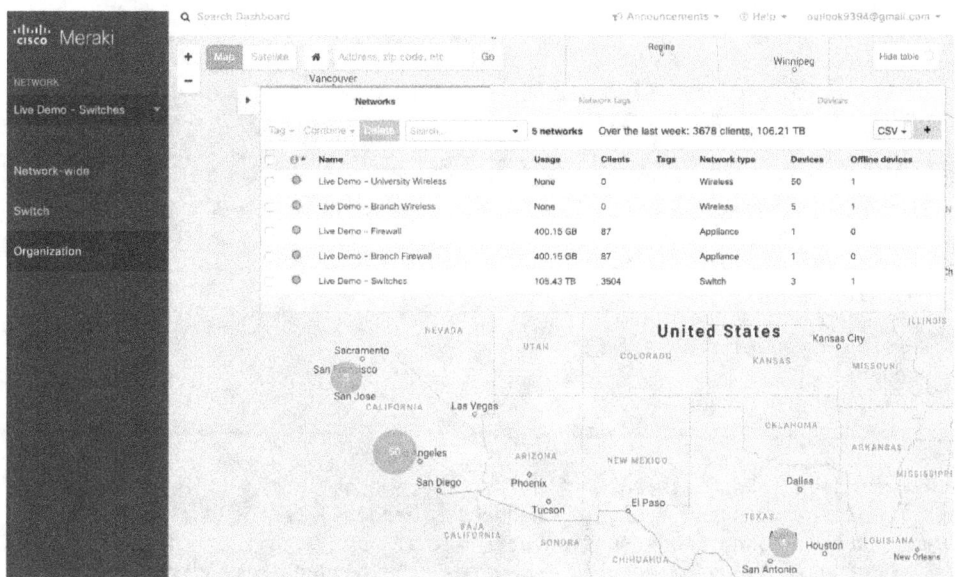

Once you're logged into your Meraki dashboard, you can simply the following REST API call to get your Organization ID. The number highlighted below is our Organization ID.

https://dashboard.meraki.com/api/v0/organizations

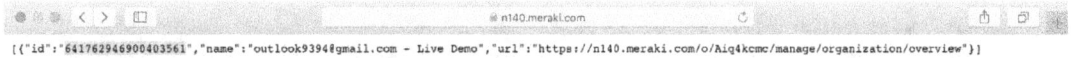

[{"id":"641762946900403561","name":"outlook9394@gmail.com - Live Demo","url":"https://n140.meraki.com/o/Aiq4kcmc/manage/organization/overview"}]

Organization ID = 641762946900403561

Workflow Task #1 – Gather existing inventory

You can gather the inventory either using the requests module (as shown below) or Meraki's API library/module which is much easier and quicker.

```python
1    import json
2    import requests
3
4    api_key = 'e1cf05af36ef9fccf579a556537112fe66a60549'
5    org_id = '641762946900403561'
6
7    def get_net_name(network_id, networks):
8      return [element
9        for element in networks
10       if network_id == element['id']
11     ][0]['name']
12
13   session = requests.session()
14   headers = {
15     'X-Cisco-Meraki-API-Key': api_key,
16     'Content-Type': 'application/json'
17   }
18   name = json.loads(session.get('https://api.meraki.com/api/v0
         /organizations/' + org_id, headers = headers).text)['name']
19   mynetworks = json.loads(session.get('https://api.meraki.com/api/v0
         /organizations/' + org_id + '/networks', headers = headers
         ).text)
20   myinventory = json.loads(session.get('https://api.meraki.com/api/v0
         /organizations/' + org_id + '/inventory', headers = headers
         ).text)
21
22   myappliances = [device
23     for device in myinventory
24     if device['model'][: 2] in ('MX', 'Z1', 'Z3', 'vM') and
           device['networkId'] is not None
25   ]
26
27   mydevices = [device
28     for device in myinventory
29     if device not in myappliances and device['networkId'] is not None
30   ]
31
32   # Print all appliances within each Network
33   for appliance in myappliances:
34     network_name = get_net_name(appliance['networkId'], mynetworks)
35   print('Network: ' + network_name)
36   device_name = json.loads(session.get('https://api.meraki.com/api/v0
         /networks/' + appliance['networkId'] + '/devices/' +
         appliance['serial'], headers = headers).text)['name']
37   print('Appliance Name: ' + device_name)
38
39   # Print all devices within each Network
40   for device in mydevices:
41     print('Network: ' + network_name)
42   network_name = get_net_name(device['networkId'], mynetworks)
43   device_name = json.loads(session.get('https://api.meraki.com/api/v0
         /networks/' + device['networkId'] + '/devices/' +
         device['serial'], headers = headers).text)['name']
44   print('Device Name: ' + device_name)
```

Code Output (truncated)

```
Network: Live Demo - Firewall
Appliance Name: Main Office
Network: Live Demo - Branch Firewall
Appliance Name: Branch office
Network: Live Demo - Branch Firewall
Device Name: Health Center, SE
Network: Live Demo - University Wireless
Device Name: Health Center, SW
Network: Live Demo - University Wireless
Device Name: Van Kampen Hall, floor 1, NE
Network: Live Demo - University Wireless
Device Name: Van Kampen Hall, floor 1, NW
Network: Live Demo - University Wireless
Device Name: Van Kampen Hall, floor 1, CE
Network: Live Demo - University Wireless
Device Name: Van Kampen Hall, floor 1, CW
Network: Live Demo - University Wireless
Device Name: Van Kampen Hall, floor 1, SE
Network: Live Demo - University Wireless
Device Name: Van Kampen Hall, floor 1, SW
Network: Live Demo - University Wireless
Device Name: Kerrwood Annex, S
Network: Live Demo - University Wireless
Device Name: Bookstore, W
Network: Live Demo - University Wireless
Device Name: Bookstore, C
Network: Live Demo - University Wireless
Device Name: Bookstore, E
Network: Live Demo - University Wireless
Device Name: Student Center, floor 1, NC
Network: Live Demo - University Wireless
Device Name: Student Center, floor 1, NW
```

We can always verify our output with what's shown in the Meraki dashboard, and it indeed it tallies up with it.

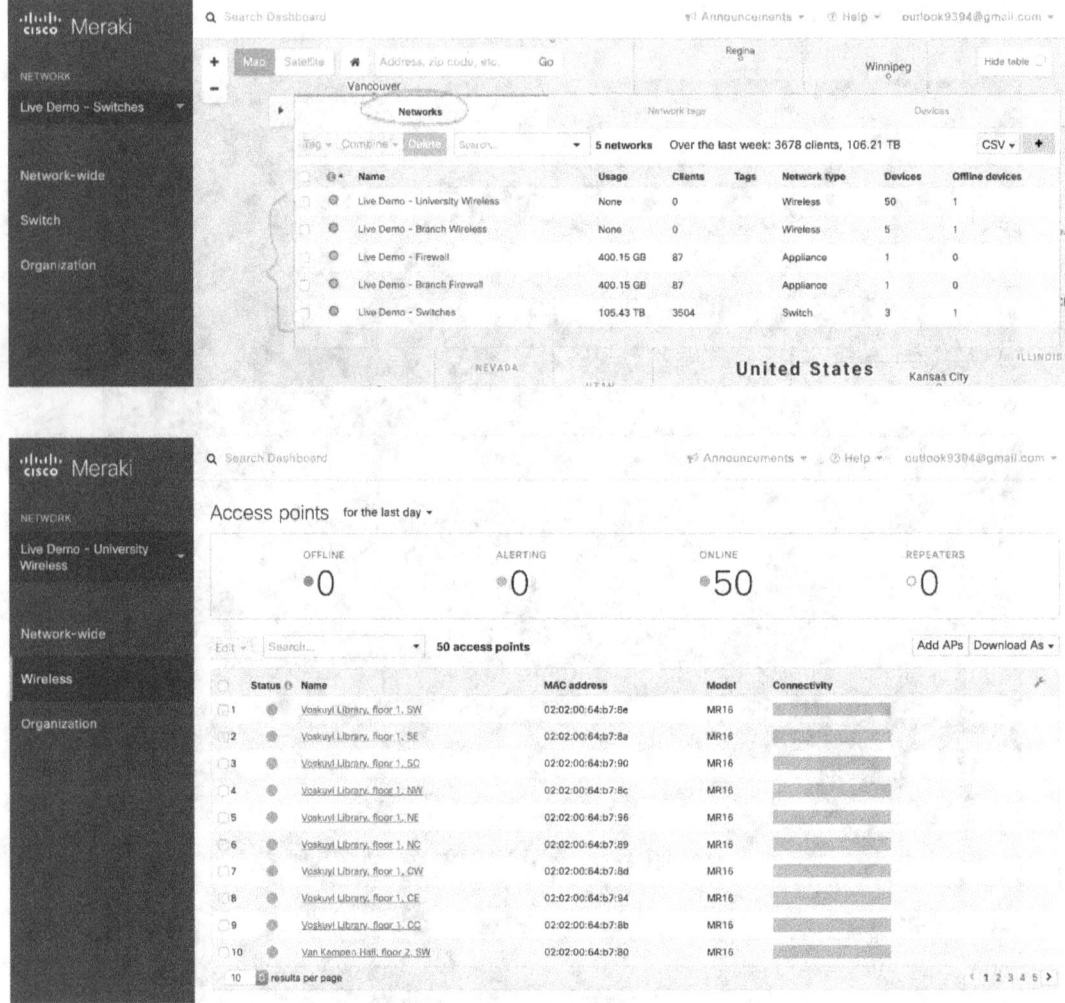

You can also save inventory or any other info that is being printed into a file by importing "sys" module and use corresponding methods such as writerow() to write.

Workflow Task #2 – Create a network

In this step, we will use Meraki's API library/module to create the network.

```
1  my_name = 'Full Stack Networker'
2  my_tags = ['WorkflowTrial', 'West', 'CA']
3  my_time = 'US/Pacific'
```

For a complete list of time zones, you can refer to Meraki's Python source file.

Python Code

```
1   from meraki import meraki
2
3   api_key = 'e1cf05af36ef9fccf579a556537112fe66a60549'
4   org_id = '641762946900403561'
5
6   # New Network Details
7   my_name = 'Full Stack Networker'
8   my_tags = ['WorkflowTrial', 'West', 'CA']
9   my_time = 'US/Pacific'
10
11  current_networks = meraki.getnetworklist(api_key, org_id)
12  network_names = [network['name']
13    for network in current_networks]
14      my_network = meraki.addnetwork(api_key, org_id, my_name,
             'wireless', my_tags, my_time)
15      my_netid = my_network['id']
16      print('New Network Details: created network {0} with network ID
            {1}\n'.format(my_name, my_netid))
```

Code Output

```
Network Operation Successful - See returned data for results

Network Added Successfully - See returned data for results

New Network Details: created network Full Stack Networker with net
work ID N_641762946900882717

>
```

Dashboard Output

Task #3 – Gather Inventory (again)

In this step, we will use Meraki's API library/module to gather inventory.

Python Code

```
1   from meraki import meraki
2   import pprint
3
4   api_key = 'e1cf05af36ef9fccf579a556537112fe66a60549'
5   org_id = '641762946900403561'
6
7   # New Network Details
8   myinventory = meraki.getorginventory(api_key, org_id)
9   pprint.pprint(myinventory, indent = 4)
```

Code Output (Truncated)

```
Inventory Operation Successful - See returned data for results

[  {  'claimedAt': None,
      'mac': '02:02:00:64:b7:68',
      'model': 'MR16',
      'name': 'Health Center, SE',
      'networkId': 'N_641762946900876737',
      'publicIp': '98.173.209.211',
      'serial': 'VRT-2207619790696'},
   {  'claimedAt': None,
      'mac': '02:02:00:64:b7:69',
      'model': 'MR16',
      'name': 'Health Center, SW',
      'networkId': 'N_641762946900876737',
      'publicIp': '98.173.209.211',
      'serial': 'VRT-2207619790697'},
   {  'claimedAt': None,
      'mac': '02:02:00:64:b7:6a',
      'model': 'MR16',
      'name': 'Van Kampen Hall, floor 1, NE',
      'networkId': 'N_641762946900876737',
      'publicIp': '98.173.209.214',
      'serial': 'VRT-2207619790698'},
   {  'claimedAt': None,
      'mac': '02:02:00:64:b7:6b',
      'model': 'MR16',
      'name': 'Van Kampen Hall, floor 1, NW',
      'networkId': 'N_641762946900876737',
      'publicIp': '98.173.209.215',
      'serial': 'VRT-2207619790699'},
   {  'claimedAt': None,
      'mac': '02:02:00:64:b7:6c',
      'model': 'MR16',
      'name': 'Van Kampen Hall, floor 1, CE',
      'networkId': 'N_641762946900876737',
      'publicIp': '98.173.209.215',
      'serial': 'VRT-2207619790700'},
```

Task #3 – Claiming an Unused Device and adding it into a Network

In this step, we will use Meraki's API library/module to claim the device into the network. When you add a new device, it needs to be claimed first. Once claimed, it can be assigned or added to a network i.e., taking ownership of it.

Python Code

```
1   from meraki import meraki
2
3   api_key = 'e1cf05af36ef9fccf579a556537112fe66a60549'
4   org_id = '641762946900403561'
5
6   # New Network Details
7   my_name = 'FSN Dmeo'
8   my_tags = ['Trial', 'West', 'CA']
9   my_time = 'US/Pacific'
10
11  # Create a network or choose an existing one(and get the ID)
12  my_network = meraki.addnetwork(api_key, org_id, my_name, 'Demo',
        my_tags, my_time)
13  my_netid = my_network['id']
14
15  myinventory = meraki.getorginventory(api_key, org_id)# Find Unused
        devices or pick one yourself that is unused
16  unused = [device
17    for device in myinventory
18    if device['networkId'] is None]
19      my_ap = unused[0]
20      my_serial = my_ap['serial']
21
22  # Our New Network doesn 't contain any device yet
23  my_network_devices = meraki.getnetworkdevices(api_key, my_netid)#
        Claim device
24  meraki.adddevtonet(api_key, my_netid, my_serial)
```

Workflow Task #4, Update device attribute

Python Code

```
 1   from meraki import meraki
 2
 3   api_key = 'e1cf05af36ef9fccf579a556537112fe66a60549'
 4   org_id = '641762946900403561'
 5
 6   # New Network Details
 7   my_name = 'FSN Dmeo'
 8   my_tags = ['Trial', 'West', 'CA']
 9   my_time = 'US/Pacific'
10
11   # Create a network or choose an existing one(and get the ID)
12   my_network = meraki.addnetwork(api_key, org_id, my_name, 'Demo',
         my_tags, my_time)
13   my_netid = my_network['id']
14
15   myinventory = meraki.getorginventory(api_key, org_id)# Find Unused
         devices or pick one yourself that is unused
16   unused = [device
17     for device in myinventory
18     if device['networkId'] is None]
19       my_ap = unused[0]
20       my_serial = my_ap['serial']
21
22   # Update Device Location
23   new_address = 'San Francisco, CA'
24   meraki.updatedevice(api_key, my_netid, my_serial, my_name, my_tags,
         address = new_address, move = 'true')
```

Identify the workflow being automated by an Ansible playbook (management packages, user management related to services, basic service configuration, and start/stop)

In this workflow, we will use an existing CI/CD pipeline that's running off of a Drone build server and make changes to our IOS devices using Ansible Playbooks. Drone executes the pipeline instructions once the "git push" takes place.

The main playbook that we use here is named "site.yml".

```yaml
 1  ---
 2  - name: Network Available
 3    hosts: all
 4    connection: local #telling ansible to run the modules locally
 5    gather_facts: false #telling ansible to not to collect variable
         information from the network devices
 6    any_errors_fatal: true #playbook execution stops if any errors
         are encountered
 7
 8    tasks:
 9      - name: Waiting 40 seconds for devices to boot up
10        command: sleep 40
11        delegate_to: localhost #setting the above command to be run
             on the host instead of the client
12          .
13      - name: Ensure all devices are up and responding. #checking all
           the devices in the inventory file to see if they are online
14        wait_for:
15          host: "{{ ansible_host }}"
16          port: "{{ port | default('22') }}"
17          delay: 5 #wait for 5 seconds before execution.
18
19  - name: Gather Info on Network
20    hosts: all
21    connection: local
22    gather_facts: false #Telling ansible to not collect variable
         information from the network devices
23
24    tasks:
25      - name: Get IOS Info
26        ios_facts:
27            host: "{{ ansible_host }}"
28            port: "{{ port | default('22') }}"
29
30
31
32  - name: Deploy Common Network Configuration
33    hosts: all
34    connection: local
35    gather_facts: false
36
37    roles:
38      - common #runs the common network configuration role playbook
```

As you can see, the main playbook, invokes yet another playbook known as "main.yml".

Main.yml

```yaml
1  - name: Get current SNMP Community Configuration
2    ios_command:
3      port: "{{ port | default('22') }}"
4      commands: "show running | inc snmp-server community"
5    register: snmp_community_before #registers the result of above
         command into this variable
6
7  - name: Remove existing SNMP Community Configuration
8    when: item != '' #runs the below commands when the
         snmp_community_before variable is not empty
9    ios_config:
10     port: "{{ port | default('22') }}"
11     lines: "no {{ item }}" #remove existing snmp community using
          the values from snmp_community_before
12   with_items: "{{ snmp_community_before.stdout_lines[0] }}"
13
14 - name: Setup SNMP Configuration
15   ios_config:
16     port: "{{ port | default('22') }}"
17     lines: #setting snmp using the variables from the group_vars
          folder
18       - snmp-server community {{ read_community }} ro
19       - snmp-server community {{ write_community }} rw
20       - snmp-server enable traps snmp linkdown linkup
21       - snmp-server enable traps snmp linkdown linkup
22       - snmp-server chassis-id {{ chassis_id }}
23       - snmp-server contact {{ contact }}
24       - snmp-server location {{ location }}
25       - snmp-server trap-source {{ mgmt_interface }}
26       - snmp-server source-interface informs {{ mgmt_interface }}
27
28
29 - name: Get current SNMP Host Configuration
30   ios_command: #getting current snmp host value and registering it
          with  snmp_hosts_before
31     port: "{{ port | default('22') }}"
32     commands: "show running | inc snmp-server host"
33   register: snmp_hosts_before
```

```
34
35 ▾ - name: Remove existing SNMP Host Configuration
36     when:  item != '' #runs the below commands when the
              snmp_hosts_before variable is not empty
37 ▾   ios_config:
38       port: "{{ port | default('22') }}"
39       lines: "no {{ item }}"
40     with_items: "{{ snmp_hosts_before.stdout_lines[0] }}"
41
42 ▾ - name: Setup SNMP Hosts
43     with_items: "{{ servers }}" #using the variable set in group_vars
44 ▾   ios_config:
45       port: "{{ port | default('22') }}"
46 ▾     lines:
47         - snmp-server host {{ item }} version 2c {{ read_community }}
                #setting the snmp server host using the variable values
                from group_vars
48
49 ▾ - name: Write config to memory #writing the config to memory
50 ▾   ios_command:
51       port: "{{ port | default('22') }}"
52       commands: "write memory"
```

Main.yml playbook helps execute changes to IOS devices in our topology, currently removing existing SNMP RW strings and replacing them with the new one that just got committed as part of the configuration changes from git.

Identify the workflow being automated by a bash script (such as file management, app install, user management, directory navigation)

Bash script is nothing but a text file that includes Linux/Unix CLIs and saved as "blah.sh" file. It is required to give this file execute permission using "chmod +x <blah.sh>" before attempt one. Shell scripts can contain variables, if/else conditionals, loops etc. much like Python. You can also schedule your scripts for execution using Cron jobs.

You can execute a shell script either locally or remotely using the following approaches.

- Transfer the script to a target machine or machines with secure copy (scp), log into remote machine using SSH and then execute
- You can pipe scripts to a remote machine using cat | ssh and execute them in a sequence with other commands
- You can store scripts on a web server or a store them in a Git repo, then log into remote host and execute the script

Performing file management tasks using Shell script

```
1   echo " "
2   echo "----Implementing Directory Management----"
3   echo " "
4   ch=0
5   while [ $choice -lt 6 ]
6   do
7           echo "Press the following to :"
8           echo "1) Create a new directory."
9           echo "2) Modify a directory."
10          echo "3) Navigate into directory."
11          echo "4) Listing directories."
12          echo "5) Exit."
13          read choice
14
15          case $choice in
16          1) echo " "
17          echo "---Creation of Directory---"
18          echo " "
19          echo "Enter the name of the directory:"
20          read name
21          mkdir $name
22          ;;
23          2) echo " "
24          echo "---Modification of Directory---"
25          echo " "
26          echo "Enter the directory to be modified:"
27          read orgdir
28          echo "Press the following to :"
29          echo " "
```

```
30        echo "1) Rename directory."
31        echo "2) Copy directory to another."
32        echo "3) Move directory."
33        echo "4) Delete directory."
34        echo "5) Exit from Modify Mode."
35        read modchoice
36
37            case $modchoice in
38            1) echo " "
39            echo "---Rename a directory---"
40            echo " "
41            echo "Enter new name for the directory:"
42            read newname
43            mv $orgdir $newname
44            ;;
45            2) echo " "
46            echo "---Copying a directory to another---"
47            echo " "
48            echo "Enter target directory:"
49            read target
50            mkdir $target
51            cp $orgdir $target
52            ;;
53            3) echo " "
54            echo "---Moving a directory---"
55            echo " "
56            echo "Enter target directory:"
57            read target
58            mkdir $target
```

```
59              mv $orgdir $target
60              ;;
61              4) echo " "
62              echo "---Deleting a directory---"
63              echo " "
64              rmdir $orgdir
65              ;;
66              5) echo " "
67              echo "---Exiting from modify mode---"
68              echo " "
69              exit
70              ;;
71              esac
72      ;;
73      3)
74      echo "---Navigation of Directory---"
75      echo " "
76      echo "Enter your choice for method of navigation :"
77      echo "1) Go to Parent Directory. "
78      echo "2) Navigate to specific directory."
79      echo "3) Exit from Navigate Mode."
80      read navchoice
81
82      case $navchoice in
83              1) echo " "
84              echo "---Parent Directory---"
85              echo " "
86              cd ..
87              pwd
```

```
88                  ;;
89                  2) echo " "
90                  echo "---Navigation to Specific Directory---"
91                  echo " "
92                  echo "Enter the target Path:"
93                  read path
94                  cd $path
95                  pwd
96                  ;;
97                  3) echo " "
98                  echo "---Exiting from Navigate Mode---"
99                  echo " "
100                 exit
101                 ;;
102                 esac
103         ;;
104         4)
105     echo "--- Listing of Directories---"
106     echo " "
107     echo "Enter your choice for method of listing :"
108     echo "1) List of directories. "
109     echo "2) List of directories and their details."
110     echo "3) Exit from List Mode."
111     read lischoice
112
113     case $lischoice in
114             1) echo " "
115             echo "---List of directories---"
116             echo " "
117             ls
118             ;;
119             2) echo " "
120             echo "---Detailed List of directories---"
121             echo " "
122             ls -l
123             ;;
124             3) echo " "
125             echo "---Exiting from List Mode---"
126             echo " "
127             exit
128             ;;
129             esac
130         ;;
131     5)echo " "
132     echo "---Exiting---"
133     echo " "
134     exit
135     ;;
136     esac
137 done
```

Shell Script Output

```
netdevops@netdevops-VirtualBox:~$ ./fmgmt.sh

----Implementing Directory Management----

Press the following to :
1) Create a new directory.
2) Modify a directory.
3) Navigate into directory.
4) Listing directories.
5) Exit.
1

---Creation of Directory---

Enter the name of the directory:
mmmm
```

```
----Implementing Directory Management----

Press the following to :
1) Create a new directory.
2) Modify a directory.
3) Navigate into directory.
4) Listing directories.
5) Exit.
4
--- Listing of Directories---

Enter your choice for method of listing :
1) List of directories.
2) List of directories and their details.
3) Exit from List Mode.
1

---List of directories---

'ansible image'      fmgmt.sh         miniconda3                        Public
CiscoIOUKeygen3f.py  gitea            Miniconda3-latest-Linux-x86_64.sh snap
config1              GitExamples      mmmm                              Templates
Desktop              GNS3             Music                             vfgggg
Documents            helloworld.sh    Pictures                          Videos
Downloads            iourc.txt        project
drone_install        just-testing     projectzip.zip
Press the following to :
1) Create a new directory.
2) Modify a directory.
3) Navigate into directory.
4) Listing directories.
5) Exit.
```

Interpret the results of a RESTCONF or NETCONF query
Interpret basic YANG models

Please refer to Chapter 3 for RESTCONF, NETCONF and YANG model request and response related topics.

Interpret a unified diff

Diff is just short for difference. In the case of Linux/Unix or coding, diff tools help spot the difference between two text or source code files. There is another related term known as a patch. Patch refers to a specific collection of diffs between files that can be applied to a source code repo or tree using the Unix utility. The word patch traces its history back to the times when punch cards were used to represent code.

Software version control solutions such as Git or GitHub track those code changes in source files and help organize a team to work together on one large codebase. Unified diffs help us visualize the changes between two versions of source code files, i.e., the original and the modified one.

Let's use an example of a Python script with the original and modified copies.

Original Python Code

```python
1   import sys, os, difflib, argparse
2   import datetime, timezone
3
4   def file_mtime(path):
5       t = datetime.fromtimestamp(os.stat(path).st_mtime,
6           timezone.utc)
7       return t.astimezone().isoformat()
8
9   def main():
10
11      parser = argparse.ArgumentParser()
12      parser.add_argument('-c', action = 'store_true',
13          default = False,
14          help = 'Produce a context format diff (default)')
15      parser.add_argument('-u', action = 'store_true',
16          default = False,
17          help = 'Produce a unified format diff')
18      parser.add_argument('-m', action = 'store_true',
19          default = False,
20          help = 'Produce HTML side by side diff '
21          '(can use -c and -l in conjunction)')
22      parser.add_argument('-n', action = 'store_true',
23          default = False,
24          help = 'Produce a ndiff format diff')
25      parser.add_argument('-l', '--lines', type = int,
26          default = 3,
27          help = 'Set number of context lines (default 3)')
28      parser.add_argument('fromfile')
29      parser.add_argument('tofile')
30      options = parser.parse_args()
31
32      n = options.lines
33      fromfile = options.fromfile
34      tofile = options.tofile
35
36      fromdate = file_mtime(fromfile)
37      todate = file_mtime(tofile)
38      with open(fromfile) as ff:
39          fromlines = ff.readlines()
40      with open(tofile) as tf:
41          tolines = tf.readlines()
```

```
42
43 - if options.u:
44     diff = difflib.unified_diff(fromlines, tolines, fromfile, tofile,
          fromdate, todate, n = n)
45 - elif options.n:
46     diff = difflib.ndiff(fromlines, tolines)
47 - elif options.m:
48     diff = difflib.HtmlDiff().make_file(fromlines, tolines, fromfile,
          tofile, context = options.c, numlines = n)
49 - else :
50     diff = difflib.context_diff(fromlines, tolines, fromfile, tofile,
          fromdate, todate, n = n)
51
52   sys.stdout.writelines(diff)
53
54 - if __name__ == '__main__':
55     main()
```

Modified Python Code

```
1    import sys, os, difflib, argparse
2    import datetime, timezone
3
4 -  def file_mtime(path):
5      t = datetime.fromtimestamp(os.stat(path).st_mtime,
6        timezone.utc)
7    return t.astimezone().isoformat()
8
9 -  def main():
10
11     parser = argparse.ArgumentParser()
12   parser.add_argument('-c', action = 'store_true',
13     default = False,
14     help = 'Produce a context format diff (default)')
15   parser.add_argument('-u', action = 'store_true',
16     default = False,
17     help = 'Produce a unified format diff')
18   parser.add_argument('-m', action = 'store_true',
19     default = False,
20     help = 'Produce HTML side by side diff '
21     '(can use -c and -l in conjunction)')
22   parser.add_argument('-n', action = 'store_true',
23     default = False,
24     help = 'Produce a ndiff format diff')
25   parser.add_argument('-l', '--lines', type = int,
26     default = 3,
27     help = 'Set number of context lines (default 3)')
28   parser.add_argument('fromfile')
29   parser.add_argument('tofile')
30   options = parser.parse_args()
31
32   parser = argparse.ArgumentParser(description = "pydiff - Tkinter
        GUI tool based on Python's difflib")
33   parser.add_argument('-p', '--paths', metavar = ('path1', 'path2'),
        nargs = 2, help = 'Two paths to compare', required = False)
34
```

```
35   args = parser.parse_args()
36
37   leftpath = args.paths[0]
38   if args.paths
39   else None
40   rightpath = args.paths[1]
41   if args.paths
42   else None
43
44   main_window = MainWindow()
45   main_window.start(leftpath, rightpath)
46 ▾ if options.u:
47     diff = difflib.unified_diff(fromlines, tolines, fromfile, tofile,
          fromdate, todate, n = n)
48 ▾ elif options.n:
49     diff = difflib.ndiff(fromlines, tolines)
50 ▾ elif options.m:
51     diff = difflib.HtmlDiff().make_file(fromlines, tolines, fromfile,
          tofile, context = options.c, numlines = n)
52 ▾ else :
53     diff = difflib.context_diff(fromlines, tolines, fromfile, tofile,
          fromdate, todate, n = n)
54
55   sys.stdout.writelines(diff)
56
57 ▾ if __name__ == '__main__':
58     main()
```

Let's now look at the diff.

```
1    1    import sys, os, difflib, argparse
2    2    from datetime import datetime, timezone
3    3
4    4    def file_mtime(path):
5    5        t = datetime.fromtimestamp(os.stat(path).st_mtime,
6    6                                   timezone.utc)
7    7        return t.astimezone().isoformat()
8    8
9    9    def main():
10   10
11   11       parser = argparse.ArgumentParser()
12   12       parser.add_argument('-c', action='store_true', default=False,
13   13                           help='Produce a context format diff (default)')
14   14       parser.add_argument('-u', action='store_true', default=False,
15   15                           help='Produce a unified format diff')
16   16       parser.add_argument('-m', action='store_true', default=False,
17   17                           help='Produce HTML side by side diff '
18   18                                '(can use -c and -l in conjunction)')
19   19       parser.add_argument('-n', action='store_true', default=False,
20   20                           help='Produce a ndiff format diff')
21   21       parser.add_argument('-l', '--lines', type=int, default=3,
22   22                           help='Set number of context lines (default 3)')
23   23       parser.add_argument('fromfile')
24   24       parser.add_argument('tofile')
25   25       options = parser.parse_args()
26   26
27   -        n = options.lines
28   -        fromfile = options.fromfile
29   -        tofile = options.tofile
30   27
31   -        fromdate = file_mtime(fromfile)
32   -        todate = file_mtime(tofile)
33   -        with open(fromfile) as ff:
34   -            fromlines = ff.readlines()
35   -        with open(tofile) as tf:
36   -            tolines = tf.readlines()
     28 +  parser = argparse.ArgumentParser(description="pydiff - Tkinter GUI tool based on Python's difflib")
     29 +  parser.add_argument('-p', '--paths', metavar=('path1', 'path2'), nargs=2, help='Two paths to compare', required=False)
     30 +
     31 +  args = parser.parse_args()
     32 +
     33 +  leftpath = args.paths[0] if args.paths else None
     34 +  rightpath = args.paths[1] if args.paths else None
     35 +
     36 +  main_window = MainWindow()
     37 +  main_window.start(leftpath, rightpath)
37   38       if options.u:
38   39           diff = difflib.unified_diff(fromlines, tolines, fromfile, tofile, fromdate, todate, n=n)
39   40       elif options.n:
40   41           diff = difflib.ndiff(fromlines, tolines)
41   42       elif options.m:
42   43           diff = difflib.HtmlDiff().make_file(fromlines,tolines,fromfile,tofile,context=options.c,numlines=n)
43   44       else:
```

The diff shows the line numbers with pluses (code added) and minuses (code removed) between the original and modified source code files. The unified diff in Linux/Unix always starts with @@.

Describe the principles and benefits of a code review process

To err is human, we all can make mistakes and when it comes to code, a review process is what we need to double-check someone else's work. It is daunting to review code that was written by someone else, but code review is the safety net to ensure code quality and reliability. Performing code reviews has benefits for the whole team. For author, it helps them receive input from others so they can learn additional best practices, or other ways code could have been implemented, even pick up on coding styles. Code reviews also provide way for knowledge transfer between developers.

There are many ways to conduct code reviews. Each one has its own benefits however most can get the job done. The most common types of code reviews are:

- Formal code review
- Change-based review
- Over-the-shoulder review
- Email pass-around review

Formal code review is where developers have a series of meetings to review the entire codebase. It allows reviewers to reach a consensus and thus better feedback. This type of review is also known as Fagan inspection, and is common in projects that use waterfall SDLC methodology. A modern version of formal code review, also known as a walkthrough, is a single meeting where developers only review code changes.

A change-based code review (or a tool-assisted review) is about reviewing the code that was recently changed due to a bug, user story, or a new feature, etc. This type of review usually involves using a peer code review tool, such as collaborator, that highlights the code changes. Change-based reviews are initiated by the developers who made the code changes.

Over-the-shoulder code review is where a reviewer looks the over the shoulder (yes, literally!) of the developer who wrote the code. The reviewer provides the feedback while the developer goes through the code line by line. The obvious drawback of this approach is that it only involves one reviewer, so the comments are not as comprehensive as they are in the case of a formal review.

Email pas-around code review is structured around the emails sent out by the SCM tools that send out automatic emails when a code check-in is made. Now, since the review is about a code change at a time, there is always a risk for missing the forest for the trees, so to speak.

Principles

There are some well-known principles when it comes to reviewing the code or what's known as a peer code review.

Commitment

Commitment is a must-have for a thorough code review, you can't just skim through it. Multiple review cycles are counterproductive.

Asking questions

If you are having difficulty in reviewing code, it likely needs to be cleaned up, or perhaps better commented or even refactored. For your review to be effective, you should feel free to ask questions.

Testing

Sometimes reading through code is not enough, so a reviewer should be willing to clone the code branch and put it through the paces. If you've a build system, it will run a series of automated tests, but your job as a reviewer goes beyond that, so feel free to go as far as breaking the code.

Comment further

Code comments are supposed to make reading easier as well as understanding the original coder's intent. If this is your code, be sure to thoroughly add comments.

Treat all code as production code

There is no time for writing code that's not written for customer facing production quality. As a reviewer, you should hold all code up to fit and finish standards.

Review code for design

Code can be reviewed for many different reasons, however practically speaking design is seldom one of them. Code design and integration matters.

Last but not least, code review process should prioritize the three important areas in this order.

1. Functionality, it must deliver the functionality it's supposed to or it's a bug.
2. Clean code that can be easily added to
3. Code efficiency for optimized run-time execution

Benefits

Code review benefits are about why the code review matters in the first place.

- Fixing bugs as soon as they arise
- It helps enforce a standardized code minimum standards compliance
- It helps non authors to understand code that they didn't write
- Consistent design and the implementation
- Enhanced security

Interpret sequence diagram that includes API calls

API sequence diagrams consist of client/server request/response control channel and data flows.

Below is an example API sequence diagram that shows an app that uses Facebook as oAuth provider. When you land a website that allows sign up using a social network (or any third-party network for that reason), generally uses oAuth behind the scenes to establish your identity and download your profile to the website to establish your account profile.

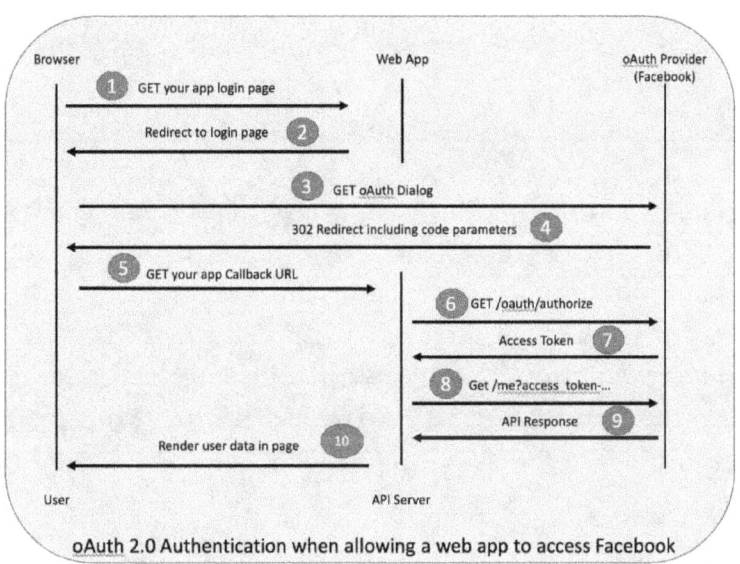

oAuth 2.0 Authentication when allowing a web app to access Facebook

Further Reading

Cisco DevNet Automation Exchange[57]
Nexus OS Programmability and Automation Overview[58]
Deploy a Docker application to Cisco Fog Director and IOx[59]
Introduction to Configuration Management[60]
Introduction to Ansible[61]

---

[57] https://bit.ly/2vZl6rd

[58] https://bit.ly/2IHRse4

[59] https://bit.ly/2wPzYd3

[60] https://bit.ly/2xrYG3f

Getting Hands On with Ansible[62]

[61] https://bit.ly/3cTZzSs

[62] https://bit.ly/2IDonAb

Chapter Summary

- YANG language is used to model data, the data here refers to configurational data, state data, RPCs, and notifications

- Each vendor, such as Cisco or Juniper, has its own YANG modules that describe how to configure their device i.e., configuration state and how to retrieve information from the device i.e., the operational state

- Controlled-based management can fully take advantage of software driven innovation esp. AI and ML in the areas of provisioning, monitoring and operations

- In contrast to simulators, emulators virtualize real network devices, so they offer more feature richness when compared to simulators. GNS3 and Cisco VIRL are examples of emulators.

- There is a big upside to VIRL which none of the other emulators such as GNS3 or EVE-NG offer, and that is access to the near latest IOS XE, IOS XR, NX OS, and ASAv software.

- Once the VIRL server is installed, you can interact with it using a client utility VM Maestro.

- Cisco pyATS bundled with Genie can be used as a test and DevOps automation tool. It provides features, solutions, and system test automation with products including routers, switches, firewalls, etc.

- Infrastructure as Code (or IaC) is a paradigm where DevOps team provision and manage a given stack for an application through software as opposed to using a manual process to configure various server hardware or operating systems.

- Configuration management tools include Ansible, Puppet, and Chef and they are well known in the DevOps circles

- Once you're logged into your Meraki dashboard, you can simply the following REST API call to get your Organization ID.

- Bash script is nothing but a text file that includes Linux/Unix CLIs and saved as "blah.sh" file. It is required to give this file execute permission using "chmod +x <blah.sh>" before attempt one.

- It is daunting to review code that was written by someone else, but code review is the safety net to ensure code quality and reliability.

CHAPTER 6 NETWORK FUNDAMENTALS

This chapter covers the following exam topics from Cisco's official 200-901 V1.0 DevNet Associate exam blueprint.

- Describe the purpose and usage of MAC addresses and VLANs
- Describe the purpose and usage of IP addresses, routes, subnet mask / prefix, and gateways
- Describe the function of common networking components (such as switches, routers, firewalls, and load balancers)
- Interpret a basic network topology diagram with elements such as switches, routers, firewalls, load balancers, and port values
- Describe the function of management, data, and control planes in a network device
- Describe the functionality of these IP Services: DHCP, DNS, NAT, SNMP, NTP
- Recognize common protocol port values (such as, SSH, Telnet, HTTP, HTTPS, and NETCONF)
- Identify cause of application connectivity issues (NAT problem, Transport Port blocked, proxy, and VPN)
- Explain the impacts of network constraints on applications

Describe the purpose and usage of MAC addresses and VLANs

Media Access Control (or MAC) address is the unique identifier that is burned in by the hardware vendor, for example a cabled or a wireless NIC, router's ethernet interface, etc. Most network cards use Registered Jack or RJ-45 connector as a physical interface to connect to a wired network.

MAC address consists of 48-bit address space, i.e., 2^48 or 281T possible combinations, and they sound plenty given that have to be unique only on a given L2 segment. 48-bit MAC address is also known as Extended Unique Identifier (EUI) EUI-48.

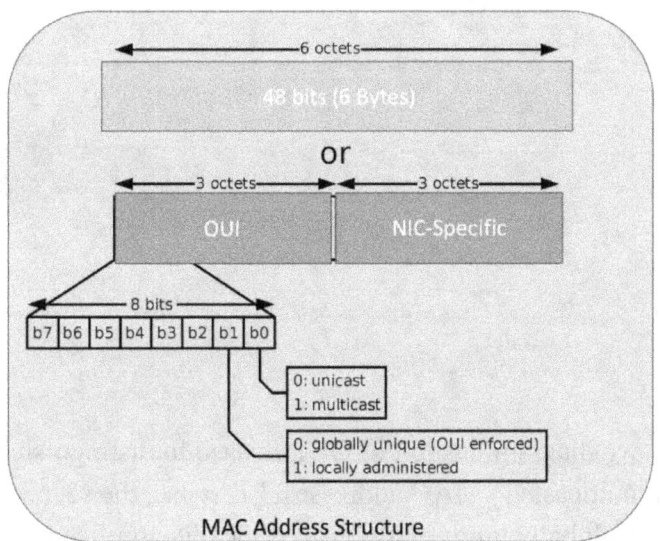

MAC Address Structure

The overall MAC address is divided into two parts, the Organizationally Unique Identifier (OUI) and NIC specific parts, each 24-bit or 3 bytes in length. OUI is unique to a vendor, such as Cisco or Apple whereas NIC specific part is assigned by the vendor itself (much like a unique serial number). OUIs are allocated by the IEEE. There is another 64-bit variant, dubbed as EUI-64, for non ethernet applications such as Zigbee, 802.15.4 or 6LoWPAN protocols.

```
MAK1-MBP:~ afaqkhan$ ifconfig en0
en0: flags=8863<UP,BROADCAST,SMART,RUNNING,SIMPLEX,MULTICAST> mtu 1500
        options=400<CHANNEL_IO>
        ether dc:a9:04:7c:7a:e7
        inet6 fe80::1c15:7704:564a:c4f8%en0 prefixlen 64 secured scopeid 0x5
        inet 192.168.1.12 netmask 0xffffff00 broadcast 192.168.1.255
        nd6 options=201<PERFORMNUD,DAD>
        media: autoselect
        status: active
MAK1-MBP:~ afaqkhan$
```

Let's run an Apple MacBook en0 MAC address (dc:a9:04:7c:7a:e7) through the Wireshark OUI lookup tool.

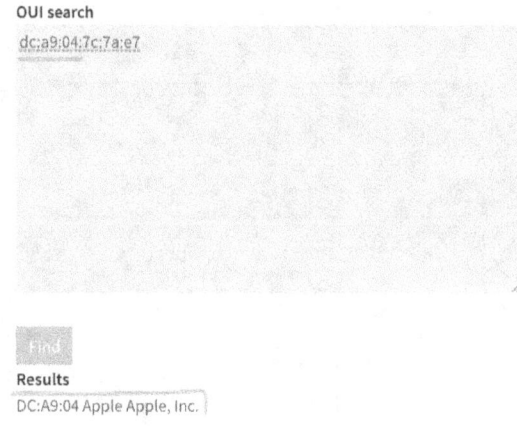

As shown in above diagram, last bit of OUI, is used to distinguish between unicast (0) and multicast (1) MAC addresses. Likewise, the second last bit, is used to identify a globally unique (0) versus a locally significant address (1).

Please note that IPv6 uses EUI-64 (defined in RFC 2373) as part of the IPv6 address, however it is still based on EUI-48. EUI-64 is constructed by adding in 0xFFFFE in between the OUI (24-bit) and NIC-specific (24-bit) MAC address portions resulting in a 64-bit long address.

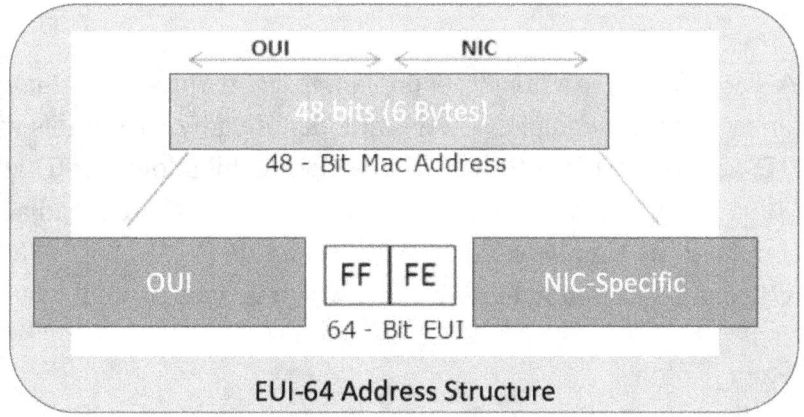

EUI-64 Address Structure

The ethernet frame consists of the following fields.

- Preamble (7 bytes of alternating 1s and 0s)
- Start of frame delimiter (1-byte field that marks the end of preamble)
- Destination Address (6-byte field contains the address of the NIC on the local network)
- Source Address (6-byte field containing the address of the of the NIC of the sending machine)
- Type (2-byte field, identifies the network layer protocols), e.g., IPv4 is 0x0800)
- Data and pad (field contains the actual data)
- Frame Check Sequence (field includes a checksum to ensure that packet was not corrupted in transit)

There are three types of network communications.

- Unicast (frame or packet is sent from one host to another)
- Broadcast (frame or packet is set from one address to all other addresses)
- Multicast (packet is sent to a specific group of devices or clients, unlike broadcast the clients must be members of a multicast group to receive transmission)

VLANs

Virtual LAN (or VLAN) is a broadcast domain that is partitioned virtually to carve out an isolated L2 segment. VLANs are identified by VLAN IDs which is a 12-bit VID field inside the IEEE 802.1Q header. 12-bit allows for ID allocation from 0 to 4095 (2^{12} - 1). While all devices within a VLAN are L2 adjacent so they can communicate simply based on ARP resolution (IP to MAC). However, inter-VLAN communication requires routine which is done by an L3 switch or a router.

Any traffic coming on a switch trunk port (ethernet port connecting a switch to another) that is not tagged with a VLAN ID, will be assigned a native VLAN tag which is VLAN ID 1 for Cisco switches. As opposed to trunk ports, access ports expect all traffic to receive untagged and will send traffic forward (or upstream) tagged with the pre-configured VLAN ID, a default ID (also ID 1 for Cisco) will be used if none configured by the administrator. In conclusion, both native and default VLAN IDs are set to 1 on Cisco devices, however, they exist in two different scenarios i.e., trunk versus access ports.

During VLAN creation process, you can set the following parameters.

- VLAN number
- VLAN name
- VLAN type
- VLAN state
- MTU

Virtual Extensible VLAN (or VXLAN) is used to create virtual overlays on top of a physical underlay. VXLAN uses MAC in IP/UDP tunneling to extend L2 segments over IP networks. VXLAN uses flood and learn mechanisms much like ethernet itself. Ethernet VPNs (or EVPNs) is a variation where VXLANs are used along with BGP to accomplish routing between endpoints.

Describe the purpose and usage of IP addresses, routes, subnet mask / prefix, and gateways

IP address is a numerical label assigned to each endpoint that is connected to a network that uses Internet Protocol (or IP). There are two variants of IP labels and protocols, one that's known as IPv4 and the other one that's known as IPv6. IPv4 and IPv6 address spaces are 32-bit and 128-bit long.

In IP nomenclature, a route is a way to reach another IP destination or a prefix. Routing is done hop-by-hop in an IP network, thus for each prefix, one or more next-hop addresses are what's needed to reach beyond an IP network or subnetwork.

An IP subnet is an isolated IP or L3 segment. Subnet is carved out of an IP network; it could be based on classful or classless boundaries which are determined by the combination of the numerical value of an IP address and the corresponding subnet mask used. Subnet masks can be written in both decimals as well as bit lengths, such as /32 (equivalent to 255.255.255.255) as shown in the output below.

You can look up the routing table using the "show ip route" command. For end hosts, such as PCs, it depends on the OS. For example, for macOS, you can view the current routing table by using "netstat -rn".

```
MAK1-MBP:~ afaqkhan$ netstat -rn
Routing tables

Internet:
Destination          Gateway            Flags      Netif Expire
default              192.168.1.1        UGSc        en0
127                  127.0.0.1          UCS         lo0
127.0.0.1            127.0.0.1          UH          lo0
169.254              link#5             UCS         en0     !
192.168.1            link#5             UCS         en0     !
192.168.1.1/32       link#5             UCS         en0     !
192.168.1.1          14:91:82:96:1d:a5  UHLWIir     en0    1171
192.168.1.12/32      link#5             UCS         en0     !
192.168.1.28         c4:95:0:9a:52:9    UHLWI       en0    1199
192.168.1.59         0:80:92:d5:2e:c3   UHLWI       en0    1150
192.168.1.86         f8:38:80:67:5c:71  UHLWIi      en0    1153
192.168.1.130        ac:cf:5c:ac:f4:39  UHLWI       en0     !
192.168.1.173        14:91:82:95:a0:e3  UHLWI       en0    1167
192.168.1.227        c4:1c:ff:25:f3:8e  UHLWIi      en0     181
192.168.1.247        14:20:5e:c2:24:f1  UHLWIi      en0    1104
224.0.0/4            link#5             UmCS        en0     !
224.0.0.251          1:0:5e:0:0:fb      UHmLWI      en0
255.255.255.255/32   link#5             UCS         en0     !
```

Gateway or default gateway, typical a router or an L3 switch, is a special type of IP address, which allows a host from one subnet to send traffic to another subnet or the internet itself (i.e., networks for which your gateway doesn't know of). In the example above, 192.168.1.1 is the default gateway IP address for en0.

There are five classes of IP addresses.

Class	Network bits	Host bits	Subnet mask
A	8	24	255.0.0.0
B	16	16	255.255.0.0
C	24	8	255.255.255.0
D	Reserved	Reserved	n/a
E	Reserved	Reserved	n/a

Describe the function of common networking components (such as switches, routers, firewalls, and load balancers)

L2 Switches are for bridging or forwarding traffic based on destination MAC address within a given L2 segment or VLAN based on CAM table which is built using the source MAC addresses. L3 switches can function both as an L2 switch as well as a router for inter-VLAN routing and many other use cases. Nexus series products represent Cisco's family of switches.

The following steps describe the switching process.

- The switch receives a frame from a source machine
- The switch stores the source MAC address and the switch port that the frame was received on into the MAC table.
- The switch checks the table for the matching destination MAC address. If there is a match, that port is used to forward the frame. If there is no match, it is flooded out of all of the switch ports (for that VLAN).

Routers route traffic across IP subnets based on destination IP address or prefix. To facilitate the propagation of routing information, routers also support various routing protocols such as OSPF, EIGRP or BGP.

Load balancers distribute traffic load across two or more links based on information within L3 or L4 headers, however in some cases even L7 or application protocol headers.

EIGRP

Enhanced Interior Gateway Routing Protocol (EIGRP) is an advanced or enhanced distance vector protocol. It uses Diffused Update Algorithm (DUAL) algorithm to calculate the shortest path a destination. It is a Cisco proprietary protocol.

Typical distance vector protocols use two pieces of information to make the best path selection to a destination network, i.e., the distance in L3 hop count and the vector which is the next-hop.

	EIGRP	IGRP	RIPv1	RIPv2
Best Path Selection Algorithm	DUAL	DUAL	Bellman-Ford	Bellman-Ford
Administrative Distance	90	100	120	120
Metric	Bandwidth, Load, Delay and Reliability	Bandwidth, Load, Delay and Reliability	Hop Count	Hop Count
Protocol Updates	Triggered	Triggered	Periodic	Triggered
Partial or Full Updates	Partial	Partial	Full	Partial

VLSM	Supported	Not Supported	Not Supported	Supported
Multi Path	Supported	Supported	Not Supported	Not Supported
Topology Table	Yes	No	No	No
Open Industry Standard	No	No	Yes	Yes

Once EIGRP builds a neighbor relationship, it builds a topology table i.e., unlike RIP or IGRP, it doesn't rely on routing table to hold all of the information it needs to operate and then installs route from this to the routing table (much like a distance-vector protocol). You can display the content of the topology table using **show ip eigrp topology** command. Topology contains both distance and vector information for each destination prefix that EIGRP knows about.

EIGRP uses minimum bandwidth and total delay to compute the routing metric. These bandwidth and delay values are what network admins have configured on the interfaces. EIGRP calculates the final metric using bandwidth, delay and a set of 5 coefficients known as K values. EIGRP speaking router wouldn't form a neighbor relationship with another L3 device if K values didn't match.

EIGRP metric = ([K1 * bandwidth + (K2 * bandwidth) / (256 - load) + K3 * delay] * [K5 / (reliability + K4)]) * 256

Where the default K values are K1=1, K2=0, K3=1, K4=0 and K5 = 0 which simplifies the metric formula to bandwidth plus delay.

EIGRP also establishes a specific jargon when it comes to path selection, and those terms include feasible distance, reported distance, and feasible successor.

Feasible distance (or the best path or FD) is the best metric along a path to a destination network. This includes the metric to the neighbor advertising the given path. Reported Distance (RD) is the total metric along the path to a destination network as advertised by an upstream neighbor. Finally, a feasible successor (FC) is a path whose reported distance is less than the feasible distance.

EIGRP supports multiple equal cost paths out of the box and you can configure it using maximum-path command. Additionally, EIGRP also supports unequal cost paths load balancing which can be configured using variance command. Unequal cost paths follow the logic that any routes with a feasible distance less than 'n' times of the successor routes feasible distance can be included in the multiple paths.

Further Reading

EIGRP Configuration Guide[63]

OSPF

Open Shortest Path First (OSPF) protocol is defined in RFC 2328 and based on link-state technology where the link is an interface on an L3 device such as a router. The state of the link is an attribute of that interface and its relationship to its neighbors. The interface attributes relevant to OSPF include the IP address, subnet mask, the type of the network, the routers that are also connected to that network and what have you.

Unlike distance vector protocols that use Bellman-Ford, OSPF uses the shortest path first (or SPF or Dijkstra SPF) algorithm to determine the shortest to all known destination networks with the help of a graph.

When an OSPF router boots up, it generates a link-state advertisement (or LSA) for that router which represents the state of links. All routers exchange their LSAs via flooding mechanism. Once the exchange is completed, every router ends up with a database that is used to calculate the shortest path to each destination. Each OSPF router uses the Dijkstra SPF algorithm to derive the shortest path tree and the result of this calculation is stored in the routing table

[63] https://bit.ly/3b7g1Ok

(or RIB). The algorithm places each router at the root of a tree and then calculates the shortest path to each destination network based on the cumulate cost needed to reach that destination.

	EIGRP	OSPF
Best Path Selection Algorithm	DUAL FSM	Dijkstra SPF
Administrative Distance	90	110
Metric	Bandwidth, Load, Delay and Reliability	Cost
VLSM	Supported	Not Supported
Authentication	Supported	Supported
Multi Path	Supported	Supported (ECMP)
Open Industry Standard	No	Yes, RFC 2328

OSPF uses interface cost as its metric, which is inversely proportional to the bandwidth of that interface, i.e., higher bandwidth means lower cost by default unless you modify it using ip ospf cost <value> command.

OSPF uses flooding to exchange link-state advertisements between routers and all routers within an area have an exact link-state database. Routers that have interfaces in multiple areas including backbone are known as Area Border Routers (ABRs). Routers that act as a gateway between OSPF and other routing protocols or other instances of the OSPF process are known as Autonomous System Border Routers (or ASBRs). OSPF finite state machine (or FSM) includes eight different states including down, attempt, init, two-way, exstart, exchange, loading and full.

OSPF addresses three classes of network types, point to point (p2p), point to multipoint (p2mp) and broadcast.

Further Reading

OSPF Design Guide[64]

BGP

BGP is an exterior gateway protocol (or EGP) so it was created from ground up to perform interdomain routing. BGP router establishes a connection using TCP to each of its neighbors. BGP router can establish two types of sessions, external or internal. If the two BGP peers reside in two different domains or autonomous systems (or ASs), the session is known as an external BGP or an eBGP session. If the two BGP peers are in the same AS, then it said to be an internal BGP or iBGP session. By default, BGP establishes a peer relationship using the IP address of the interface closest to the peering router. However, BGP peers can use neighbor update-source command to source BGP packets from another interface if so desired.

BGP routers can receive multiple paths to the same destination but BGP router uses the best path selection algorithm and would only install the best route in the routing table. BGP assigns the first valid path as the current best path, but then BGP compares the best path with the next path in the list until BGP reaches the end of the list.

Best Path Selection Criteria

Here is the sequence of best path selection algorithm, however, keep in mind that a lot of these tests can be overridden or even bypassed altogether based on the various BGP knobs and options available on a Cisco router.

1. Prefer the path with the highest WEIGHT (Cisco proprietary)
2. Prefer the path with the highest LOCAL_PREF (default value is 100)

---

[64] https://bit.ly/2RPY1Ao

3. Prefer the path that was locally originated via network or aggregate commands
4. Prefer the path with the shortest AS_PATH
5. Prefer the path with the lowest origin type
6. Prefer the path with the lowest MED
7. Prefer eBGP over iBGP
8. Prefer the path with the lowest IGP metric to the BGP next hop (best path is already selected at this point)
9. Optionally, if BGP Multipath is configured, then continue further.
   a. When two best paths exist, prefer the path that was received first (the older one)
   b. Prefer the route that comes from the BGP router with the lowest router ID
   c. If the originator or the router ID is same for multiple paths, prefer the path with the minimum cluster list length
   d. Prefer the path that comes from the lowest neighbor address

Neighbor Relationships

iBGP Configuration

iBGP peers are supposed to be in the same AS hence there is no requirement for them to be directly connected. BGP assumes that Intra AS routing is already taken care of by an IGP. iBGP speakers must either be fully meshed, or a route reflector must be used.

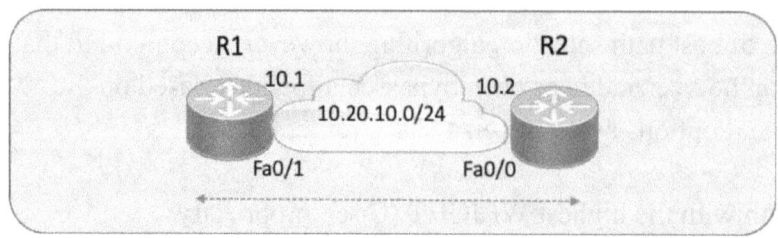

iBGP Configuration

#R1

```
interface fa0/1
 ip address 10.20.10.1 255.255.255.0
!
router bgp 400
```

eBGP Configuration
neighbor 10.20.10.2 remote-as 400

```
#R2
interface fa0/0
ip address 10.20.10.2 255.255.255.0
!
router bgp 400
 neighbor 10.20.10.1 remote-as 400
```

eBGP Configuration

Unlike iBGP, and in case of eBGP, the two peers must be directly connected.

#R1

```
interface fa0/1
 ip address 10.20.10.1 255.255.255.0
!
router bgp 300
neighbor 10.20.10.2 remote-as 400
```

#R2

```
interface fa0/0
ip address 10.20.10.2 255.255.255.0
!
```

```
router bgp 400
 neighbor 10.20.10.1 remote-as 300
```

Further Reading

BGP Configuration Guide[65]

Interpret a basic network topology diagram with elements such as switches, routers, firewalls, load balancers, and port values

Network topology is about how the various networking products are interconnected, i.e., routers, switches, firewalls, and load balancers.

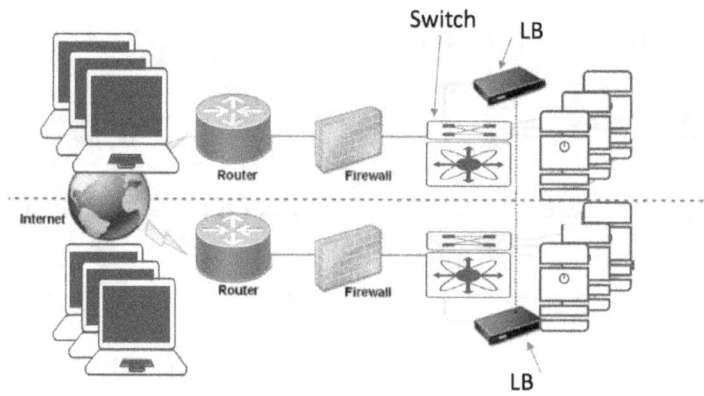

Generally, this is how a typical (however simplified) network topology looks like when a large site (say Campus HQ) is connected to the Internet. Behind the routers, you have a pair of firewalls and then a pair of switches that connect the servers and the load balancers.

---

[65] https://bit.ly/2tjonkS

Describe the function of management, data, and control planes in a network device

You can divide a networking device into four distinct logical groups as far as traffic to/from or through a device is concerned.

1. Data plane (traffic that is not sourced or destined from/to the device, i.e., transit traffic)
2. Control plane (traffic sourced or destined from/to the device, traffic type used for the creation and operation of the network such as BGP, OSPF, and ARP)
3. Management plane (technically same as control plane traffic but for network management such as TFTP, SSH, SNMP, FTP, NTP, etc.)
4. Services plane (a special case of data plane traffic but in this case, router is involved in modifying the packet header or payload, such as GRE, QoS, NAT, etc.)

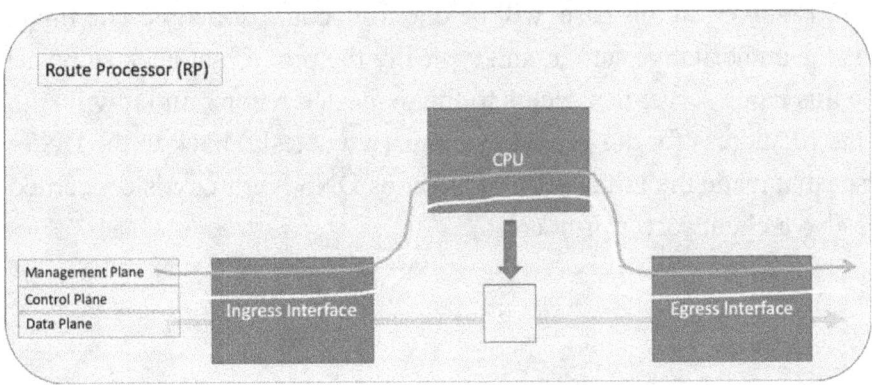

Describe the functionality of these IP Services: DHCP, DNS, NAT, SNMP, NTP

The Dynamic Hosting Configuration Protocol (or DHCP) is one of the many network management protocols used on IP networks, typically running on a server, dynamically assigns IPv4 addresses and other related network configurations (such as subnet mask, gateway IP address, etc.) to each device on that network.

DHCP is a client/server protocol, where the client is the device that needs an IP address assignment, and the server is the entity that governs the assignment being sought. All DNS communication, by default, takes place in cleartext.

Domain Name System (or DNS) is a network management protocol organized in a hierarchical and decentralized fashion to resolve IP device names to their IP addresses. When you browse a website say www.tesla.com, it is a series of DNS servers that help resolve it to its IP address e.g., 209.133.79.61. The series of name servers involved in fully resolving www.tesla.com into the corresponding IP address or addresses would typically include four servers.

It starts with the DNS recursor (aka DNS resolver) which makes further DNS queries on the client's (in this case PC with the browser) behalf. Recursor will contact the root server which points to an even more specific location, i.e., TLD server. TLD server, in this case, will be one for ".com" domains. The final name server is the authoritative server, and typically the proverbial buck stops here because this name server has access to the requested record, and it will simply return the IP address for the given hostname (www.tesla) back to the DNS precursor that made the initial request as far as DNS hierarchy is concerned. DNS is also a client/server protocol.

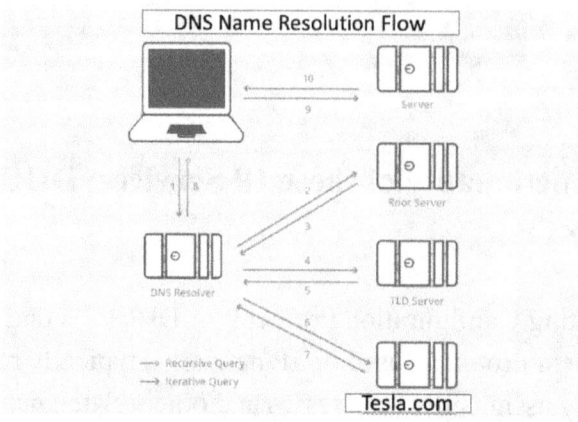

```
MAK1-MBP:~ afaqkhan$ nslookup www.tesla.com
Server:         192.168.1.1
Address:        192.168.1.1#53

Non-authoritative answer:
www.tesla.com   canonical name = www.tesla.com.edgekey.net.
www.tesla.com.edgekey.net        canonical name = e1792.dscx.akamaiedge.net.
Name:   e1792.dscx.akamaiedge.net
Address: 184.30.231.116
```

Network Address Translation (NAT)

Network Address Translation (or NAT) comes in many different forms, but in all variations, it is still about translating IP addresses with or without the help of TCP/UDP ports. First, there is NAT and Port Address Translation (PAT).

NAT can be configured in two ways, static and dynamic. Static NAT is the simplest form of NAT where only one to one translation of IP addresses is involved. With static NAT, translations forever stay in the translation table and never time out once they are configured by the network admin. To remove entries from the translation table, you've to remove the static NAT statements from the configuration.

Dynamic NAT is similar to static NAT in the sense that it is still one to one NAT i.e., between an inside local and inside global address. However, the mapping of an inside local to an inside global address happens dynamically. For dynamic NAT to work, you have to set up a pool of inside global IP addresses. The dynamic entry only stays in the translation table so long as there is some traffic, in the absence of traffic the entries time out.

What if you had more local addresses and less global addresses? Enter PAT. PAT allows a specific UDP or TCP port on a global address to be translated to a specific port on a local address. Static PAT, much like static NAT, is where you specify the translation rules within the configuration. PAT (or NAT overload) is a way to hide an entire RFC1918 IP address space behind a single public globally routable IP address (it could also be a few global IP addresses as opposed to one!).

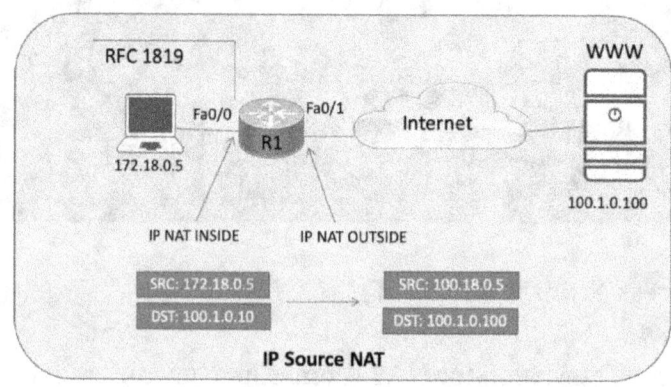

IP Source NAT

Static NAT

Router(config)#interface fa0/0
Router(config-if)#ip nat inside

Router(config)#interface fa0/1
Router(config-if)#ip nat outside

Router(config)#ip nat inside source static 172.18.0.5 100.18.0.5

Router#sh ip nat translations

Pro	Inside global	Inside local	Outside local	Outside global
--	100.18.0.5	172.18.0.5	---	---

Dynamic NAT

Router(config)#interface fa0/0
Router(config-if)#ip nat inside

Router(config)#interface fa0/1
Router(config-if)#ip nat outside

Router(config)#ip nat pool dynamic-ip 100.0.16.1 100.0.16.6 prefix-length 29
Router(config)#ip access-list standard client-list
Router(config-std-nacl)#permit 172.18.0.0 0.0.0.15

Router(config)#ip nat inside source list client-list pool dynamic-ip

After some traffic matches those NAT rules, you can notice the following.

Router#sh ip nat translations

Pro	Inside global	Inside local	Outside local	Outside global
icmp	100.16.1:2	172.18.0.1:2	100.1.0.100:2	100.1.0.100:2
tcp	100.16.2:35694	172.18.0.2:35694	100.1.0.100:80	100.1.0.100:80
tcp	100.16.1:56185	172.18.0.1:56185	100.1.0.100:80	100.1.0.100:80
---	100.16.1	172.18.0.1	---	---
---	100.16.2	172.18.0.2	---	---

Static PAT

Router(config)#interface fa0/0
Router(config-if)#ip nat inside

Router(config)#interface fa0/1
Router(config-if)#ip nat outside

Router(config)#ip nat inside source static tcp 172.17.0.5 80 88.88.88.88 80
Router(config)#ip nat inside source static tcp 172.17.0.6 22 88.88.88.88 666

Router#sh ip nat translations

Pro	Inside global	Inside local	Outside local	Outside global
tcp	88.88.88.88:80	172.18.0.5:80	---	---
tcp	88.88.88.88:666	172.18.0.6:22	---	---

PAT (NAT Overload)

Router(config)#interface fa0/0
Router(config-if)#ip nat inside

Router(config)#interface fa0/1

Router(config-if)#ip nat outside

Router(config)#ip access-list standard client-list
Router(config-std-nacl)#permit 172.18.0.0 0.0.0.255
Router(config)#ip nat inside source list client-list interface fastethernet0/1 overload

After some traffic matches the PAT rules, you can witness the following.

Router#show ip nat translations
Pro Inside global   Inside local   Outside local   Outside global
tcp 88.88.88.88:7921   172.18.0.2:7921   95.100.96.233:443   95.100.96.233:443
tcp 88.88.88.88:8651   172.18.0.5:8651   173.194.44.18:80   173.194.44.18:80
tcp 88.88.88.88:8652   172.18.0.111:8652 173.194.44.18:443
173.194.44.18:443
tcp 88.88.88.88:8653   172.18.0.223:8653 173.194.70.84:443
173.194.70.84:443
udp 88.88.88.88:64116 172.18.0.222:64116 8.8.8.8:53   8.8.8.8:53
udp 88.88.88.88:64756 172.18.0.223:64756 8.8.4.4:53   8.8.4.4:53

Simple Network Management Protocol (SNMP)

Simple Network Management Protocol (or SNMP) is an IP protocol responsible for collecting and organizing, in a tree-like fashion, information about the devices being managed. It can also be used to modify those objects to change a device's behavior. It uses UDP ports 161 and 162.

SNMP has been around for over 30 years. Over this time, it has been the de-facto way to monitor networks. It worked great when networks were small and polling a device every 15-30 minutes met operational requirements. SNMP MIBs are a type of data model defining a collection of information that is organized in a hierarchical format that is used along with SNMP. Anyhow, SNMP did work great for monitoring devices every few minutes, but it never caught on for configuration management purposes due to custom or proprietary MIBs.

In addition to SNMP, there has always been the network command-line interface or CLI. Access to the CLI happens via console, Telnet, or SSH, and it has been the de-facto way of managing the configuration of networking devices for the past 20+ years.

Network Time Protocol (NTP)

Network Time Protocol (or NTP) is an IP networking protocol responsible for synchronizing clock information between systems. NTP is designed to synchronize the time on a network. It uses UDP to transport packets. An NTP network receives its time from an authoritative time source such as an atomic clock attached to a time server. NTP distributes this time across the network. NTP servers use UDP port 123 to talk to each other and to communicate with NTP clients.

NTP client makes a transaction with its server each polling interval. It uses the concept of a stratum to describe the distance in hops between a machine and an authoritative time source. Devices running NTP prefer another device that has the lowest stratum number. General, it is possible to achieve 10ms drift over long distances (WAN) and 1ms for LAN.

NTP servers associate with each other in one of three modes.

1. Client/server
2. Active/Passive
3. Broadcast

The client/server is the most common internet use case. In this setup, a client or dependent server can be synchronized to a group member, but no group member can synchronize to the client or dependent server.

Symmetric active/passive is useful for configurations where a group of low stratum peers operates as backups for each other.

Broadcast or multicast mode is where clients can be configured to use broadcast or multicast modes. It allows clients to use a single configuration to associate with multiple servers.

Recognize common protocol port values (such as, SSH, Telnet, HTTP, HTTPS, and NETCONF)

SSH, Telnet, HTTP, HTTPS, and NETCONF protocols all use IANA assigned TCP ports for communication as far as the server or service-side is concerned.

Protocol	Encrypted?	TCP Port(s)
SSH	Yes	22
Telnet	No	23
HTTP	No	80
HTTPS	Yes	443
NETCONF	Yes	830

Identify cause of application connectivity issues (NAT problem, Transport Port blocked, proxy, and VPN)

Application connectivity issues that have to do with NAT primarily boil down to NAT device (typically a router or a firewall) not able to handle the IP address (and/or port) translation inside the application protocol header. This leads to broken connectivity where application just times out.

To resolve this issue, NAT device must be made aware (if possible, if not replaced with one that is) of how to handle IP address and/or port handling, also known as Application Layer Gateway (ALG). Examples of protocols that require ALG support within the NAT device are your typical unified communication protocols such as H.323 or SIP.

Transport Port Blocked

Application connectivity issues can also arise from blocked TCP/UDP port, typically by firewalls. A TCP/UDP port can range from 0 to 65,535 (it is a 16-bit field within the transport headers). Most of the important services that we discussed earlier use ports from 0 to 1023. If your firewall is blocking a port that your application is trying to use to reach a server/service, the application attempt will simply fail. Here is the list of most common ports that are part of the 0-1023 space.

Protocol Name	Transport (TCP/UDP) Ports Used
FTP (File Transfer Protocol)	20
Secure Shell (SSH)	22
Simple Mail Transfer Protocol (SMTP)	25
Domain Name System (DNS)	53
Hypertext Transfer Protocol (HTTP)	80
Hypertext Transfer Protocol Secure (HTTPS)	443
Post Office Protocol (POP3)	110
Internet Message Access Protocol (IMAP)	143

Depending on the OS or the device, you can easily scan for blocked and open ports. There are also bunch of third-party tools that you can use such as Nmap or even SolarWinds Free Port scanner.

Device	Scan CLIs for open/closed ports

Windows PC	Local Host: netstat -a -n Windows Native FW: netsh firewall show state netsh firewall show config Intermediary FW: netstat -ano | findstr -i SYN_SENT
macOS machine	You can use Network Utility to scan for both locally and intermediary blocked ports.
Linux machine	You can use netstat or nmap utility from CLI.

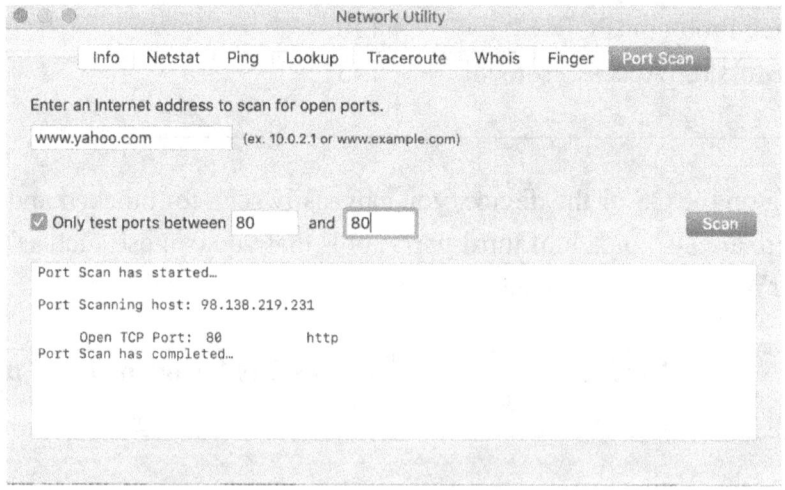

Proxy

Proxy servers can be used for performing the functions of NAT and firewall including blocking the TCP/UDP ports. The most popular proxy servers in use today are Squid (Linux) and Windows Web Application Proxy (Windows

Server). Proxies can be deployed either as a forward proxy or a reverse proxy. A forward proxy is used by the client such as a web browser to connect to a service whereas reverse proxy is used by the server, for example, a web server. Forward proxies are placed in the same network as the clients requesting services through them, whereas reverse proxies and the actual web servers are almost always on separate networks. Cloud Access Security Broker (or CASB) solutions make use of both forward and reverse proxy functions.

Today, proxy servers (much like VPNs) are used by third-party providers to help folks hide their real (ISP assigned) IP address when browsing the Internet. For example, hide.me, hidester, or proxysite.com.

VPN

Virtual Private Network (or VPNs) are used to encrypt communication between two endpoints, typically between a client and a server. Almost all medium to large Enterprises worldwide use VPN clients (from vendors like Cisco such as AnyConnect VPN) for encrypting communication between a roaming client (such as a laptop) and the company's intranet, for example, to download emails or browse intranet websites.

VPN services are also commonly used today to hide IP address when browsing the Internet (much like proxies). The most common VPNs are NordVPN, ExpressVPN, IPVanish, etc.

Explain the impacts of network constraints on applications

Every time you access a web server, your communication (IP/TCP/HTTP protocol headers and payloads) traverse several intermediary networking devices, such as switches, routers, access points, firewalls, and load balancers. Keeping this mind all design assumptions and limitations that exist in the network by definition may result in some constraints on the application traffic.

The most common types of constraints the network put on applications include the following.

Network Metric	Application Metrics
Bandwidth	Performance
Latency and Jitter	perceptual user experience
QoS	user experience
Availability or HA	application uptime

Solutions such as Cisco AppDynamics can offer a detailed view into application performance and root cause analysis of application related issues.

Troubleshooting common network connectivity issues

You can perform network troubleshooting by following the OSI layer in a bottoms-up fashion.

- Ensure that the client is connected via an ethernet cable or Wi-Fi. In case of Wi-Fi, make sure that the client is connected to the nearest wireless access point.
- Make sure that client and the switch it is connected to, are able to learn MAC addresses (use arp and "show mac address-table" on a Cisco switch to view MAC table)
- For network layer, make sure that the client has obtained an IP address from the DHCP server. You can verify connectivity to the IP address using ping network utility. You can view IP addresses on a Linux or macOS machine using "ifconfig". You can verify L3 connectivity one hop at a time.
- For transport layer, you need to verify the TCP/UDP port(s) in question for the service. You can use utilities like curl and telnet.

Further Reading

Networking basics and software-defined networks[66]

Networking topologies and models[67]

IPv4 Addresses and subnets[68]

Network Programmability Basics Video Course[69]

---

[66] https://bit.ly/3aKj3ql

[67] https://bit.ly/2xpwWfE

[68] https://bit.ly/2W6XBlH

[69] https://bit.ly/2THyXg3

Chapter Summary

- 48-bit MAC address is also known as Extended Unique Identifier (EUI) EUI-48.
- The overall MAC address is divided into two parts, the Organizationally Unique Identifier (OUI) and NIC specific parts, each 24-bit or 3 bytes in length.
- Virtual LAN (or VLAN) is a broadcast domain that is partitioned virtually to carve out an isolated L2 segment.
- An IP subnet is an isolated IP or L3 segment.
- Enhanced Interior Gateway Routing Protocol (EIGRP) is an advanced or enhanced distance vector protocol. It uses Diffused Update Algorithm (DUAL) algorithm to calculate the shortest path a destination. It is a Cisco proprietary protocol.
- Open Shortest Path First (OSPF) protocol is defined in RFC 2328 and based on link-state technology where the link is an interface on an L3 device such as a router
- BGP is an exterior gateway protocol (or EGP) so it was created from ground up to perform interdomain routing.
- Services plane (a special case of data plane traffic but in this case, router is involved in modifying the packet header or payload, such as GRE, QoS, NAT etc.)
- DHCP is a client/server protocol, where the client is the device that needs an IP address assignment, and the server is the entity that governs the assignment being sought
- Network Time Protocol (or NTP) is an IP networking protocol responsible for synchronizing clock information between systems.
- Proxy servers can be used for performing the functions of NAT and firewall including blocking the TCP/UDP ports.